麦积山石窟手册

马英莲 赵萍霞 著

中央编译出版社

图书在版编目（CIP）数据

麦积山石窟手册 / 马英莲，赵萍霞著. -- 北京：中央编译出版社，2025. 3. -- ISBN 978-7-5117-4812-6

Ⅰ. K879.24

中国国家版本馆CIP数据核字第202408P7T8号

麦积山石窟手册

责任编辑	张　科
责任印制	李　颖
出版发行	中央编译出版社
地　　址	北京市海淀区北四环西路69号（100080）
网　　址	www.cctpcm.com
电　　话	（010）55627391（总编室）　（010）55627312（编辑室） （010）55627320（发行部）　（010）55627377（新技术部）
经　　销	全国新华书店
印　　刷	北京盛通印刷股份有限公司
开　　本	880毫米×1230毫米　1/32
字　　数	337千字
印　　张	15
版　　次	2025年3月第1版
印　　次	2025年3月第1次印刷
定　　价	98.00元

新浪微博：@中央编译出版社　　微　信：中央编译出版社（ID：cctphome）
淘宝店铺：中央编译出版社直销店（http://shop108367160.taobao.com）（010）55627331

本社常年法律顾问：北京市吴栾赵阎律师事务所律师　闫军　梁勤
凡有印装质量问题，本社负责调换，电话：（010）55627320

本书获得天水师范学院科研项目资助

天水师范学院 2021 年麦积山石窟艺术研究项目"麦积山石窟智慧旅游汉英二维码导览应用研究"（项目号：MJS2021-03）

全国重点文物保护单位

内容简介

本书共分为三章,系统地介绍了麦积山石窟的历史、艺术价值及其文化传播。第一章通过梳理历史文献,作者详细阐述了麦积山石窟的基本概况、重要历史事件及其在佛教艺术史上的重要地位。第二章针对原麦积山石窟解说词存在的信息序列混乱、语言措辞过于正式等问题,作者运用哈蒂姆和梅森的语篇分析模式,从背景信息、主题信息、引申与拓展三个维度,以汉英双语形式推介了15个特窟和70个普窟,以适应全球化语境的需求。其中,引申与拓展部分不仅列举了各洞窟间相似的建筑风格、主题内容和造像特征,还收录了西方汉学家翻译的相关麦积山石窟历史文献,使读者能够比较不同语境下译者对同一汉语文本的诠释。第三章则介绍了麦积山石窟的附属遗存——瑞应寺和舍利塔的基本情况,以及所藏石碑和杜甫诗词等内容。

本书以读者易于接受的方式,生动地讲述了洞窟造像、壁画、建筑及相关传说,旨在传播麦积山石窟的艺术文化,同时为石窟导游和研究者提供了丰富的文献基础和范式参考。

前　言

本书为天水师范学院 2021年麦积山石窟艺术研究项目"麦积山石窟智慧旅游汉英二维码导览应用研究"（项目号：MJS2021-03）成果。在系统概述麦积山石窟的历史、艺术价值及其附属遗存的基础上，本书选取了麦积山石窟的15个特窟和70个普窟作为研究对象。每个洞窟的介绍均包含背景信息、主题信息、引申与拓展三个部分，并以汉英双语对照的形式呈现。敦煌研究院麦积山石窟艺术研究所董广强研究员和他的团队承担了汉语文本撰写工作和洞窟图片的拍摄和编辑，天水师范学院外国语学院项目组完成英语翻译。

本书约18万字，其中第二章麦积山石窟汉英解说词主要由马英莲完成，约10万字。赵萍霞负责第一章麦积山石窟概述、第三章麦积山石窟附属遗存以及第二章引申与拓展部分的翻译，约8万。

为方便读者阅读以及导游推介洞窟中的佛像群，本书中"左"和"右"指的是佛像的左右两边。

在此，特别感谢天水师范学院科研处为本书提供经费支持，感谢敦煌研究院麦积山石窟艺术研究所董广强研究员和他的团队的辛勤付出，其撰写的汉语介绍文本确保了解说词的专业性和准确性。最后，衷心感谢家人对我们翻译工作的支持与理解。

目 录

第一章　麦积山石窟概述 / 001

第二章　麦积山石窟汉英解说词 / 015

第1窟 / 024	第28窟 / 154	第76窟 / 242	第128窟 / 346
第2窟 / 030	第29窟 / 158	第78窟 / 248	第133窟 / 350
第3窟 / 036	第30窟 / 162	第80窟 / 254	第135窟 / 364
第4窟 / 044	第31窟 / 166	第85窟 / 258	第136窟 / 372
第5窟 / 070	第35窟 / 170	第90窟 / 262	第139窟 / 376
第7窟 / 078	第36窟 / 174	第92窟 / 266	第140窟 / 380
第8窟 / 082	第37窟 / 178	第93窟 / 270	第141窟 / 384
第9窟 / 086	第43窟 / 182	第94窟 / 274	第142窟 / 388
第10窟 / 092	第44窟 / 188	第98窟 / 278	第146窟 / 394
第11窟 / 096	第48窟 / 194	第100窟 / 282	第147窟 / 398
第12窟 / 100	第50窟 / 198	第101窟 / 286	第148窟 / 402
第13窟 / 106	第51窟 / 200	第102窟 / 290	第155窟 / 406
第14窟 / 112	第53窟 / 204	第105窟 / 294	第162窟 / 410
第15窟 / 116	第54窟 / 206	第112窟 / 298	第163窟 / 414
第17窟 / 120	第55窟 / 210	第114窟 / 302	第165窟 / 420
第20窟 / 124	第58窟 / 214	第115窟 / 306	第168窟 / 424
第22窟 / 128	第59窟 / 218	第117窟 / 310	第169窟 / 436
第23窟 / 132	第60窟 / 222	第121窟 / 314	第172窟 / 440
第24窟 / 136	第62窟 / 226	第122窟 / 320	第191窟 / 444
第25窟 / 140	第69窟 / 230	第123窟 / 324	
第26窟 / 144	第72窟 / 234	第126窟 / 330	
第27窟 / 150	第74窟 / 238	第127窟 / 334	

第三章　麦积山石窟附属遗存 / 451

瑞应寺 / 452

舍利塔 / 468

参考文献 / 470

CHAPTER ONE

第一章

麦积山石窟概述

针对麦积山石窟的概述，主要基于史书记载。主要目标为通过分析历史文献了解麦积山石窟基本情况、重要历史事件和石窟的重要性。

一

麦积山石窟基本情况

南宋学者祝穆在《方舆胜览》第六十九卷中提到"天水军"时，介绍麦积山"在天水县东百里。状如麦积，为秦地林泉之冠。姚秦时建瑞应寺，在山之后，姚兴凿山而修，千龛万象，转崖为阁，乃秦州胜景。"该文献描述了麦积山石窟的地理位置、山形、开凿时间、洞窟数量、崖阁建筑特征和社会地位。

《太平广记》第三百九十七卷中，引《玉堂闲话》的描述更加具体："麦积山者，北跨清渭，南渐两当，五百里冈峦，麦积处其半。崛起一石块，高百万寻，望之团团，如民间积麦之状，故有此名。其青云之半，峭壁之间，镌石成佛，万龛千室，虽自人力，疑其鬼功。隋文帝分葬神尼舍利函于东阁之下石室之中。有庾信铭记，刊于岩中。"《古记》中云："六国共修。"自平地积薪，至于岩颠，从上镌凿其龛室神像，功毕，旋拆薪而下，然后梯空架险而上。其上有散花楼、七佛阁、金蹄银角犊儿。这篇散文除了描述麦积山石窟的地理位置、山的名称由来、开凿时间等基本情况，还描写了开窟造像的构建方法，尤其突出了麦积山悬崖陡峭险峻的特征。

The general introduction of Maijishan Caves is mainly based on historical records. The main objective is to get a general idea of the basic information, the important historical events and the significance of grottoes Grottoes by analyzing the historical documentations.

I

The Basic Information of Maijishan Caves

According to "Tianshui Prefecture" in *An Overall Survey of Scenic Spots Across the Country*, Sec. 69 by Zhu Mu of the Southern Song Dynasty, "Maijishan lies 100 miles southeast of Qinzhou, shaped like a grain stack. It is known as the first scenic spot in Qinzhou for its forests and springs. Ruiying Temple was built at the foot of the hill during the Later Qin Dynasty (AD 383-417). And then the ruler Yao Xing began to excavate cliffs to build thousands of niches and figures, especially those chambers open to the cliff face, It is a famous historical site in Qinzhou." The document describes the geographical location, the shape of the hill, the time of the excavation, the number of caves, the architectural characteristics of caves open to the cliff face and social status of the Maijishan Caves.

A more detailed description can be seen in *The Records of the Taiping Era*, Sec. 397 from *Idle Talks from Jade Hall* The Maijishan, to the north of which is the clear Weishui River and on the south of which is the Liangdang County, is in the middle of the five hundred-li mountains. The Maiji (meaning in English grain stack) Mountain is so called because it is a solitary peak, which is very high and looks round, like a folk grain stack. Many niches and shrines were carved on the high cliffs of the Maijishan, and although this was done by manpower, sometimes we suspect it was ghost's work. Emperor Wen of the Sui Dynasty buried the case, in which part of the relics of Zhi Xian (智仙), the Buddhist nun, was contained, in the stone chamber under the East Pavilion, which can be seen in the rock, in which the inscription of Yu Xin was carved. It was said in *Ancient Records* that the Maijishan Caves were the joint construction of six kingdoms. Wood was piled up from the flat ground to the top of the rock and then shrines and statues were chiseled and carved from the top. After the work was finished, the wood was removed gradually and the ladders were set for people to climb up, which looked dangerous. There are the Sanhua (scattering flowers) Building, the Seven-Buddha Pavilion and the Calf with Golden Hooves and Silver Horns on the cliff of the Maijishan. In addition to describing the basic information of the geographical location, the name origin and the time of the excavation of the hill, this essay also demonstrates the construction methods of the excavating of cave shrines and image making, especially emphasizing the characteristics of steep, precipitous cliff at Maijishan.

二

麦积山石窟重要历史事件

冯国瑞[1]在《大事年表》中详细记录了麦积山历史上发生的重要事件。已知的麦积山历史，始于公元420年至公元422年《高僧传》第十一卷《玄高传》中记载的文字，"高乃杖策西秦，隐居麦积山，山学百余人，崇其义训，禀其禅道。时有长安沙门释昙弘，秦地高僧，隐在此山，与高相会，以同业友善。时乞伏炽磐，跨有陇西，西接凉土。有外国禅师昙无毗，来入其国，领徒立众，训以禅道"。

最早的有确切纪年的开窟题记，记载了公元502年张元伯对现在的第115窟的开窟造像情况。在第127窟发现的一块北魏残碑，记述了公元503年至公元516年期间"洛阳刘姓沙弥法生在麦积，请良匠加工造龛一所"。同一时期，秦州太守王宗在第166窟造像、绘壁。同在公元503年至公元516年期间，"陈益生、贾伏生等合造第110窟、塑像、绘壁；李道生全家造第159窟、塑像、绘壁；姜小晖全家造第160窟、塑像、绘壁"。公元539年"西魏皇后乙弗氏卒，凿麦积崖为龛而葬，号寂陵"，这一事实证明了这一圣地的重要性。公元552年，乙弗氏丈夫西魏文帝元宝炬去世，她的儿子元钦即位，"自麦积崖迁乙弗氏后，合葬永陵（今西安）皇陵"。

麦积山石窟历史上最引人注目的事件之一发生在公元566年和公元568年之间，当时秦州的大都督李允信为悼念亡父而造七佛阁，并采用"薄肉塑"与绘塑结合的装饰技法。这就是位于东崖

---

[1] 冯国瑞. 麦积山石窟志 [M]. 天水：天水报社印刷厂承印本，1989:99-108.

II

The Important Historical Events of Maijishan Caves

Feng Guorui recorded the important events in the history of Maijishan in details in the *Section of the Event Chronology*. The known history of Maijishan dates from *Biography of Xuangao*, sec.11 in *Biographies of Famous Monks*. The famous monk Xuangao arrived in the Western Qin with a cane and lived in Maijishan, gathering a hundred pupils around him in the mountain. His disciples advocated his doctrines and practiced meditation in Zen Buddhism. At that time another famous monk Shi Tanhong from Chang'an (modern Xi'an) who just secluded himself in the mountain joined Xuangao. The two monks worked and taught together friendly. The territory of the Western Qin extended to Longxi and connected Liangzhou to the west under its third ruler Qifu Zhipan (AD 412-438). Qifu Zhipan invited Indian monk Dharmaksema to his country to teach the disciples and preach the Zen Buddhism.

The earliest dated inscription of AD 502 records that Zhang Yuanbo, a minor officer, cut a cave now is called Cave 115 and made images in it. A stone tablet that broken of the Northern Wei Dynasty found in Cave 127 describes during AD 503 and AD 516, a Luoyang novice monk Liu Fasheng invited the skilled craftsmen to excavate a cave at Maijishan. At the same period, Wang Zong, the governor of Qinzhou, made sculptures and painted on the walls in Cave 166. In AD 503 to AD 516, Cave 110 was excavated, in which sculptures were modelled and paintings were drawn by Chen Yisheng, Jia Fusheng and others jointly. Cave 159 was excavated by Li Daosheng's family, and Cave 160 was excavated by Jiang Xiaohu's family". In AD 539 Empress Wen, Yifu (AD 510-540) of the Western Wei Dynasty died, she was buried in the niche chiseled on the cliff of Maijishan, which was later called the Silent Mausoleum. The fact proves the significance of this holy site. In AD 552, her husband Yuan Baoju, Emperor Wen of the Western Wei Dynasty died. Her son Yuanqin was enthroned as the emperor. He removed her mother's body from Maijishan and buried Empress Wen and Emperor Wen together in the Yongling Mausoleum.

One of the most remarkable events in the history of Maijishan Caves occurred between AD 566 and AD 568, when Li Yunxin, the senior military commander of Qinzhou, built the Seven Buddha Cave to memorize his father, and adopted the decorative technique of "painting and sculpture". This is Cave 4 at the eastern cliff, the largest and most impressive cave at Maijishan. In AD 583, Emperor Wen of the Sui Dynasty followed the pious spirit of King Ashoka and ordered that "each temple must be built at the foot of every famous mountain and pagodas must be constructed in more than one hundred prefectures". From the figures of the history of the Sui Dynasty, we are

的第4窟，是麦积山规模最大和最令人印象深刻的洞窟。公元583年，隋文帝效仿阿育王的虔诚精神，降旨"名山之下，各为立寺，一百余州立舍利塔"。从隋朝历史的数字中可以了解到全国佛教发展的巨大规模："度尼僧二十三万人，立寺三千七百九十二所，写经四十二藏（经指《大藏经》），一十三万二千八十六卷，修故经三千八百五十八部，造像十万六千五百八十躯。"隋朝在麦积山的广泛活动既包括开凿新崖窟和造像，也包括修理和复原旧崖窟和造像。

公元604年，朝廷降诏在麦积山"敕葬神尼舍利，建宝塔，赐净念寺"。这些舍利塔和寺庙是否在公元618年隋朝灭亡之前就已建成，不得而知。然而据记载，在唐朝建立后不久，即公元618年至公元629年期间，"敕应乾寺"虽然后来被重建，而且有了不同的名字（瑞应寺），但这座寺庙就已矗立在麦积山脚下。

发生在公元708年的地震毁坏了寺庙和宝塔，公元734年的地震更是"殷殷有声，折而复合，经时不止，坏庐舍殆尽，压死四千余人"。公元759年，诗圣杜甫辞去长安附近的华州司功参军的职务，来到秦州，想隐居于此。他在秦州待了不满四个月，却写了二十首歌咏当地山川风物的杂诗，抒发了自己的伤时感事之情。公元763年，安史之乱后，吐蕃攻占长安，陇右随后沦陷，吐蕃族接管麦积山。

公元911年，"天水王仁裕登西崖万佛堂（即现在的第133窟，'碑洞'），题诗"。窟内壁诗文已亡。公元923年—公元924年，蜀主王衍"远幸秦州，游麦积山。前秦州节度判官蒲禹卿谏阻，因为天水地远，峻恶难行。险栈欹云，危峰插汉，麦积崖无可瞻恋。后主竟不从之。王仁裕和韩昭谓随行唱和事"。直到宋大中祥符二年（公元1009年），迥觉大师来到麦积山"寻旧基圣迹，构精蓝"。也许迥觉大师的虔诚得到了回报，因为宋代大观年间（公元1107年），"遍山花卉盛开，进灵芝"。

able to know the huge scale of the Buddhist development all over the country. There were 230 thousand tonsured nuns and monks, 3,792 temples were built, 42 sutras (referring to the Tripitaka) were copied among 132,086 volumes, 3,858 ancient sutras were revised, and 166,580 sculptures were repaired". The extensive activities of the Sui Dynasty at Maijishan included the excavation of new caves and new images-making, as well as the repair and restoration of old caves and sculptures.

In AD 604, the imperial court commanded to bury the relics left after the cremation of a saintly monk at Maijishan, so the pagoda to deposit the relics for worship was constructed, and the temple was granted the name of the Jingnian Temple". Whether the pagoda and the temple were built before the extinction of the Sui Dynasty in AD 618 is unknown. However, it is recorded that shortly after the establishment of the Tang Dynasty, from AD 618 to AD 629, the temple was named the Yingqian Temple by imperial decree. Although it was rebuilt later and had a different name (the Ruiying Temple), it still stands at the foot of Maijishan.

The earthquake in AD 708 destroyed the temple and the pagoda. In the earthquake of AD 734, people could hear faint sounds underground, the surface above ground broke and closed again, and the shocks lasted for a long time. Most of the houses were badly damaged, and more than 4,000 people lost their lives. In AD 759, Du Fu, China's greatest poet, gave up the power of the military in Huazhou, near Chang'an, went to Qinzhou, hoping to live in seclusion here. He stayed in Qinzhou for less than four months, but he wrote 20 unclassified poems about the local mountains, rivers, sceneries, folk customs, and historical sites, expressing his unhappy feelings in troubled times. In AD 763, after the An Shi Rebellion, the Tibetans captured Chang'an, occupied Longyou later, and the Tibetans took over Maijishan.

In AD 911, Wang Renyu, a native of Tianshui, ascended the Cave of a Myriad Buddha on the western cliff (now Cave 133, "Cave of the Steles") and wrote a poem on the wall. The text of the poem on the wall of the cave was lost. From AD 923 to AD 924, Wang Yan, the king of the Kingdom of Shu wanted to make a long-distance tour to Qinzhou and visit Maijishan. Pu Yuqing, the former Administrative Assistant to the Military Commissioner of Qinzhou presented a memorial to the emperor to prevent his journey, because Tianshui was far away from Chengdu, located in a remote area and the roads were rough and difficult to move. The rough plank roads uprised as high as white clouds, the peaks rose steeply into the sky. There was nothing worth seeing and remembering at Maijishan. The king did not take his suggestion, and insisted on his going to Tianshui followed by Wang Renyu and Han Zhao, who were ordered to write poems of presenting in reply. It was not until the second year of the Dazhong era (AD 1009), the monk Jiongiue came to Maijishan to seek the old foundation of the temple and rebuilt it. Perhaps the Master's devoutness was rewarded, because in the first year of the Daguan era of the Song Dynasty (AD 1107), flowers of Ganoderma lucidum bloomed all over the mountain.

尽管在公元1003年、公元1007年和公元1027年都发生了灾难性的地震，但在十一世纪，麦积山再次处于繁荣状态。考古工作者挖掘了一些新的洞窟，并对造像进行了大量的维修和重塑。例如公元1035年，"当寺山主沙门惠珍及太原王秀等，募集重妆塑山脚下应乾寺东西两阁佛像"。公元1068年，"寺僧委铁壁入内，升座讲演宗乘，敕赐圆通禅师"。这表明，麦积山的寺庙再次兴旺起来了。公元1070年的碑文记载，"李师中等人登山刻石"；公元1081年，"陕西转运副使蒋之奇在登牛儿堂（第5窟）刻石"；公元1091年和公元1095年，"阁令、薛适登七佛阁（第4窟）刻石"。三年后，麦积山遭遇饥荒，寺庙也变得破败不堪。

但在公元1101年，"寺主僧智俐在山顶再建舍利塔"。虔诚再次得到了回报，因为六年后"绝顶阿育王塔旁产灵芝三十八本，秦州经略陶龙图进上"。宋徽宗视此事吉祥，随赐寺院名"瑞应寺"，即"预示好兆头的寺庙"，或"许愿灵验的寺庙"。公元1107年，一些访客留下的题记之后，一百年来麦积山再无任何记录。

公元1208年，麦积山下的农民遭受饥荒，"李实、强德、张均等起义，驱逐寺僧占有大量之仓粮硇畜。公元1209年，李实等事败，天水军压制赔还，旋将寺田收冲营田"。这些寺田两次易手，但在公元1224年被四川安抚兼制使归还。在公元1520年、公元1535年、公元1560年、公元1564年、公元1567年、公元1579年和公元1590年，绅士们供奉神龛，或雕刻诗词题记，或两者兼而有之。今天，在东崖石窟中可见的大量作品都属于这些时期。但记录中也提到了公元1543年至公元1559年之间的一场严重火灾以及几次地震。

关于十七世纪和十八世纪的记录很少，大部分都是类似的灾难、断断续续的修理和复原。例如公元1631年，"礼县李春晖等贴完三大佛"。在公元1662年至公元1670年间，圆慧和尚重建了山顶的佛塔，另

Overview of Maijishan Caves

Although disastrous earthquakes occurred in AD 1003, AD 1007 and AD 1027, Maijishan was prosperous once again in the 11th century. Some new caves were excavated and a large number of sculptures were restored and remodelled. For example, Huizhen, the host of the Yingqian Monastery, and Wang Xiu, a worshipper from Taiyuan, Shanxi Province, raised funds to repair and redecorate the images in the two side halls of Yingqian Temple at Maijishan of AD 1035. In AD 1068, the monk Wei Tiebi was invited to the imperial court to give lectures on Buddhism and was granted Zen Master Yuantong by Emperor Shenzong in the Song Dynasty. This shows that the temple at Maijishan was thriving once again. The inscription of AD 1070 records that Li Shizhong and his friends ascended the mountain and carved stones. In AD 1081, Jiang Zhiqi, the Deputy Forwarding Magistrate of Shaanxi carved stones in Cave of the Bull (Cave 5). In AD 1091 and AD 1095, Yan Ling and Xue Shi mounted the Seven Buddha Cave (Cave 4) and carved stones. Three years later, Maijishan suffered from a famine, and the temple was also in ruins.

But in AD 1101, the chief monk Zhili reconstructed the Pagoda of Asoka on the top of the mountain. Devoutness was rewarded again, because six years later, 38 Ganoderma lucidums grew near the pagoda on the mountaintop, and Tao Longtu, the Qinzhou Military Commissioner, sent them to the imperial court. Ruiying Temple was granted later by Emperor Huizong of the Song Dynasty to memorize this auspicious event, namely the "Temple of Good Omens", or "Temple of Efficacious Fulfillment for Vows". There were no records for a hundred years at Maijishan, after those inscriptions left by some visitors in AD 1107.

In AD 1208, the peasants around Maijishan suffered from famine. Li Shi, Qiang De, Zhang Jun and others rose up and expelled the monks from the Ruiying Temple and occupied a large number of stored grain and livestock. In AD 1209, Li Shi and other rebels were caught, and the Tianshui Army suppressed the compensation, and collected the farmlands of the temple as army field. These farmlands of the temple changed hands twice, but were returned by the Sichuan Military Commissioner in AD 1224. In AD 1520, AD 1535, AD 1560, AD 1564, AD 1567, AD 1579, and AD 1590, gentries offered shrines, or carved poems and inscriptions, or both. A large number of works visible today in the caves of the eastern cliff belong to this period. But the records also mentioned a serious fire and several earthquakes between AD 1543 and AD 1559.

There are rare records in the 19th and 18th centuries, mostare similar disasters, intermittent repairs and restorations. In AD 1631, for example, Li Chunhui from Li County and others finished the covering the three Great Triads on the Eastern Section with gold foil. Between AD 1662 and AD 1670, the monk Yuanhui rebuilt the pagoda at the top of the mountain, and another monk Jiongjue restored the Ruiying Temple at the foot of the mountain. In AD 1764, Qinzhou magistrate Fei Tingzhen allotted the regular grain tribute in Ruiying Temple. The most famous visitor to Maijishan in the 18th century was Bi Yuan (AD

一位迥觉大师则修复了山脚下的瑞应寺。公元1764年,"秦州知州费廷珍开除瑞应寺常住田地粮"。十八世纪,麦积山最著名的访客是清代官员、学者毕沅(公元1730年—公元1797年)。公元1866年,西北民族战争迫使"居民避居洞窟"。其中包括陇南书院山长任其昌以及其他绅士题诗刻石。

此后,麦积山再次被遗忘,直到公元1920年,一位"天水天主教堂意国教士揭取第4窟,即'散花洞'壁画"。公元1941年,天水籍学者冯国瑞与友人入山考察,开创了麦积山石窟开窟近一千六百年来,第一次由专业人士对石窟文化进行科学考察和深入研究的新篇章,并对洞窟做了编号,随后写成《麦积山石窟志》发行于世。

《甘肃石窟志》❶介绍了中华人民共和国成立后,专业人士对麦积山石窟的两次考察。1952年9月至10月,由中央人民政府文化部组织,中央美术学院、西北军政委员会文化部、敦煌文物研究所三单位组成的考察团对重点洞窟进行了历时30余天的摄影、测绘和临摹工作,共编号石窟157个。

1953年7月,中央人民政府文化部社会文化事业管理局组织了以吴作人为团长的麦积山石窟勘察团。勘察团在32天的工作中,写出《麦积山石窟勘察团工作报告》和《麦积山勘察团工作日记》。研究者们编录的《麦积山石窟内容总录》共编录了194四个窟龛,比前述勘察团的录编新增37个窟,除10多个窟因窟内不通,情况不明外,余者每个编号洞窟内容均涉及窟形、时代、建筑、造像、壁画、题记诸方面。此次编号一直沿用至今。

二十世纪九十年代,麦积山石窟艺术研究所对所有洞窟做了细致的调查档案,并对有些窟龛重新编号,包括王子洞窟区,现共编号窟龛211个。

---

❶ 敦煌研究院、甘肃省文物局. 甘肃石窟志 [M]. 兰州:甘肃教育出版社, 2011: 277-278.

1730-1797), an official and scholar of the Qing Dynasty. In AD 1866, the great rebellion of Muslims in the northwest forced residents to live in the caves. Among them were Ren Qichang, the head of Longnan Literary Academy, and other gentries who wrote poems and carved on the walls.

Later, Maijishan was forgotten again until 1920, when an Italian missionary from Tianshui Catholic Church removed the paintings from Cave 4–Cave of the Scattered Flowers. In 1941, Feng Guorui, a scholar from Tianshui, visited Maijishan with his friends and began the scientific investigation first made by professionals, which has a groundbreaking significance to the culture of caves since Maijishan Caves were excavated for nearly 1600 years. They gave the numbers to caves, subsequently a book was published in the same year under the title *The Caves of Maijishan*.

The Caves of Gansu (2011: 277-278) introduces the two explorations of the Maijishan Caves after the establishment of the People's Republic of China. From September to October in 1952 Maijishan was explored by a Survey Team. The team was organized by the Ministry of Culture of the Central People's Government, consisting the Central Academy of Fine Arts, the Ministry of Culture of the Northwest Military and Political Commission, and the Dunhuang Cultural Relics Research Institute. They were able to photograph, measure and make replications of some important caves within more than 30 days, and numbered 157 caves totally.

In July of 1953 the Social and Cultural Administration of the Ministry of Cultural Affairs of the Central People's Government sent a team to carry out a more thorough survey of Maijishan Caves under Wu Zuoren. *The Report of the Survey Team at Maijishan Caves* and the *Diary of the Survey Team at Maijishan Caves* were finished within 32 days. Complete Record of Maijishan Caves by researchers numbered a total of 194 caves, to which another 37 new ones were added than what the Survey Team did. The contents of numbered caves cover types, dates, architectures, sculptures, paintings and inscriptions, except that more than ten caves have still not been reached, and no one yet knows what treasures of sculptures and paintings they may contain. The number of caves remains today.

In the 1990s, a complete survey of all caves at Maijishan was made by the Art Research Institutethe of Maijishan Caves and renumbered some of the caves and niches, including the Prince's Cave. There are totally 211 numbered caves today.

三

麦积山石窟的重要性

麦积山石窟始建于后秦，后经北魏、西魏、北周、隋朝和唐朝连续开凿。宋代没有开挖新窟，但重修了大部分北朝洞窟和部分元朝、明朝、清朝洞窟。麦积山现存编号洞窟211个，分为西崖、东崖和王子洞三部分，其中西崖142个、东崖54个、王子洞15个，共有造像7200多身，壁画近1000平方米。

因大多数造像是北朝泥塑，所以麦积山被誉为"北朝雕塑博物馆"。其系统而完整的北朝造像对了解中国佛教艺术的发展状况及其规律具有重要意义。受外来艺术影响，其北魏早中期泥塑造像具有较强烈的神格化特征。而在北魏晚期，当其早期外国艺术的影响在中国传统艺术的影响下逐渐消退，体现出浓厚的民族化、民间化色彩的雕塑风格。北魏晚期造像不仅形神兼备，而且技艺精湛，堪称当时佛教造像的楷模，达到了北朝泥塑艺术的最佳水平，也反映出北朝佛教的高度兴盛与发展，更体现了当时艺术创作者的聪明才智与高度成就。虽然现存壁画很少，但一些北朝时期的经变画，如西方净土变、维摩诘变、涅槃变、法华变等是目前我国石窟寺中保存最早的北朝大型经变画，也是研究佛教经变画演变过程的十分珍贵的资料。麦积山石窟的佛教艺术是我国古代丰富文化遗产中的宝贵财富。

III

The Significance of Maijishan Caves

The excavating of cave shrines at Maijishan began in the Later Qin Dynasty, and the work continued there intermittently in the Northern Wei Dynasty, the Western Wei Dynasty, the Northern Zhou Dynasty, the Sui Dynasty and the Tang Dynasty. No new caves were excavated in the Song Dynasty, but most caves of the Northern Dynastiy were rebuilt. Part of the Yuan Dynasty, the Ming Dynasty and the Qing Dynasty was also reconstructed. With 211 numbered caves at Maijishan, it is divided into three sections: the western cliff, the eastern cliff and the Prince Cave, among which 142 caves on the western section, 54 Caves on the eastern cliff, and 15 caves on the Prince Cave. It contains more than 7,200 sculptures, and paintings of nearly 1,000 square meters.

For most of the sculptures are clay in the Northern Dynasty, Maijishan is praised as "the Sculpture Museum of the Northern Dynasty." Its systematic and complete sculptures of the Northern Dynasty are important to the understanding of the development of Buddhist art in China. The surviving clay sculptures of early and middle Northern Wei Dynasty have a distinct feature of the divine under the foreign art influence. While for those of late Northern Wei Dynasty, when their early foreign art influences receded gradually under the influence of traditional Chinese art and their style and colouring became distinct Chinese and secularization. These features are both all extremely lifelike and of great technical skills. They appear to be a refined example of the Buddhist sculptures at that time, reaching the finest level of clay sculpture art in the Northern Dynasty. They also reflect the high prosperity and development of Buddhism in the Northern Dynasty, and the intelligence and high achievement of the artistic creators at that time. Although very few wall-paintings have survived, some sutra illustration paintings of the Northern Dynasty, such as the Illustration to the Pure Land, Vimalakirti Sutra Illustration, Nirvana Sutra Illustration Painting and Illustration of Saddharma-pundarika are the earliest large-scale sutra illustration paintings of the Northern Dynasty preserved in the cave temples in China, and are also very precious materials for the evolution of Buddhist sutra illustration paintings. The Buddhist art of Maijishan Caves is a precious wealth in the rich cultural heritage of ancient China.

CHAPTER TWO

第二章

麦积山石窟汉英解说词

自二十世纪四十年代以来，随着国内学术界对麦积山石窟研究的兴起，日本和英美学者也相继出版了画册和专著，承载着丰富佛教文化内涵的英语介绍文本成为向国内外读者传播石窟文化的重要媒介。麦积山石窟英语介绍文本指附于麦积山石窟景点介绍、画册介绍和旅游宣传图册的情景性英文片段[1]，其中具有代表性的有《汉英雕塑画册》[2]《汉英旅游手册》[3]《汉英画册》[4]《汉英导游词》[5]以及麦积山石窟景区制作的汉英解说牌。

一

麦积山石窟英语介绍文本语篇特征分析

本书对拍摄到的麦积山石窟英文介绍文本按照哈蒂姆和梅森（Hatim & Mason）[6]语篇分析模式从背景信息和主题信息划分，方便读者了解其语篇结构特征。两组第5窟英文介绍文本见表1和表2。

---

[1] 马英莲. 麦积山佛教石窟介绍文本英译研究 [J]. 天水师范学院学报, 2023(1)：112-119.
[2] 何静珍、陈玉. 麦积山石窟艺术丛书（第一辑）[M]. 兰州：甘肃人民美术出版社, 1997：1-60.
[3] 天水市文化和旅游局. 天水旅游 [M]. 天水市文化和旅游局, 2019：39.
[4] 天水画册编辑委员会. 天水画册 [M]. 甘肃人民出版社, 1989：20.
[5] 高亚芳、秦斌峰. 英语甘肃导游 [M]. 中国旅游出版社, 2008：29-33.
[6] HATIM, B. & MASON, I. Discourse and the Translator [M]. Shanghai：Shanghai Foreign Language Education Press, 2001：223.

表1　麦积山石窟第5窟英语介绍文本1

序列	名称	第5窟	Cave 5
背景信息	名称来源	俗称"牛儿堂"。因其廊上塑一立于卧牛背上之天王而得名。	Commonly referred to as the Bull Hall, named for the Heavenly King standing on a lying bull.
主题信息	造像	此窟有三个佛龛，中龛一佛二弟子四菩萨为隋代作品，左右龛各一佛二菩萨均为初唐作品。	This grotto includes three niches, of which, the middle one with one Buddha, two disciples and four Bodhisattvas was built in the Sui Dynasty, and both the left and right niche with one Buddha and two Bodhisattvas were built in the early Tang Dynasty.
	壁画	廊前正壁右上方有西方净土变壁画及供养人数十身，造型优美，是麦积山初唐壁画的代表作。	On the upper right of front wall in front of the corridor are the mural painting of Pure Land and tens of people of offering with elegant pattern, which are the representative works of mural paintings of the early Tang Dynasty in Maijishan.

（选自天水麦积山石窟景区英语解说牌）

表2　麦积山石窟第5窟英语介绍文本2

序列	名称	第5窟	Cave 5
背景信息	开凿时间	隋代（公元581年—公元618年）始凿，初唐完成。	Started in the Sui Dynasty (AD 581-618); and completed at the beginning of the Tang Dynasty,
	俗称	"牛儿堂"。	this grotto, commonly referred to as the Bull Hall
	形制	三间四柱式崖阁。	a three-room and four-column type cliff pavilion
主题信息	造像特征	现有隋、唐两代泥塑造像15身，三龛主尊为三世佛，历经重修。隋代造像清俊优祥，初唐造像圆润秀丽。中龛外踏牛天王，孔武雄健，气势不凡。	Currently, there are 15 clay statues made in the dynasties of Sui and Tang; the major Buddha of the three niches is the third period Buddha. The grotto has been rebuilt several times. The statues made in the Sui Dynasty are pretty and gracious, and the statves made in the early period of Tang Dynasty are mellow, full and comely. Outside the middle niche, the bull is fierce and vigorous and has an extraordinary imposing manner.
	壁画特征	现存壁画约70平方米。廊外正壁右上方的"西方净土变"及廊顶的奔马图，构图严谨，施色艳丽，为唐代绘画的上乘之作。	The area of existing mural painting is about 70 square meters. The Pure Land Sutra Painting at the top-right side of front wall outside the corridor and the Running Horses at the corridor top are scrupulously composed and flamboyantly colored, and are the excellent painting works of the Tang Dynasty.

（选自天水麦积山石窟景区英语解说牌）

（一）麦积山石窟第5窟英语介绍文本内容分析

从表1和表2可以看出，该文本语篇内容由背景信息和主题信息两个序列组成。表1背景信息中解释了"牛儿堂"名称的由来，主题信息阐述了窟中造像和壁画的数量和时代。表2背景信息介绍了开凿时间、俗称和形制，主题信息不仅描述窟中造像和壁画的数量和时代，还介绍了特征。但两组例子未提及洞窟位置和社会地位。

（二）麦积山石窟第5窟英语介绍文本译文分析

语体比较正式，有较长的复合句。如"The Pure Land Sutra Painting at the top-right side of front wall outside the corridor and the Running Horses at the corridor top are scrupulously composed and flamboyantly colored, and are the excellent painting works of the Tang Dynasty."此长句由连词"and"连接，介绍了壁画的位置、内容、时代和特征。

在具体翻译中，译者采用纽马克（Newmark）[1]"语义翻译"策略，即在目的语语言结构和语义许可的范围内，把原作者在原文中表达的意思准确地再现出来。其按源语语篇语序一字不差地翻译，在相应的汉语介绍文本基础上一一对应翻译。例如："隋代、初唐"没有补充公元纪年信息。忠实汉语文本的译文与英语语境下相关平行文本的写作风格有着很大的差异，难以满足目标语受众的信息期待和阅读习惯。这在很大程度上影响了译文在目的语读者中的接受，从而制约着麦积山石窟文化的世界传播。

---

[1] Newmark, P. Approaches to Translation [M]. New York: Prentice Hall, 1981:39.

第二章 麦积山石窟汉英解说词

二

英语语境下石窟英语介绍文本语篇特征分析

习近平总书记于2019年8月视察敦煌时强调，要"更加积极主动地学习借鉴世界一切优秀文明成果"。要让麦积山佛教石窟文化走出去，就要把肇始以来的海外研究著述系统译入国内，为国内研究提供文献基础和范式参照。在众多介绍石窟的国外网站中，《印度阿旃陀石窟英语介绍文本》(*Bharat Online.com: Ajanta Caves*)被选为参考模板。该文本除了与麦积山石窟英语介绍文本功能对等、文本类型对应外，还有另外两个原因。其一，作为佛教石窟鼻祖对麦积山石窟雕塑和壁画有很大影响。其二，英语是印度官方语言之一，印度旅游景点英语介绍文本语篇结构与英美国家一致。阿旃陀石窟第1窟英语介绍文本背景信息和主题信息序列见表3。

表3 印度阿旃陀石窟第1窟英语介绍文本分析

序列	名称	Cave 1
背景信息	地理位置	The first cave that we come across as we enter the Ajanta Cave Temple, has been named as Cave 1.
	开凿时间	It is believed to date back to the 6th and 7th century.
	社会地位	and has been adorned with auspicious motifs on its doorway.
主题信息	主要景观	Here you can see the paintings on the interiors and exteriors of the caves, including different images.
	壁画	For example, Great Buddha, a Goddess on the upper left corner of the shrine doorway, a Cherubic Dwarf, a Bodhisattva believed to be Padmapani Avaokitesvara, Bodhisattva Vajrapani, Four Deers with a Common Head, Lovers, a Dark Princess believed to be an Andhra Princess, a Dancing Girl with Musicians, a Princess Reclining by a Pillar, a Maid seated on the Ground, Proceedings in a Persian Court, the Golden Geese, the Pink Elephant, a Bull Fight, etc.
	造像（补充）	Lord Buddha has a preaching posture with Bodhisattvas on either side and five disciples and a wheel flanked by deers at the base of the pedestal suggests symbolically Buddha's first sermon at Sarnath.

(Bharat Online. com: Ajanta Caves)

（一）阿旃陀石窟第1窟英语介绍文本内容分析

表3显示，该文本内容也由背景信息和主题信息两个序列组成。语篇信息结构依次按照：背景信息（地理位置、开凿时间、社会地位）和主题信息（主要景观、壁画）层层推进，重点突出主题信息的传递，背景信息描述完整。增强了文本的可接受性，能够实现信息有效传递。

在背景信息中，依次介绍了第1窟位于"U"形山坳的入口处，开凿于公元六至七世纪，龛门左右两侧绘持莲花菩萨和持金刚菩萨。持莲花菩萨是阿旃陀石窟壁画中最著名的代表作。在主题信息中，可以欣赏内部几乎全部绘有不同形象的壁画装饰并详细介绍了主要人物和场景。

该介绍文本没有提及位于正壁中央的主尊佛说法像，作者参考其他资料补充了龛内造像场景：主佛结跏趺坐，双手施说法印，两侧胁持菩萨和五个弟子，基座上的双鹿和法轮象征着佛陀在鹿野苑的第一次布道。

（二）阿旃陀石窟第1窟英语介绍文本结构分析

该介绍文本介于口语和书面语两级之间的混合语体。除了Padmapani（莲花手菩萨）、Vajrapani（金刚手菩萨）等佛教词汇难懂外，文本多用英语基本词汇。结构松散的句子体现口语特点（a Maid seated on the Ground, Proceedings in a Persian Court, the Golden Geese, the Pink Elephant, a Bull Fight），如名词短语（Four Deers with a Common Head, a Dancing Girl with Musicians, a Princess Reclining by a Pillar）。

三

基于参考模板的麦积山石窟汉语介绍文本

为使麦积山石窟英语介绍文本符合更多读者的阅读习惯,项目团队先参考阿旃陀石窟介绍文本模板撰写汉语文本,该项工作由敦煌研究院麦积山石窟艺术研究所董广强研究员和他的团队承担。团队成员分为两组,分别查找英文和日语资料,按照哈蒂姆和梅森语篇结构模式从背景信息、主题信息和引申与拓展三个序列组织文本内容。在编写过程中,力求达到:语言规范,文字准确,结构严谨,内容层次符合逻辑。多用日常浅显易懂的书面语词汇和短句,穿插相关洞窟传说、民间故事、诗词和名家评论,阐述同类洞窟的异同。突出每个洞窟的代表性特征和重要性。照顾国内外读者的阅读习惯,多补充解释性信息以便更好地了解造像和壁画。

以第5窟汉语介绍文本为例。该介绍文本内容由背景信息、主题信息和引申与拓展三个序列组成。背景信息中介绍了第5窟的位置(东崖最上层西端)、解释了"牛儿堂"名称的由来(因中龛的外侧塑踏牛天王)、开凿时间(隋朝)并补充(公元581年—公元618年)和社会地位(现存极少的隋代原作和唐代造像,壁画中的供养人形象为研究唐代绘画、服饰提供了宝贵的资料)。

主题信息重点突出了洞窟形制(崖阁式洞窟)、客观具体地描述了造像数量、时代和特征(三龛内十四尊七世纪初到七世纪中期),壁画位置、时间和特征(廊顶和廊正壁上方、三龛内及左右龛楣、龛顶部七世纪中期)。最后推介二十则访客题记,体验明代在东侧开凿仅容一人而通往第4窟("散花楼")的过洞。大量使用名词性短语,遵循了书面语与口语相结合的表达方式。

引申与拓展中生动形象地描述了有关"小有洞天"通道的天水民谣和开挖历史以及"踏牛天王"造像的传说,增添了地方特色,达到了传播石窟文化的目的。

该汉语介绍文本与英语语境下石窟介绍文本的写作风格一致,满足目标语受众的信息期待和阅读习惯。用国内外读者熟悉的方式讲述麦积山石窟造像、壁画和相关民谣和传说。

四

基于参考模板的麦积山石窟英语介绍文本

麦积山石窟介绍文本英译选择规约性翻译策略。第5窟中"小有洞天(A Hole of Another Scenery)"、"踏牛天王(the Heavenly King standing on the back of a crouching bull)"等专有名词和天水民谣"千佛廊,万佛堂,鹞子翻身牛儿堂。(the Thousand Buddhas Corridor, the Cave of a Myriad Buddha, the sparrow hawk turns its body in the Cave of the Bull.)"的英译尽量符合英语的表达习惯。其中"小有洞天"镌刻在通往第4窟的石洞门顶上。道教称"洞天"为神仙所居住的地方,含有洞中另有一个天地的意思。在具体的语境中,当访客在第5窟("牛儿堂")穿过仅容一人低头通过的石洞时,抬头就看见宏伟壮观的第4窟(散花楼),好像是另一个景色。因此"小有洞天"英译为A Hole of Another Scenery。

英译文本还采用介于口语和书面语之间的混合语体。多用英语基本词汇、结构松散的句子和主动语态。第5窟这样介绍窟内题记：该窟残存二十则题记。访客在三龛口、内外壁、台座、前廊洞口潦草地墨书题记、留名。大部分清晰可辨。(There are twenty inscriptions left by visitors in the cave. Visitors might have written dedications and roughly scratched their names with a brush on the entrances, inner and outer walls, thrones in three niches, gate of the tunnel in gallery. Most of them are clearly legible.)

第 1 窟 卧佛洞

第1窟位于东崖最东端,开凿于北魏(公元386年—公元534年),造像为明代(公元1368年—公元1644年)、清代(公元1636年—公元1912年)重塑。该窟是麦积山唯一的涅槃洞窟,俗称"卧佛洞"。

该窟是三间四柱的崖阁建筑,窟中有一尊侧卧的涅槃像、十尊面目神情各异的泥塑造像、一则柱头题记、一幅墨书对联。

形制:该洞窟宽7.75米、高2.35米、深2.27米,是一个三间四柱、平面横长方形平顶窟。柱子为石胎雕凿,外部裹泥皮,没有上彩,截面为八边形,每个柱子下有圆形覆莲状素面柱础。柱子上方有一些仿木结构建筑的构件。

造像:六世纪的原作已经破坏无存。现存明代重塑造像十二身,清代重妆颜色。正壁坛台上塑释迦牟尼涅槃像,其头、身后,及足侧塑十大弟子及一身供养人。

正壁的涅槃像,身长5.96米、高1.1米。右侧卧,头枕于右手,下方有柱形枕头,枕边缘有回形纹饰。面部较宽,细眉下弯,眼睑稍凸,双目微闭。眼珠部分破损。鼻梁较宽平,双唇边缘塑出凸起轮廓。身着半披肩袈裟,上沥粉堆塑龙凤、云纹和牡

第二章 麦积山石窟汉英解说词

Cave 1 Cave of Reclining Buddha

Cave 1 is located at the extreme east end of the eastern cliff, and was excavated in the Northern Wei Dynasty (AD 386-534). The sculptures were remodelled in the Ming (AD 1368-1644) and Qing (AD 1636-1912) dynasties. The cave is the only Nirvana Cave at Maijishan, commonly known as Cave of Reclining Buddha.

In the cave, visitors will enjoy a chamber of three openings open to the cliff face, with its lintel supported by four stone pillars, a roof carved in relief in the rock above it, an image of the Nirvana of Reclining Buddha, ten sculptures modelled in clay with different attitudes, an inscription on top of the pillar, and a pair of couplets written with a brush. Details are as follows.

Type: The cave is 7.75 meters wide, 2.35 meters high and 2.27 meters deep. It is a horizontal rectangular cave with a flat ceiling, of three openings and its lintel supported by four stone pillars which are built up in clay plaster over a core of rock, unpainted, with an octagonal cross section, and each pillar has a circular column base in the form of an upside-down lotus. Some imitation wood architectural components are placed above them.

Sculptures: The original works of the sixth century has been badly damaged and disappeared. Twelve sculptures remodelled in the Ming Dynasty have survived, and repainted in the Qing Dynasty. An image of the Nirvana of Sakyamuni lies on the base of the main wall, surrounded by his ten disciples and a donor at his head, his rear, and his feet on each side.

The Nirvana of Buddha on the main wall is 5.96 meters long and 1.10 meters high. He lies on the side, with the right hand under the head, below is a cylindrical pillow decorated with fret on its edge. With wider face, thin curved eyebrows, slightly bulging eyelids, his eyes are slightly closed, eyeballs are partially damaged, with flatter nasal bridge, and bulging contours at the edges of the lips. He is wearing the robe partially covering the shoulder,

丹等装饰图案，下身着裙系带。左臂直伸平放于左侧身体上，双足前部裸露。

卧佛周围围绕十个弟子。其中第一身弟子高1.42米、宽1.18米，青年形象，神情沉静，双手合十，手指残失。内着交领衫，中层着交领衣，外着袒右袈裟，左肩有环形扣。结跏趺坐于佛头顶侧。第二身弟子为老者形象，位于佛头后侧，嘴角下垂，右手抚摸佛头，左手裹衣角托下颏。其余弟子身高与第一身弟子大致相当，神态各异。围绕卧佛的塑像双眼珠均残失。

在佛的脚部位置有一身供养人，高1.27米。头戴冠，面部长圆，鼻梁较宽平，嘴角轻微上扬。左手残失，右手抚摸佛趾。内着交领衫，外着圆领宽袖紫红蟒袍，上半身服饰装饰有祥云、龙纹等图案，下半身服饰有道教的八卦图案。

壁画：窟内残存团花图案、菱形纹饰、双线网格纹图案、花卉、云纹等，以石青、石绿、褚红、白色、朱砂为主。

题记：东侧柱头上墨书："张锡、张进乾隆五十八年四月初二日进香。"

对联：窟门中间两柱门内侧以粉白色书写对联，左侧柱为：幽洞悬崖翠竹苍松千古秀；右侧柱为：灵水名山鸟语花香四时新。

which is decorated with the patterns of dragons and phoenixes, clouds and peonies. His lower body is robed in a dress with a sash tied around the waist. His left arm extends and rests on the left side, leaving the front of the feet bare.

The Reclining Buddha is surrounded by his ten disciples. Among them, the first disciple is 1.42 meters tall and 1.18 meters wide. He is a calm, youthful image of a monk, whose palms are together (the hand gesture of namaskar), but his fingers have disappeared. He wears an open cross-collar shirt, over which is an open cross-collar garment, and the outer robe thrown over the left shoulder or the upper throwing a strong diagonal across the body, leaving the right side of the body and shoulder bare with a looped button on the left shoulder. He seats on the side of Buddha's head in a pose of deep yogic meditation, with the legs tightly locked, the soles of both feet uppermost. The second disciple is an elder image, who is at the rear of the Buddha's head. With drooping corners of mouth, his right hand touches the Buddha's head, while resting his chin on his left hand holding the corner of the robe. The height of rest of the disciples is roughly identical to that of the first disciple, with different expressions and attitudes. All the eyeballs of the sculptures around the Reclining Buddha are missing.

At the foot of the Buddha, there is a donor of 1.27 meters high, wearing a crown, with round face, flatter nasal bridge, the corners of the mouth slightly up. His left hand has disappeared, while his right hand is touching the Buddha's toes. He wears an open cross-collar robe, over which is a purplish red garment with the round collar and long loose sleeves. The upper garment is decorated with patterns of auspicious clouds, dragons and other patterns, and the lower garment is adorned with the pattern of the Taoist Eight Trigrams.

Paintings: The remaining patterns of Neolamarckia cadamba, prism, double lined grid, flowers and clouds, etc survive in the cave. The colours on a light ground consist today chiefly of the mineral blue, deep emerald green, reddish-brown, white and cinnabar.

Inscription: An inscription is written on the capital of the east side with a brush: The pilgrimage for Zhang Xi and Zhang Jin on the second of April in the 58th year of the reign of Emperor Qianlong in the Qing Dynasty (AD 1797).

Couplets: A pair of couplets is visible on the inner side of the two pillars in the center of the door inscribed in pink and white. The one on the left side pillar reads: Secluded caves, the overhanging cliffs, verdant bamboos and green pines can be so beautiful for thousands of years, while the other on the right side pillar reads: The magical streams, the famous hill, the chirping of birds and the fragrance of flowers have taken on an entirely new look.

引申与拓展

该窟正壁涅槃造像是表示释迦牟尼去世时的情景。相关内容可参考第12窟、第26窟和第127窟"涅经变"。佛教认为,世间的各种生命都在不停地轮回,而"涅槃"则是脱离了这个轮回,进入了不生不灭的最高境界。该洞窟是横长方形,虽然六世纪的原作雕塑已经不存在了,但是从这个洞窟的形制分析,六世纪的造像还是涅槃造像,也就是佛躺卧的形象。

该洞窟的建筑是模仿中国传统的木结构建筑形式,但仅仅是模仿了柱子以及相关的结构形式,屋顶没有雕凿出来。

卧佛,明代

Extension and Elaboration

The image of the Nirvana of Buddha on the main wall in the cave illustrates the scene of the death of Sakyamuni. You can consult the related contents of "Nirvana Sutra Illustration Painting" in Cave 12, Cave 26 and Cave 127. Buddhism believes that all kinds of life in time are constan reincarnation, and "Nirvana" is separated from this reincarnation and enters the highest realm of eternal and immortal. It is a horizontal rectangle. Although the original sculptures modelled in the sixth century no longer exist, the analysis of the type of the cave shows that the image of the Nirvana of Buddha is the original sculpture modelled in the sixth century, that is, the image of the Nirvana of Reclining Buddha.

The architectural form of this cave is modelled after the traditional Chinese wooden structure, but it only imitates the pillars and related structures, and the ceiling has not been carved out.

第 2 窟 狮子洞

第2窟位于东崖东端，开凿于西魏（公元535年—公元556年）。洞窟中已经完全没有西魏时期塑像和壁画的痕迹，现存均为十七至十八世纪重塑或重绘。因洞窟正中现有一身形似狮子的神兽，亦被附近的信众称为"狮子洞"。

该窟是麦积山石窟中唯一一个八面坡帐形洞窟，窟内有十六尊木骨泥塑造像，十七至十八世纪的彩绘壁画。

形制：该洞窟是平面横长方形、倒梯形顶，高3.14米、宽6.1米、深3.74米。前壁开有窟门，窟门下部为竖长方形，上部为低圆拱形，整体保存完整。正壁前左右两侧各有一长方形低坛基，坛基上各筑多层"工"字形台座。左右佛座前侧中央分别塑青狮和白象。顶部中央位置为一个相对较小的平面，四周是斜向的倒梯形，在转角和各个面的相交接位置均雕凿有半圆形的结构，象征着这种形式建筑的骨架。

造像：窟内现存造像二十八身，其中木骨泥塑十六尊，影塑十二身。洞窟中已经完全没有西魏时期（六世纪中期）塑像的痕迹，现存均为明清（十七至十八世纪）补修或重塑。该窟内的主尊是地藏菩萨，东侧是文殊菩萨，西侧是普贤菩萨；另外，在东西两

Cave 2 Cave of the Lion

Cave 2 is located at the east end of the eastern cliff and was excavated in the Western Wei Dynasty (AD 535-556). However, no traces of sculptures and paintings modelled in the Western Wei Dynasty can be seen in the cave and what remains are all remodelled or repainted in the 17th and 18th centuries. For a lion-like divine beast remains in the center of the cave, it is also called "Cave of the Lion" by the nearby worshipers.

In this cave, visitors can enjoy the unique tent-shaped cave with eight sloping sides at Maijishan Caves, 16 sculptures of clay modelled on a wooden armature, and painted murals from the 17th and 18th centuries. Details are as follows.

Type: The cave is a plane horizontal rectangular with an upside-down trapezoidal ceiling, 3.14 meters high, 6.10 meters wide, and 3.74 meters deep. There is a door in the front wall, with a lower of vertical rectangular and an upper of low chaitya arch, and the whole is preserved intact. On each side an I-shaped throne in multi-layer is supported on a rectangular low base on the left and right sides in front of the main wall. A green lion and a white elephant are modelled respectively in the front center on each side of the throne. The central ceiling retains a relatively small panel, surrounded by a sloping topdown trapezoid. A semicircle structure is carved at the corner and the intersection of each surface, symbolizing the framework of this form of architecture.

Sculptures: 28 sculptures survive in the cave among which 16 images of clay modelled on a wooden armature and 12 figures modelled in relief. Traces of sculptures modelled in the Western Wei Dynasty (the mid-sixth century) in the cave are invisible, and what remains are all repaired or remodelled in the Ming and Qing dynasties (the 17th and 18th centuries). The main image is Ksitigarbha Bodhisattva, Manjusri Bodhisattva on the east and Samantabhadra Bodhisattva on the west. His two attendants — Monk Daoming stands on the east and Elder Min on the west. An envoy leads a lion by holding the rope around its neck, another five sculptures in front of the left and right walls symbolize the different Kings in hell.

侧立有道明和尚和闵公立像。在狮子的前方，还有一身牵狮子的使者，在左右两壁前各位五身象征着地狱中各种王者的塑像。

地藏菩萨高1.03米。头戴花冠，面容方圆，双耳垂肩，上身裸露，胸部丰满挺拔。着披巾，挂璎珞，下着装饰华丽的革带系裙。双手置于胸前作说法印，结跏趺坐于仰莲花座上，莲花座由足踏四朵莲花神兽驮着。神兽高1.59米。神兽目视前方，口大张，露齿与舌，颈上饰有铃铛，身上有圆状凸起。

第2窟昆仑奴

牵狮子的使者形象十分精彩，此人形象是北方草原上人物像，高1.23米。传说来自遥远的昆仑山，所以俗称"昆仑奴"。其头戴卷沿毡帽，毡帽上饰有连珠纹。隆额高鼻，眼窝深陷，眼珠突出，胡须卷曲上翘；胸腹爆圆，形貌古怪。内着紧身短衣，外罩披肩，衣袖上卷至肘间，穿长筒靴。双腿作弓箭步，右手持琉璃珠，左膝跪压一圆球。

左侧站立道明和尚，高1.56米，青年形象，面容清秀，双手在胸前合十。内着交领衣，外罩袈裟，穿白袜和白底黑鞋。右立闵公，高1.55米，老年形象，头戴双翅冠，白眉白须，目视前方。双手合十。内着交领衣，外罩交领长袍，足穿白底黑靴。

两侧墙壁前的地狱王者形象基本相同，均头戴笼冠。着交领衣袍，腰围玉带，双手握于胸前而立。

洞窟顶部长方形藻井内壁每壁各三身影塑坐佛，共十二身。结

第二章　麦积山石窟汉英解说词

Ksitigarbha Bodhisattva is 1.03 meters high. She is wearing a crown, the round face carved with pendulous ears, naked above the waist, and a plump and straight chest. Her broad scarves hang over the shoulders, with a heavy garland of jewels round the neck, and the lower body is robed in a dress with an elaborate leather sash tied around the waist. With his hands on his chest in gesture of preaching (Vitarka mudra), he seats on a throne of upturned lotus-petal in a pose of deep yogic meditation, with the legs tightly locked, the soles of both feet uppermost. The throne is supported by a divine beast stepping four lotuses, which is 1.59 meters high. It looks straight ahead, with the mouth widely open, leaving teeth and tongue exposed. It hangs a string of bells round the neck, with round bulgings on the body.

The image of the envoy leading a lion by holding the rope around its neck is very splendid. This is the figure on the northern grassland, with 1.23 meters high. The legend goes that he comes from the distant Kunlun Mountain, so he is commonly known as "Kunlun Slave". He wears a felt hat with rolled brim, which is decorated with a beaded pattern. He has bulging forehead and tall nose, deep-set eyes, protruding eyeballs, beards curling upward; His extremely swelling chest and abdomen make the exotic appearance. He is dressed in a short tight-fitting coat, with the outer shawl covering both shoulders, sleeves rolling up to the elbow, on boots. Two legs are in a lunge position, with the right hand holding glass beads, and his left leg kneeling on a ball.

Monk Daoming standing on the left is 1.56 meters high, a youthful image, with delicately modelled features, with clasped hands. He wears an open cross-collar garment, and is robed in an upper garment that completely covers his body, on white socks and black shoes with white soles. While Elder Min standing on the west is 1.55 meters high, an elderly image, with a double wing crown, white eyebrows and beard, looking straight ahead, with clasped hands. He wears an open cross-collar garment, over which is a closed full-body garment with crossed-collar, on black boots with white soles.

The images of the Kings in hell in front of the two walls are almost identical, wearing the cage crowns. They wear the open cross-collar garments with a jade belt tied around the waist, standing with two hands holding together in front of chest.

Three seated Buddhas modelled in relief can be seen on each sloping side of the panels a on rectangular caisson ceiling, and there are 12 sculptures in all. They seat on the double-reverse lotus thrones in a pose of deep yogic meditation, with the legs tightly locked, the soles of both feet uppermost. They are robed in the outer robes thrown over the left shoulder or the upper throwing a strong diagonal across the bodies, leaving the right side of the body and shoulder bare.

Paintings: Paintings related to hell are visible on the left and right walls of the cave. Five to a side, there are ten in all. Yama seats in the hall with a hanging valance painted with flower patterns. There is a long table in front of him, on which lies a pen holder, documents, a lot of pot and other items.

跏趺坐于仰覆莲座上，着袒右式袈裟。

壁画：在洞窟的左右壁，绘有和地狱有关的壁画，左右各五幅，共十幅。阎君坐于帐幔下，帐幔上绘有花纹。阎君身前有案几，案几上绘有笔架、文书、签筒等物品。

地狱十王审判亡者魂魄的画面，让人异常恐怖。那些生前作恶多端的人到地狱后遭到严酷的审判，有刀山剑林、牛头马面以及各种各样的酷刑。

顶部壁画中央方格绘一红色圆形，圆形中绘一菩萨，戴花冠，面容饱满。着红色袒右式袈裟，结跏趺坐于莲花座上。八面坡分别绘有八个不同的道教的八卦符号。

引申与拓展

道明和尚与闵公是地藏王菩萨身边的侍者。道明和尚是唐代一个信奉地藏菩萨的僧人，在晚期的地藏信仰中，信徒都会供奉他的塑像，闵公是道明和尚的父亲，是地藏菩萨的忠实信徒。

在传说中，地狱中一共是十位王者，如果人生前做恶事太多，就会在地狱中受到这些王的审判，并且受到各种酷刑的折磨。佛教希望用这种方式制止或减少人们作恶。

道教的八卦形象和洞窟内的佛教内容没有直接的关系，可能是窟顶位置刚好分为八块，而工匠就在窟顶绘制了八个道教的符号。

这个洞窟内的造像组合并不符合佛经中的各种描述，将各种不同信仰的人物放置在一个洞窟内。这和十七至十八世纪信徒对佛经的理解不深、佛教和世俗生活更密切结合在一起等社会现象有密切关系。

The pictures of ten Kings of Hell trying the souls of the dead are horrifying. Those who have committed all kinds of evil deeds in their previous lives are put into the hell and are severely tried, such as climbing the mountain of swords, stabbed with swords, tortures suffered by two devils in animal forms (one with the head of an ox and the body of a human being, the other with the face of a horse and the body of a human being) and all kinds of cruel punishments.

Painting in the central panel on the ceiling retains a red circle containing a bodhisattva, wearing a corolla, full face. She is robed in the red robe thrown over the left shoulder or the upper throwing a strong diagonal across the body, leaving the right side of the body and shoulder bare, sitting on the lotus throne in a pose of deep yogic meditation, the legs tightly locked, the soles of both feet uppermost. Eight different symbols of Taoist Eight Trigrams can be seen on each of the eight sloping sides.

Extension and Elaboration

Elder Min and Daoming are attendants of Ksitigarbha Bodhisattva. Daoming is a monk in the Tang Dynasty who believes in Ksitigarbha Bodhisattva. In the late Ksitigarbha belief, the Statue of Ksitigarbha is dedicated. Elder Min, the father of Daoming, both are faithful worshipers of Ksitigarbha Bodhisattva.

In the legend, there are ten Kings in hell. If people practice too many evil deeds in their previous lives, they will be severely tried in hell, and will be tortured by various cruel punishments. Buddhism wishes to prevent or reduce people from practicing evil deeds in this way.

There is no direct relationship between the symbols of Taoist Eight Trigrams and the contents of Buddhist in the cave. It may be that the ceiling just bears eight sloping sides and the craftsmen painted eight Taoist symbols on the ceiling of the cave.

The group of sculptures in the cave is an unorthodox version of descriptions in the Buddhist sutras, and various figures of different beliefs are placed in a cave. This is closely related to two social phenomena. One might possibly have been suggested by the worshipers in the 17th and 18th centuries who misread the Buddhist sutras, the other is the closer integration of Buddhism and secular life.

第3窟 千佛廊

第3窟位于麦积山石窟东崖中上部，俗称"千佛廊"，因其廊道上下现存六排共二百九十七身石胎泥塑坐佛，即"千佛"造像而得名。始凿于北周（公元557年—公元581年），宋（公元960年—公元1279年）、明（公元1368年—1644年）重修，是一座仿照宫殿、园林中的长廊，也是麦积山石窟唯——座长廊式阁道。

该窟是中国石窟中唯一的长廊式洞窟，六排二百九十七尊石胎泥塑造像，十则残存题记。一眼望去，这些佛像的身高和造型似乎大体相同，细观每身佛像的发式、表情、手印、坐姿、袈裟等各不相同。

形制：该洞窟是大型"人"字坡顶长廊式崖阁建筑，坐北朝南。阁道整体水平凿刻，东西全长36.5米、进深2.7米，共有十四间，廊顶中间雕有月梁十三道，月梁中央雕出驼峰，驼峰之上有替木和脊檩，内壁上雕出檐檩。两坡之间凿出圆形六七根椽子连接脊檩和檐檩，前檐大部崩塌。窟门与第168窟台阶相连。

造像：廊道上方分布两排共九十二身坐佛，下方四排共二百身坐佛。廊道外侧与左前部残存上下两层，上层三身，下层两身。造像大小基本相等，均高0.93米，宽0.6米，厚0.19米，每排造像下方有分隔的横栏，高0.95米，栏台高0.28米，廊道第二排与第三排

Cave 3　Thousand Buddhas Corridor

Cave 3 is located in the upper middle part of the eastern cliff at Maijishan Caves, commonly known as "Thousand Buddhas Corridor". Because 297 seated Buddhas, the Thousand Buddhass, modelled in clay plaster over a core of rock in six rows survive on the upper and lower parts of its corridor. It was initially excavated in the Northern Zhou Dynasty (AD 557-581) and repaired in the Song (AD 960-1279) and Ming (AD 1368-1644) dynasties. It is a corridor modelled after palaces and gardens, and it is the unique gallery with long corridor at Maijishan Caves.

In this cave, visitors can observe the unique long corridor in caves in China, 297 seated Buddhas modelled in clay over the conglomerate of the cliff itself in six rows, with ten surviving inscriptions. They might look to a casual observer as though their heights and modellings are almost identical, but if you watch carefully you will find each of them bears different hair style, expression, mudra, pose, robe and so on. Details are as follows.

Type: It is a huge south-facing recess with an inverted Y-shaped ceiling and a long corridor. The gallery is carved in horizontal as a whole, with a total length of 36.50 meters from east to west, the vertical depth of 2.70 meters. There are 14 openings in all, 13 crescent beams are carved on the central ceiling of the corridor with a camel-hump shaped support in the cent, above which a *timu* (a narrow member inserted in the lu tou as an auxiliary half kung to support the bracket arm) and a ridged purlin are placed, an eave purlin is carved in the inner wall. The ridged purlin and the eave purlin are connected by six or seven round rafters hollowed between the two sloping sides, and most of the front eaves have fallen away. The cave door is connected to the stairs of Cave 168.

Sculptures: There are two rows above the corridor containing 92 seated Buddhas in all and four rows retaining 200 seated Buddhas altogether below the corridor. The outside of the corridor and the left front remain two tiers, with three seated Buddhas above and two seated Buddhas below. The size of the sculptures is almost identical, with all 0.93 meters high, 0.6 meters wide and 0.19 meters thick. Below each row of sculptures there is a divider with 0.95 meters high and the terrace of 0.28 meters high. The terrace between the seated Buddhas

坐佛的分隔栏台高约0.6米。廊道下部四排造像除少数塑像泥皮脱落外，绝大多数保存基本完好。廊道上方两层造像小部分面部泥皮脱落，较为完整地保存宋代重修原貌。

廊道上方两排上部佛像石胎结构较清晰，低平肉髻和五官，颈部较短，上身宽平，手臂较长，环于腹前。上身紧贴壁面，身后有圆形项光，石胎上可见袈裟及覆莲座的阴刻线。北周原作泥塑已不可辨，外层现可见宋代重修作品，低平肉髻，有肉髻珠。佛像发髻有磨光、水波纹和旋涡纹三种形式，间隔塑做。面部丰满，前额平阔，有泥质半珠形白毫相，下层一排白毫均残毁不存。眉骨突出，阴刻弯眉，双眼眼角上翘，微曲下视。鼻梁适中，唇分四瓣，双耳垂肩，绘有胡髭。内着僧祇支，外着双领下垂或圆领袈裟，施以赭红、石绿和浅黄色。袈裟右侧衣角或搭于

第3窟上部两排千佛

in the second row and the third row of the corridor is about 0.6 meters high. Except few thin skin of clay plaster has fallen away in the four rows below the corridor, with most figures being particularly well preserved. Very little sculpture of the facial thin skin of clay plaster has peeled off in the two rows above the corridor, which more completely retains the original plaster restored in the Song Dynasty.

The structures of the cores of rocks in the two rows of the upper Buddhas above the corridor are clearly visible, with the low flat ushnishas right on the top, and facial features, short necks, broad and smooth upper bodies, with longer arms resting on their abdomens. The upper bodies cling to the wall, having the circular aureoles behind them, the incised lines of the robes and the upside-down lotus thrones can be seen on the core of rock. The clay plaster of the original work modelled in the Northern Zhou Dynasty is barely legible, only the refurbished works of the Song Dynasty there survive on the outer layer with the low flat ushnishas right on the top, the beads between the buns and the bottom hair. There are three types of hairstyles: a polished, a water wavy, a spiral-shaped topknot carved at intervals. They have full faces, broad and smooth foreheads, and their white hair between the brows is carved in clay plaster in semicircular, leaving those in the lower rows destroyed. They bear protruding eyebrow bones, incised arched brows, the corners of eyes upwards, with eyes slightly curved and looking downward. They are of moderate nose bridges, the four-petalled lips, large ears with pendulous lobes, moustached. They wear inner vests

第3窟上部两排千佛

左肩，或搭于左肘或于左胸前结环垂挂，下摆于莲花座前分四瓣状下垂。双手施禅定印，结跏趺坐于莲花座。千佛双手结印分三种形式相间隔，或掌心向上置于腿部，或掌心向内覆于腿部外侧，或拢于袖中置于腿部。部分造像袈裟"田相"上绘有石绿色白边的卷草图案。

廊道下方四排坐佛，基本保持原作，表面均有磨蚀。除部分造像被桩孔打破，其余保存较为完整。坐佛均为磨光低平肉髻，面相方圆，眉间未塑出白毫相，细眉凸起，眼鼻适中，嘴唇稍小，脖颈稍短，肩宽体长。内着僧祇支，外着双领下垂袈裟，阴刻衣纹较为舒缓。双手施禅定印，结跏趺坐。上排坐佛袈裟下摆为较平的素面，最下一排袈裟下摆呈莲瓣状。以赭石和现呈黑色的颜料绘出圆形项光和袈裟边缘。

第3窟下部四排千佛

covering the left shoulder and armpits, either in the upper garments that completely cover their bodies, with U-shaped collar falling to the chest, the corner of the robe on the right either resting on the left arm, or the robes of round collar, colouring in reddish-browns, stone green and light yellow. The corners of the robes on the right rest either on the left shoulder or on the left elbow or hang on the left chest in a loop, and the hem cascades over their lotus thrones in four large petals. They are seated with legs tightly locked in a yogic pose on the lotus thrones, and their two hands perform the dhyana mudra. Three forms of the Thousand Buddhas are carved at intervals, either resting on the laps with the palms up, or beside the laps with the palms inward, or on the laps concealing the clasped hands in the sleeves of robes. Some of the "paddy-field design" robes are adorned with the pattern of white edged roll grass in stone green.

The seated Buddhas in the four rows below the corridor remain basically original works, and all the surfaces have been eroded. Except that some of the sculptures have been broken by the pile holes, the rest seems to be intact. They all wear the polished low flat ushnishas right on the top, with the round faces, no white hair between the brows, the arched and raised eyebrows, moderate eyes and noses, smaller lips, shorter necks, broad shoulders and long physiques. They wear inner vests covering the left shoulder and armpits, the upper garments that completely cover their bodies, with U-shaped collar falling to the chest, the corner of the robe resting on the left arm, the smooth incised drapery. They are seated with legs tightly locked in a yogic pose on the lotus thrones, and their two hands perform the dhyana mudra. The hems of the seated Buddhas in the upper row are flatter without carvings or patterns, while those in the lowest row are adorned with lotus petals. The circular aureoles and hems of robes are drawn in ochre and black.

Inscriptions: There are ten inscriptions left by visitors in the cave. Visitors might have written dedications and roughly scratched their names on the bodies or beside seated Buddhas with a brush. Among which the one on the 29th seated Buddha reads: "The dedication carved on intercalary August 26th in the third year of Longqing in the Ming Dynasty (AD 1569) is here by Zhang Ruiquan of Qinzhou." The more clearly legible. Others have inscriptions of Ming and Qing dynasties with names or dates subsequently worn or rubbed off.

Extension and Elaboration

Literally, the Thousand Buddhas Corridor at least has a thousand Buddhas, but actually there are not so many, only six rows of 297 seated Buddhas in all. Figures of the Thousand Buddhass are one of the major themes in the art of the caves at Maijishan, which play a

题记：该窟残存十则题记。访客在坐佛身上、身旁潦草地墨书题记、留名。其中第二十九身左边墨书题记："隆庆三年闰八月二十六日秦州张瑞泉到。"字迹清晰可辨，其他明朝和清朝题记人名或纪年被磨掉或擦掉了。

引申与拓展

千佛廊，并不是长廊塑有一千尊佛，千佛指三世十方诸佛群像。千佛造像是麦积山石窟艺术题材之一，对洞窟起装饰作用。窟顶和四壁上层，塑像和说法图四周画小千佛，使洞窟形成一个四处有佛的佛国天堂，使整窟显得气势雄伟。

decorative role in the caves. The small Thousand Buddhass are often carved on the ceiling, the upper part of the four walls of the cave, around sculptures and Sakyamuni's preaching, making the cave a Buddha paradise with Buddhas everywhere and the whole cave pretty magnificent.

第4窟 散花楼

第4窟位于麦积山石窟东崖最高位置，位于第13窟"东崖大佛"上方，距地面45米。在公元566年和公元568年期间，当时秦州的大都督李允信为悼念亡父而建造。因后室七列龛里各有一身主尊佛，组成七佛龛，七龛内供奉"过去七佛"，通常称"上七佛阁"。又因五代文学家王仁裕（公元880年—公元956年）《玉堂闲话》中称之为"散花楼"而得名。该洞窟是麦积山石窟外观规模最大、最宏伟的崖阁式窟，也是唯一由南北朝文学家庾信（公元513年—公元587年）制铭的洞窟。这个虔诚开凿的洞窟是提到麦积山时最重要的文学参考题材。

该窟外观宏大，属于崖阁建筑，现存大中型泥塑佛、弟子、菩萨、力士、文殊、维摩诘等造像计七十五身（其中两身塑像破损为多个残块）以及石胎浮塑"天龙八部"护法八身和影塑小千佛七百五十七身，共计造像八百四十身。这些造像多经后代重修或重塑及妆銮。廊顶及龛外正壁上方的北周壁画，其中龛上方前五幅将绘画与薄塑融合的"薄肉塑"飞天壁画富于立体感以及七龛内壁画。该洞窟大约有四十则残存题记，七龛龛楣之上悬挂的明制牌匾，明代时期，在西侧开凿仅容一人而通往第5窟（"牛儿堂"）的过洞。

形制：该窟在开凿设计时是按照六世纪时期宫殿建筑的形式开凿的，平面长方形、七间八柱、单檐庑殿顶式崖阁，坐北朝南，前廊后室结构。前廊通高16米、廊高8.65米、面阔31.4米、进深4.1米。最初在栈道栏杆的位置有八根粗大的柱子，因为公

Cave 4　Pavilion of Scattered Flowers

Cave 4 is located at the highest point on the eastern cliff above the triad of Cave 13, 45 meters from the ground. Between AD 566 and AD 568 when Li Yunxin, the senior military commander at Qinzhou, had seven Buddha niches hollowed out in memory of his father. Because each bears a seated Buddha on the main wall, consisting of "Seven Buddhas Cave". The seated Buddhas are the Seven Buddhas of the Past, so it is usually called "the Upper Seven Buddhas Halls". Also the poet Wang Renyu of Five Dynasties (AD 880-956) described it as "Pavilion of Scattered Flowers" in his work *Idle Tales of the Jade Hall*. It is a huge chamber, the most ambitious excavation at Maijishan, for which the unique inscription written by Yu Xin (AD 513-587), a litterateur of the Northern Dynasty. This pious excavation was the subject of the most important literary reference to the sacred site.

In this cave, visitors can see the huge chamber open to the cliff face, 75 large and medium-sized Buddhas, disciples, bodhisattvas, dvarapalas, Manjushri and Vimalakirti of clay (Fragments of two sculptures remain.), as well as eight guardians of "Demi Gods and Semi Devils" carved in relief over a core of rock, and 757 small Thousand Buddhass moulded in relief, there are 840 in all. Most of these sculptures have been rebuilt or remodelled and redecorated by their descendants. The ceiling frescoes of the gallery and the upper part outside the niche were made in the Northern Zhou Dynasty, among which five flying apsaras "adorned with painting and sculpture" at the front above the niche achieved a strong three-dimensional effect, as well as wallpaintings on the walls inside the seven halls. You can also observe 40 surviving inscriptions, the about wooden horizontal plaque engraved in the Ming Dynasty (AD 1613) above the lintels of the seven halls, and experience the tunnel to the west leading to Cave 5 (Cave of the Bull) dug in the Ming Dynasty, which allows one person pass through only by crawling. Details are as follows.

Type: The cave was excavated in the form of palace buildings in the sixth century. It is a huge plane rectangular south-facing chamber open to the cliff face, with the lintel supported by stone pillars, and a single-eaved hip roof carved in relief in the rock above. Originally eight stone pillars supported a roof carved from the living rock, making a gallery of seven openings open along the front, behind which dug a row of seven halls. The gallery is 16 meters from the ground, 8.65 meters from ceiling to floor, with the room width of 31.40 meters and the vertical depth of 4.10 meters. The whole of the front of the hall has fallen away by the severe earthquake of AD 734 in the Tang Dynasty, taking with it the floor and

第4窟外景

第4窟"薄肉塑"飞天

元734年地震的缘故,中间的六根柱子和对应的地面、屋顶等都塌毁了,我们在山根下的堆积层里还可以看见个别残断的柱子。前廊右壁凿开一洞,通第5窟。通道口高1.5米、宽0.75米、深2.94米。

站在洞窟中间位置向左右两侧观望,可以看到在洞窟两侧靠近山体的位置还各有一根粗大的石柱子。柱高7.25米,八面形,为了适应视觉效果,柱子的直径从下向上逐步缩小,在柱子的下边有直径超过两米的覆莲柱础。柱头雕大斗,大斗上雕额枋,其上部又雕齐心斗和散斗;斗上雕替木和木撩檐枋;再上部雕水平伸出的扁檐椽。殿顶雕正脊两端鸱尾,屋面筒瓦瓦垄。前廊左右壁上方各开一敞口小龛。廊顶各间原凿平棋六块,共计四十二块,现存两稍间六块,其余已塌毁。

第4窟"薄肉塑"飞天

the row of six rock-hewn columns, leaving only the engaged two columns at the ends. We can also see some fragments of pillars at the bottom of the mountain. A tunnel was cut to the west wall of the gallery leading to Cave 5. The entrance is 1.50 meters high, 0.75 meters wide and 2.94 meters deep.

Standing in the middle of the cave and looking to the left and right, you can see a huge stone pillar on each side near the rock. With the height of 7.25 meters, octagonal cross section, they are receded from the top to the bottom to meet the visual requirements, at the bottom of which there is an upside-down lotus column base with more than two meters in diameter. A cap block is placed on the capital, a lintel or architrave is placed on the cap block above, and a central block and a small block are placed above; a *timu* and a wooden eave purlin are erected on the brackets; and then the horizontal extension of the flat eave rafters is carved above. A *chiwei* (a decorative component shaped like an owl's tail) is decorated at both ends on the main ridge of the roof, with rows of round tiles. Above the east and the west ends of the front gallery stands a small open niche on the cliff face. Originally six recessed panels were cut in the ceiling of the gallery of seven openings, there are 42 panels in all. Today, only the ends of the coffered ceiling containing six panels survive, of which the whole of the panels has collapsed.

At the rear of the pillars stands seven large quadrangle halls in a row, which imitate the

在柱子的后方位置,则是七间方正的房屋,这种房屋是模仿六世纪室内装饰性的"帐"来雕凿的。龛形大小基本相同,平面方形、四角攒尖顶龛,近方形门。龛高5.06~5.42米,壁高约4.3米、宽4.2米、进深4.2米。龛门上方雕出龙、凤、象首等动物形象,口含由珠宝、铃铛等构成的长流苏。

龛内雕出八边形帐柱、帐杆,下有覆莲柱础,帐柱和帐杆相交接处雕出莲花,窟顶中央也有一大朵莲花。

造像:该窟现存泥塑、石胎浮塑和影塑造像,共计八百四十身,分布在前廊左右两侧、前廊左右耳龛、七龛外左右两侧壁面、七佛龛内。

前廊左右两侧。站在洞窟中央位置向左右看,可以看到东西两侧各有一身大力士形象,这是十二世纪的雕塑作品。左力士,高四米,头向左前扭,束高髻,颈挂璎珞,帔帛覆肩,腰系战裙,戴臂钏、腕环、脚镯,赤足站石台座上;右手握拳屈肘上举过头,左手屈肘向下拄金刚杵,怒目圆睁,张口做呵斥状。右力士,高4.3米,

第4窟左力士

第4窟右力士

interior decoration of a "tent" in the sixth century. Their types and sizes are identical, a flat square quadrangle niche with a pyramidal roof, subquadrate door. The niche is 5.06-5.42 meters high, and the wall is about 4.30 meters high, 4.20 meters wide and 4.20 meters deep. They are 5.06-5.42 meters high, and the wall about 4.30 meters high, 4.20 meters wide and the vertical depth of 4.20 meters. Above the door of the seven halls are adorned with the heads of dragons, phoenixes and elephants with long hanging tassels of jewelry, bells in their mouths at both ends.

The octagonal tent poles, and tent columns are carved on the ceiling and four corners. The round column bases are placed in the form of an upside-down lotus below. A lotus flower is carved at the junction of the column and the pole, and there is a large lotus flower in the center of the ceiling.

Sculptures: 840 sculptures survive in the Upper Seven Buddhas Halls, which are built up in clay, in shallow relief over a core of rock, and in relief. They are distributed at the left and right ends of the gallery, a niche at left and right end of the gallery, the walls on the left and right outside the Seven Buddhas halls, and inside the Seven Buddhas halls.

In the left and right ends of the gallery standing in the center of the cave and looking from left to right, you can see a huge image of dvarapala modelled in the 12th century at each end. The dvarapala at left end is four meters high, with head twisting to the front left, wearing his hair in a high ushnisha right on the top, a heavy garland of jewels round the neck, broad scarves hanging over the shoulders, the waist wrapped with battle skirt, wearing armlets, wrist rings, anklets, standing on the stone base barefoot; His right arm is raised over the head with a clenched fist, while his left arm extends downward, holding a vajra, eyes round open in fury attitude, with mouth open in a scolding manner. The dvarapala at right end is 4.3 meters high, wearing a circular ushnisha right on the top and a high crown with a small seated Buddha image. His left arm is raised above with a clenched fist, while his right arm extends downward with a half clenched fist. He stands with head high and shoulders squared, leaving lips closed, looking fiercely ahead. The two dvarapalas are powerfully modelled, especially their faces and bulging muscles.

There is a niche at left and right end of the gallery. A niche carved above the rear wall of dvarapala at each end of the gallery contains Vimalakirti at the east end, and Manjushri at the west end. These sculptures in the niches are relatively late and were modelled by worshipers around the 15th century. Vimalakirti is 1.05 meters high, while Manjushri 1.6 meters high. And each has an attendant, with 1.22 meters to 1.4 meters tall. In the niche Vimalakirti has plump face, high brow bone, eyes half-open, wearing an inner garment with a collar folded across in front, an outer loose-sleeved robe, the left hand rests on knee, holding his fan in his right hand, the upper body slightly leaning upon a table, sitting on a square high pedestal, his almost regal attitude suggesting an elder image. A maid is standing on his right, looking up, with round face and broad shoulders. Her hair is braided and looped up on either side of her head, her left hand in clenching fist, the right hand hangs down. She wears a dress with long loose sleeves, and a long dress on the lower body. She is

环形高髻，戴化佛冠。左手屈肘上举紧握拳，右手屈肘向下半握拳，昂首挺胸，双唇紧闭，怒视前方。两身力士造型坚实有力，尤其面部、胸肌的塑作起伏变化大。

　　前廊左右耳龛。在力士后方墙面上方，各有一个小耳龛，其中东侧龛内的造像是维摩诘居士，西侧龛内的造像是文殊菩萨。这两个龛内塑像时代比较晚，是十五世纪前后信徒塑做的。维摩诘高1.05米，文殊高1.6米。他们的两侧各有一侍者站立，身高1.22～1.4米。维摩诘面相丰硕，眉骨高隆，双目半睁，内穿交领衫，外穿宽袖长袍，左手抚膝，右手执麈尾，上身微前倾，踞坐方形高台上，神态潇洒似一长者形象。其右侧立侍女，抬头仰视，面圆肩宽，梳分瓣双髻，左手握拳，右手下垂。外穿长袖衣，下着长裙。体态丰盈，神情专注，在聆听维摩诘讲经说法。

第4窟文殊菩萨耳龛　　　　　　　　　　第4窟维摩诘耳龛

full, looks intently, listening to the teaching of Vimalakirti.

In the walls on the left and right outside the seven Buddha halls, we can see eight guardian figures "Demi Gods and Semi Devils". The inner structure is carved on the conglomerate of the cliff itself for a rough armature, and the outer specific parts of the body is modelled in clay over. The images are carved after the army warriors in sixth century. We can see the thin skin of clay plaster in two or even three overlapping layers, which is the result of the restoration of the believers in the Tang and Song dynasties. Although restored, they retain their original appearances. Now most of the clay has fallen off, leaving the core of rock carved in the Northern Zhou Dynasty exposed. The first and the eighth guardians are lateral, each foot supported by an atlantid half crouched. Five heavenly kings in the middle are frontal, standing on bases decorated with squatting lions, Earth God and so on. Among them, the third figure is tall and stout, wearing a tiger helmet, the round face with raised brows, eyes round open in a fury attitude. Wearing a heavy collar, with shoulder protection, the waist is wrapped with short skirt. Holding a sword in his left hand, wearing bracelets in the right hand, he steps on the back of the Earth God barefoot, showing a brave and mighty attitude. Above him are bodhisattvas painted in the Tang Dynasty.

Inside the seven Buddha halls, the interior of Niche 1 contains three seated Buddhas flanked by two standing disciples and six bodhisattvas. Niches 2, 4, 6 and 7 show a seated Buddha flanked by two standing disciples and six bodhisattvas. Niches 3 and 5 retain a seated Buddha and eight standing bodhisattvas. Each niche of seven halls bears a seated Buddha on the main wall, who are the Past Seven Buddhas with 2.37 meters to 2.5 meters high. The style is similar to something solid and full. Bodhisattva and disciples in each niche are 2.76 meters to 3.1 meters tall. Except two bodhisattvas in each niche of Niche 1 and Niche 2 have collapsed and damaged, the rest of the statues are intact. These figures of Buddhas and bodhisattvas were all rebuilt in the 12h century, as the previous ones were destroyed by an earthquake in AD 734. But the motifs on their costume we see were repainted by local donors in the 18th or 19th century.

Among figures of disciples, the Kasyapa on the left side of the main wall in Niche 1 is the most impressive. He is 2.8 meters tall, with the square face carved with pendulous ears, wrinkles on his forehead, bulging cheekbones, sunken eye sockets, shrivelled lips, exposed muscles and bones of the neck, jagged ribs on chest, all suggesting an old age. He is robed in an upper garment that completely covers his body, with a U-shaped collar falling to the chest, the lappet of the robe resting on the left arm, while his waist is wrapped in long skirt, with a band tied at the abdomen falling in a knot. The combination of painting and sculpture has shaped the image of the old monk Kasyapa.

Among figures of bodhisattvas, the two on the walls on either side of the entrance in Niche 6 are the most outstanding. They are 2.96 meters high, of very similar type: with a high crown, oval face, slant-eyed, the white hair between their brows (urnalaksana), high bridged nose with large nostrils, a heavy garland of jewels round the neck, broad scarves hanging

第4窟"天龙八部"浮雕

在七龛外左右两侧墙面上,雕刻八身"天龙八部"护法形象。内部结构是在岩石上雕刻出大致骨架,外侧的具体部位用泥来塑做。其形象是仿照六世纪军队武士形式雕刻的。我们可以看到有两层甚至三层泥皮的叠压,这是唐宋信众重修的结果。尽管重修但原貌仍存,现大部泥塑脱落,北周石胎暴露在外。第一身和第八身侧面向内,足下各有一半蹲力士托举,中间五身天王为正面塑像,足下塑蹲狮、地神等。其中第三身像形体魁梧,戴虎头盔,圆脸,眉上扬,双目圆睁做愤怒状。戴宽项圈,着护肩,系短裙。左手握剑,右手戴镯,赤足踩地神背上,表现出勇猛威武的神态。其上方有唐代所绘菩萨等。

七佛龛内。列龛内,第1龛为三佛、二弟子、六菩萨组合;第

over the shoulders. They wear the short robs adorned with raised swirls on the chest, the lower tight-fitting garments with revers at the waist, and stand on the round lotus pedestals barefoot. The left-side bodhisattva ties a broad sash adorned with ornaments at the waist. While the right-side bodhisattva hangs a pair of bands tied around the waist falling in a knot over the lower abdomen. Their drapery shows a combination of smooth curve and rotating arc, and incised lines of the raised drapery. The technique of gelled patterning and gilding was used to redecorate in the Ming Dynasty, and the colors were extremely bright.

There are Thousand Buddhass modelled in relief. A large number of small seated Buddhas modelled in relief are carved on the upper part of each of the front, left and right walls in seven halls. Some Buddhas in each hall have been peeled away, and still 757 Buddhas survive in three horizontal rows on each wall. A single Buddha modelled in the relief is 0.2 meters high, wearing a low flat ushnisha right on the top. They are robed in the inner vests (samkaksika) covering the left shoulder and armpits, the cassocks, sitting with legs tightly locked in a yogic pose. A large halo is decorated with the canopy with a hanging valance, and long hanging string of pearls and tassels on each side. Thousand Buddhass modelled in relief are divided into two types: one is those whose hands are elevated to the chest level and the lotus Sumeru thrones supported by dvarapalas, and the other is those whose two hands perform the dhyana mudra and the lotus Sumeru thrones supported by two lions. The two types appear alternatively among three rows of Thousand Buddhass. They are arranged neatly, with highly decorative. These small seated figures in relief are modelled in the sixth century. They are not made in insolation, but in moulds with the clay spreading over, are finally applied to the walls. This method can make small figures in mass production. After careful observation, we find that the seated Buddhas are not modelled in one image, but actually in four types, each with different details, but the height and width are identical, making it more conducing to arrange on the wall.

Paintings: On the whole, the paintings in the cave can be divided into two parts. The first part refers to those in the gallery, while the second part is ones in the seven halls. Those on the ceiling of the gallery and on the main walls outside the seven halls are the original works of the Northern Zhou Dynasty (AD 557-581), while those on the ceiling and walls in the seven halls are repainted by worshipers in the 15th and 16th centuries.

There are paintings on the ceiling of the gallery. Some paintings of the sixth century are preserved in the panels on the ceiling. Originally there are 42 panels in all, all have been damaged by the earthquakes, leaving only six panels. Because they were not exposed to the sun, colours were not badly faded, to large extent they have retained their pristine freshness of colour and clear images in six century. The images chiefly contain bodhisattvas, disciples, divines, courtyard buildings, carriages, etc. Around and in the center of the picture are decorated with motifs of four-petal fragrant flowers with stems, honeysuckles and auspicious clouds, colouring in a bluish grey tint, a stone green, a reddish-brown and gingery and so on. A picture is painted to the inner left of the west side, which is said to depict the scene of "Queen and Prince Returning to the Palace". The combination of intersection and scattered

第4窟第1龛牌匾　　　　　　　第4窟第2龛牌匾

2、第4、第6、第7龛为一佛、二弟子、六菩萨组合；第3和第5龛为一佛、八菩萨组合；七龛正壁主尊各为一坐佛，是为"过去七佛"，七坐佛高2.37～2.5米，风格大体相同，敦厚丰满。各龛菩萨、弟子，身高2.76～3.1米。除第1、第2龛各有两身菩萨倒塌残损外，其余塑像均完好。这些佛像和菩萨像，都是在十二世纪重修的，因为之前的造像都在公元734年的地震中被破坏了。但是我们看到的佛像、菩萨像身体服饰表层的各种花纹，则是十八或十九世纪由当地的供养人重新绘制的。

弟子，以第1龛正壁左侧的迦叶最传神。高2.8米，方面大耳，前额有皱纹，颧骨隆起，眼窝深陷，嘴唇干瘪，颈间筋骨外露，两胸肋骨嶙峋，显现老相。外穿双领下垂袈裟，衣襟搭于臂，腰系长裙，腹前结带下垂。刻、塑结合，塑造了苦修老僧迦叶的形象。

菩萨，以第6龛左右壁近门两菩萨最突出。二菩萨高2.96米，造型基本相似：高花冠，椭圆脸，眼角上挑，眉间白毫相，隆鼻露孔，颈挂璎珞，帔帛顺两臂下垂。上穿短襦，胸有凸起旋涡饰纹，下着紧身翻腰长裙，跣足立圆莲台上。其中左菩萨腰系宽带，有佩饰，右菩萨腰系双股丝带，腹前作结。菩萨衣纹由流畅曲线和旋转

第4窟第3龛牌匾　　　　　　　　　　　　第4窟第4龛牌匾

perspectives is adopted to form the composition of the figures of horses and carriages, leaving the marching direction of the red horse might look to an observer as though it was opposite from different angles and the changes are marvelous. Two panels containing figures and buildings on the west: the upper right corner in one panel illustrates the scene of "The Construction of the Hall of Three Seasons", a remaining courtyard surrounded by flowers, trees, and the winding corridors. The lower right corner in the same panel consists of four or five figures wearing the small crowns, the short robs, and the long dresses. The other panel describes a courtyard with tower gates containing more than ten people. Outside, warriors with the upper body bare and barefoot, wear shorts, holding weapons in their hands on patrol. Among the paintings on the east side, one panel is considered as the scene of "Heavenly Beings Riding on Dragons", with four flying apsaras guiding ahead, followed by disciples, bodhisattvas and attendants flying among the clouds, or stepping on the lotus platforms, or standing barefoot. Several female donors holding flowers survive at the corner of the other panel, elegantly modelled.

Flying apsaras "adorned with sculpture and painting" are above the main wall of the gallery. A row of seven large wallpaintings of flying apsaras painted on the corresponding walls of each hall above the main wall of the gallery are original works of the Northern Zhou Dynasty. Each contains four flying apsaras in painting and sculpture, symmetric on both sides, in trapezoidal arrangement, there are 28 in all. Each ranges from 1.50 to 1.80 meters in height and from 2.90 to 3.50 meters wide. Among which the first five from left to right are "Painting Adorned with Sculpture and Painting", and the last two are plane murals. They are thinly clad, their scarves fluttering in the wind, and they are flying towards each other in the falling flowers and rain. It depicts the scene of the celestial musicians dancing while playing strung and drumming instruments. Paintings of No.1, No.3, No.5 and No.7 show the different images of the celestial musicians playing instruments, some are playing horn, ocarina, flute, *sheng* (bamboo organ) and pan-pipes, some are beating drums and gongs, and others are playing zither, *konghou* (an ancient plucked stringed instrument), *ruanxian* (a plucked stringed instrument) and *pipa* (guitar).

第4窟第6龛主佛

弧线组成,并在凸起褶纹上加刻阴线一道,明代曾用沥粉贴金的技法重妆,色彩异常鲜艳。

影塑千佛。每个方形房间的正、左、右壁上部位置,都有大量的小型坐佛,每壁均为横向三排,各龛均有剥取痕迹,现存七百五十七身。每尊的高度为20厘米左右,低平肉髻。内着僧祇支,外穿袈裟,结跏趺坐。后大背光上有饰帷幔华盖,左右璎珞、流苏下垂。影塑千佛分为双手抚胸、力士莲花须弥座和禅定印、双狮莲花须弥座两类。三排千佛中两类型相间出现。排列整齐,极富装饰性。这些小坐佛都是六世纪的影塑作品,它们不是单独塑做的,而是用泥制模具翻制后再贴到墙面上。这样的方法可以大批量制作小型佛像。众佛像并非一种形象,而是有四种,各自在细节上都有所区别,但高度和宽度等都是一致的,这样更有利于在墙面上

第二章　麦积山石窟汉英解说词

第4窟第6龛左菩萨

第4窟第6龛右菩萨

排列。

壁画：窟内壁画整体上可以分为两部分，第一部分为前廊壁画，第二部分为后室七龛壁画。前廊壁画包括廊顶和七龛外正壁上方的壁画是北周时期（公元557年—公元581年）的原作，而七前廊廊顶和七龛外正壁上方的壁画是北周时期（公元557年—公元581年）的原作，而七龛内部各个位置的壁画则是经过了十五世纪和十六世纪信徒的重绘。

廊顶壁画。在廊顶部的方格内保存一些六世纪的壁画，原有42块，因地震现仅存六块，皆有破损。这些壁画由于没有经受阳光直射等，所以颜料褪色不是很严重，较大程度保持了六世纪的色彩。多绘以菩萨、弟子、天人等形象及庭院式建筑、马车等，画面周围及中间也是以带茎四瓣香花及忍冬纹祥云装饰。所用颜料有石青、石绿、土红、姜黄等。西侧靠里偏左所绘，一说为"母子还宫"，

第4窟廊顶壁画

Wallpaintings of No.2, No.4 and No.6 bear the different images of votive flying apsaras, those at the four corners are either holding a lotus flower, or holding a tray of offerings, or holding a long-handled incense burner in one hand and scattering flowers with the other hand. This "Painting Adorned with Sculpture and Painting" achieves a strong three-dimensional effect.

Paintings of 60 square meters on the interior ceilings of the seven halls are just visible, repainted in the Ming Dynasty, but still retain its original style of the Northern Zhou Dynasty. Most are Buddha Sermon Illustrations, Buddha Worship Pictures, and sutra illustration paintings of Illustration to the Pure Land and Nirvana Sutra Illustration Paintings. Below them also retain paintings of the Tang Dynasty. The faces of the figures, tree branches and the contours of houses are subtly modelled in very shallow relief, suggesting a strong three-dimensional sense.

The paintings inside the seven halls have been rebuilt many times, we can just make out the works of worshipers modelled in the 15th and 16th centuries. The basic content is the scene of Sakyamuni's preaching and so on. The lower layers of them still show traces of their sixth-century decoration.

Plaques: Above the door of the seven halls hangs four plaques inscribed with the phrases "Bodhi Field" "The Holy One from the West" "Wisdom Shining Everywhere", and "The

第4窟窟顶

其中的车马人物，运用交点透视和散点透视结合构图，使红马前进的方向从不同位置观察截然相反，变化奇妙。西侧两方人物建筑图：一方右上角绘"建三时殿"，残存一庭院，围绕有花草树木、回廊。右下角有四五个头戴小冠，身穿短襦、长裙的人物。另一方绘有门楼庭院，内有十余人，庭院外有袒身赤足、穿短裤的武士，手持武器巡视。东侧所绘，其中一方有人认为是"诸天普乘"，四身飞天前方导引，其后众弟子、菩萨及侍从相随乘云前进，或脚踩莲台，或赤足站立。另一方的一角残存数身持花女供养人，体态优美。

前廊正壁上方的薄肉塑壁画。前廊上方诸龛对应的壁面上，绘有七幅大型飞天壁画，北周原作。每幅绘塑四身飞天，左右对称，呈梯形排列，合计二十八身。每幅壁画高1.5～1.8米，宽2.9～3.5米。其中从左至右前五幅为"薄肉塑"壁画，后两幅为平面壁画。每身飞天衣裙轻薄，帔帛飘扬，于飞落花雨中相向飞行，描绘出天宫伎乐在弦管鼓乐的演奏下翩翩起舞的场景。第1、第3、第5、第7幅为伎乐飞天演奏乐器，有吹胡角、埙、笛、笙和箫的，也有击腰鼓、敲锣的，还有抚琴，弹箜篌、阮咸和琵琶的不同形象。第2、第4、第6幅为供养飞天，画面四角飞天或手持莲花，或手托供果盘，或一手握长柄香炉、一手散花等，形象各异。将薄塑与绘画融合的"薄肉塑"壁画富于立体感。

后室七龛内顶部壁画60平方米，明重绘，但仍有北周风格。七龛顶部多绘说法、礼佛图，也有净土、涅槃等经变壁画。其下还有唐代壁画。画面中有人物面部、树枝及屋宇轮廓等采用浅浮雕技法，立体感强。

七龛内侧的壁画则是经历了多次的重修，可见的壁画大约是十五世纪至十六世纪信徒的作品。基本内容是佛说法图等。在这些壁画的下层，隐约可见六世纪壁画的痕迹。

Supreme Art of Sculptures" respectively. They were written by the calligraphers at the request of the worshipers in the 16th and 17th centuries. They are all in praise of the Buddha.

Among them, above the lintel of Niche 4 hangs a wooden horizontal plaque inscribed with "The Most Magnificent Scenery", of which a limestone horizontal board inscribed with "Wonders at Maijishan" on the cliff face over its lintel. Each character can be as big as two or three chis (尺, a unit of length <3 chi=1 meter>), with pure gold embedded in them, which are more obviously seen from a distance. Their calligraphy is vigorous and upright, just like *Shiping Gong Zaoxiang Ji* (a stone carving calligraphy work)". Next to the four characters are five characters "Tian Xiong He Ying Xie", and the dynasty is unknown. Finally you can experience the tunnel to the west leading to Cave 5 dug in the Ming Dynasty, which can only allow one person to walk lowering his head. Above it hangs a wooden horizontal board inscribed with "A Hole of Another Scenery".

"The Supreme Art of Sculptures" is the most famous plaque of "the Pavilion of Scattered Flowers". It was written by litterateur Wang Liaowang of the Ming and Qing dynasties. When he was young, he read too widely and hoped to serve his country, but he suffered a total dislocation of his life for dynastic changes. When he was over 70 years old, he returned to his hometown Longxi. He spent most of his time sitting in deep meditation and worshiping Buddhas in different temples. He made a practice of reciting poetry and writing odes, leaving many works of art. When he came to Maijishan, he was moved by the Buddha figures modelled over a thousand years and splendid scenery, so he wrote "The Supreme Art of Sculptures" with a brush, expressing his realm of understanding the world thoroughly and his mind like still water. It means the Prajna Paramita, which is the supreme mantra in *The Heart Sutra*. This is also the most accurate description of the Maijishan Caves, the supreme art of sculptures.

Inscriptions: There are approximately 40 inscriptions left by visitors in the cave. Visitors might have written dedications and roughly scratched their names with a brush on the inner walls on both ends of the gallery, legs of the heavenly kings, pillars, an inner walls of the seven halls. Most contents of them are clearly legible.

牌匾：在七龛的外侧门口上方位置，悬挂着四块牌匾，分别为"西来圣人""菩提场""慧光普照"和"是无等等"，都是十六世纪甚至十七世纪信徒请当时的书法家撰写，对佛的赞颂词句。

其中第4龛龛楣木匾"是无等等"上部有石灰质牌匾一方，曰"麦积奇观"。每字大可二三尺，嵌以赤金，远视更显。书法挺劲如《始平公》。旁题"天雄赫瀛书"，朝代不明。前廊右壁下方贴地面凿有一洞连接第5窟"牛儿堂"，上刻"小有洞天"牌匾一方。

"是无等等"是"散花楼"最有名的一块牌匾。作者是文学家王了望。他一生跨越明清两朝，少时饱读诗书，盼望为国效力，却因改朝换代，颠沛流离。在他年逾古稀时，回到故乡陇西，来往于寺院之间，参禅礼佛，吟诗作赋，留下许多艺术作品。当他来到麦积山，被这里静立千年的佛像和"麦积烟雨"的秀美风光所打动，于是提笔写下"是无等等"，以表达自己看透世间、心如止水的境界。"是无等等"出自《心经》，赞叹佛法至高无上，这也是对麦积山石窟最确切的描述，雕塑艺术造诣的至高无上。

题记：该窟残存近四十则题记。访客在前廊耳龛内壁、天王腿部、立柱、七佛龛内壁面潦草地墨书题记、留名。多数内容可辨。

引申与拓展

七佛阁前廊正壁洞口上方的飞天壁画采用了"薄肉塑"绘塑结合技法。飞天的头部与手部等肌体暴露部分均用一层薄泥塑出，凸起在画面上，而飘曳的衣裙和飞舞的彩带画面全部采用彩绘而成。这些飞天可以追溯到北周时期（公元557年—公元581年）。这种装

Extension and Elaboration

The technique of painting and sculpture may be seen in the flying apsaras over the entrances to the Seven Buddhas Halls of Cave 4. Here head, arms and other exposed parts of the body are subtly modelled in very shallow relief, while garments and trailing scarves are merely painted on the wall. These are stylistically dateable in the Northern Zhou Dynasty (AD 557-581). This decorative technique really became popular in the contemporary art world of the 20th century, combining different materials and techniques, which is called installation art. But it is a miracle that ancient Chinese artists made such amazing attempts 1500 years ago.

The excavation of the massive chamber requires a lot of manpowers, material and financial resources and can not be completed by ordinary worshipers. Researchers have found some clues in an ancient book, *Yu Zishan Collected Works*, which is a collected works by a famous litterateur Yu Xin in the sixth century. Among which *The Inscription of the Seven-Buddha Niche on the Maiji Cliff in the Tianshui Prefecture of Qinzhou* was preserved in it. It is a dedicatory inscription for "the Seven Buddhas Halls" written by Yu Xin shortly after its completion at the request of the Chief Governor of Oinzhou. According to the content of the inscription, we can assume that the cave was dug around AD 570.

The poet Yu Xin (AD 513-581), a native of Henan province who had become celebrated at the Southern Liang Court in Nanjing where he held a high military appointment. At the request of Li Yunxin, he wrote an inscription for the "Seven Buddhas Cave", preserved in his collected works, which he prefaced with the following words: "The Maijishan is a famous mountain in the Longshan Mountain system, and among many beautiful peaks to the west of the Yellow River, with its peak high and its valley deep. Like Mount Lingjiu, Maiji mountain is a sacred place of Buddhist teachings. Here you can trace the footprints of the Zen masters who have made painstaking efforts and contributions to the construction of temples in the Maijishan; they are like cranes and stars in the sky. The narrow mountain roads are dangerous and suddenly come to an end. The clouds are like the wings of big rocs, and sometimes they suddenly obstruct the sky; the trees are like the moon, and the branches seem to touch the sun when they swing. Therefore, monks from far away came to the Maijishan to carve caves in the mountain, and built the Maijishan into a pure land of Buddhists. In the stone room, monks worshipped Vimalakirti (Bodhisattva), and then they will become immortal and walk in the wind; in the Buddhist niches on the mountain they worshipped the Bodhisattva, and then they will ascend to heaven.

Li Yunxin, the governor of the Qinzhou Prefecture, had a profound understanding of the path to Buddhism by virtue of his good roots planted in his previous life, so he ordered on the south cliff of the Maijishan to cut the road by erecting high ladders, and respectfully build the Seven-Buddha Nich for his dead father. It's like carving river water, like processing crystal. The leisurely

饰技法在二十世纪的当代艺术界才真正流行起来，将不同的材质和技法进行结合，称之为"装置艺术"。但在1500年前的中国古代艺术家就有了如此惊人的尝试，是一个奇迹。

这个洞窟规模宏大，需要投入大量的人力、物力、财力才能完成，不是一般的信徒能够完成的。研究者从一本古代典籍《庾子山文集》中找到了一些线索。这本典籍是六世纪一名著名的文学家庾信的作品集，其中有一篇《秦州天水郡麦积崖佛龛铭》，是庾信为秦州大都督李允信在麦积山开凿七佛阁所做的铭文。而根据铭文内容，我们可以推定这个洞窟开凿在公元570年前后。

庾信（公元513年—公元581年），河南人，在南京的南凉朝廷中声名显赫，并被拜为建康令。应李允信之请庾信为"七佛阁"撰写了一篇铭文，他在序言中写道：

"麦积崖者，乃陇底之名山，河西之灵岳。高峰寻云，深谷无量。方之鹫岛，迹循三禅；譬彼鹤鸣，虚飞六甲。鸟道乍穷，羊肠或断。云如鹏翼，忽已垂天；树若桂华，翻能拂日。以上序奇境是以飞锡遥来，度杯远至，疏山凿洞，郁为净土。拜灯王于石室，乃假驭风；礼花首于山龛，方资控鹤。

"大都督李允信者，籍于宿植，深悟法门。乃于壁之南崖，梯云凿道，奉为王父造七佛龛。似刻浮檀，如冰水玉，从容满月，照耀青莲。影现须弥，香闻仍利。如斯尘野，还开说法之堂；犹彼香山，更对安居之佛。昔者如来追福，有报恩之经；菩萨去家，有思亲之供。敢缘斯义，乃作铭曰：

'镇地郁盘，基乾峻极。

石关十上，铜梁九息。

百仞崖横，千寻松直。

and soothing full moon shines on the Buddha's eyes. The Buddha statue reveals Sumeru and smells the fragrance of heaven. In this earthly world, there is also a place where masters can explain the Dharma to the monks in the world. Like the Fragrant Mountain, we still have the Buddha who lives in peace. In the past, the Tathagata made merits for the dead, and there were scriptures to repay the kindness; when the Bodhisattva left home, there were offerings to miss his parents. I hope to follow this ritual system, so I made this inscription:

The Maijishan is the main mountain of the local area, with deep twists and turns, standing high above the sky. The Maijishan Caves are based on rock cliffs. There are ten layers on top of each other, and they are connected by plank roads, like copper beams, which make people breathless when they climb up. The Maiji cliff is very wide and the tall pine trees are straight. The moon borrows its way, and the sun flies back. During the construction, various vehicles were loaded with materials for digging into the mountain and caves, and shuttled back and forth; skilled craftsmen were busy setting up ladders to build the Buddhist niches and the connecting plank roads. The Buddhist niches and grottoes on the cliff are brightly lit in the sun, like overlapping star rivers, gorgeous and winding. There are many scriptures on the cliff, and many Buddha images in the niches. The frescoes and caisson in the niches are gorgeous and exquisite, like the fairy hall with the carved moon and the beautiful hall with carved mirrors. The incense accumulates the incense of trees. The stone walls were carved across, and the mountain beams were dug silently. The dharma drum is like thunder, and the lingering incense flies to the sky. The clear spring water flows through the valley paved with colored stones, and the light breeze comes slowly, like blowing a stone bed, green and dust-free, sounding the piano leisurely. The Maijishan is really a treasure place where celestial spirits are gathered, and a good mansion for storing scriptures. In spring orchids bloom, and in autumn the Zen houses are enveloped by red leaves, with fragrant forests, spring flowers and plenty of rain. In winter ice valley, silver sand, the silvery sight of snow and ice-covered carved mountain buildings and stone rooms are more beautiful and moving. The Maijishan in the misty rain is particularly beautiful. Here folks follow the customs of the Ji County and the land west of the Yellow River. The sound of water swallows, and the mountains are steep and strange. The Buddha dharma covering everything like a cloud is always here, and the wisdom of the Buddha shines throughout the Maijishan. The Maijishan is always a palace inhabited by Gods, free from the chaos of the worldly world."

Readers can compare partial English translation of *The Inscription of the Seven-Buddha Niche on the Maiji Cliff in the Tianshui Prefecture of Qinzhou. The Preface* from *The Cave Temples of Maichishan* by Michael Sullivan, "The military governor Li Yunxin was deeply imbued with the precepts of Buddhism. He had a path like a ladder to the clouds constructed on the southern face of the rock, and had the niches of the Seven Buddhas carved as a temple-offering for the repose of his father's soul. The work could be compared to the carving of sandalwood, the fashioning of stream-jade. Its splendour looks like the full moon or the refection of the blue lotus, evoking the majesty of Mount Sumeru, and the comfort of sweet-smelling incense. Even in this wild place there are now halls where the Law is preached. As on the Fragrant Mountains, here too we can meditate before the divine images.

阴兔假道，阳乌回翼。
载辇疏山，穿龛架岭。
纠纷星汉，回旋光景。
壁累经文，龛重佛影。
雕轮月殿，刻镜花堂。
横镌石壁，暗凿山梁。
雷乘法鼓，树积天香。
潄泉珉谷，吹尘石床。
集灵真馆，藏仙册府。
芝洞秋房，檀林春乳。
冰谷银沙，山楼石柱。
异岭共云，同峰别雨。
翼城馀俗，河西旧风。
水声幽咽，山势崆峒。
法云常住，慧日无穷。
方域芥尽，不变天宫。'"

读者可以比较迈克尔·苏立文（Michael Sullivan）[1]对《秦州天水郡麦积崖佛龛铭并序》的部分英译。"大都督李允信者，籍于宿植，深悟法门。乃于壁之南崖，梯云凿道，奉为王父造七佛龛。似刻浮檀，如冰水玉，从容满月，照耀青莲。影现须弥，香闻仍利。如斯尘野，还开说法之堂；犹彼香山，更对安居之佛。载辇疏山，穿龛架岭。纠纷星汉，回旋光景。壁累经文，龛重佛影。雕轮月殿，刻镜花堂。横镌石壁，暗凿山梁。"

---

[1] SULLIVAN, M. Cave Temples of Maichishan[M]. London: Faber & Faber, 1969:5-6.

It is as if one were to mount a carriage and pierce the mountain, carving out great niches, bestriding the peak ridge, an infinite medley of stars overhead and all the land spinning around far below. The walls are covered with inscriptions taken from holy scripture; in the niches are multiplied the representations of the Buddhas. A Moon-Disc Palace and a Hall of Mirrored Flowers are carved. The wall of rock is cut across on a broad face, and chambers are carved in the darkness of the mountain peak."

第 5 窟 牛儿堂

第5窟位于东崖最上层西端，与第4窟相邻，二窟间有隧道相通，距地面70余米，是麦积山石窟能登临洞窟中相对位置最高的一处洞窟。中龛的外侧塑牛天王，也称"牛儿堂"。开凿于隋朝（公元581年—公元618年），现存麦积山石窟为数极少的隋代原作和唐代造像，壁画中的供养人形象为研究唐代绘画、服饰提供了宝贵的资料。

该窟为一个崖阁式洞窟，三龛内有十四尊七世纪初到七世纪中期的造像，廊顶和廊正壁上方、三龛内及左右龛楣、龛顶部，有七世纪中期壁画、二十则访客题记。东侧有明代开凿的仅容一人能通往第4窟（"散花楼"）的过洞。

形制：该窟前开三间四柱窟廊，后凿三龛。前廊平面呈长方形，平基顶。高9米、宽15米、深6.5米。最初建筑的外观形制为仿宫殿式洞窟，但洞窟的前部在公元734年的天水大地震中受到破坏，四根柱子以及连带的地面在地震中塌毁，仅余靠近东侧山体的半根四方石柱，在这半截柱子上方，有模仿木结构建筑的构件。前廊左壁凿开一洞，通第4窟。通道口高1.5米、宽0.75米、深2.94米。

廊后壁开凿有三个大型的佛龛，其中中间的佛龛平面呈圆形、穹隆顶，顶高5.5米、宽5.9米、进深4米。前面有窟门，比较宽大，十六世纪左右的佛教信徒采用竹子泥墙的方式砌筑了一道简单的篱

Cave 5　Cave of the Bull

Located at the highest point of the west end of the eastern cliff, Cave 5 (Cave of the Bull) is adjacent to Cave 4, which are connected by a tunnel. With over seventy meters from the ground, Cave 5 becomes the highest cave in the Maijishan Caves that can be accessed. For a bull carved outside the central niche, it also called "Cave of the Bull". It was built in the Sui Dynasty (AD 581-618), and very few original works of the Sui Dynasty and the sculptures of the Tang Dynasty survive. The images of the donors in the wallpaintings provide valuable materials for the study of the paintings and the style of costume in the Tang Dynasty.

In the cave visitors will enjoy a chamber open to the cliff face, fourteen sculptures modelled from the early to the middle of the seventh century in three niches, wallpaintings drawn from the middle of the seventh century on the ceiling and above the central wall of the gallery, the interior of three niches and twenty inscriptions the lintels on each niche, and the ceiling of the three halls. There is a the tunnel leading to Cave 4 (Pavilion of Scattered Flowers) on the east side in the Ming Dynasty, which allows only one person to pass through. Details are as follows.

Type: This is a chamber open to the cliff face, in which four stone pillars supported a roof carved from the living rock, making a gallery of three openings at the front, and a row of three halls dug behind. The gallery is plane-horizontal rectangular with a flat-topped ceiling. The ceiling is 9 meters high, 15 meters wide and 6.5 meters deep. The exterior of the original building was modelled after palatial caves. However, the front of the gallery has been damaged by the Tianshui earthquake in AD 734, taking with it the grounds of four stone pillars, and leaving only half the engaged square pillar at the eastern end, above which components mimicing wooden structures are placed. A tunnel was cut to the left wall of the gallery leading to Cave 4. The entrance is 1.50 meters high, 0.75 meters wide and 2.94 meters deep.

Three large niches are excavated in the back wall behind the gallery. Among which a flat circular niche with the "dome of heaven" ceiling is cut in the center, with the ceiling of 5.5 meters high, 5.9 meters wide, the vertical depth of 4 meters. There is a door in front,

笆墙。左右两侧各开一平面马蹄形圆拱龛,高3.3米、宽2.7米、进深1.6米。各龛都有莲瓣形和圆拱形双重龛楣,左右两侧有龛柱,柱头塑火焰宝珠和莲花。

造像:三龛主尊组合为三世佛。其中中龛一佛、二弟子、四菩萨为隋代所塑,左右两龛内各为唐代塑一佛、二菩萨。中窟门外右侧塑踏牛天王。窟内现存造像十四身。

中窟主佛圆塑,身高5米,螺髻,有肉髻珠,眉间有白毫。内着僧祇支,外披通肩袈裟,腰间束带。右手作降魔印,左手与愿印,结跏趺坐于须弥座上。左右二胁侍弟子高3.2米,左侧为老年形象,右侧为少年形象。均身披袈裟,跣足立于圆形莲台上。

弟子之外各两身胁侍菩萨,高3.2~3.4米,戴花冠。下穿裙,裙腰外翻。帔帛绕臂或垂于膝际,跣足立于圆莲台上。左龛主尊为倚坐的弥勒佛,高3米,两侧胁侍菩萨身高2.65米。右龛主尊为结

第5窟第1龛

which is relatively wide. A simple hedge with a muddy wall by dried bamboos was built by Buddhist worshipers around the 16th century. A horseshoe-shaped niche with a chaitya arched ceiling is just visible on each end, with 3.3 meters high, 2.7 meters wide, and vertical side of 1.6 meters. Each niche hangs double lintels adorned with a lotus petal and a chaitya arch, pillars are erected on each end, and the flaming pearls and lotus are moulded on the capitals.

Sculptures: A group of principal Buddhas in three niches are Dipankara (the Buddha of Past), Sakyamuni (the Buddha of Present) and Maitreya (the Buddha of Future). The central niche contains a Buddha flanked by two disciples and four bodhisattvas modelled in the Sui Dynasty, while two niches on each side bear a Buddha flanked by two bodhisattvas modelled in the Tang Dynasty. A Heavenly King (lokapala) is standing on the back of a crouching bull on the right outside the entrance of the central niche. There are 14 sculptures in all.

The principal Buddha in the central niche is modelled in the round, with five meters tall, the spiral-shaped topknot, a bead between the bun and the bottom hair, the white hair between their brows (urnalaksana). He is robed in an inner vest (samkaksika) covering the left shoulder and armpits, an upper garment that completely covers his body and hangs in heavy folds round his shoulders, a sash tied round the waist. With his right hand in the mudra of the earth touch, and his left hand in the varada mudra, he sits with legs tightly locked in a yogic pose on a Sumeru throne. Two attendant disciples on each side are 3.2 meters high. Kasyapa standing on his left is an elderly image, while Ananda standing on his right is a young image. Both of them are dressed in robes, standing on the circular lotus platforms barefoot.

第5窟第3龛

珈趺坐，身高2.65米，两侧胁侍菩萨同左龛。中龛外左侧天王像，脚下踏一牛，天王高3.6米，高鼻深目。上着铠甲，下着战裙，双手紧握，稳健地站在牛犊背上。脚下的牛犊高0.8米，牛首昂起，眼睛注视着前方，鼻翼大张，仿佛正在喷吐着粗气，仰起的颈部及身体其他部位有着极强的力量感。左右两龛的造像为麦积山石窟现存为数极少的唐代造像，弥足珍贵。

壁画：保存约70平方米。三龛内及左右龛楣均为明代重绘，左侧间右壁及右侧龛顶、平棋保存部分唐代作品。廊顶西侧平棋绘天马图，马居中，四足奔腾，前有摩尼宝珠，后绘一头象，左右绘飞天，画面表现的应为佛传故事情节。施色以赭红为主。廊正壁上方西侧唐代绘西方净土变。中龛顶部绘说法图及供养人行列。供养人分三列，左侧为女供养人，右侧为男供养人，是研究唐代绘画、服饰等方面十分重要的形象资料。

题记：该窟残存二十则题记。访客在三龛口、内外壁、台座、前廊洞口潦草地墨书题记、留名。大部分清晰可辨。

引申与拓展

该窟"小有洞天"，通道可通第4窟。现在从"散花楼"穿过石洞来到"牛儿堂"非常容易。在这之前游人必须借助固定在两座洞窟间崖壁木桩上的铁索链荡过去，在落地的一瞬间还要翻身挺腰站稳身形。天水民谣"千佛廊，万佛堂，鹞子翻身牛儿堂"，就是对飞身激荡的形象生动描述。一明朝秦州州官，挑战在"散花楼"用"鹞子翻身"的姿势游荡到"牛儿堂"，可是却没有勇气荡回去。

Outside disciples on each side stands two attendant bodhisattvas, 3.2 meters to 3.4 meters high, chapleted. Their lower bodies are robed in the dresses with reverses at the waist. Their broad scarves cover both shoulders and fall down, either up through the armpits or down to the knees, they stand on the circular lotus platforms barefoot. The principal Buddha in the left niche is a seated Maitreya with legs pendent, 3 meters high, while two attendant bodhisattvas on each side are 2.65 meters tall. The principal Buddha in the right niche sits with legs tightly locked in a yogic pose on a Sumeru throne, with 2.65 meters high, two attendant bodhisattvas on each side are identical with those in the left niche. The Heavenly King (lokapala) on the right outside the central niche standing on the back of a crouching bull is 3.6 meters high, high nose and sunken eyes. With the upper body clad in armor, the waist is wrapped with battle skirt, clenched hands, standing on the back of a crouching bull steadily. The bull at his feet is 0.8 meters high, with its head raised, looking ahead, his nostrils flared, in gasping for breath. The upturned neck and other parts of the body are powerfully modelled. Those in two side niches are very few surviving sculptures modelled in the Tang Dynasty at Maijishan Caves, which are very precious.

Paintings: About 70 square meters survive. The interior of three niches and the lintels on two side niches are redecorated in the Ming Dynasty. Four panels are carved on each ceiling of the central chamber and the chamber on the right end. The surviving wallpaintings on the right wall in the chamber on the left end, and panels carved on the ceiling in the chamber on the right end are the works of the Tang Dynasty. The figure of the Heavenly Horse is painted in the panel on the west, with the galloping heavenly horse in the center of the picture, the cintamans in front, an elephant behind, flying apsaras on each side. The painting illustrates the scene of the life story of the Buddha, colouring chiefly in reddish-browns. On the west above the main wall of the gallery depicts Illustration to the Pure Land of the Tang Dynasty. The scene of Sakyamuni's preaching and a group of donors on the ceiling of the central niche are just visible. The donors are divided into three columns, with females on the left and males on the right, which are very important image data for the study of paintings and the style of costume in the Tang Dynasty.

Inscriptions: There are twenty inscriptions left by visitors in the cave. Visitors might have written dedications and roughly scratched their names with a brush on the entrances, inner and outer walls, thrones in three niches, gate of the tunnel in gallery. Most of them are clearly legible.

Extension and Elaboration

The tunnel inscribed with "A Hole of Another Scenery" leads to Cave 4. Now it is very easy to move from "Pavilion of Scattered Flowers" by the tunnel to the west leading to "Cave of the Bull", which was dug in the Ming Dynasty. Before that visitors have to swing back and forth by the iron cable chain fixed in the stakes into the cliff face between the two

众随从只得请石匠凿洞,州官才从洞里爬了出来。后来这个洞窟逐渐扩大,成了现在的面貌,游人爬行就可以通过,并特地在洞口顶上镌刻了十七世纪书法家甘茹书写的"小有洞天"四个大字。

该窟"踏牛天王"造像更像是一个避除震灾的祈祷,在国内外石窟中实属罕见。传说这头"金角银蹄"的卧牛犄力大无比,它只要一动,天水地区就会发生地震。于是天王牢牢踏在牛背之上,不让它乱动。自此以后,天水地区从未发生过严重的地震。

第5龛踏牛天王

caves, turning their bodies as soon as they landed. The folk song in Tianshui "the Thousand Buddhas Corridor, the Cave of a Myriad Buddhas, the sparrow hawk turns its body in the Cave of the Bull" describes this dangerous action vividly. A governor in Qinzhou of the Ming Dynasty challenged to swing from "Pavilion of Scattered Flowers" to "Cave of the Bull" in the posture of turning his body like a sparrow hawk, but he lacked the courage to swing back. His followers had a hole hollowed out to let the governor climb over. With further excavations, the tunnel takes its present look, visitors can pass through only by crawling. Above which hangs a wooden horizontal board inscribed with four characters "A Hole of Another Scenery" which means "As if there is another world inside the cave." by the calligrapher Gan Ru in the 17th century.

The figure of "the Heavenly King standing on the back of a crouching bull" is more like a prayer for earthquake relief, which is rare among the caves in and outside China. Legend has it that this crouching bull with "gold horns and silver hoofs" was very powerful, its every move would cause an earthquake in the area of Tianshui. So the Heavenly King firmly stepped on its back, leaving it crouching all the time. Severe earthquakes never shook the area of Tianshui ever since.

第5窟菩萨

第 7 窟

第7窟位于东崖东端，开凿于北周（公元557年—公元581年）。该窟是麦积山石窟中另一处在北周时期最盛行的"七佛题材"造像的洞窟。

该窟为四角攒尖顶窟，有七尊坐佛像，一则题记。

形制：该洞窟平面方形，高2.5米、宽1.96米、进深1.96米。方形窟门。窟内正壁凿圆拱形龛，左右壁凿通长台座，地面正、左、右前有"凹"字形低坛基。

造像：窟内正壁龛内塑一佛，左右壁各塑三佛，共计七身。

正壁佛，高0.81米。水涡纹低肉髻，方圆脸，眉骨突出，眼窝下陷，目下视，鼻头尖，四瓣嘴。短颈宽肩，体态较丰满。内着僧祇支，外着双领下垂袈裟。左手置膝，掌心贴膝，右手施无畏印。结跏趺坐于龛内低坛座上。

左右壁各三佛，均高0.82米。磨光低平肉髻，眉骨突出，细目下视，小鼻大耳，嘴角微微上翘，带有笑意。其中左右壁外侧的两身头微微转向窟口，结跏趺坐于台座上。

壁画：原窟顶及四壁均彩绘壁画，因自然侵害和受烟熏严

Cave 7

Cave 7 is located at the east end of the eastern cliff, and was excavated in the Northern Zhou Dynasty (AD 557-581). It is another cave with its most prevailing theme of the Seven Buddhas in the Northern Zhou Dynasty at Maijishan.

In the cave visitors will enjoy a cave with the "dome of heaven" ceiling, figures of seven seated Buddhas, and an inscription written with a brush. Details are as follows.

Type: It is a square cave with the "dome of heaven" ceiling, 2.50 meters high, 1.96 meters wide, the vertical depth of 1.96 meters, and a square door. A chaitya arched recess is carved into the main wall, an inseparate pedestal set on each of the side walls, and a low concave base is cut around the ground of each front of the main wall, the left wall and the right wall.

Sculptures: A seated Buddha occupies a shallow niche cut into the main wall, with three seated Buddhas set in a row on each of the side walls. There are seven figures in all.

The Buddha on the main wall is 0.81 meters high, with water-wave-shaped low ushnisha right on the top, the square face carved with raised eyebrow bone, sunken eye sockets, downcast eyes, pointy nose, and four-flap mouth. With short neck and broad shoulders, the figure is modelled a little fuller. He is robed in an inner vest (samkaksika) covering the left shoulder and armpits, an upper garment that completely covers his body, with U-shaped collar falling to the chest, the corner of the robe resting on the left arm. The left hand rests on knee, and the right hand performs abhaya mudra. The Buddha is seated on the low throne in the shallow niche in a pose of deep yogic meditation, with the legs tightly locked, the soles of both feet uppermost.

Three seated Buddhas on each of the side walls are all 0.82 meters high. They wear the low

重，原绘壁画隐约可见，绘有红色长方形边框、火焰纹项身光轮廓等痕迹。

题记：左壁近门，第一与第二佛中间壁墨书："大中十年？"

引申与拓展

该窟左右壁坛台上各并列三尊坐佛的奇特排列形式，与另一座北周第12窟相同，代表"过去七佛"。其中正壁龛内为释迦牟尼佛，左右壁为"过去六佛"。其敦厚的北周风貌依旧明显。

flat ushnishas right on the top, with raised brow bones, small eyes looking downward, small noses and pendulous ears, mouth slightly upturned with a smile. Among them, the two Buddhas on each of outer side walls are seated with legs tightly locked in a yogic pose on the long pedestal thrones, turning their heads slightly to the entrance.

Paintings: Badly suffered from weathering and blackened with smokes, original coloured paintings drawn on the ceiling and four walls are barely visible. Traces of the contour of the aureoles and mandorla decorated with the red rectangular outer borders and flaming motifs can just be made out.

Inscription: There is an inscription left by visitors with a brush on the left wall near the door, the central wall between the first and the second Buddha: "The ten years of Dazhong in the Tang Dynasty (AD 856)？

Extension and Elaboration

The unusual arrangement of three seated Buddhas in a row on each of the side walls is identical with another Cave 12 in the Northern Zhou Dynasty, which represent the Seven Buddhas of the Past. Among them, the Sakyamuni Buddha occupies his own recess on the main wall, the six Buddhas of the past on each of the side walls. Their massiveness of the Northern Zhou Dynasty is apparent.

第 8 窟

第8窟位于东崖东端,开凿于隋朝(公元581年—公元618年)。

该窟为平面长方形、穹隆顶小龛,有三尊造像,三则墨书题记。

形制:该洞窟高1.5米、宽1.46米、进深0.75米。正壁凿台阶式高台基,下坛台正中伸出莲花座高0.08米。龛形基本保存完好,龛内壁面泥皮大多剥落,现仅存台座右侧及左壁部分泥皮。

造像:正壁塑一身坐佛,左右壁各塑一身胁侍菩萨,共计三身。

主佛,高1.18米。磨光低平肉髻,方圆脸,双眼下视,双耳平贴。内着僧祇支,外着双领下垂袈裟。袈裟上彩绘"田相"纹,并夹有花卉装饰。左手握袈裟一角贴于胸前,右手自然下垂,掌心贴于右膝上。倚坐于高台座上,双足踏仰莲。

左右壁菩萨,均高1.16米。跣足立于圆形台上。左壁菩萨右手上抬胸侧,掌心托宝珠,右壁菩萨右手下垂提净瓶。

Cave 8

Cave 8 is located at the east end of the eastern cliff, and it was excavated in the Sui Dynasty (AD 581-618).

In the cave visitors will see a small plane rectangle niche with the "dome of heaven" ceiling, three sculptures, and three inscriptions written with a brush. Details are as follows.

Type: It is a small plane rectangle niche with the "dome of heaven" ceiling, with 1.5 meters high, 1.46 meters wide and 0.75 meters deep. The high stepped base was cut on the main wall, a lotus pedestal of 0.08 meters high sprung from its center below. The niche is basically well preserved, and most thin skin of clay plaster on the inner wall of the niche has peeled away, leaving only those on the right side of the throne and partial on the left wall.

Sculptures: A seated Buddha is modelled on the main wall, with two attendant bodhisattvas on each of the side walls. There are three sculptures in all.

The principal Buddha is 1.18 meters high. He has a polished low flat ushnisha right on the top, the square face carved with downcast eyes, flanked by flattened ears. He wears an inner vest (samkaksika) covering the left shoulder and armpits, and an upper garment that completely covers his body, with U-shaped collar falling to the chest, the corner of the rob resting on the left arm. The robe is adorned with coloured "paddy-field design" with flowers decoration. The left hand is placed on the chest holding the corner of the robe, and the right hand rests on knee. He is seated with legs pendent against a wall and feet resting on an upside-down lotus buds.

The height of the bodhisattva on each of the side walls is 1.16 meters. They stand on the

壁画：现存约0.3平方米。原正、左、右三壁可能均彩绘壁画，因壁面原有泥皮剥落严重，仅存少许。佛身后两侧各彩绘一身单膝跪于椭圆形蒲团上的供养菩萨，佛右侧泥皮上可辨一身弟子。

题记：三则题记分别写在右壁近门、前廊东侧洞口上方。

circular platforms barefoot. The left-wall bodhisattva raises her right hand to the chest, with a pearl on the palm, while the bodhisattva on the right wall holds a vase (kalasa) in her right hand.

Paintings: About 0.3 square meters, paintings survive. The original main, left and right walls might have been covered by coloured paintings, of which original thin skin of clay plaster has severely peeled away, leaving only a few. A votive bodhisattva of half-kneeling half-squatting on oval hassock is made on each side behind the Buddha, and a disciple on the thin skin of clay plaster on the right of the Buddha is legible.

Inscriptions: There are three inscriptions left by visitors with a brush on the right wall near the door, above the entrance on the east of the gallery.

第 9 窟

第9窟位于东崖东端,紧邻东崖大佛。因其位于麦积山石窟可到达范围内的中段,且一字排开分布有七个佛龛,每龛各供一佛而称"中七佛阁",开凿于北周时期(公元557年—公元581年),是一座大型栈桥式崖阁。

该窟为北周时期的崖阁建筑,十九身宋代重修的精美雕塑作品以及明(公元1368年—公元1644年)、清(公元1616年—公元1912年)时期的重彩壁画,十则墨书题记。

形制:该洞窟高4.95米、宽24.1米、深4.65米,并列七个大型佛龛,前部原有木构建筑,后因地震前部全部塌毁,现存为1980年按照原来木结构形制重新建造了钢筋混凝土栈阁加固。

造像:该窟内造像经宋代重塑,明清重新妆彩。七个大型佛龛中每龛中各供一佛,共七佛。正中第4龛内为一佛二弟子,其余各龛均为一佛二菩萨。目前共保存塑像二十一身,均为泥塑。

第4龛塑释迦牟尼和他两个弟子迦叶和阿难。释迦牟尼坐在方形的佛座上,头顶布满小螺纹,前有肉髻珠,面型圆润,短颈。内穿僧祇支,外穿双领下垂袈裟。结跏趺坐,双手分别做无畏印和与愿印。佛面部色彩变色严重,多为从红色变为黑色。

Cave 9

Cave 9 is located at the east end in the eastern cliff, adjacent to the great triad on the east face. Because it is the middle-accessible eastern cave with seven niches cut in a row, each containing a Buddha, it is usually called "the Middle Seven Buddhas Halls". It was excavated in the Northern Zhou Dynasty (AD 557-581), is a large trestle chamber open to the cliff.

In the cave visitors will enjoy the chamber open to the cliff built in the Northern Zhou Dynasty, with 19 exquisite sculptures remodelled in the Song Dynasty, redecorated paintings in the Ming (AD 1368-1644) and Qing (AD 1616-1912) dynasties, and ten inscriptions written with a brush. Details are as follows.

Type: The cave is 4.95 meters high, 24.1 meters wide and 4.65 meters deep. Seven large niches are excavated in a row, and all their original wooden buildings in the front have fallen away by the earthquakes. The concrete shallow niche was rebuilt after its original wooden structures by the reinforcement work in 1980.

Sculptures: All were remodelled in the Song Dynasty and redecorated in the Ming and Qing dynasties. Each of the seven large niches contains a Buddha, with seven Buddhas in all. The central Niche 4 retains a Buddha flanked by two disciples, and others are a Buddha with standing bodhisattvas on either side. The total 21 sculptures modelled in clay survive in the cave.

The figures modelled in Niche 4 are Sakyamuni and his two disciples Kasyapa and Ananda. Sakyamuni is seated on a square throne, the hair and ushnisha arranged in tight curls, a bead between the ushnisha and the bottom hair, the round face and short neck. He wears an inner vest covering the left shoulder and armpits, an upper garment that completely covers his body, with U-shaped collar falling to the chest, the lappet of the robe resting on the left arm. He is seated with legs tightly locked in a yogic pose on a long pedestal throne,

第9窟外廊

佛右侧迦叶高2.65米,老年形象,面庞清瘦并布满皱纹,神情严肃,双手抱拳于胸前。内着僧祇支,外穿双领下垂袈裟,呈现出一个以苦修行的老者形象。佛左侧阿难,面容清秀,双手合十于胸前。身穿袈裟,衣着华贵,上有祥云、龙、凤、花卉等图案。左右两侧的三个大龛塑像都是一佛二菩萨,造像风格和第4龛差别不大。

壁画:龛内壁画均为明清重绘,多为护法形象,色彩保存相对较好。在第4龛主佛的上部,有火焰宝珠和迦楼罗的形象。迦楼罗是一种神话中的鸟,通常被描述为鸟翅人面。第4龛顶部绘共命鸟,为双头童子形象,鸟翅鸟爪,新奇别致。

第9窟第1龛、第2龛、第3龛、第4龛佛与菩萨

with right hand in abhaya mudra and left hand in varada mudra. The badly faded colours on the face of the Buddha consist today chiefly of a red faded to black.

Kasyapa standing on the right of the seated Buddha, with 2.65 meters high, is an elderly image with thin and wrinkled face, solemn manner, one clenched fist in the other hand at the chest. He is robed in an inner vest (samkaksika) covering the left shoulder and armpits, an upper garment that completely covers his body, with U-shaped collar falling to the chest, the lappet of the robe resting on the left arm. The image depicts an old ascetic monk. Ananda standing on the left of the seated Buddha, and he bears delicately modelled features, with clasped hands. He wears a voluminous robe richly adorned with auspicious clouds, dragons, phoenix, flowers and other patterns. Three large niches on either side contain a seated Buddha flanked by two standing bodhisattvas, their style of image-making is almost identical to that in Niche 4.

Paintings: The paintings in the niches were all redecorated in the Ming and Qing dynasties, most of which are guardian figures, and they have retained their pristine freshness of colour. The images of the flaming pearl and Garuda are visible above the principal Buddha in Niche 4. Garuda is a mythological bird usually described as having a human face with the wings of a bird. On the ceiling of Niche 4 is Jivajivaka in the figure of the double-headed boy with unbelievable wings and claws.

题记： 十则题记分别写在窟内壁、菩萨胸前。

引申与拓展

该窟与第4窟同属于麦积山石窟"七佛题材"造像的洞窟。七佛又称"过去七佛"，据佛经典籍解释，"七佛"是指释迦牟尼佛与在他出现之前悟得正觉的六位佛尊，依次为毗婆尸佛、尸弃佛、毗舍浮佛、拘留孙佛、拘那含牟尼佛、迦叶佛。但是在一般石窟开凿中，都会把释迦牟尼佛放在中间位置。

第9窟第4龛迦楼罗与双头童子壁画

Inscriptions: There are ten inscriptions left by visitors with a brush on the inner walls of the niches, on the chests of the bodhisattvas.

Extension and Elaboration

The theme of the Seven Buddhas in the cave is identical to Cave 4 at Maijishan. The Seven Buddhas are also known as the "Seven Buddhas of the Past". According to Buddhist scriptures, the "Seven Buddhas" refers to Sakyamuni, the last of the "Seven Buddhas" and other six of the "Seven Buddhas" who had attained the supreme Enlightenment and become the Buddhas before him. They are Vipasyin, Sikhin, Visvabhu, Krakucchanda, Kanakamuni, Kasyapa and Sakyamuni. But in the general excavation of caves, the Sakyamuni Buddha occupies the central place.

第 10 窟

第10窟位于东崖东部,东侧为崖面,西邻第13窟东崖大佛。开凿于隋朝(公元581年—公元618年)。

该窟为平面马蹄形、穹窿顶窟,七尊造像,窟顶千佛壁画,四则墨书题记。

形制:该窟高2.1米、宽2.02米、进深1.7米。有圆拱形甬道。窟内正壁正中塑一方形台座,左右两壁凿通长低坛基。窟形保存完好,窟内泥皮基本保存相对完整。

造像:正壁塑一身坐佛,左壁塑三身菩萨,右壁正中塑一身弟子,其左右侧各塑一身菩萨,共计七身。

正壁主佛,高1.64米。光头,双眼微启下视,绘胡须,宽肩挺腹。内着僧祇支,外着双领下垂袈裟。结跏趺坐于方形台座上。

左右壁五身菩萨类型非常相似:均高1.5米以上,高冠。一只胳膊曲于胸前,另一只胳膊贴腿下垂,立于圆形莲台上。衣着与主佛相同。

中间弟子,高1.55米。足蹬圆口履立于圆形莲台上。主佛、菩

第二章　麦积山石窟汉英解说词

Cave 10

Cave 10 is located at the east part of the eastern cliff, to its east is the cliff surface and the west is adjacent to Cave 13 the Great Triad on the Eastern Face, and it was excavated in the Sui Dynasty (AD 581-618).

In the cave visitors will see a plane horseshoe-shaped niche with the "dome of heaven" ceiling, seven sculptures, paintings of the Thousand Buddhas on the ceiling and four inscriptions written with a brush. Details are as follows.

Type: It is a plane horseshoe-shaped niche with the "dome of heaven" ceiling, flat horseshoe shape, with 2.1 meters high, 2.02 meters wide and 1.7 meters deep. There is a chaitya-arched passage. A square throne is cut on the center of the main wall, with an inseparate low platform on each of the side walls. The cave is well preserved, and the thin skin of clay plaster is almost intact.

Sculptures: A seated Buddha is modelled on the main wall, with three bodhisattvas on the left wall, a disciple flanked by two bodhisattvas on the right wall. There are seven figures in all.

The principal Buddha on the main wall is 1.64 meters high. He is bald, with slightly open and downcast eyes, moustache, broad shoulders and a slightly swollen abdomen. He is robed in an inner vest covering the left shoulder and armpits, an upper garment that completely covers his body, with U-shaped collar falling to the chest, the lappet of the robe resting on the left arm. He sits on the square throne in a pose of deep yogic meditation, the legs tightly locked, with the soles of both feet uppermost.

Five bodhisattvas on each of the side walls are of very similar type: over 1.5 meters high, with a high crown. One arm is raised, the other flung back against the leg, standing on the

萨和弟子均内着僧祇支，外着双领下垂袈裟。衣着与主佛相同。

壁画：现存约11平方米，因风化剥蚀，所绘内容大部分模糊不可辨。窟顶正中绘圆莲，以圆莲为中心四周绘四层千佛，仅可辨认外形。

题记：四则题记分别写在窟内壁及窟顶。

circular lotus platform. Their costumes are identical with the principal Buddha.

The central disciple is 1.55 meters high, standing in roundmouth shoes on the circular lotus platform. The Buddha, bodhisattvas and disciple are all robed in an inner vests covering the left shoulder and armpits, an upper garment that completely cover their bodies, with U-shaped collar falling to the chest, the lappet of the robe resting on the left arm. His costume is identical with the principal Buddha.

Paintings: About 11 square meters survive. Due to suffered from weathering, they have peeled away, and most of the contents of the paintings are ambiguous. A lotus flower is painted on the central place of the ceiling. Round the lotus flower sunburst at the center are the Thousand Buddhass in four layers which only external contour lines can just be made out.

Inscriptions: There are four inscriptions left by visitors with a brush on the inner walls of the niche and its ceiling.

第11窟

第11窟位于东崖东部,东侧为摩崖刻字"麦积山"。开凿于北周(公元557年—公元581年),宋朝(公元960年—公元1279年)、明朝(公元1368年—公元1644年)重修。

该窟为平面方形、四角攒尖顶窟,有十一尊造像、山水画、花卉壁画,十三则墨书题记。

形制:该窟高2.98米、宽2.85米、进深2.88米。窟内四角和壁面转折处雕凿有半圆形帐柱。前壁开方形甬道。窟内正、左、右三壁通长凿"凹"字形低坛基。

造像:窟内三壁原塑像已无存。现存正壁塑一佛二胁侍弟子,左右二壁各塑四身菩萨,共计十一身。其中右侧弟子为明代增塑外,其余均系宋代重塑,明代妆銮。

正壁主佛,通高1.88米。水波纹发髻,双眼微启下视。内着僧祇支,外着双领下垂袈裟。左手掌心向下,平贴于左膝上,右手施说法印,结跏趺坐于方形台座上。袈裟下摆分三瓣自然垂于台座前。

左侧弟子,高1.63米。老者形象,双手抱拳于胸前,足穿圆头鞋。右侧弟子,高1.7米。少年形象,双手胸前合十。二弟子均外着袒右袈

Cave 11

Cave 11 is located at the east part of the eastern cliff, with three characters "Maiji Shan" carved on the cliff face on its east, and it was originally excavated in the Northern Zhou Dynasty (AD 557-581) and repaired in the Song Dynasty (AD 960-1279) and the Ming Dynasty (AD 1368-1644).

In the cave visitors will see a flat square niche with the "dome of heaven" ceiling, 11 sculptures, paintings of landscapes and flowers, 13 inscriptions written with a brush. Details are as follows.

Type: It is a flat square niche with the "dome of heaven" ceiling, with 2.98 meters high, 2.85 meters wide and 2.88 meters deep. Semicircular tent pillars are carved at the four corners of the cave and the turning point of the walls. There is a square passage on the front wall. A low concave base is cut on the main wall with an inseparate concave base on each of the side walls.

Sculptures: The original figures on three walls modelled in the Northern Zhou Dynasty have all disappeared. The cave now has a Buddha flanked by two attendant disciples on the main wall, four bodhisattvas on each of the side walls. There are 11 figures in all. Among them, the disciple on the right was added in the Ming Dynasty, the rest were remodelled in the Song Dynasty and redecorated in the Ming Dynasty.

The principal Buddha on the main wall is 1.88 meters high. He has a water-wavy topknot, downcast eyes with slightly open. He wears an inner vest (samkaksika) covering the left shoulder and armpits, an upper garment that completely covers his body, with U-shaped collar falling to the chest, the lappet of the robe resting on the left arm. His left hand rests on knee, his right hand is in gesture of preaching (Vitarka mudra), and he sits on the square throne with the left leg lying over the right leg. The drapery cascades over his knees,

裟，立于低坛台上。左右壁八身菩萨类型非常相似：均高1.9米左右，戴宝冠，跣足立于坛台上。

壁画：现存面积约10平方米，均系明代重新彩绘。佛绘圆形项光，底层隐约可见莲瓣形身光。弟子及左右壁菩萨绘圆形项光，底层均绘火焰纹，菩萨项光之上画砖纹墙壁装饰，下绘云朵。前壁门内门楣上绘数树木、山水、人物等。窟顶正中绘莲花，其余三斜披均各绘牡丹一朵。

题记：十三则题记分别写于门楣、左右壁上方、佛座、窟顶上。

引申与拓展

该窟东侧摩崖题刻"麦积山"，与悬崖上的岩石颜色一致，需要久视才能区分。字体苍古俊逸，属于北魏（公元386年—公元534年）的书法风格。从远处看，每个字可能有八九尺大，肯定不可能用毛毡拓。应该由西魏（公元535年—公元556年）或北周（公元557年—公元581年）人书写。国内摩崖大字没有能超过这三个字的。

covering the throne in three large petals.

The disciple on the left is 1.63 meters high, an elderly image with one clenched fist in the other hand at the chest, in shoes with round toe. The disciple on the right is 1.70 meters high, a young image, with clasped hands. Both disciples are robed in the outer robe thrown over the left shoulder or the upper throwing a strong diagonal across the body, leaving the right side of the body and shoulder bare, standing on the low platforms. Bodhisattvas on each of the side walls are of a very similar type: about 1.9 meters high, with a high crown, standing on the platform barefoot.

Paintings: The cave retains paintings about ten square meters, which were all repainted in the Ming Dynasty. The Buddha has a circular aureole behind him, and the lotus petal-shaped mandorla on the bottom layer is subtly visible. The disciples and bodhisattvas on each of the side walls are under circular nimbuses too, painted with a flaming pattern on the bottom layer. Above the nimbuses of these bodhisattvas have bricks for wall decoration, with the clouds below. The inner lintel into the front wall is painted with trees, landscapes, figures, etc. We can see a lotus on the center of the ceiling, a peony on each of three slopping panels.

Inscriptions: There are 13 inscriptions left by visitors with a brush on the lintels, above the left and right walls, the throne of the Buddha, and the ceiling.

Extension and Elaboration

The three characters "Mai Ji Shan" are carved on the cliff face on its east, with the same color as the rock on the cliff, and it takes a long time to tell them from the rock. They are vigorous and simple, beautiful and unrestrained, and belong to the style of the calligraphy in the Northern Wei Dynasty. Seen from a distance, each character can be as big as eight or nine chis, so it is bound to be impossible to be rubbed with felt. These three characters should be written by the people of the Western Wei Dynasty (AD 535-556) or the Northern Zhou Dynasty (AD 557-581). None of the big cliff characters in China can exceed these three ones.

第12窟

第12窟位于东崖东端,开凿于北周(公元557年—公元581年),明代(公元1368年—公元1644年)重修。该窟是麦积山石窟另一处北周最盛行的"七佛题材"造像的洞窟,七佛排列与第7窟相同,是麦积山北周窟龛形制和造像保存最完整洞窟之一。

该窟为平面方形、四角攒尖顶窟,十一身敦厚的北周造像,窟顶"涅槃变"和"揭钵图"经变画,十二则墨书题记。

形制:该洞窟是一个小型窟,宽1.76米、高2.3米、进深1.74米,洞窟整体保存完整。窟前壁有方形甬道,窟内四壁角及顶部塑石胎泥塑帐柱,正壁开一圆拱形龛,左右壁各开凿一字排开通长基座。

造像:窟内造像保存完整,均为北周原作。正壁龛内一身坐佛,龛外两侧各一身站立胁侍菩萨,左右壁基座上各并列三身坐佛,前壁甬道两侧各一身弟子,共计十一身造像。这组泥塑造像虽经明代重新妆彩,但其敦厚的北周风貌依存。

正壁龛佛高1米,体态挺拔敦厚,低平肉髻,方圆面型,双目下视。内着僧祇支,外披双领下垂袈裟。双手抚胸前作说法状,结跏趺坐于佛龛内。佛身后有圆形头光及身光。

第二章　麦积山石窟汉英解说词

Cave 12

Cave 12 is located at the east end of the eastern cliff, was originally excavated in the Northern Zhou Dynasty (AD 557-581) and repaired in the Ming Dynasty (AD 1368-1644). It is another cave with its most prevailing theme of the Seven Buddhas at Maijishan, the arrangement of Seven Buddhas is identical to Cave 7. It is one of the most intact cave shrines and sculptures made in the Northern Zhou Dynasty at Maijishan.

In the cave visitors will appreciate a flat square niche with the "dome of heaven" ceiling, 11 massive sculptures modelled in the Northern Zhou Dynasty, sutra illustration paintings of Nirvana Sutra Illustration Paintings, Raising the Alms-bowl on the ceiling, 12 inscriptions written with a brush. Details are as follows.

Type: It is a small flat square niche with the "dome of heaven" ceiling, with 1.76 meters wide, 2.30 meters high, 1.74 meters deep, and the whole cave is intact. There is a cave passage on the front wall. The tent columns in clay plaster over a core of rock are carved on the ceiling and four corners. It has a chaitya arched recess cut into the main wall, and an inseparate pedestal cut in a row on each of the side walls.

Sculptures: The sculptures in the cave are intact, which are the original works of the Northern Zhou Dynasty. A recess cut into the main wall contains a seated Buddha flanked by two standing bodhisattvas on each side of the shrine, with three seated Buddhas cut in a row on the inseparate pedestals on each of the side walls, a disciple on each of the side walls of the passage on the front wall. There are eleven sculptures in all. Although these clay figures were under the refurbishing of the Ming Dynasty, their massiveness is apparent.

The Buddha carved into the niche on the main wall is one meter high, tall and straight and solid, wearing a low flat ushnisha right on the top, the square face carved with downcast eyes. He wears an inner vest covering the left shoulder and armpits, an upper garment that completely covers his body, with U-shaped collar falling to the chest, the lappet of the robe

菩萨面相丰润，弯眉细目。头戴莲花宝冠，上身袒露，颈饰桃形项圈，璎珞垂至膝下。下着翻腰长裙，双手置于胸前，持宝罐或莲花，跣足立于覆莲台之上。

左右壁六身坐佛神情姿态与正壁佛似同，只是体量稍微变小。内着僧祇支，外着双领下垂袈裟或通肩袈裟。双手禅定印，结跏趺坐于通长基座上。

前壁左右弟子光头，面庞丰圆，弯眉高鼻，神态虔诚恭敬。内着僧祇支，外着袒右田相式袈裟。左弟子双手合十于胸前，右弟子双手交叠于腹前，立于半圆形覆莲台上。

壁画：窟内保存壁画约7.5平方米，原北周壁画已无存，现壁画（包括头光、背光等）皆为明代重绘，保存完整，内容丰富。窟

第12窟左侧弟子像

resting on the left arm. His two hands are elevated to the chest level in gesture of preaching, and he sits with the left leg lying over the right leg on the throne. There is a circular nimbus and a mandorla behind him.

The bodhisattva has the full face carved with arched brows sweeping above gently opened almond eyes. He wears the lotus crowns, with the upper body bare, a peach-shaped collar round the neck, the heavy garlands of jewels hanging down the shin. He is robed in the long dress with reverses at the waist, and his two hands are elevated to the chest level either holding a jar or lotus in his hands, standing on the upside-down lotus pedestals barefoot.

The expression and attitude of the six seated Buddhas on each of the side walls are identical with the Buddha on the main wall, but a slightly sagging contour. They wear the inner vests covering the left shoulder and armpits, either the upper garments that completely cover their bodies, with U-shaped collar falling to the chest, the lappet of the robe resting on the left arm or the upper garments that completely cover their bodies and hang in heavy folds round his shoulder. They are seated with legs tightly locked in a yogic pose on the inseperate pedestal, and their two hands perform the dhyana mudra.

Paintings: About 7.5 square meters survive in the cave. The original works made in the Northern Zhou Dynasty has disappeared, and the present works (including nimbus and mandorla, etc.) is a restoration of the Ming Dynasty, which are intact and in the richness of its pictorial content. The four panels on the ceiling respectively contain stories of sutra illustration of Nirvana Sutra Illustration Paintings, and Raising the Alms-bowl.

"Nirvana Sutra Illustration Paintings" are painted on the back and the left panels on the ceiling. In the center of the back panel, the Buddha lies on his right side on a couch, surrounded by his ten mourning disciples, of which Kasyapa makes obeisance at the feet of the Buddha on the footside of the couch. Above the picture, a Buddha stands among the clouds depicting the scene of the Buddha's last preaching. The left panel illustrates the scene that the Buddha is seated on the lotus pedestal in gesture of preaching, with five disciples holding flowers on both sides, a stone stool set in front of him, above which an incense burner is put, in front of which a lay worshipper kneeling on the ground.

"Raising the Alms-bowl" is painted on the right panel of the ceiling, depicting the story of the karma of Hariti, the Mother of Demons. Here Ksitigarbha Bodhisattva as a Buddha is seated with legs tightly locked in a yogic pose on the throne, with a big vat in front, inside which we can see a figure floating, surrounded by four demons, with fierce features, exposed sharp teeth, holding guns and bows, meting out cruel punishments.

Inscriptions: There are twelve inscriptions left by visitors with a brush on the inner wall above the door and the right wall.

顶四披分别绘有"涅槃变""揭钵图"等经变故事。

"涅槃变"绘于窟顶后披和左披内。后披正中绘释迦横卧于佛床上，十大弟子围在声旁，床尾处绘迦叶探视佛足。上方云气中一立佛，表现释迦临终说法情景。左披绘有佛祖释迦以说法状端坐于莲台之上，身旁两侧持花弟子五人，面前摆石凳香炉一处，炉前有一俗装信徒伏地跪拜。

"揭钵图"位于窟顶右披处，描绘鬼子母因缘故事。画面中佛装地藏菩萨结跏趺坐，面前置大瓮一口，内里可窥见有人浮动，瓮周边围绕恶鬼四身，相貌狰狞、尖牙外露，持枪张弓，操持刑具。

题记：十二则题记分别写于窟门内壁上方和右壁上。

引申与拓展

该窟左右壁坛台上各并列三尊坐佛的奇特排列形式与另一座北周第7窟相同，代表"过去七佛"。其中正壁龛内为释迦牟尼佛，左右壁为"过去六佛"。其敦厚的北周风貌依旧明显。

"揭钵图"描写《宝积经》中的故事。该窟"揭钵图"是对中土自宋元开始流行的这一图像的继承和发展，是麦积山唯一的鬼子母因缘壁画。

该洞窟前壁门楣上有牌匾一方，上刻"蓬莱洞"三字。这个名字带有道教特点，与该窟佛教内容完全不一致。可以看出当时普通信众对佛、道之间的区别并不是太在意。

Extension and Elaboration

The unusual arrangement of three seated Buddhas in a row on each of the side walls is identical with another Cave 7 in the Northern Zhou Dynasty, they represent the Seven Buddhas of the Past. Among them, the Sakyamuni Buddha occupies his own recess on the main wall, the Six Buddhas of the past on each of the side walls. Their massiveness of the Northern Zhou Dynasty is apparent.

Raising the Alms-bowl illustrates the story from *Sutra of the Heap of Jewels*. It shows the inheritance and development of the same theme since the Song and Yuan dynasties in the Central Plains, is the only image about the karma of Hariti in the paintings at Maijishan Caves.

On the lintel into the front wall, there is a plaque inscribed with three characters "Peng Lai Dong". Bearing Taoist characteristics, it is completely inconsistent with the contents of Buddhist in the cave. It can be seen that the ordinary believers at that time did not care too much about the difference between Buddhism and Taoism.

第 13 窟 东崖大佛

第13窟位于东崖中部，始凿于隋代（公元581年—公元618年），宋代（公元960年—公元1279年）重修。因三尊摩崖高浮雕像，也被称为"东崖大佛"，是麦积山现存最大的一组摩崖大佛造像，一佛二菩萨三尊形式是麦积山石窟最常见的造像构图主题。

本窟为麦积山石窟最大的一佛二菩萨石胎泥塑造像，是直接在崖面上雕凿的大型造像。壁画中的佛和菩萨头光，三则题记。

形制：该窟是摩崖龛，高15.7米、宽17.81米。

造像：一佛二菩萨悬立崖面，除了头部之外，其他体态挺拔之中略显敦厚。中间主佛高15.7米，螺纹肉髻，面形丰满，两眼下视。内着僧祇支，腰间束带打结下垂，外着垂领式袈裟。双手已失，双腿下垂庄严地倚坐于方形座上。佛双膝以下泥皮全部剥落，石胎外露，岩层表面可见规则排列的方形桩孔。

两侧菩萨均高13米。佛左侧菩萨头戴高花冠。面容方圆饱满，弯眉长目，嘴角上扬。饰长条形耳坠。挺胸鼓腹。左手托莲花于颈前侧，右手放置于腹部。上身有帔帛，下着翻腰长裙，跣足立于仰莲台上。佛右侧菩萨，耳戴环形饰。姿态略同于左菩萨。左手提净瓶垂于左腿前侧，右手端于胸腹前。

Cave 13　Great Triad on the Eastern Cliff

Cave 13 is located in the middle of the eastern cliff, was initially excavated in the Sui Dynasty (AD 581-618) and repaired in the Song Dynasty (AD 960-1279). It is also called "Great Triad on the Eastern Cliff" for the three colossal figures modelled in high relief on the cliff face. They are the largest colossal group carved on the cliff face at Maijishan. A seated Buddha flanked by two standing bodhisattvas is the most common theme of the iconographic schemes at Maijishan.

In the cave visitors can enjoy the largest figures at Maijishan more closely, with a seated Buddha flanked by two standing bodhisattvas built up in clay plaster over a core of rock, the three colossal figures carved in high relief on the cliff face. The nimbuses in paintings are behind the Buddha and bodhisattvas, and there are three inscriptions. Details are as follows.

Type: It is an open niche on the cliff face, with 15.7 meters high and 17.81 meters wide.

Sculptures: A seated Buddha flanked by two standing bodhisattvas is modelled on the cliff face, except for the heads, the relief is rather huge and straight with a little bit solid. The principal Buddha is 15.7 meters high, with the hair and ushnisha arranged in tight curls, the full face carved with downcast eyes. He is robed in an inner vest covering the left shoulder and armpits, with a sash tied round the waist falling in a knot, an upper garment that completely covers his body, with U-shaped collar falling to the chest, the lappet of the robe resting on the left arm. He is seated with legs pendent on a square throne in a dignified attitude, with two hands a disappeared. All thin skin of clay plaster below the knees of the Buddha has peeled away, leaving the core of rock exposed, and we can see the square pile holes set regularly on the surface of the rock.

The flanking bodhisattvas are 13 meters high. The bodhisattva on the Buddha's left wears a high corolla, with the round and full face carved with arched brows sweeping above gently opened almond eyes. The plump lips with a clearly defined bowed outline. She has long striped earrings, squared shoulders and slightly swollen abdomen with the left hand

第13窟东崖大佛

壁画：佛及菩萨头光。佛头光为圆形，一共三圈。其中中间一圈纹带上绘小坐佛，内穿僧祇支，外穿垂领式袈裟，作禅定印，结跏趺坐。

题记：该窟存三则题记。菩萨衣褶处刻有公元1517年，公元1519年和公元1633年的题记。

引申与拓展

二十世纪八十年代初期，在修复佛头时发现一白瓷碗和一卷《金刚光明经》。

其珍贵之处在于碗的外侧题记，内容为"甘谷工匠高振同，是绍兴二十七年八月廿五日"，这条题记至少为我们提供了两条信息：一是重修大佛的工匠来自邻近的甘谷县；二是重修的年代是南宋绍兴二十七年，这为研究麦积山石窟的历史情况提供了不可多得的文字资料。工匠把佛经放在佛的头部的做法称之为"装藏"，寓意着佛的思想和灵魂，在宋代以后的佛教造像艺术中是很普遍的习俗。

公元734年，秦州大地震对大佛表面泥层破坏较大。南宋绍兴十五年至绍兴二十七年（公元1157年），麦积山僧人重新募款重塑。现在所见的大佛表层，就是南宋重修所作。

is elevated to the neck level holding out a lotus flower, while the reverses hand rests in the abdomen. With the broad scarf comes over the shoulders, she is robed in a long dress with revers at the waist, standing on the upturned lotus platform barefoot. The bodhisattva is on the Buddha's right, wearing circular earrings. The attitude is almost identical with the left-hand figure. The left hand hangs down in the front of the left leg holding a vase, and the right hand is elevated to the chest level.

Paintings: The Buddha and bodhisattvas have nimbuses behind them. The Buddha is under circular nimbus of three bands. Among which the central band bears small seated Buddhas. They are robed in the inner vests covering the left shoulder and armpits, the upper garments that completely cover their bodies, with U-shaped collar falling to the chest, the lappet of the robe resting on the left arm. They are seated with legs tightly locked in a yogic pose on the throne, with their two hands in the dhyana mudra.

Inscriptions: There are three inscriptions of AD 1517, AD 1519 and AD 1633 carved on folds of the drapery of the bodhisattvas.

Extension and Elaboration

In the early 1980s, a white porcelain bowl and a volume of *the Sutra of Golden Light* were found in the restoration of the Buddha's head.

What precious lies the inscriptionin written with a brush on the outside of the bowl by the ancient craftsman, which is a dedication by a certain Gao Zhentong, a craftsman from Gangu county, and the date is on August 25th of the 27th year of Shaoxing period in the Song Dynasty (AD 1157). It at least provides two information, one is the place where the craftsman is from, the other is the date of restoration, which is rare documentation in studying the history of Maijishan Caves. The practice of placing the sutras on the head of the Buddha by the craftsmen is referred as "Storing", implying the thought and soul of the Buddha. It is a common convention in the art of Buddhist sculptures after the Song Dynasty.

The thin skin of clay plaster of the Giant Buddha was heavily damaged possibly by the severe earthquake of Qinzhou in AD 734. From the 15th to the 27th year of Shaoxing period in the Song Dynasty (AD 1157), monks at Maijishan raised funds again to remodel him, and the present work is a restoration of the Song Dynasty.

第 14 窟

第14窟位于东崖中上部,开凿于隋代(公元581年—公元618年),明代(公元1368年—公元1644年)重修。其力士造像仍保留了隋朝简约和力感的特色。

该窟为一座平面方形、四角攒尖顶窟,有两身腰肢半扭的菩萨和一身力感的力士造像。三则刻画或墨书题记。

形制:该窟高3.41米、宽3.70米、残深2.18米。前部受到地震影响坍塌。正壁开一个圆拱形大龛,龛外侧有装饰性的龛楣和龛柱。

造像:窟内现存正壁龛内一佛,龛外左右两侧各一胁侍菩萨,左壁一力士,共计四身。

主佛高1.19米,低平肉髻,方面大耳。结跏趺坐。右臂屈肘上举,手指部分已经残损。

两身胁侍菩萨腰肢半扭,笑意微露,就像当地农妇劳动之余的小憩,显得安详舒坦。

左壁力士高1.86米,眼睛圆睁,戴项圈,上身袒露。颈部静脉曲张,宽肩挺胸,两臂残断。浑身肌肉的力量感很强身体向左侧成

第二章 麦积山石窟汉英解说词

Cave 14

Cave 14 is located at the upper middle part of the eastern cliff, was originally excavated in the Sui Dynasty (AD 581-618) and repaired in the Ming Dynasty (AD 1368-1644). The dvarapala retains the original simplicity and power of the Sui Dynasty.

In the cave visitors will appreciate a niche with the "dome of heaven" ceiling, two bodhisattvas in the triple bend of the body, a powerfully modelled dvarapala, three inscriptions carved or written with a brush. Details are as follows.

Type: It is a flat square niche with the "dome of heaven" ceiling, with 3.41 meters high, 3.70 meters wide and residual deep of 2.18 meters. Partial of its front has fallen away by the earthquakes. A large chaitya arched recess is cut into the main wall, with decorative lintel and columns outside.

Sculptures: A Buddha occupies a recess cut into the main wall, with two flanking attendant bodhisattvas standing outside the recess, a dvarapala on the left wall. There are four sculptures in all.

The principal Buddha is 1.19 meters high, wearing a low flat ushnisha right on the top, the square face flanked by pendulous ears. He is seated with legs tightly locked in a yogic pose on the throne. His right hand is elevated to the chest level, leaving partial fingers damaged.

Two attendant bodhisattvas stand in the triple bend of the body, their slight smiles convey the a sense of peace and comfort, just like the local women taking a short break after work.

The dvarapala on the left wall is 1.86 meters high, with eyes round open in a fury attitude, a collar round the neck, the upper body exposed. He has bulging muscles on the neck,

弓形，显得非常威武不可侵犯。

题记：该窟残存三则题记。访客墨书或刻于正壁龛内左侧上方、左壁力士后、右壁。

引申与拓展

该窟力士造像保留了隋朝简约和力感的特色。腰肢半扭的菩萨写实、个性突出。多采用大体积、大块面的塑作手法，给人以概括简洁、厚重饱满的印象，为唐代雕塑艺术的辉煌发展拉开了序幕。

broad shoulders and straight chest, with two arms broken. The strong strength shows in the muscles, the body turning to the left into a bow, giving an impression of powerful and offensive.

Inscriptions: There are three inscriptions left by visitors in the cave. Visitors might have written dedications above the left of the recess cut into the main wall with a brush or carved behind the dvarapala, and on the right wall.

Extension and Elaboration

The dvarapala retains the original simplicity and power of the Sui Dynasty. Bodhisattvas in the triple bend of the body bear a high realism, with outstanding personalities. They are carved on large masses and massive surfaces, and give a viewer the impression of simple, thick and solid, presenting a splendid development of the sculpture art of the Tang Dynasty.

第 15 窟

第15窟位于东崖中部西侧,开凿于北魏(公元386年—公元534年),宋代(公元960年—公元1279年)、明代(公元1368年—公元1644年)重修,是麦积山一座五佛龛。

该窟中有三尊宋代、两尊明代坐佛,正壁佛座后明代彩绘卷云图案。

形制:该窟为一个平面方形、"人"字坡顶窟。前部受到地震影响坍塌。地面凿低坛基。正、左、右三壁各设一方形基座,正壁两侧各砌一小基座。

造像:窟内正、左、右三壁各塑一宋代坐佛,正壁主佛两侧各塑一稍小明代坐佛,共计五身。

正壁和左右壁三佛,方圆脸大耳,弯眉细目,平视,丰肩袒胸。内着僧祇支,束带腰部打结下垂,外着双领下垂袈裟。结跏趺坐于长方形台座上。身后彩绘项身光、卷云图案。其中正壁佛,水波纹发髻,双手施禅定印。左右壁佛,螺髻,左手抚膝,右手施无畏印。

Cave 15

Cave 15 is located at the west side of the middle part in the eastern cliff, was originally excavated in the Northern Wei Dynasty (AD 386-534), and repaired in the Song Dynasty (AD 960-1279) and the Ming Dynasty (AD 1368-1644). It is a five Buddhas niche at Maijishan.

In the cave, visitors will appreciate three seated Buddhas in the Song Dynasty and two in the Ming Dynasty. Behind the base of the main wall, colourful eurly clouds were painted in the Ming Dynasty Details are as follows.

Type: It is a flat square niche with an inverted Y-shaped ceiling. Partial of its front has fallen away by the earthquakes. A low base is cut around the ground. A square pedestal throne is built on each of the main wall and the side walls, and a smaller throne is set on either side of the flanking walls.

Sculptures: A seated Buddha is modelled in the Song Dynasty on each of the main wall and two flanking walls, with a smaller seated Buddha in the Ming Dynasty on either side of the principal Buddha on the main wall. There are five sculptures in all.

Three Buddhas on the main wall and the left and right walls have the round and square faces flanked by pendulous ears, with arched brows sweeping above gently opened almond eyes, looking straight ahead, with broad shoulders and bared chests. They are robed in inner vests covering the left shoulder and armpits, a band tied at the waist falling in a knot, the upper garments that completely cover their bodies, with U-shaped collar falling to the chest, the lappet of the robe resting on the left arm and down to the left knee. They are seated with legs tightly locked in a yogic pose on the rectangle thrones, backed by coloured aureoles and mandolas adorned with motifs of curly clouds. Among them the Buddha on the main wall wears a topknot with water wavy, and two hands perform the dhyana mudra.

正壁左右侧佛,发型、衣着、坐姿、项身光与正壁佛相同,体格略小。左手置于腹部,右手举于胸前,双手皆失。

引申与拓展

该窟"人"字坡顶形制与第3窟相同。

The Buddhas on the left and right walls have the spiral-shaped topknots, and their left hands rest on knees, and their right hands in the abhaya mudra.

The hairstyle, clothes, sitting posture, aureole and mandorla of the Buddhas on either side of the main wall are identical with those of the principal Buddha, only smaller in size. Their left hands are placed on the abdomen, while the right hands are elevated to the chest level, leaving two hands missing.

Extension and Elaboration

The type of flat square niche with an inverted Y-shaped ceiling in the cave is identical with that in Cave 3.

第 17 窟

第17窟位于东崖中部,开凿于北魏(公元386年—公元534年)。

该窟中有五身泥塑造像、六身影塑造像。

形制:该窟是平面方形、平顶窟,大部分坍塌。正、左、右三壁各开一圆拱形大龛,正、左壁龛内设方形基座。正壁和左右壁两侧各凿一圆拱形小龛,共四小龛。正、右壁两侧各建一两层小坛台。

造像:正、左壁龛内各塑一身坐佛,正壁龛外两侧各残存一身弟子。左壁两侧各塑一胁侍菩萨。正、右壁两侧两层小坛台上嵌四身影塑坐佛和一身弟子,共计十一身。

正、左壁龛佛,磨光高肉髻,面形长圆,弯眉细目,高鼻大耳,面带微笑。内着僧祇支,外着双领下垂袈裟。左手施与愿印,右手无畏印。结跏趺坐于"工"字形高台座上,下摆呈三瓣垂覆于座前。身后绘圆形项光及莲瓣形身光。

正壁左右侧弟子,均头失。衣着与主佛相同。其中左弟子,左

Cave 17

Cave 17 is located at the middle part of the eastern cliff, and was excavated in the Northern Wei Dynasty (AD 386-534).

In the cave visitors will appreciate five clay sculptures, six figures in relief. Details are as follows.

Type: It is a flat square niche with a flat ceiling, most have fallen away. A large chaitya arched niche is carved on each of the main wall and the side walls, and a square throne is set on each of the main wall and the left wall. Four recesses are carved into each of the main wall and the left and right walls. Two-tier ledges are cut on either side of the main wall and the right wall.

Sculptures: A seated Buddha is modelled in each of the niche on the main wall and the niche on the left wall, and a disciple stands on both sides outside the niche on the main wall. An attendant bodhisattva stands on each side of the left wall. Four seated Buddhas and a disciple in relief are inserted on the two-tier ledges cut on either side of the main wall and the right wall. There are 11 figures in all.

The Buddhas in each niche on the main wall and the left wall wear the polished high topknots, with the oval faces carved with arched brows sweeping above gently opened almond eyes, the high nose flanked by pendulous ears, smiling. They are robed in the inner vests covering the left shoulder and armpits, the upper garments that completely cover their bodies, with U-shaped collar falling to the chests, the lappet of the robe resting on the left arm. With the right hands in the abhaya mudra and the left hands in the varada mudra, they sit in dhyanasana on the I-shaped high thrones with the hem covering in three petals.

手举于肩部。右弟子，双手残损。

左壁左右侧菩萨，戴扇形花冠，五官与主佛相似。内着僧祇支，下着长裙。帔帛从双肩下垂至膝部上卷搭于肘部后下垂。其中左菩萨，左手提桃形法器于腹前，右手举于肩部，手残损。右菩萨，右手握物举于肩部。

正壁小坛台上嵌三身影塑坐佛和一身影塑弟子，右壁小坛台一身影塑坐佛，均无头。

引申与拓展

该窟主佛头像在国内巡展。清秀的面庞上露出隐隐的一丝微笑，是典型北朝秀骨清像之风。

There are circular aureoles and lotus petal-shaped mandorlas behind them.

The disciples on either side of the main wall have lost their heads. Their clothing is identical with that of the principal Buddha. Among which the left-hand disciple raises his left hand to the shoulder level, the right-hand disciple, with hands missing.

The attendant bodhisattvas on either side of the left wall have the fan-shaped corollas, their features are similar to those of the principal Buddha. They are robed in an inner vests covering the left shoulder and armpits, the long dresses on the lower bodies. Their broad scarves come over the shoulders and fall down to the knees and up again rest on the arms and down again. Among them, the left-hand bodhisattva places her left hand to the abdomen level carrying a peach-shaped object, while her right hand is lifted to the shoulder level with hand damaged. The right-hand bodhisattva holds an object to the shoulder level in her right hand.

Three seated Buddhas and a disciple in relief are inserted on the little ledges of the main wall and a seated Buddha in relief on the little ledges of the right wall, all headless.

Extension and Elaboration

The head of the principal Buddha in the cave has taken part in the itinerant exhibition in China. There is a ghost of a smile on his graceful face, is a typical style of the long and slender figure and delicately modelled features in the Northern Dynasty.

第 20 窟

第20窟位于东崖中部西侧,开凿于西魏(公元535年—公元556年)。该窟是麦积山模仿第44窟主佛西魏文皇后乙弗及西魏佛"女相化"的另一个例子。

该窟中有四身泥塑造像,右壁两则墨书题记。

形制:该窟是平面方形、平顶窟,窟顶和右壁前部塌毁。正、左壁各设一方形台座。

造像:正壁塑一坐佛二菩萨,左壁塑一身坐佛,共四身。

正、左壁佛,旋涡纹肉髻,面形长圆,细眉杏眼微启,薄唇大耳,面带微笑。内着僧祇支,外着双领下垂袈裟。结跏趺坐于方形台座上,右足显露在外,下摆覆盖座前呈两瓣重叠下垂。其中正壁佛,右手施无畏印,左手施与愿印,手指均残。左壁佛,双手施禅定印。

主佛两侧菩萨,戴三花冠,面形方圆,宽项圈。上身袒露,下着长裙,胸前结带下垂。其中左菩萨,右手举花于胸前,左手握圆形玉璧于腿侧。右菩萨,手势刚好相反。

Cave 20

Cave 20 is located at the west side of the middle part in the eastern cliff, and was excavated in the Western Wei Dynasty (AD 535-556). It is another example of imitating the principal Buddha Empress Wen, Yifu of the Western Wei Dynasty in Cave 44 and the Buddhas with "Feminine Appearance" modelled in the Western Wei Dynasty at Maijishan.

In the cave visitors can enjoy four sculptures modelled in clay, and two inscriptions with a brush on the right wall. Details are as follows.

Type: It is a flat square niche with the flat ceiling, and the ceiling and the front of the right wall have fallen away. A square pedestal is set on each side of the main wall and the left wall.

Sculptures: A seated Buddha flanked by a bodhisattva holds the main wall, with a seated Buddha on the left wall. There are four figures in all.

The Buddhas on the main wall and the left wall wear the spiral-shaped topknots, the oval faces carved with arched browns sweeping above gently opened almond eyes. He has a thin slip and flanked by pendulous ears, with a smile. They are robed in the inner vests covering the left shoulder and armpits, the upper garments that completely cover their bodies, with U-shaped collar falling to the chest, the corner of the robes resting on the left arm. They are seated in a pose of deep yogic meditation, with the legs tightly locked, the sole of the right foot uppermost on the square thrones with the hems covering in layered two large petals. Among them the right hand of the Buddha on the main wall performs the abhaya mudra and his left hand in the varada mudra. The two hands of the Buddha on the left wall are in dhyana mudra.

The bodhisattvas on each side of the Buddha wear the three lotus petal-shaped crown, with a round face, a broad collar around the neck. They are robed in lower garments, with a band

题记：访客在右壁留有两则墨书题记。

引申与拓展

该窟主佛面容秀美，长眉细目，面带微笑，体态端庄优雅。其"女相化"与被誉为"东方美人"的第44窟主佛西魏文皇后乙弗相同。这种清新近人、温婉秀丽的风格，既受到北魏晚期的影响，又由雕塑师与赞助者的审美趣好决定。

tied at the chest falling in a knot, leaving the upper bodies bare. Among which the right hand of the bodhisattva on the left is lifted at the chest holding a flower and the left hand hangs down with a circular jade beside the thigh. The gesture of the right-hand bodhisattva is just the opposite.

Inscriptions: There are two inscriptions with a brush left by visitors on the right wall.

Extension and Elaboration

The principal Buddha of the cave has a pretty face carved with arched brows sweeping above gently opened almond eyes, smiling, in a dignified and elegant attitude. His "Feminine Appearance" is identical with that of the principal Buddha Empress Wen, Yifu of the Western Wei Dynasty in Cave 44, which is known as the "Oriental Beauty". This kind of fresh and approachable, gentle and beautiful style is not only influenced by the late Northern Wei Dynasty, but also determined by the aesthetic interest of the sculptors and sponsors.

第22窟

第22窟位于东崖中部西侧，开凿于北周（公元557年—公元581年）。主佛整体艺术风格和面部表情与第44窟主佛西魏文皇后乙弗有很大的相似性，是工匠模仿第44窟建造的洞窟之一。

该窟中有三身泥塑造像。

形制：该窟是平面方形、平顶窟。前部已坍塌，现只残存后部分。正壁开一圆拱形龛，龛内设一"工"字形基座，地面作低坛基。龛外左侧建一坛基。

造像：正壁龛内塑一身坐佛，龛外左侧塑一身弟子、一身菩萨，共计三身。

正壁佛，低平肉髻，圆脸，眉间白毫相，细眉凤眼，高鼻厚唇。内着僧祇支，外着通肩袈裟。右手施无畏印，左手施与愿印。结跏趺坐于"工"字形台座上，右足显露在外，下摆呈两片垂于座下。身后彩绘圆形项光内有放射线同心圆，莲瓣形身光左侧一飞天二弟子，右侧二飞天一菩萨痕迹。以石绿、石青、赭红为主调。虽有残损，但色泽仍鲜丽。

左侧弟子和菩萨，圆脸，体格修长。头微微转向主佛，立于坛

Cave 22

Cave 22 is located at the west side of the middle part in the eastern cliff, and was excavated in the Northern Zhou Dynasty (AD 557-581). The overall artistic style and facial expression of the principal Buddha are very similar to those of the principal Buddha Empress Wen, Yifu of the Western Wei Dynasty in Cave 44. It is one of the caves built by craftsmen imitating Cave 44.

In the cave visitors will enjoy three clay sculptures. Details are as follows.

Type: It is a flat square niche with the flat ceiling, and the front of the cave has fallen away, now only leaving the rear part. The main wall contains a chaitya arched shallow bay in which an I-shaped throne is set, and a low base is cut around the ground. A platform is built on the left outside the niche.

Sculptures: A seated Buddha occupies a niche cut into the main wall, outside which a disciple and a bodhisattva stand on the left. There are three figures in all.

The Buddha on the main wall has a low topknot, the round face is carved with the white hair between the brows, the arched browns sweeping above gently opened almond eyes, high nose and full lips. He wears an inner vest covering the left shoulder and armpits, an upper garment that completely covers his body and hangs in heavy folds round his shoulders. With the right hand in the abhaya mudra and the left hand in the varada mudra, he sits in dhyanasana, the sole of the right foot uppermost on the I-shaped throne with the hem covering in two large petals. There is the coloured circular aureole composed of a concentric circle with radioactive lines, and the lotus petal-shaped mandorla behind him, where we can see the traces of a flying apsara and two disciples on the left, two flying apsaras and a bodhisattva on the right, with colours chiefly of a bluish grey tint, a deep emerald green and a reddish-brown. Although badly damaged, they have retained their pristine freshness of colour.

基上。项光和身光形状与主佛相同。其中弟子，内着僧祇支，外着袒右袈裟。左手握衣角于胸前，右手提小布袋于腿侧。菩萨，束扇形发髻。肩部有圆形饰物，戴项圈、臂钏。上身袒露，下系长裙。披帛搭肩垂于腹前穿环绕臂垂下。左手自然下垂握帛带，右手持莲蕾于胸前。

引申与拓展

第44窟是麦积山最经典和最漂亮的洞窟之一，有非常厚重的历史文化。与西魏文皇后乙弗相关联，《北史·后妃传》有详细记载。在此之后，麦积山出现了一批模仿第44窟的洞窟，该窟是其中之一。

该窟正壁主尊佛衣与第141窟二佛相同，均着褒衣博带演化式佛衣。前者领口向上略微收紧，掩去了内着的僧祇支和带饰，后者右领襟敷搭左臂和左肩，胸系带结下垂。

The disciple and the bodhisattva on the left have the round faces, slender and long-legged. They stand on the platforms, turning their heads slightly to the principal Buddha. The shape of the aureoles and mandorlas is identical with that of the principal Buddha. Among them, the disciple is robed in an inner vest covering the left shoulder and armpits, with the outer robe thrown over the left shoulder or the upper throwing a strong diagonal across the body, leaving the right side of the body and shoulder bare. The left hand is placed on the chest holding the corner of the robe, the right hand hangs down beside the thigh carrying a small cloth handbag. The hair of the bodhisattva is tied in a fan-shaped topknot. The shoulders are decorated with circular ornaments, with a collar around the neck and armlets on the arms. The upper body is exposed, and the lower body is robed in the long dress. The scarf covers both shoulders and falls down to pass through a ring over the lower abdomen, then up through the armpits and down again. He hangs down the left hand naturally holding a ribbon, with a lotus bud in the right hand at the chest.

Extension and Elaboration

Cave 44 is one of the most classic and beautiful caves at Maijishan, with a very profound history and culture. It is related to Empress Wenn, Yifu of the Western Wei Dynasty, and the details are in *History of the Northern Dynasty· Records of the Historian Biography of Imperial Concubine*. In the following years, a number of caves imitating Cave 44 appeared at Maijishan, the cave is one of them.

The robe of the principal Buddha on the main wall is the same as the two Buddhas of Cave 141, all robed in the evolution of the loose gowns with wide girdles. The collar of the former is upward with slightly tightened, concealing the inner vest and sash, while the right lappet of the latter rests on the left arm and the left shoulder, with a band tied at the chest falling in a knot.

第 23 窟

第23窟位于东崖中部西侧,开凿于北魏(公元386年—公元534年)。主佛典雅飘逸,是北魏晚期特征比较突出的士人形象。

该窟中有两身泥塑造像,主佛左右两侧及左右壁上部绘千佛,正壁下部两侧绘女供养人,窟顶正中绘一圆莲。

形制:该窟是平面方形、平顶窟,前部因地震坍塌。正壁设一方形基座。

造像:正壁塑一坐佛,右壁一胁侍菩萨,共计两身。

正壁坐佛,面貌清秀。半球形高肉髻,长方脸微含笑意,高鼻细眼。内着僧祇支,腰带于腹前打结下垂,外着双领下垂袈裟。双臂前伸,双手均残。结跏趺坐于方形台座上,下摆呈四瓣垂于座上。身后浮塑宽带同心圆项光,莲瓣形大身光边缘绘火焰纹、忍冬纹。下部两侧各绘一身弟子及菩萨。色彩的痕迹仍然存在,主要为石青、石绿和赭红。

右侧菩萨,头戴花冠,长发披肩,高鼻小嘴。身材修长,上身袒露。斜披络腋,下着长裙。帛带自双肩绕臂贴墙壁呈圆弧状垂

Cave 23

Cave 23 is located at the west side of the middle part in the eastern cliff, and was excavated in the Northern Wei Dynasty (AD 386-534). The principal Buddha is elegant and graceful, which is a more prominent image of clerisy with characteristics in the late Northern Wei Dynasty.

In the cave visitors will enjoy two clay sculptures, with the Thousand Buddhas painted on either side of the principal Buddha and the upper part of the flanking walls, the figures of female donors on each side of the lower part of the main wall, and a circular lotus in the center of the ceiling. Details are as follows.

Type: It is a flat square niche with the flat ceiling, and the front of the cave has fallen away by the earthquakes. The main wall contains a square throne.

Sculptures: A seated Buddha is modelled on the main wall, and an attendant bodhisattva stands on the right wall. There are two figures in all.

The seated Buddha on the main wall has delicately modelled features, with a hemispherical high topknot, long square face with slightly smiling, high nose and gently opened almond eyes. He is robed in an inner vest covering the left shoulder and armpits, with a sash tied at the abdomen falling in a knot, an upper garment that completely covers his body, with U-shaped collar falling to the chest, the lappet of the robe resting on the left arm. Both arms are stretched forward with two hands damaged. He sits in dhyanasana on the square throne with the hem of the robe covering in four large petals. There is a concentric circular aureole with broad rim, and a large lotus petal-shaped mandorla in relief is behind him, with the flame motif and honeysuckle on the outermost border. A disciple and a bodhisattva are painted on each of its lower sides. Traces of colour remain, chiefly in a bluish grey tint, a stone green, and a reddish-brown.

下。左手提桃形法器置于左胯，右手举一莲花于右胸前。面向佛，跣足立于半圆形莲台上。身后项身光只残留少部分火焰纹。均白粉作底，施色为石青、石绿、赭红等。

壁画：主佛左右两侧及左右壁上部绘千佛，身后有项身光。身着双领下垂袈裟。施禅定印，结跏趺坐。正壁下部台座两侧共绘六身女供养人，在侍从们的簇拥下拱手似持一莲花面佛而立。在这群人的后面，六位侍者持羽葆。供养人束高发髻，身穿圆领广袖衫，衣袖垂至膝际，下系长裙。窟顶正中绘一圆莲，周围环绕六个小圆莲，外缘绘有花卉及奔跑的小鹿等。

引申与拓展

该窟正壁下部两侧六身彩绘女供养人，在服饰特点和人物布局方面充分体现出当时胡汉融合的特殊社会历史风格，真实再现了秦州地区北朝贵族女性礼佛场景。这组美丽的组像与第127窟西方净土变中一群上层社会女性形象相似，只是规模较小。

The bodhisattva on the right has the hair gathered high encircled by a diadem and falling down the back, with a high nose and a small mouth. She is slender and long-legged, with the upper body bare. She is robed in the upper throwing a strong diagonal across the body, leaving the right side of the body and shoulder bare, a long dress on the lower body. The scarf comes from shoulders and hangs down through the armpits flung against the walls in circular arcs. The left hand hangs down beside the hip carrying a peach-shaped ritual instrument, and the right hand is raised to the chest holding a lotus. She stands on a semicircular lotus platform barefoot towards the Buddha. Only a small part of the flame motif remains in the aureole and mandorla behind her. Their underpainting is white, colouring in a bluish grey tint, a stone green, and a reddish-brown.

Paintings: The Thousand Buddhas is painted on either side of the principal Buddha and the upper part of the flanking walls have aureoles and mandorlas behind them. They are robed in the upper garments that completely cover their bodies, with U-shaped collar falling to the chest, the lappet of the robe resting on the left arm. With two hands in dhyana mudra, they are seated in dhyanasana on the thrones. Six female donors on each side of the throne below the main wall stand with the right hand into a fist and the left hand held straight against the fist towards the Buddha holding a lotus, with their attendants. At the back of the group six attendants hold a parasol over the each head of them. They wear the high topknots, wearing the round collar garments with long loose sleeves down to the knees, with the long dresses on the lower bodies. A circular lotus in the center of the ceiling is surrounded by six small round lotuses, with flowers and running deer on the outer rim.

Extension and Elaboration

The characteristics of the costume and the layout of the figures of six coloured female donors on each side of the lower part of the main wall fully reflect the special social and historical style of the fusion between the Hu and the Han at that time. It truly recurs the scene of the noble women in Qinzhou worshipping the Buddha in the Northern Dynasty. This beautiful group images are similar to those of the group of women of high rank in Illustration to the Pure Land in Cave 127, only on a small scale.

第24窟

第24窟位于东崖中部,开凿于隋朝(公元581年—公元618年)。该窟保存了麦积山石窟为数不多的隋朝造像。

该窟是类似草原游牧民族毡帐的石窟,窟内有四身木骨架泥塑和一身木雕弟子像。

形制:该窟是一个平面马蹄形、穹窿顶窟,高2.84米、宽2.9米、深2.13米,窟门口部分因地震塌陷。

造像:窟内正中泥塑一坐佛,左侧塑一身菩萨和一身木雕菩萨,右侧塑一身弟子及一身菩萨,共五身造像。

主佛高1.3米,顶部螺纹状低肉髻,面形方圆,两眼微睁。上身内着僧祇支,腰间系带,外穿双领下垂袈裟,一角搭于左臂。右手食指指向前方施期克印,左手抚膝,结跏趺坐于方形佛座上。

左侧菩萨高1.56米,戴冠,戴项圈。斜披络腋,下穿裙,袒胸露双臂。左手屈肘于胸前,右手垂于身侧,站在圆形莲台上。左侧木雕菩萨高1.65米,五官模糊。

右侧弟子高1.55米,衣着与主佛相同。右手牵衣角自然下垂,

Cave 24

Cave 24 is located at the middle part of the eastern cliff, and was excavated in the Sui Dynasty (AD 581-618). It preserves few rare sculptures modelled in the Sui Dynasty in the Maijishan Caves.

In the cave visitors can enjoy the niche similar to the tents of the nomads on the grassland, with four sculptures of clay modelled on a wooden armature and a disciple of wood carving. Details are as follows.

Type: It is a flat horseshoe-shaped niche with the "dome of heaven" ceiling, with 2.84 meters high, 2.90 meters wide and 2.13 meters deep. Partial of its entrance has fallen away by the earthquakes.

Sculptures: A seated Buddha is modelled in clay in the center of the niche, with a bodhisattva in clay and a bodhisattva of wood carving on its left, a disciple and a bodhisattva of clay on its right. There are five figures in all.

The principal Buddha is 1.30 meters high, the hair and ushnisha arranged in tight curls, and the round face with eyes slightly open. He is robed in an inner vest covering the left shoulder and armpits, a sash tied round the waist, an upper garment that completely covers his body, with U-shaped collar falling to the chest, the lappet of the robe resting on the left arm. His right hand is raised in tarjani mudra, and the left hand rests on knee. He is seated with legs tightly locked in a yogic pose on square high throne.

The bodhisattva on the left is 1.56 meters high, wearing a crown and a collar round the neck. She is robed in the upper throwing a strong diagonal across the body, leaving the right side of the body and shoulder bare, and a long dress on the lower body, leaving the chest

第24窟主佛

左手屈肘向前,脚穿圆头鞋站在莲花台上。右侧菩萨高1.52米,头顶平铺莲瓣形发髻。斜披络腋,帔帛自双臂垂至腹部于膝部上卷绕臂下垂。左手屈肘上举,手托供品(但手中的供品已失),右手垂于身侧,跣足立于圆形莲台上。

引申与拓展

该窟内的塑像原作均未上彩,露出泥质本身的色调,表面也未发现色彩脱离的痕迹。推断最初塑做的时候就没有上色,表现出一种简单、质朴的美感。木雕菩萨的形式、高度和其他的泥塑差别较大,可能不是同时期的作品,是后世补配的造像,这种塑像形式更便于移动,并且对细节雕刻比较模糊,可能是需要在表面增加细泥。袈裟表面的衣纹使用了阶梯式的褶皱,更具动感。

and arms bare. Her left arm is raised to the chest, the right hand hangs down beside the thigh, standing on the circular lotus platform. Her neighbour bodhisattva of wood carving is 1.65 meters high, whose features are too damaged to make out.

The disciple on the right is 1.55 meters high, whose clothing is identical with that of the principal Buddha. His left arm is raised, the right hand hangs down holding the corner of the robe, standing on the circular lotus platform in shoes with round toe. His neighbour bodhisattva is 1.52 meters high, with the hair and ushnisha arranged in lotus petals. She is robed in the upper throwing a strong diagonal across the body, leaving the right side of the body and shoulder bare. The broad scarves come from the shoulders and hang down to the lower abdomen, then over the knees and up through the armpits and down again. Her left arm is raised holding out an offering (which has disappeared), and the right hand hangs down beside the thigh, standing on the circular lotus platform barefoot.

Extension and Elaboration

The original sculptures in the cave are all unpainted, the soil colour is distinct, and there is no traces of faded colours on the surface. It might have been that they are uncoloured right at the beginning of the modelling, giving an impression of simple and plain. The bodhisattva of wood carving is quite different from other sculptures of clay in style and height. Presumably it is not a works of the same date, but an added figure later, which is more convenient to move. And more ambiguous details of the carving suggest that the fine clay is presumably not spread over the wooden armature. The drapery on the surface of the robe hangs in layered symmetrical folds, with an easy rhythmic movement.

第 25 窟

第25窟位于东崖中部，开凿于隋代（公元581年—公元618年），明代（公元1368年—公元1644年）重修。龛内雕塑一尊十五世纪麦积山石窟最大的坐姿菩萨。

该窟内有一尊麦积山石窟最大的坐姿菩萨，佛项光、身光和佛座绘云朵的壁画，一则刻画题记。

形制：该龛是一个大型马蹄形、圆拱顶龛，高4.6米、宽3.72米、深1.56米，龛的前部位置有坍塌。

造像：该窟正壁仅存一身坐姿菩萨。

正壁坐姿菩萨高2.97米，头戴高花冠，冠的正中有一尊小坐佛像。颈部项链下垂串珠、玉佩等作为装饰。上身裸露，但是有宽大的披巾覆盖着双肩和两侧臂膀。下身穿着长裙，在裙边有二龙戏珠纹饰，在腰间有系带，系带在腹部结成花结并下垂。菩萨结跏趺坐在"工"字形须弥座上。须弥座束腰部镂空雕刻，有六根四棱角柱，柱头上有摩尼宝珠，下有覆莲柱础，柱与柱之间雕刻出拱门，拱门浮塑缠枝忍冬纹。须弥座制作精巧，造型独特，为麦积山各代佛座中较为突出的一个。

第二章　麦积山石窟汉英解说词

Cave 25

Cave 25 is located at the middle part of the eastern cliff, and was originally excavated in the Sui Dynasty (AD 581-618), repaired in the Ming Dynasty (AD 1368-1644). It contains the largest seated bodhisattva modelled in the 15th century in the Maijishan Caves.

In the cave visitors can enjoy the largest seated bodhisattva at Maijishan, paintings on the aureole and mandorla behind the Buddha, the clouds on the throne, and a carved inscription. Details are as follows.

Type: It is a large horseshoe-shaped niche with a chaitya arched ceiling, with 4.6 meters high, 3.72 meters wide and 1.56 meters deep. Its front part has fallen away.

Sculptures: A seated bodhisattva survives on the main wall.

The seated bodhisattva on the main wall is 2.97 meters high, wearing a high corolla with a small seated Buddha image in the middle. A string of pearls and jade pendants hang from a heavy collar round the neck, the upper body is bare, but the broad scarf covers the shoulders and arms. The lower body wears a long dress adorned with the pattern of two dragons playing with a pearl on its hem, a sash tied round the waist falling in a knot over the abdomen. He is seated with legs tightly locked in a yogic pose on the I-shaped Sumeru throne, a base of upside-down lotus petals over a waist above a further tier of upturned lotus-petals. Among which its concave waist is a hollowed-out work supported by six quadrangular columns, the cintamans is placed on the capital, while the column bases in the form of an upside-down lotus, painted interlocking honeysuckle motif in relief supporting the chaitya-arch stand on top of the pilasters. The modelling of the throne is exquisite and unique, which is more outstanding among those in different generations at Maijishan.

壁画：龛内均为明代重绘，壁面上部分残存有菩萨水波纹形头光及小部分椭圆形身光。周围绘有祥云图案，以石青、石绿、褚红为主色调。

题记：佛座左侧有一则刻画题记，内容是：公元1364年，侯氏兄弟请寺院的僧人作为自己的导师对该窟进行了重新妆彩。另外从题记文字中可以看到，有一位出家前为木匠的僧人作为主要参与者参加了此次妆彩。

引申与拓展

该窟坐姿像可能是着菩萨装的弥勒佛，具有明显的菩萨大乘特点。在佛教传统中"未来佛弥勒是目前居住在兜率宫（六天之第四天）的菩萨"，是继释迦牟尼佛之后来到我们这个娑婆世界教化众生的下一位佛。造像具有强烈的神生兜率、信仰弥勒的思想，反映了这一时期麦积山石窟造像的特点和思想内涵。

Paintings: The pictures were all repainted in the Ming Dynasty, and partial water wavy aureole and fragments of oval mandorla behind the bodhisattva remain on walls. They are surrounded by auspicious clouds, chiefly in a bluish grey tint, a stone green, and a reddish-brown.

Inscription: There is an inscription carved on the left of the throne, the content indicates that in AD 1364, the Hou brothers redecorated the niche guided by the monks of the temple. In addition, a monk who had been a carpenter before mainly participated the work.

Extension and Elaboration

The seated figure in the cave might be Maitreya as a bodhisattva, bearing obvious characteristics of the Bodhisattva Mahayana. In Buddhist tradition "Maitreya-the future Buddha is presently a bodhisattva residing in the Tushita heaven (the fourth of the six heavens) ", is the immediate successor to Sakyamuni Buddha to teach and transform sentient beings in this Saha World. There is a strong thought that Maitreya descends from the Tushita Heaven and the Maitreyan faith, reflecting the characteristics and ideological connotations of the sculptures at Maijishan Caves during this period.

第 26 窟

第26窟位于东崖中部，开凿于北周（公元557年—公元581年），宋朝（公元960年—公元1279年）重修。该窟是保存麦积山石窟北周最典型的造像，窟顶"涅槃变"场景与第12窟相似。

该窟体现了北周原作与宋朝（公元960年—公元1279年）重修造像风格，窟内有六尊木骨泥塑和六身浮塑飞天，窟顶"涅槃变"和彩绘千佛，七则刻于壁上的题记。

形制：该窟平面方形、四角攒尖顶窟，宽3.24米、高3.68米、残进深1.73米，洞窟前部在地震中残损，目前仅存洞窟建筑的二分之一。窟内四壁顶部相交处雕有圆莲。正壁开一圆拱形龛，左右壁前有通长的佛座。

造像：正壁龛内塑一身坐佛，龛外两侧各塑一身胁侍菩萨。左壁塑一身坐佛，其佛座前端浮塑两身飞天，右壁塑两身坐佛，其佛座前端浮塑四身飞天，共计十二身造像。其中正壁的一佛二菩萨和左壁的一佛是北周原作。

正壁佛高1.06米，头残失。内着僧祇支，外着双领下垂袈裟。右手说法印，左手与愿印，结跏趺坐于莲花座上。

Cave 26

Cave 26 is located in the middle part of the eastern cliff, and it was originally excavated in the Northern Zhou Dynasty (AD 557-581) and repaired in the Song Dynasty (AD 960-1279). It preserves the most typical sculptures modelled in the Northern Zhou Dynasty at Maijishan. The scene depicted in "Nirvana Sutra Illustration Painting" on the ceiling is similar to that of Cave 12.

In the cave visitors can enjoy the style of image-making between the original works of the Northern Zhou Dynasty and the restorations of the Song Dynasty (AD 960-1279), with six figures of clay modelled on a wooden armature and six flying apsaras in relief, "Nirvana Sutra Illustration Painting" and the coloured Thousand Buddhas on the ceiling, and seven inscriptions carved on the walls. Details are as follows.

Type: It is a flat square niche with the "dome of heaven" ceiling, with 3.24 meters wide, 3.68 meters high, and 1.73 meters deep. The front has fallen away by the earthquakes, leaving only half of the building. A circular lotus is carved at the intersection between the ceiling and four walls. There is a large chaitya arched recess cut into the main wall, and an inseperate throne in front of the left and right walls.

Sculptures: A seated Buddha occupies the niche cut into the main wall, outside which an attendant bodhisattva stands on each side. A seated Buddha is modelled on the left wall with two flying apsaras in relief on the front of the throne, while on the right wall, two Buddhas are seated on the throne with four flying apsaras in relief on the front. There are twelve figures in all. Among them, the Buddha flanked by two bodhisattvas on the main wall and the Buddha on the left wall are the original works of the Northern Zhou Dynasty.

The Buddha on the main wall is 1.06 meters high, and the head is missing. He is robed in an inner vest covering the left shoulder and armpits, an upper garment that completely covers his body, with U-shaped collar falling to the chest. He is seated in dhyanasana on a

右侧菩萨头戴化佛冠,颈戴宽项圈。双手佩手镯,身挂串珠璎珞。斜披络腋,下身着翻边长裙。宽大的帔帛自双肩垂下,从腹前穿环,垂至双腿之间上折绕臂。跣足立于圆形莲台上。左侧菩萨与右侧菩萨大致相同,只是头已残失。

左右壁三佛均高1.2米,低平肉髻。内着僧祇支,外着通肩袈裟。双手施禅定印,结跏趺坐于台座上。右壁的两身佛像经过宋代重修,可以看到明显的附加泥层。

左右壁佛座前端,六身浮雕伎乐,姿态和手持的乐器都不相同。限于佛座的高度,这些伎乐都是坐姿,或打鼓,或弹拨古筝,或吹奏排箫。

壁画:现存面积约12平方米,位于窟顶披面及正、左、右三壁上部。

在窟顶正面斜面上绘制《涅槃变》,画面分为两部分。在中间位置一尊佛坐在彩色华盖下的"工"字形台座上,身穿袈裟,左右拥簇弟子、菩萨、供养人、力士等。这是佛最后一次说法的场景。在左下角位置,佛右肋侧身而卧于长榻上,众多的弟子拥簇在周围呈哭泣状。画面左侧树下,放置着一口棺木。这是佛去世时的场景。在这些画面的周围点缀着树木、山石等。空中有一些飞天人物。在前景中佛陀两边凡界男女神情或悲恸,或愕然,或惊诧。右上方树丛中的一群人可能代表前来吊唁的地方名流,佛派阿难告诉他们佛将会在当夜入灭的消息。

在各个壁面的靠上位置,绘制有三排千佛形象,这些千佛形象都比较简单,都呈坐姿,禅定印,身穿的袈裟颜色相互间隔穿插,可见有黑、褐色等。

题记:该窟存七则刻于壁上的题记。

lotus throne, with his raised right hand showing the vitarka mudra, his lowered left hand in varada mudra.

The bodhisattva on the right wears a high crown with a small seated Buddha image, a wide collar round the neck. The wrists are decorated with bracelets, with a heavy garland of jewels hanging in a loop from both shoulders. She is dressed in the upper throwing a strong diagonal across the body, leaving the right side of the body and shoulder bare, the long dress with reverses at the waist on the lower body. The broad scarves come over the shoulders and down to pass through a large pi-disc over the lower abdomen then down into the hollow between the legs and up through the armpits. She stands on the circular lotus platform. The bodhisattva on the left is almost identical with that on the right, but the head has disappeared.

The three Buddhas on the left and right walls are all 1.20 meters high, with low flat topknots. They wear the inner vests covering the left shoulder and armpits, the upper garments that completely cover their bodies and hang in heavy folds round the shoulders. They sit in dhyanasana on the thrones with hands resting on the laps. The two Buddhas on the right wall are restorations of the Song Dynasty, in which you can see obvious thin skin of clay plaster in overlapping layers.

The front of the throne on each of the side walls bears six celestial musicians in relief, which are different in attitudes and instruments. Limited to the height of the thrones, they are modelled in seated posture, either playing drums, or a zither or pan-pipes.

Paintings: About 12 square meters survive. They are on the slope sides of the ceiling and above the front wall, the left wall and the right wall.

Nirvana Sutra Illustration Painting on the front slope side of the ceiling is visible, composed of two parts. In the center of the picture a Buddha is seated on an I-shaped throne under a coloured canopy, wearing a long robe of a monk, surrounded by disciples, bodhisattvas, donors, and dvarapalas, etc. The scene is the last preaching of the Buddha. In the lower left corner, Sakyamuni lies on his right side on a couch, surrounded by his mourning disciples and followers. On the left there is a bier under the tree. The scene is the death of the Buddha. Trees and rocks are scattered here and there. Some flying apsaras are riding in the sky. In the foreground to either side earthly beings bear expressions either of grief, or sadness, or surprise. A group among the trees, upper right, perhaps represents the local notables to whom Ananda was sent to tell of the Buddha's approaching death.

In the upper part of each wall retains three rows of images of the Thousand Buddhas. The modellings of these figures are simple, all with a seated posture and in dhyana mudra. The colours of the robes are painted at intervals, of which the traces of black, brown, etc. are visible.

引申与拓展

　　该窟壁面上部出现成排彩绘千佛。佛教将世界划分为多个时空，每个世界都会有众多的人成佛。"千"在这里是众多的意思，不是确定的一千。信徒绘制众多的千佛图像也是希望自己能够成为其中的一员。

　　该窟佛座前端出现浮塑飞天。详情可参考第4窟"散花楼"绘塑结合技法。

Inscriptions: There are seven inscriptions carved by visitors on the walls.

Extension and Elaboration

The images of coloured Thousand Buddhas appear on the ceiling in the cave. Buddhism divides the world into multiple time and space, and there will be many people in each world to become Buddhas. "Thousand" here means many, not the definite one thousand. Worshipers draw many images of Thousand Buddhas and hope to become one of them.

Flying apsaras in relief appear on the front of the thrones. You can consult the technique of painting and sculpture in Cave 4 (Pavilion of Scattered Flowers).

第 27 窟

第27窟位于东崖中部,开凿于北周(公元557年—公元581年)期间。窟顶新出现了北周壁画"法华经变"。

该窟中有北周原作"法华经变"和城池壁画,六尊宋代(公元960年—公元1279年)重塑造像,五则墨书题记。

形制:该窟是平面方形、四角攒尖顶,宽3.27米、高3.31米、进深2.1米,洞窟前部因地震坍塌。正、左、右壁各开一个平面马蹄形穹隆顶龛(均浮塑龛楣及半圆形龛柱,柱础为覆莲,柱头为仰莲,正中塑火焰宝珠)。

造像:窟内目前保存四佛二菩萨泥塑造像,共六身,均在宋代重塑或改塑。

正壁佛高1.41米,方圆脸。内穿僧祇支,外穿双领下垂式袈裟。结跏趺坐于方形台座上。佛身项光为六世纪原绘,项光由同心圆形构成,莲瓣形身光上绘有火焰纹等,颜色以赭红、石青为主。

左胁侍菩萨束高发髻,面形方圆。袒上身,颈戴宽项圈,双手佩手镯。下着长裙,披帛从双肩下垂后于腹前穿璧成"X"形。左

第二章 麦积山石窟汉英解说词

151

Cave 27

Cave 27 is located in the middle part of the eastern cliff, and it was excavated in the Northern Zhou Dynasty (AD 557-581), "Lotus Sutra Illustration Painting" of the Northern Zhou Dynasty first appears on the ceiling in the niche.

In the cave visitors can enjoy the original works of "Lotus Sutra Illustration Painting" and the city in the Northern Zhou Dynasty, six figures restored in the Song Dynasty (AD 960-1279), and five inscriptions with a brush. Details are as follows.

Type: It is a flat square niche with the "dome of heaven" ceiling, with 3.27 meters wide, 3.31 meters high, 2.10 meters deep, and the front has fallen away by the earthquakes. A horseshoe-shaped niche with the "dome of heaven" ceiling is cut into the main wall and each of the side walls. Each of them contains a lintel in relief above, supported by semi-circular columns. The column base is adorned with upside-down lotus-petal, while the capital with upturned lotus-petal, and the flaming pearl in the center.

Sculptures: The cave contains four Buddhas and two bodhisattvas made of clay plaster. There are six figures in all, which are all restorations or remodellings of the Song Dynasty (AD 960-1279).

The Buddha on the main wall is 1.41 meters high, with a square and round face. He wears an inner vest covering the left shoulder and armpits, an upper garment that completely covers his body, with U-shaped collar falling to the chest. He is seated in dhyanasana on a square throne. The aureole and mandorla behind the Buddha are the original works of the sixth century, with the concentric circles on the aureole and lotus petal-shaped mandorla decorated with a flame motif, chiefly in a reddish-brown and a bluish grey tint.

手抚胸,右手垂于身侧。右胁侍菩萨风格与左胁侍菩萨相同,仅右手贴于胸前,左手垂于身侧提一桃形璧。

左右壁龛内坐佛身穿圆领袈裟。结跏趺坐,双手结禅定印。

壁画:现存面积约7平方米。正、左、右三壁及龛内壁画残损较为严重,多已剥落成碎片状,内容模糊不清。窟内顶部彩绘保存较好,描述场面壮观的"法华经变"。释迦、多宝并坐于华盖下,有圆形头光。内着僧祇支,外着双领下垂袈裟。施说法印,结跏趺坐于台座上。两侧各有一弟子站立,其下方各有一菩萨站立。右菩萨下方站立一弟子。

窟顶西坡的壁画中绘一城池,城门、城墙、城楼、角楼、城内建筑等,城内外有众多的人物形象。这个建筑利用透视法,细致准确地反映出了北周时期的建筑。

题记:该窟在正左右壁上存五则墨书题记。

引申与拓展

该窟窟顶绘"法华经变",表现形式为释迦、多宝佛并坐谈法,是较为早期的"法华经变"。《法华经》图像是北朝佛教造像的主流,法华思想影响着北方地区大部分的佛教石窟开凿和造像。释迦、多宝两佛并坐是"法华经变"中最常见和最有代表性的场景之一。

The attendant bodhisattva on the left has a tall topknot, with a square and round face. The upper body is bare, with a wide collar round the neck, the wrists are decorated with bracelets. The lower body wears a long dress, the scarf hangs from the shoulders down to pass through a large pi-disc over the lower abdomen, leaving a shape of "X". The left hand is elevated to the chest level and the right hand hangs down beside the thigh. The style of the right-hand bodhisattva is identical with that of the left, with only the right hand lifting to the chest level and the left hand falling down beside the thigh holding a peach-shaped jade.

The seated Buddhas in each of the side niches wear the robes of round collar. They are seated in dhyanasana on the thrones in dhyana mudra.

Paintings: About seven square meters survive. Those on the main wall and each of the side walls have suffered badly, they have peeled away in many places only retaining fragments, and the contents of which are too damaged to make out. Those coloured drawings on the ceiling are preserved well, depicting the spectacular sight of "Lotus Sutra Illustration Painting". Here Sakyamuni and Prabhutaratna share the same throne under the canopy, backed by circular aureole. They wear the inner vests covering the left shoulder and armpits, the upper garments that completely cover their bodies, with U-shaped collar falling to the chest. They are seated in dhyanasana on the pedestals in vitarka mudra. A disciple stands on each side, below which stands a bodhisattva. A disciple stands below the bodhisattva on the right.

The paintings on the west slope of the ceiling illustrate a city with gates, walls, towers, corner towers, and buildings within the city, with numerous figures inside and outside the city. This building is painted using perspective, reflecting the architecture of the Northern Zhou Dynasty in a detailed and an accurate way.

Inscriptions: There are five inscriptions left by visitors with a brush on the main wall, the left wall and the right wall.

Extension and Elaboration

"Lotus Sutra Illustration Painting" on the ceiling in the cave represents a rather early version of Sakyamuni and Prabhutaratna sharing the same throne. Iconography of the *Lotus Sutra* is the mainstream of Buddhist sculptures in the Northern Dynasty, the concept of which affects most buddhist cave excavations and image-makings in the northern regions. Sakyamuni and Prabhutaratna sharing the same throne are one of the most common and representative scenes in "Lotus Sutra Illustration Painting".

第 28 窟

第28窟位于东崖下部,开凿于北魏(公元386年—公元534年),宋代(公元960年—公元1279年)、明代(公元1368年—公元1644年)、清代(1636年—公元1912年)重修。因其位于下段,且与第29窟和第30窟一字排开分布有七个佛龛,每龛各供一佛,所以又称"下七佛阁"。

该窟内有宋代重塑的十身造像。

形制:该窟是单檐庑殿顶崖阁,三间四柱,为前廊、后室结构。后壁并排开凿三个马蹄形穹隆顶龛。

造像:中间龛内塑一佛二弟子和二胁侍菩萨,左右两龛各塑一佛二菩萨(一身菩萨像残损),共十身造像。

三佛均束螺髻,圆脸。内着僧祇支,外着双领下垂袈裟。结跏趺坐于方形台座上。其中,左右龛佛双手结禅定印。

中间龛内左侧弟子迦叶颧骨隆起,怒目粗眉,肋骨突出,显现老相。右侧弟子阿难面形饱满圆润,青年形象。

五身菩萨均束高发髻、弯眉杏眼。上身袒露,戴项圈。斜披络腋,外着大衣,下着长裙。

Cave 28

Cave 28 is located at the lower part in the eastern cliff. It was originally dug in the Northern Wei Dynasty (AD 386-534) and repaired in the Song (AD 960-1279), Ming (AD 1368-1644) and Qing (AD 1636-1912) dynasties. Because it is in the lower part with seven niches each containing a Buddha cut in a row, a niche in Cave 29, three niches in each of this cave and Cave 30, they are also called "the Lower Seven Buddhas Halls".

Visitors can appreciate ten sculptures remodelled in the Song Dynasty. Details are as follows.

Type: It is a chamber open to the cliff face, with the lintel supported by stone pillars, and a single-eaved hip roof carved in relief in the rock above. It has four stone pillars supporting the roof, making the gallery of three openings along the front. It is composed of a gallery at the front, the shaft at the rear. Three horseshoe-shaped niches with the "dome of heaven" ceiling are cut into the rear wall in a row.

Sculptures: The central niche holds a Buddha flanked by two disciples and two attendant bodhisattvas on each side, and a Buddha attended by two attendant bodhisattvas in each of the flanking niches (with a bodhisattva damaged). There are ten figures in all.

Three Buddhas wear spiral-shaped topknots, the round faces. They are robed in inner vests covering the left shoulder and armpits, upper garments that completely cover their bodies, with U-shaped collar falling to the chest, the lappet of the robe resting on the left arm and down to the left knee. They sit in dhyanasana on square thrones. Among them, the two hands of the Buddha in each flanking niches are in dhyana mudra.

The disciple Kasyapa on the left in the central niche has bulging cheekbones, with the fierce eyes below thick brows, protruding ribs, all suggesting an elder image. The disciple Ananda on the right bears a full, rounded face, a young image.

引申与拓展

该窟与第4窟、第9窟、第29窟和第30窟同属于麦积山石窟"七佛题材"造像的洞窟。

Five bodhisattvas are with high topknots, with the faces carved with arched brows sweeping above gently opened almond eyes. Their upper bodies are bare, with collars round the necks. They are robed in the upper throwing a strong diagonal across the body, leaving the right side of the body and shoulder bare, the overcoats and long dresses on the lower bodies.

Extension and Elaboration

The theme of the Seven Buddhas in the cave is identical to that in Cave 4, Cave 9, Cave 29 and Cave 30 at Maijishan.

第29窟

第29窟位于东崖下部,开凿于北周(公元557年—公元581年),明代(公元1368年—公元1644年)、清代(1636年—1912年)重修。因其位于下段,且与第28窟和第30窟一字排开分布有七个佛龛,每龛各供一佛,所以又称"下七佛阁"。

该窟内有明清重塑的三身造像。

形制:该窟是平面半圆形、平顶摩崖敞口大龛。

造像:正壁塑一佛,左右两侧各塑一身菩萨,共三身造像。佛束螺髻,圆脸,突目。内着僧祇支,外着双领下垂袈裟。结跏趺坐于方形台座上。右手抚膝,左手置于腹前。

两身菩萨均戴冠,圆脸。上身袒露,戴串珠项圈。外着大衣,下着贴腿长裙。其中左侧菩萨坐卧象上,右侧菩萨坐卧狮上。三身造像衣着上均塑沥粉堆金龙凤、云纹等装饰图案。

Cave 29

Cave 29 is located at the lower part in the eastern cliff. It was originally dug in the Northern Zhou Dynasty (AD 557-581) and repaired in the Ming (AD 1368-1644) and Qing (AD 1636-1912) dynasties. Because it is in the lower part with seven niches each containing a Buddha cut in a row, three niches in each of Cave 28 and Cave 30, a niche in this cave, they are also called "the Lower Seven Buddhas Halls".

Visitors can appreciate three sculptures remodelled in the Ming and Qing dynasties. Details are as follows.

Type: It is a large semicircle open niche on the cliff face with a flat ceiling.

Sculptures: A Buddha flanked by a bodhisattva on the left and right sides are modelled on the main wall. There are three figures in all.

The Buddha wears a spiral-shaped topknot, the round face with bulging eyes. He is robed in an inner vest covering the left shoulder and armpits, upper garment that completely covers his body, with U-shaped collar falling to the chest, the lappet of the robe resting on the left arm and down to the left knee. He sits in dhyanasana on a square throne. His right hand rests on knee, and the left hand is put on the abdomen.

Two bodhisattvas wear high crowns with the round faces. Their upper bodies are bare, with collars of a string of beads round the necks. They are robed in overcoats and long dresses on the lower bodies melting the legs. Among which the left-hand bodhisattva sits on a crouching elephant, while the right-hand bodhisattva sits on a crouching lion. The robes of three figures are decorated with the patterns of dragons, phoenixes and clouds. The technique of embossed painting and gilding craft was used here.

引申与拓展

　　该窟与第4窟、第9窟、第28窟和第30窟同属于麦积山石窟"七佛"题材造像的洞窟。

Extension and Elaboration

The theme of the Seven Buddhas in the cave is identical to that in Cave 4, Cave 9, Cave 28 and Cave 30 at Maijishan.

第30窟

第30窟位于东崖下部,开凿于北魏(公元386年—公元534年),宋代(公元960年—公元1279年)、明代(公元1368年—公元1644年)、清代(1636年—公元1912年)重修。因其位于下段,且与第28窟和第29窟一字排开分布有七个佛龛,每龛各供一佛,所以又称"下七佛阁"。

该窟内有宋代重修的二十一身造像,左龛壁面和中龛沿留有两则墨书题记。

形制:该窟是单檐庑殿顶崖阁,三间四柱,为前廊、后室结构。后壁并排开凿三个圆拱形龛。

造像:三龛内各塑一佛,左右两侧各有三身胁侍菩萨,共二十一身造像。

三佛均束螺髻,方圆脸,宽肩。内着僧祇支,外着双领下垂袈裟。结跏趺坐于方形台座上,薄衣贴体。其中正龛佛右手无畏印,左手施与愿印,左右龛佛双手结禅定印。

十八身菩萨均束高发髻,椭圆形脸,弯眉杏眼。上身袒露,戴项圈。斜披络腋,外着袈裟,下着长裙。

题记:左龛壁面和中龛沿留有两则墨书题记。

Cave 30

Cave 30 is located at the lower part in the eastern cliff. It was originally dug in the Northern Wei Dynasty (AD 386-534) and repaired in the Song (AD 960-1279), Ming (AD 1368-1644) and Qing (AD 1636-1912) dynasties. Because it is in the lower part with seven niches each containing a Buddha cut in a row, three niches in each of Cave 28 and this cave, a niche in Cave 29, they are also called "the Lower Seven Buddhas Halls".

Visitors can appreciate 21 sculptures restored in the Song Dynasty, two inscriptions with a brush on the wall of the niche on the left and the border of the central niche. Details are as follows.

Type: It is a chamber open to the cliff face, with the lintel supported by stone pillars, and a single-eaved hip roof carved in relief in the rock above. It has four stone pillars supporting the roof, making the gallery of three openings open along the front. It is composed of a gallery at the front, the shaft at rear. Three chaitya arch shafts are cut into the rear wall in a row.

Sculptures: A Buddha is flanked by three attendant bodhisattvas on the left and right sides occupying each of the three niches. There are 21 figures in all.

Three Buddhas wear spiral-shaped topknots, square faces, and broad shoulders. They are robed in inner vests covering the left shoulder and armpits, upper garments that completely cover their bodies, with U-shaped collar falling to the chest, the lappet of the robe resting on the left arm and down to the left knee. They sit in dhyanasana on square thrones, thinly clad with robes melting into the bodies. Among them, the right hand of the Buddha in the central niche performs the abhaya mudra and the left hand in the varada mudra. The two hands of the Buddha in each flanking niches are in dhyana mudra.

18 bodhisattvas are with high topknots, with the oval faces carved with arched brows sweeping above gently opened almond eyes. Their upper bodies are bare, with collars round the necks.

引申与拓展

　　该窟与第4窟、第9窟、第28窟和第29窟同属于麦积山石窟"七佛题材"造像的洞窟。

They are robed in the upper throwing a strong diagonal across the body, leaving the right side of the body and shoulder bare, outer robes and long dresses on the lower bodies.

Inscriptions: There are two inscriptions left by visitors with a brush on the wall of the niche on the left and the border of the central niche.

Extension and Elaboration

The theme of the Seven Buddhas in the cave is identical to that in Cave 4, Cave 9, Cave 28 and Cave 29 at Maijishan.

第31窟

第31窟位于东崖中部，开凿于北周（公元557年—公元581年），隋代（581年—公元618年）重修。窟内存六世纪末十方佛原作。

该窟正壁有两层六世纪末十尊影塑坐佛。

形制：该窟是平面长方形、平顶敞口龛。

造像：正壁两层贴十尊影塑坐佛，右壁影塑菩萨一尊（无头），共十一身造像。

十尊影塑坐佛分别着袒右袈裟、通肩袈裟和双领下垂袈裟。结跏趺坐，双手结禅定印或者说法印。其中两尊台座下各刻一坐姿力士，其余八尊台座下各刻一踏莲狮子。右壁影塑菩萨内着僧祇支，下着长裙。双手相叠于腹前，跣足而立。

Cave 31

Cave 31 is located at the middle part in the eastern cliff. It was originally dug in the Northern Zhou Dynasty (AD 557-581) and repaired in the Sui Dynasty (AD 581-618). It contains the unrestored works on the Buddhas of the Ten Quarters in the end of the sixth century.

Visitors can appreciate ten seated Buddhas of the end of the sixth century modelled in relief in two rows on the main wall. Details are as follows.

Type: It is a small rectangle open niche on the cliff face with a flat ceiling.

Sculptures: Ten seated Buddhas modelled in relief in two rows are applied on the main wall, with a relief bodhisattva (headless) on the right wall. There are eleven figures in all.

Ten Buddhas in relief wear either the outer robes thrown over the left shoulder or the upper throwing a strong diagonal across the body, leaving the right side of the body and shoulder bare or upper garments that completely cover their bodies and hang in heavy folds round their shoulders or upper garments that completely cover their bodies, with U-shaped collar falling to the chest, the lappet of the robe resting on the left arm and down to the left knee. They sit in dhyanasana on a square thrones with their two hands either in dhyana mudra or in vitarka mudra. Among which each of the two seats is decorated with a seated atlantid, while the other eight are carved with a lion stepping on a lotus. The bodhisattva in relief on the right is robed in an inner vest covering the left shoulder and armpits, and a long dress on the lower body. With two hands holding together to the abdomen level, she stands barefoot.

引申与拓展

　　该窟与第142窟同属于麦积山石窟"十方佛题材"造像的洞窟。

Extension and Elaboration

The theme of the Buddhas of the Ten Quarters in the cave is identical to that in Cave 142 at Maijishan.

第 35 窟

第35窟位于东崖中部，开凿于北周（公元557年—公元581年）、宋朝（公元960年—公元1279年）、元朝（公元1271年—公元1368年）重修，龛内坐佛为保存不多的元朝造像。

该窟中有两身分别塑于元代和北周的坐佛，绘有五尊佛及菩萨的说法图壁画。

形制：该窟是一个平面方形、四角攒尖顶小窟，高2.63米、宽2.68米、深2.65米。正壁开一圆拱形龛，龛外有浮塑的莲瓣形龛楣。

造像：正壁龛内塑一身元代坐佛，右壁残存一身从第6窟移入的北周小坐佛，共计两身。

正壁龛内坐佛高0.56米，顶作螺肉髻，面容沉静。身着袒右袈裟。施禅定印，双手惨毁。结跏趺坐于双层"工"字形仰覆莲台座上。佛身后头光和身光装饰模制莲花瓣、火焰宝珠、花朵、卷草等。

右侧地面放置小坐佛一身，高0.57米，为北周塑作。低平肉髻，面型方圆。内着僧祇支，外穿双领下垂袈裟。结跏趺坐。右手

Cave 35

Cave 35 is located in the middle part of the eastern cliff, and it was originally excavated in the Northern Zhou Dynasty (AD 557-581), repaired in the Song Dynasty (AD 960-1279) and the Yuan Dynasty (AD 1271-1368). The seated Buddha in the niche is a rare sculpture of the Yuan Dynasty.

In the cave visitors can enjoy two seated Buddhas modelled in the Yuan Dynasty and the Northern Zhou Dynasty respectively, paintings of the scene of Sakyamuni's preaching containing five Buddhas and bodhisattvas. Details are as follows.

Type: It is a flat square niche with the "dome of heaven" ceiling, with 2.63 meters high, 2.68 meters wide and 2.65 meters deep. A small chaitya arched recess is cut into the main wall with a lotus petal-shaped lintel.

Sculptures: A seated Buddha modelled in the Yuan Dynasty is cut into the niche on the main wall, and the right wall remains a small seated Buddha modelled in the Northern Zhou Dynasty, which was moved into from Cave 6. There are two figures in all.

The seated Buddha cut into the niche on the main wall is 0.56 meters high, with the hair and ushnisha arranged in tight curls, the serene face with meditative expression. He is robed in the outer robe thrown over the left shoulder or the upper throwing a strong diagonal across the body, leaving the right side of the body and shoulder bare. He performs dhyana mudra with two hands missing. He is seated in dhyanasana on the I-shaped double reverse lotus throne. The aureole and mandorla behind the Buddha are decorated with lotus petals, flaming pearls, flowers, and curly grass made in moulds.

A small seated Buddha placed on the ground on the right is 0.57 meters high, which is the original works of the Northern Zhou Dynasty. He wears low flat topknot, with square

心向内放在胸前，左手置于左膝。

壁画：窟顶部残存北周原作壁画，因烟熏严重仅模糊可辨一些人物。窟顶四披绘《说法图》。正披上模糊可见坐佛、菩萨、弟子等。左披正中一佛，左右各立两身菩萨等。前披正中为一佛坐在圆覆莲座上，左右立数身弟子。右披上依稀可辨华盖下有一坐姿的菩萨，左右各立二弟子四菩萨。

引申与拓展

麦积山元代洞窟很少，元代造像更加稀有。该窟坐佛和第48窟四臂观音均为藏传佛教密宗造像，具有重要的历史及考古价值。

and round face. He wears an inner vest covering the left shoulder and armpits, an upper garment that completely covers his body, with U-shaped collar falling to the chest. He is seated in dhyanasana on a pedestal. The right hand is elevated to the chest level with the palm inward, and the left hand rests on knee.

Paintings: The ceiling remains the original works of the Northern Zhou Dynasty. As they are badly smokeblackened, we can only see some ambiguous figures. The scene of Sakyamuni's preaching appears on the ceiling with four sloping panels. A seated Buddha flanked by standing bodhisattvas and disciples and so on can vaguely make out on the main panel. A seated Buddha flanked by two standing bodhisattvas occupies the left panel. In the center of the front panel is a Buddha seated on a circular throne with upside-down lotus-petal, flanked by several standing disciples. On the right panel there is a seated bodhisattva flanked by two standing disciples and four bodhisattvas under a canopy, which is barely discernible.

Extension and Elaboration

There are few caves cut in the Yuan Dynasty at Maijishan Caves, and sculptures of the Yuan Dynasty are even more rare. Both the seated Buddha in the cave and the a Four-Armed Kwan-Yin in Cave 48 are the sculpture of esoteric Tibetan sects, which have important historical and archaeological values.

第 36 窟

第36窟位于东崖中部,开凿于北周,宋代重修,是宋代比较重要的七佛龛,造像具有敦厚质朴、珠圆玉润的北周特点。

　　该窟内有八身泥塑造像,窟顶残存一佛头及二身供养人、三壁上方彩绘小坐佛。

　　形制:该窟是平面方形、四角攒尖顶,前壁因地震塌毁。正、左、右三壁前有低坛基。正壁开一圆拱形龛,左右壁前凿通长台座。顶部及四壁角各雕凿半圆形石胎泥塑帐杆和帐柱及圆莲装饰。

　　造像:正壁龛内塑一身坐佛,左右侧各塑一身胁侍菩萨。左壁塑三身坐佛,右壁现存两身坐佛,共计八身。

　　正壁佛,磨光低肉髻,前有肉髻珠,方脸细眉,双眼微启下视,挺鼻厚唇,粗颈。内着僧祇支,外着双领下垂袈裟。左手施与愿印,右手施无畏印。结跏趺坐于龛内,袈裟下摆分两片悬垂于龛前。身后彩绘圆形项光和莲瓣形身光,饰有宽带、忍冬纹等装饰图案。

Cave 36

Cave 36 is located at the middle part of the eastern cliff, and was originally excavated in the Northern Zhou Dynasty (AD 557-581), and repaired in the Song Dynasty (AD 960-1279). It is an important seven Buddhas cave in the Song Dynasty. The sculptures carry the characteristics of kindness and simplicity, roundness and plumpness in the Northern Zhou Dynasty.

In the cave visitors will enjoy eight clay sculptures, remainings of a head of the Buddha and two donors painted on the ceiling, and coloured small seated Buddhas above the three walls. Details are as follows.

Type: It is a flat square niche with the "dome of heaven" ceiling, and the front wall has fallen away by the earthquakes. A low concave base is cut around the ground in front of the main wall and the two side walls. A shallow chaitya arched recess is cut into the main wall, and an inseperate pedestal is set in front of the left and right walls. The semicircular tent poles and columns decorated with circular lotus in clay plaster over a core of rock are carved on the ceiling and four corners of walls.

Sculptures: The niche on the main wall holds a seated Buddha flanked by an attendant bodhisattva. Three seated Buddhas are modelled on the left wall and two seated Buddhas survive on the right wall. There are eight figures in all.

The Buddha on the main wall has a polished low topknot, a bead between the topknot and the bottom hair, the square face carved with arched brows, downcast eyes slightly open, high nose and full lips, broad neck. He is robed in an inner vest covering the left shoulder and armpits, an upper garment that completely covers his body, with U-shaped collar falling to the chest, the lappet of the robe resting on the left arm and down to the left knee. With the right hand in the abhaya mudra and the left hand in the varada mudra, he sits in dhyanasana on the throne in the niche with the hem covering in two large petals. There are the coloured circular aureole and lotus petal-shaped mandorla adorned with motifs of broad band and honeysuckle in relief behind him.

正壁左右侧菩萨，磨光圆形发髻，长发垂肩，花冠缺失。圆脸，双眼微启下视，嘴角略上翘，戴宽项圈。上着僧祇支，下身着翻边长裙。帛带自肩部下垂至膝前上卷搭臂下垂，跣足立于仰覆莲台上。其中左侧菩萨，右手执一莲花于胸前，左手自然下垂于身侧手中执一圆形物。右侧菩萨，左臂托举宝珠于胸前，右手托左肘。

左右壁五佛，体格小于主佛。圆脸，弯眉细眼，高鼻小嘴，颈短粗。身体修长，腹部凸出。着通肩袈裟。双手施禅定印，结跏趺坐于台座上，袈裟下摆分两片悬垂于座前。其中左壁三佛，低肉髻。右壁二佛，宋代重修，水波纹发髻。

壁画：窟顶右披残存一佛头及二身供养人。正、左、右三壁上方彩绘二排着通肩袈裟的小坐佛。

引申与拓展

该窟与第4窟、第9窟、第28窟、第29窟、第30窟和第141窟同属于麦积山"七佛题材"造像的洞窟。

第二章　麦积山石窟汉英解说词

The bodhisattvas on either side of the main wall wear the polished circular topknots, with the hair gathered high and falling down the backs with the diadem missing. The round faces are carved with downcast eyes slightly open, with the corners of the mouth slightly raised, and the broad collars around the necks. They are robed in the inner vests covering the left shoulder and armpits, the long dresses with revers at the waist on the lower bodies. Their broad scarves come over the shoulders and down in loops over the lower abdomen, then up resting on the elbows and down again, they stand on double reverse lotus bases barefoot. Among them, the left-hand bodhisattva holds a lotus at the chest in her right hand, the left hand hangs down naturally carrying a circular object. The left arm of the right-hand bodhisattva is lifted to the chest level holding a pearl, which is supported by the right hand on the elbow.

The five Buddhas on the left and the right walls are smaller in size than the principal Buddha. Their round faces are carved with arched brows sweeping above gently opened almond eyes. They have high noses and small mouths, short and broad necks. They are slender and long-legged, with bulging abdomens. They are robed in upper garments that completely cover their bodies and hang in heavy folds round their shoulders. With two hands in dhyana mudra, they sit in dhyanasana on the thrones with the hem covering in two large petals. Among which the three Buddhas on the left wall have the low topknots. The two Buddhas on the right wall remodelled in the Song Dynasty bear water wavy topknots.

Paintings: A head of the Buddha and two donors painted on the right panel of the ceiling survive. Coloured small seated Buddhas in two rows are drawn above the three walls, which are robed in upper garments that completely cover their bodies and hang in heavy folds round their shoulders.

Extension and Elaboration

The theme of the Seven Buddhas niches is identical to that in Cave 4, Cave 9, Cave 28, Cave 29, Cave 30 and Cave141 at Maijishan.

第 37 窟

第37窟位于东崖中区入口处,开凿于隋代(公元581年—公元618年)。该窟内保存一尊丰满夸张的隋代菩萨像。其双臂交叉放在胸前,安详的形象中透出庄重与纯真是典型的隋代作品。

该窟是类似草原游牧民族毡帐的石窟类型,窟内有一身倚坐佛像和一位虔诚的菩萨造像。

形制:该窟是平面马蹄形、圆拱顶,高2.8米、宽2.45米、深1.63米。地震造成前部微损。

造像:正壁塑一身坐佛,右壁塑一身菩萨,共两身造像,均为木骨泥塑。

主佛倚坐于方形台座上,脚踩半圆形莲台。高2.1米,头顶有螺旋状肉髻。面型方圆,眼珠为镶嵌宝石,双耳垂肩。身穿通肩袈裟,左手手指残损,右手残失。

右壁菩萨高1.85米,束高发髻,戴花冠,束发丝带飘于两肩。面庞丰满,眉弯目细。上身袒露,双肩披大衣,颈部佩戴宽项圈,胸前佩戴璎珞。下身穿长裙,双臂交叉抚于胸前。

Cave 37

Cave 37 is located at the entrance of the middle part in the eastern cliff and was dug in the Sui Dynasty (AD 581-618). It preserves a full and exaggerated bodhisattva of the Sui Dynasty. Folding her arms over her chest, the serene image bears the blending of noble and genuine, which is a typical works of the Sui Dynasty.

In the cave visitors can enjoy the niche similar to the tents of the nomads on the grassland, a Buddha is seated with legs pendent and a pious bodhisattva. Details are as follows.

Type: It is a horseshoe-shaped niche with a chaitya arched ceiling, with 2.8 meters high, 2.45 meters wide and 1.63 meters deep. Its front has been slightly damaged by earthquakes.

Sculptures: A seated Buddha is modelled on the main wall, with a bodhisattva on the right wall. There are two figures of clay modelled on a wooden armature in all.

The main Buddha is seated with legs pendent on a square pedestal and feet resting on a semi-circular lotus bud. He is 2.1 meters high, with the hair and ushnisha arranged in tight curls. With a square and round face, his eyeballs look like the inlaid gems, flanked by pendulous ears. He wears an upper garment that completely covers his body and hangs in heavy folds round his shoulder. The fingers of the left hand are damaged, and the right hand is missing.

The bodhisattva on the right wall is 1.85 meters high, wearing a high topknot, chapleted, with the hairband hanging over the shoulders. The full face is carved with arched brows sweeping above gently opened almond eyes. The upper body is bare, the outer shawl covers both shoulders, with a wide collar round the neck, a heavy garland of jewels hangs down the chest. The lower body wears a long dress, and she folds her arms over her chest.

引申与拓展

隋朝皇帝杨坚及其家族曾经长期在草原生活,所以在审美方面有较浓厚的北方草原风气。这种审美自然对普通民众的审美造成较大的影响。该窟就是模仿草原上毡帐开凿,都是和皇室推崇的游牧民族审美有关。

第37窟胁侍菩萨

第二章　麦积山石窟汉英解说词

Extension and Elaboration

Emperor Yang Jian and his royal family of the Sui Dynasty once lived on the grassland for a long time, so they preferred the aesthetic of northern grassland. This naturally has a greater impact on the beauty of the common people. The excavation of the cave imitates the tents of the nomads on the grassland, associated closely with the royal family's praise for the aesthetic of the nomads.

第43窟 魏后墓

第43窟位于东崖中区，西邻第44窟，开凿于西魏（公元535年—公元556年），五代（公元907年—公元960年）和宋代（公元960年—公元1279年）重修。因西魏皇后乙弗氏（公元510年—公元540年）葬在该窟，号"寂陵"，俗称"魏后墓"，文帝死后迁葬于永陵，仅余空窟。该窟是一座墓窟和佛龛相结合的洞窟，其前享堂后墓室的结构、丰润的造像风格和不同空间的造像组合安排对后续麦积山开窟造像产生了一些具体的影响。

该窟是一座墓窟建筑，窟内有十身造像，三则壁上墨书或刻画题记。

形制：该窟是单檐庑殿顶大型崖阁，三间四柱，高6.1米、宽6.65米、深7.3米，为前廊、享堂、后室结构。享堂为平面马蹄形穹隆顶大龛，其左右壁各开一圆拱壁龛，后室为后壁正中凿一盝顶龛。

造像：窟内前廊内左右两次间宋代各塑一身力士，前室正中为宋代塑一尊倚坐佛像，左右侧为五代（宋重修）各塑一身菩萨。前室正壁上方高浮雕二身供养菩萨，椅背头各塑一条龙头。后室内左侧立一件西魏石雕佛，共计十身（含龙头塑像）。

前廊左右力士均高2.5米以上。头戴花冠，双目圆睁。上身袒露，肌肉凸起。披帛搭于双肩绕臂随风飞扬。下着战裙，身躯扭动。腕戴镯，脚戴环，跣足立于台基上。其中左力士呈张口怒状表

Cave 43

Cave 43 is located in the middle part of the eastern cliff, to its west is Cave 44. It was originally dug in the Western Wei Dynasty (AD 535-556) and was repaired in the Five Dynasties (AD 907-960) and the Song Dynasty (AD 960-1279). Because Empress Wen, Yifu (AD 510-540) of the Western Wei Dynasty was at first buried in the cave entitled Silent Tomb, commonly known as the Tomb of Empress Wen of the Western Wei Dynasty, but later her body was disinterred and buried at Yongling Mausoleum after the death of Emperor Wen, leaving the tomb empty. It is a blending of a tomb and a shrine. The structure of the entrance chamber and rear shaft, the style of plump image-makings and the arrangement of figures in different spaces have some specific effects on the subsequent cave excavations and image-makings at Maijishan.

In the cave visitors can enjoy a blending of a tomb and a shrine, ten sculptures, three inscriptions written with a brush or carved on the walls. Details are as follows.

Type: It is a huge chamber open to the cliff face, with the lintel supported by stone pillars, and a single-eaved hip roof carved in relief in the rock above. It has four stone pillars supporting the roof, making the gallery of three openings along the front. It is 6.1 meters high, 6.65 meters wide, 7.3 meters deep, composed of a gallery at the front, the entrance chamber in the middle, the shaft at rear. The entrance chamber is a large flat horseshoe-shaped niche with the "dome of heaven" ceiling, a chaitya arched niche is cut into each of the side walls, and a tent-style shaft is cut into the center of the rear wall.

Sculptures: A dvarapala modelled in the Song Dynasty stands on each of the side openings in front gallery, and a Buddha of the Song Dynasty is seated with legs pendent in the central of the entrance chamber with a bodhisattva made in the Five Dynasties and restored in the Song Dynasty standing on each side. A head of dragon is modelled on each side of the Buddha suggesting the back of the throne, from behind which two votive bodhisattvas in high relief rise up above the main wall in the entrance chamber. On the left of the shaft stands a stone Buddha of Western Wei Dynasty. There are ten sculptures in all (including the heads of dragons).

Both dvarapalas on each side of the gallery are over 2.5 meters high, chapleted, with the eyes round open in fury attitude. The upper bodies are bare with bulging muscles. The scarves come from the shoulders and down through the armpits fluttering in the wind. The lower

情，左手托金刚杵搭于肩部，右手手指张开向左上挥动。右力士，头部向左侧扭动，双唇紧闭。左手拄金刚杵立于脚下（已残损），右手握拳上扬至头部。

前室主佛，高2.5米。螺髻，面形方圆，细眼弯眉。大耳，宽肩挺胸。体态端庄，神情肃穆。内着僧祇支，外着双领下垂袈裟。右臂屈肘向上前举至胸部，左手抚膝。倚坐于"工"字形台座上，双脚各踩莲台。

主佛身后壁面高浮雕供养菩萨均头戴高冠，面形圆润，弯眉。其中左侧供养菩萨左手托净瓶于胸。右侧供养菩萨双手合十。两龙头昂首相向而视。

二胁侍菩萨面形方圆，眉眼细长，大耳小嘴。上着圆领窄袖短襦，项部束带打结，外着圆领半袖衣。斜披络腋，腹前作结下垂。两胸前衣纹为凸起的旋涡状。下着翻边紧身长裙。臂戴钏，腕绕环。身体呈微微"S"形扭头向佛，双足残损，立于方形台座上。其中左菩萨头顶有残损，冠饰遗矢。左手托于胸前，右手自然下垂，双手手指均残损。右菩萨高发髻，双手置于胸前，右手手指残失。

后室内石雕佛，佛头部及上部背光残损。内着僧祇支，外着双领下垂袈裟。左手置于左膝，右臂屈肘平置、右手残损。倚坐台上，双足下有半圆形台。左右两侧各有一身弟子穿袈裟，双手拢于腹前。

题记：该窟存三则墨书或刻于壁上的题记。

bodies wear the battle skirts with a slight bend of the bodies. Their arms are decorated with bracelets, they stand on the platforms barefoot with anklets. Among which the dvarapala on the left keeps mouth open in a scolding manner, his left hand holds out a vajra resting on the shoulder, while his right hand waves to the upper left with fingers extended. The head of the right-hand dvarapala twists to the left, leaving lips closed. His left hand holds a vajra at the feet (damaged), and his right arm is raised above the head with a clenched fist.

The Buddha occupying the entrance chamber is 2.5 meters high. He has spiral-shaped topknot, the round face carved with arched brows sweeping above gently opened almond eyes. He is flanked by pendulous ears, with broad shoulders and stiff chest. He sits in dignified attitude with a serene expression. The Buddha wears an inner vest covering the left shoulder and armpits and an outer garment that completely covers his body, with U-shaped collar falling to the chest, the corner of the robe resting on the left arm. His right hand is elevated to the chest level, and the left hand rests on the knee. He is seated with legs pendent on an I-shaped throne and feet resting on two lotus buds.

Both of the two votive bodhisattvas on the main wall behind the Buddha in high relief wear high crowns with full face carved with arched brows. Among which the bodhisattva on the left elevates her left hand to the chest level holding a vase. The palms of the right-hand bodhisattva are pressed together at the chest. The two dragons raise their heads highly facing opposite directions.

Two attendant bodhisattvas have round faces carved with long brows sweeping above gently opened almond eyes. They are flanked by pendulous ears and small mouth. They wear the short robs with a roll collar and close-fitting sleeves, which have a knot round the neck, and a coat with half-arm sleeves. They are dressed in the upper throwing a strong diagonal across the body, leaving the right side of the body and shoulder bare, with a band tied at the chest falling in a knot. The drapery on the chests is cut with raised whirlpool motif. They are robed in long dresses with reverses at the waist. Their arms are decorated with bracelets, rings encircling the wrists. With the slightly swaying curves of their bodies, and their heads slightly turning towards the Buddha, they stand on the square platforms with damaged feet. Among them, the top head of the bodhisattva on the left is damaged, and the crown is missing. The left hand raises to the chest, the right hand naturally hangs down beside the thigh, leaving fingers of two hands damaged. The right-hand bodhisattva bears a high topknot, and his hands are raised to the chest with the fingers of the right hand lost.

The head and the upper part of the mandorla of the stone Buddha in the shaft have been damaged. He wears an inner vest covering the left shoulder and armpits and an outer garment that completely covers his body, with U-shaped collar falling to the chest, the corner of the robe resting on the left arm. The left hand rests on the knee, and the right arm is elevated to the chest level with the right hand damaged. He is seated with legs pendent on a throne and feet resting on a semicircular base. On each side stands a disciple wearing robes, with clasped hands over the abdomens.

引申与拓展

该窟特别引人注目,两身胁侍菩萨身体微扭与第62窟菩萨相同。该窟与第4窟长廊两端都雕塑了坚实有力的力士像,显示了宋代佛教艺术的高超水平。

该窟因西魏文皇后乙弗的悲情故事而出名。她在麦积山出家为尼,起初"卒后凿麦积崖为龛而葬"。公元552年,其丈夫西魏文帝去世,她儿子元钦即位,"自麦积崖迁出后,合葬永陵(今西安)皇陵"。这一事实证明了当时圣地麦积山的重要性。为麦积山石窟增添了浓厚的人文内涵,也让其造像艺术充满了人性。与其相邻的第44窟是一座纪念西魏文皇后乙弗的专属洞窟。

Inscriptions: There are three inscriptions written with a brush or carved by visitors on the walls.

Extension and Elaboration

The two remarkable attendant bodhisattvas in the slightly swaying curves of the body are identical with those in Cave 62. Both Cave 43 and Cave 4 were embellished with magnificent dvarapalas at either end of their terraces, showing the superb level of the Buddhist art in the Song Dynasty.

The cave is famous for the tragic story of Empress Wen, Yifu of the Western Wei Dynasty. She lived at Maijishan as a nun and was at first buried in this cave, specially carved out for her when she died in AD 540. In AD 552, her husband Emperor Wen of the Western Wei Dynasty died. Her son Yuanqin was enthroned as the emperor, who removed her mother's body from Maijishan and buried Empress Wen and Emperor Wen together in the Yongling Mausoleum. This fact proved the importance of the sacred site Maijishan at that time. It increases a strong humanistic connotation to the Maijishan Caves, and also makes its art of sculptures full of humanity. Its neighbouring Cave 44 is specially carved out for Empress Wen, Yifu of the Western Wei Dynasty in memory of her.

第 44 窟

第44窟位于东崖中区,东邻第43窟,开凿于西魏(公元535年—公元556年),五代(公元907年—公元960年)和宋代(公元960年—公元1279年)重修。该窟是一座纪念西魏文皇后乙弗(公元510年—公元540年)的专属洞窟。坐佛是麦积山最为有名的作品之一,其逼真的造型是文皇后乙弗的真容像。

该窟内有四身泥塑造像,其中面带微笑、具有女性面容的坐佛和其水波纹裙摆独具特色,令人深刻印象。

形制:该窟原为平面方形、四角攒尖顶,高2.4米、宽3.1米、深1米。前部因地震塌毁,现存洞窟后部及龛形。正壁开一圆拱形浅龛。

造像:正壁龛内塑一身坐佛,龛外两侧各塑一身胁侍菩萨,左壁塑一身立弟子,共计四身泥塑造像。自窟前部崩塌千百年来,虽受到潮湿气候和烈日暴晒的影响,但大都完好且衣着颜色可见石青、石绿等色彩。表现了当时工匠非凡的雕塑才能和高超的制泥技巧。

正壁主佛,高1.56米。旋涡纹高肉髻,面形长圆,细眉杏眼微启,薄唇,大耳,面带微笑。内着僧祇支,外着双领下垂袈裟。右手施无畏印,左手施与愿印,结跏趺坐于台座上,右足显

第二章　麦积山石窟汉英解说词

Cave 44

Cave 44 is located in the middle part of the eastern cliff, to its east is Cave 43. It was originally dug in the Western Wei Dynasty (AD 535-556) and was repaired in the Five Dynasties (AD 907-960) and the Song Dynasty (AD 960-1279). It is specially carved out for Empress Wen, Yifu (AD 510-540) of the Western Wei Dynasty in memory of her in AD 540. The seated Buddha is one of the most famous works of Maijishan, and the realistic modelling suggests that Empress Wen, Yifu is actually portrayed.

In the cave visitors can enjoy four sculptures modelled in clay. You will be impressed with the smiling seated Buddha with feminine face, and the rippling curves at the hem. Details are as follows.

Type: It is originally a flat square niche with the "dome of heaven" ceiling, 2.4 meters high, 3.1 meters wide, 1 meter deep. The front has fallen away by the earthquakes, leaving only the rear part and the contour of the cave. A shallow chaitya arched recess is cut into the main wall.

Sculptures: A seated Buddha occupies a niche cut into the main wall, flanked by a bodhisattva on each side, and a disciple stands on the left wall. There are four figures modelled in clay in all. Since the collapse of the front for thousands of years, although they have badly suffered from the wetter climate and greater exposure to the sun, most of them are intact and their robs have retained their pristine freshness of colour in a bluish grey tint and a stone green on clothing. It shows the extraordinary sculpture talents and superb claymaking skills of the craftsmen at that time.

The Buddha on the main wall is 1.56 meters high with a spiral-shaped topknot, an oval face carved with arched browns sweeping above gently opened almond eyes. He has a thin slip and flanked by pendulous ears with a smile. He is robed in an inner vest covering the left shoulder and armpits, an upper garment that completely covers his body, with U-shaped collar falling to the chest, the corner of the robe resting on the left arm. The

第44窟正壁一佛二菩萨

露在外。衣纹在膝盖前自然下垂呈对称"U"形或者阶梯式分布，裙摆上形成水波纹的衣褶。

主佛两侧菩萨均高1.3左右，面形方圆。双腕戴镯，跣足而立。上身袒露，下着长裙。其中左菩萨束花冠，戴项圈，左手提颈瓶，右手握飘带。右菩萨左手提如意，右手屈肘于腹部。

右壁弟子，高1.4米。面形长圆，着通肩袈裟。双手合十，双足穿云头履而立。

引申与拓展

该窟和相邻的第43窟均以西魏文皇后乙弗的悲剧而闻名。为让乙弗氏从悲惨的一生中解脱，善良的雕塑家把其塑成面带微笑

Buddha is seated in a pose of deep yogic meditation on the throne, the legs tightly locked, the sole of the right foot uppermost, his right hand in the abhaya mudra and his left hand in the varada mudra. The drapery cascades over his knees, covering the throne in layered symmetrical folds ending in rippling curves at the hem.

The bodhisattva on each side of the Buddha is about 1.3 meters high, with the round faces. Their arms are decorated with bracelets, and they stand on the platforms barefoot. They are robed in lower garments, leaving the upper bodies bare. Among which the bodhisattva on the left bears a corolla and a collar round the neck, holding a vase in her left hand and a ribbon in her right hand. The right-hand bodhisattva holds a *ruyi*, an S-shaped ornamental object in her left hand and her right hand is raised to the abdomen.

The disciple on the right wall is 1.4 meters high. The face is oval, wearing an upper garment that completely covers his body and hangs in heavy folds round his shoulder. The palms are pressed together at the chest, standing in cloud head shoes.

Extension and Elaboration

The cave and its neighbouring Cave 43 are all famous for the tragedy of Empress Wen, Yifu of the Western Wei Dynasty. To be free from the miserable life of Yifu, she was modelled into a Buddha with a smile by the kindhearted sculptors, which is the praise of her dedication to the country and the representation of King Wudu's devotion to his mother. The details are as follows in *History of the Northern Dynasty· Records of the Historian Biography of Imperial Concubine*.

It is said in *History of the Northern Dynasty· Records of the Historian Biography of Imperial Concubine* that Yifu, Empress Wen (AD 510-540) of Emperor Wen (AD 535-551) of the Western Wei Dynasty, was from Luoyang, the Henan Province. In the first year of Datong of Emperor Wen (AD 535), she was granted empress. The empress was fond of thrift by nature, lived a simple life and had no hobbies for dress and playthings. The empress was also kind and tolerant without jealousy, and the emperor valued her even more. She bore twelve boys and girls, but only the prince and Yuan Wu, King Wu Du, survived. At that time, the capital of the Western Wei Dynasty was just established in Guanzhong, and it was necessary to fight eastward, but when Rouran invaded the border of the Western Wei Dynasty from the north, and Emperor Wen had no time for the northern expedition, so the emperor married to appease Rouran and re-accepted Empress Dao. Empress Wen gave up her seat as a queen to live in another palace and became a nun. But Empress Dao still had suspicions about her, so Empress Wen moved to the Qinzhou Prefecture again and lived with her son King Wu Du, the governor of the Qinzhou. Although Emperor Wen

的佛，是对其为国献身的奉献精神的赞许，是武都王对母亲至孝之心的体现。《北史·后妃传》详细记载如下。

"文帝文皇后乙弗氏，河南洛阳人。大统元年册为皇后。后性好节俭，蔬食故衣，珠玉罗绮，绝于服玩。又仁恕不为嫉妒之心，帝益重之。生男女十二人，多早夭，唯太子及武都王戊存焉。时新都关中，务欲东讨，蠕蠕寇边，未遑北伐，故帝结婚以抚之，于是更纳悼后。后逊居别宫，出家为尼。悼后犹怀猜忌，复徙后居秦州，依子秦州刺史武都王。帝虽限大计，思好不忘。后密令养发，有追还之意。然事秘禁，外无知者。六年春，蠕蠕举国度河，前驱已过夏。颇有言虏为悼后之故兴此役。帝曰：'岂有百万之众，为一女子举也？虽然，致此物论，朕亦何颜以见将帅耶？'乃遣中常侍曹宠赍手敕，令后自尽。后奉敕挥泪谓宠曰：'愿至尊享千万岁，天下康宁，死无恨也。'因命武都王前，与之决，遗语皇太子，辞皆凄怆，因恸哭久之。侍御咸垂涕失声，莫能仰视。召僧设供，令侍婢数十人出家，手为落发。事毕，乃入室引被自覆而崩。年三十一。凿麦积崖为龛而葬。神躯将入，有二丛云先入龛中，顷之一灭一出，后号寂陵。及文帝山陵毕，手书云：'万岁后欲令后配飨'。公卿乃议，追谥曰文皇后，附于太庙。废帝时，合葬于永陵。"

dismissed Empress Wen for the sake of national importance, he did not forget his feelings for her. Later, he secretly ordered Empress Wen to grow her hair, so that she would come back. But this matter was secret, the outsiders didn't know. In the spring of the sixth year of Datong, the State of Rouran crossed the Huanghe River with the strength of the whole state and its vanguard troop passed the Hu Xia State (AD 407-431). It was quite said that the Rouran State launched this battle for the sake of Empress Dao. Emperor Wen said, "There is no reason for millions of troops to wage war for a woman. Even so, because of the public opinion caused by Empress Wen, what face do I have to meet the generals?" Emperor Wen could only send Cao Chong, one of his intimate minister, to send his handwritten edict to Yifu and let her kill herself. After receiving the emperor's order, Empress Wen said to Cao Chong with tears in her eyes, "May the emperor enjoy thousands of years of life, and the world will be healthy, so even if I die, there will be no regrets." Then she ordered King Wu Du to come to see her, bid farewell to him, and left her last words to the crown prince. What she said was sad and sorrowful, so she cried bitterly for a long time. The attendants cried bitterly and could not look up at her. The monks were called and sacrifices were displayed and dozens of maids were ordered to become nuns and she shaved their hair with her own hands. When everything was properly handled, she entered the room and pressed herself to death with quilts. She was only 31 years old when she died. Yifu was buried in the niche chiseled on the Maiji cliff. When Yifu's coffin was about to be put into the niche, two clumps of clouds first entered the niche, and soon one cloud disappeared and the other came out, and the grotto was later called the Silent Mausoleum. After the construction of Emperor Wen's mausoleum was completed, Emperor Wen wrote with his own hands: "After my death, I want Yifu to be worshipped together." Then high-ranking officials and ministers held discussions and added a posthumous title to Yifu, Empress Wen and raised her memorial tablet to the Tai Temple and attached it to the memorial tablets of his ancestors and offered sacrifices. When Yuan Qin was the emperor, he buried the past empress and the past emperor in the Yongling Mausoleum.

第 48 窟

第48窟位于东崖下部，开凿于北周时期（公元557年—公元581年），元代（公元1271年—公元1368年）重修。一尊元代四臂观音是藏传密宗造像，是了解元代北方地区藏传佛教不可多得的材料。

该窟为并列双龛，两身风格迥异的密宗造像以及两身力士造像，东龛壁上一则题记。

形制：该洞窟为长方形浅廊式，正壁并列开两个圆拱顶双龛。高2.25米、宽3.2米、深1.9米。每龛均塑尖拱形龛楣和龛柱，覆莲础，火焰宝珠莲花柱头。正壁双龛基本完整，长廊壁面及龛内壁面泥皮大部分已脱落。

造像：在两个相对独立的龛中供奉两个主尊一佛一菩萨，为元代作品，是典型的佛教密宗造像，龛外两身力士为北周原作，共四身造像。

东侧龛内塑四臂观音高0.42米，是典型的密宗造像。束宝塔式发髻，面相饱满，上身袒露，下着轻盈长裙，体态浑圆。前两手于胸前合十，后两手屈肘向上。下着长裙，裙裾覆盖双膝。结跏趺坐于束腰式仰覆莲台上。身后浮雕莲瓣形多重身光，正中间顶部有宝相花，两侧各有兽头，兽头上各刻有一对狮子。

Cave 48

Cave 48 is located on the lower part of the eastern cliff, and it was originally dug in the Northern Zhou Dynasty (AD 557-581) and repaired in the Yuan Dynasty (AD 1271-1368). A Four-Armed Kwan-Yin modelled in the Yuan Dynasty is the sculpture of esoteric Tibetan sects, which is a rare material for getting ideas of Tibetan Buddhism in the northern areas of the Yuan Dynasty.

In the cave visitors can enjoy a pair of niches in a row, two sculptures of esoteric sects in different styles and two dvarapalas, an inscription on the wall in the eastern niche. Details are as follows.

Type: It is a rectangular niche with a shallow gallery, and two niches with a chaitya arched ceiling are cut in a row into the main wall. It is 2.25 meters high, 3.2 meters wide and 1.9 meters deep. Each of them contains a lintel in pointed arch above, supported by columns. The column base is adorned with upside-down lotus-petals, while the capital with upturned lotus-petals, and the flaming pearl in the center. They are almost intact, most thin skin of clay plaster on the walls of the gallery and the walls in niches has peeled away.

Sculptures: Two main images of a Buddha and a bodhisattva modelled in the Yuan Dynasty occupy their own niche, which are typical sculptures of esoteric Buddhism sects. Two dvarapalas outside the niche are the original works of the Northern Zhou Dynasty. There are four sculptures in all.

The Four-Armed Kwan-Yin occupies the eastern niche with 0.42 meters high, which is a typical works of esoteric sects. Wearing a high topknot in pagoda style with the full face, the upper body is bare, the lower body is robed in a thin long dress, and she is plump. The front palms are pressed together at the chest, and the rear arms are raised. The lower body is dressed in a long dress, and the hems cascades over her knees. She is seated in dhyanasana on the I-shaped double-reverse lotus throne. Backed by the lotus-petalled mandorla of multiple bands, at the center of which is a lotus flower motif over the head of Kwan-Yin in relief, below it bear two beast heads with two lions above, one on each side.

西侧龛内一坐佛。高0.47米，磨光高肉髻，面型扁圆，肩阔膀圆。着偏右袒袈裟，结跏趺坐于莲台。台座及身光与四臂观音相同，也属于密宗造像。

双龛中间及正壁右侧角各立一力士。中间力士高1.04米。头发呈火焰状，怒目圆睁，獠牙凶煞，颈部筋骨分明。突胸鼓腹，穿外翻边短裙。左力士高1.1米，高发髻，高颧骨，下颌上翘。全身肌肉健硕。左残臂置于腹前，右手握拳屈肘侧身举过头顶。上身袒露，下着过膝长裙。

题记：东龛壁上一则题记。

引申与拓展

佛教密宗造像在中国流行比较晚，且派别较多。比较重要的是藏传密宗，在元代比较流行，其主要影响区域在西藏。随着文化交流以及元朝皇帝的支持，该窟的密宗造像就是在这种背景下产生的。

四臂观音是藏传佛教崇奉的重要菩萨之一，在藏族人民心目中有着极其崇高的地位。在藏族传统绘画中，四臂观音是广为采用的神佛题材。世界上唯一供奉四臂观音菩萨的寺庙位于中国西南四川省阿坝藏族自治区金川县，该寺始建于公元七世纪，自此吸引了世界各地的藏传佛教信徒。

把两个佛龛并列开凿在一起的做法有一定的政治背景。最早出现在云冈石窟，是为当时的皇帝和皇太后分别开凿的洞窟。这两个洞窟之间无论是内在关联还是外在的形式联系度很密切。后来形成一种定式，在各个石窟中多有出现。

The western niche holds a seated Buddha. He is 0.47 meters high, with a polished high ushnisha right on the top, flat round face, broad shoulders and round arms. He is robed in the outer robe thrown over the left shoulder or the upper throwing a strong diagonal across the body, leaving the right side of the body and shoulder bare. He is seated in dhyanasana on the lotus throne. The throne and mandorla are identical with those of the Four-Armed Kwan-Yin. The figure also belongs to the esoteric sects.

Two dvarapalas stand between two niches and at the right corner of the main wall respectively. The central dvarapala is 1.04 meters high with a flaming hairstyle, eyes round open in fury attitude, ferocious fangs and bulging muscles on the neck give a fierce expression. With swelling chest and abdomen, the lower body is robed in a battle skirt with reverses at the waist. The dvarapala on the left is 1.1 meters high, wearing a high topknot, prominent cheekbones and raised jaw. The muscles of the whole body are powerfully modelled. The left remaining arm rests on the abdomen, and the right arm raises over the head with a clenched fist. The upper body is bare, a long dress on the lower body falling over the knees.

Inscription: Visitors left an inscription on the wall in the eastern niche.

Extension and Elaboration

Sculptures of esoteric Buddhism sects became popular late in China and have many schools. More important is the esoteric Tibetan sects, which were popular in the Yuan Dynasty, and its main influential area was in Tibet. With the cultural exchange and the support of Emperors in the Yuan Dynasty, it also developed in the mainland. The sculptures of esoteric sects in the cave were made under this background.

The Four-Armed Kwan-Yin is one of the important bodhisattvas worshipped by Tibetan Buddhism and has an extremely lofty position in the minds of the Tibetan people. In the traditional Tibetan paintings, it is a widely adopted theme of deities and Buddhas. The only temple that hosts the shrine to the Four-Armed Avalokitesvara bodhisattva in the world is located in Jinchuan County, Aba Tibetan Autonomous Region, southwest China's Sichuan Province. The temple was built in the seventh century and attracted Tibetan Buddhism worshipers all around the world ever since.

The practice of digging two Buddhist niches together has a certain political background. It first appeared in Yungang Grottoes, dedicated to the Emperor and the Empress Dowager respectively. The two niches are closely related in both internal and external forms. Later, it develops into a convention, which often appears in various caves.

第50窟

第50窟位于东崖下部,开凿于隋代(公元581年—公元618年),宋代(公元960年—公元1279年)重修。现存麦积山石窟唯一的一尊宋代僧人造像,该像做工粗糙。

该窟内有一身宋代僧人像。

形制:该洞窟为较浅的圆拱龛,高2.35米、宽2.55米、深1.25米。

造像:窟内仅保存一身僧人塑像,高1.01米,面形长圆,弯眉垂眼,眼内镶嵌黑色琉璃珠。身穿袈裟,结跏趺坐于方座之上。

引申与拓展

与第90窟僧人像相比较,可以感受到宋代佛教艺术的高超水平。在山脚下的寺院中,保存着一块十三世纪的碑刻,记录到一位名叫法秀的僧人于公元1068年到皇宫里面为皇室人员讲授佛法。皇帝特别给麦积山石窟赐予了很多特权,包括大量的土地,成为麦积山石窟发展的最大支持。所以当时寺院的僧人对法秀都很尊重,并塑像纪念。

Cave 50

Cave 50 is located on the lower part of the eastern cliff, and was originally dug in the Sui Dynasty (AD 960-1279) and repaired in the Song Dynasty (AD 960-1279). The unique figure of the monk modelled in the Song Dynasty at Maijishan Caves remains in the cave which is a crude work.

In the cave visitors will enjoy a figure of the monk modelled in the Song Dynasty. Details are as follows.

Type: It is a shallow chaitya arched recess with 2.35 meters high, 2.55 meters wide, 1.25 meters deep.

Sculpture: The cave retains a figure of the monk with 1.01 meters high, with the oval face, curved brows and downcast eyes inlaid with black glass beads. He wears a voluminous robe, is seated in dhyanasana on the square pedestal.

Extension and Elaboration

Visitors can compare the superb level of Buddhist art in the Song Dynasty among the monks in Cave 90. The monastery lay at the foot of Maijishan preserves a stone with inscriptions embedded in the wall, which records that in AD 1068 the monk Faxiu was invited to the imperial court to give lectures on Buddhism. The emperor granted many special privileges to Maijishan Caves, including lands, which were the biggest support for the development of Maijishan Caves. All the monks of the monastery show their respect to Faxiu and he is actually portrayed in memory of him.

第51窟

第51窟位于西崖底部,是麦积山石窟开凿位置最低的洞窟。开凿于后秦(公元384年—公元417年),明代(公元1368年—公元1644年)重修,是麦积山石窟现存早期洞窟之一。

该窟内有七身明代重修造像和壁画。

形制:该洞窟是一个平面方形、平顶敞口龛,高4.45米、宽3.90米、深3.15米。窟内各壁面交接处均为圆弧形,正壁两侧上方各开一耳龛。这种在正壁两侧上方各开凿一个小龛的做法是麦积山石窟初期洞窟的特征之一,其文化源流可以追溯到犍陀罗地区的建筑形式。

造像:正壁有一坐佛二弟子二菩萨,左右壁各有一身坐佛。窟内现存造像七身,均为明代重修。

正壁坐佛高2.58米,顶作低肉髻,面型圆润。内着僧祇支,外穿双领下垂袈裟。结跏趺坐于高基座上,双臂屈肘上举,双手残损。头后有绘制的水波纹头光。

左侧弟子迦叶高1.86米,面相苍老。内穿僧祇支,外着袒右袈裟,袈裟上有田字方格,双手合十于胸前。右侧弟子阿难高1.86

Cave 51

Cave 51 is located at the bottom of the western cliff, and is at the lowest position of the excavations at Maijishan Caves. It was originally dug in the Later Qin Dynasty (AD 384-417) and repaired in the Ming Dynasty (AD 1368-1644), and is one of the surviving early caves at Maijishan Caves.

Visitors will enjoy seven sculptures and paintings restored in the Ming Dynasty. Details are as follows.

Type: It is a square open niche on the cliff face with flat ceiling, 4.45 meters high, 3.90 meters wide and 3.15 meters deep. It contains a circular arc junction of each wall. A small niche is carved above each end of the main wall, which is one of the characteristics of the early caves of Maijishan Caves, and its cultural origin can be traced back to the architectural form of Gandhara area.

Sculptures: The main wall holds a seated Buddha flanked by two disciples and two bodhisattvas, and a seated Buddha on each of the side walls. There are seven figures in all, which are all restorations of the Ming Dynasty.

The seated Buddha on the main wall is 2.58 meters high. He bears a low topknot and a full face. He is robed in an inner vest covering the left shoulder and armpits, an upper garment that completely covers his body, with U-shaped collar falling to the chest, the corner of the robe resting on the left arm. The Buddha sits in dhyanasana on the high throne, his two arms are raised to the chest level with two hands damaged. There is a water-wavy aureole behind him.

The disciple Kasyapa on the left is 1.86 meters high, an elder image. He wears an inner vest covering the left shoulder and armpits, the outer robe thrown over the left shoulder

米，面容清秀。内穿僧祇支，外穿袒右袈裟。双手交叠置于胸前，左手残损。

左右两菩萨高2.1米，均束高发髻，戴花冠，颈戴华丽的项链。上身袒露，下身内穿左肩系带长裙，外穿双领下垂袈裟。天衣覆肩，菩萨双手残损。头后有绘制的圆形头光，由两个深浅不一的土红色同心圆组成。

左右壁坐佛均高于2.5米，顶作低圆肉髻。上身袒露，衣着与左右两菩萨相同。结跏趺坐于基座上，佛头部后方绘制有圆形的头光。其中左壁坐佛右手抚胸，左手置于左腹前。右壁坐佛左手置于左膝上，左手残损。右手作无畏印，五指部分残损。

壁画：该窟壁画面积现存约为18平方米。顶部绘制鸟首人身的迦楼罗、童子、飞天、仙鹤及乐器等图案。佛两侧画天王及帝释天。左右壁绘天王四身。

引申与拓展

该窟是麦积山石窟开凿位置最低的洞窟，也是麦积山石窟现存最早的洞窟。因为在这个位置开凿石窟位置便利，不需要特别架设栈道等设施，所以是最优先选择的位置。同时也为后期信徒重修提供了便利。我们需要仔细分辨才可以区分出早期开凿的一些痕迹。

or the upper throwing a strong diagonal across the body, leaving the right side of the body and shoulder bare which is adorned with coloured "paddy-field design". The palms are pressed together at the chest. While the right-hand disciple Ananda is 1.86 meters tall, bearing delicately modelled features. He is robed in an inner vest covering the left shoulder and armpits, the outer robe thrown over the left shoulder or the upper throwing a strong diagonal across the body, leaving the right side of the body and shoulder bare. He lifts the two hands to the chest, his palms with fingers extended and touching each other, his left hand broken.

The bodhisattvas on each side are 2.10 meters high with the high topknots, wearing corollas and the richly adorned collar round their necks. With bared upper bodies, they are robed in the inner dresses with the band tied on the left shoulder, the upper garments that completely cover their bodies, with U-shaped collar falling to the chest, the corner of the robe resting on the left arm. The outer shawl covers both shoulders, and their two hands have been damaged. Each bears a circular aureole behind them, composed of two concentric circles in varying shades of earth red.

The seated Buddhas on each of the side walls are over 2.5 meters higher with the low topknots. Their upper bodies are bare, their clothing is identical with that of the bodhisattvas on each side. They sit in dhyanasana on the thrones, each holding a circular aureole behind them. Among which the Buddha on the left wall puts his right hand on the chest, and his left hand rests on the lap. The broken left hand of the Buddha on the right rests on knee, while his right hand in the abhaya mudra with partial fingers damaged.

Paintings: It covers an area about 18 square meters. Garuda, a mythological bird usually described as having a human form with the head of a bird is painted on the ceiling and other motifs of lotus boys, flying apsaras, cranes and musical instruments. The Heavenly Kings and the Indra appear on each side of the Buddha. Each of the side walls contains four Heavenly Kings.

Extension and Elaboration

Lying at the lowest position of cave excavations at Maijishan, it is a surviving early cave at Maijishan Caves. Because it is convenient to dig the caves in this location, there is no need to set up a special ladder and other facilities, so it is called the most preferred location. But at the same time it also provides convenience for the restorations of the later worshipers. We need to carefully distinguish some traces of the early excavations.

第 53 窟

第53窟位于西崖下部,开凿于北魏(公元386年—公元534年),北周(公元557年—公元581年)、宋代(公元960年—公元1279年)重修。主佛为纯朴浑厚的秦州青年形象。

该窟内有一尊北周塑佛。

形制:该窟是圆拱形、敞口小龛。正壁设有一方形基座。

造像:正壁残存一身坐佛。

正壁佛,磨光低肉髻,面形方圆,眉间有白毫相,弯眉细目,镶嵌珠石眼珠。高鼻大耳,绘八字胡。内着僧祇支,外着双领下垂袈裟。左手抚膝,右手说法印。结跏趺坐于方形台座上。宋代在面部进行过部分补塑。胸部、右手腕有几处残破的小洞。身后绘圆形项光。

引申与拓展

该窟主佛与第60窟主佛一样,为圆润饱满的秦州青年形象。

Cave 53

Cave 53 is located at the lower part of the western cliff. It was originally dug in the Northern Wei Dynasty (AD 386-534) and repaired in the Northern Zhou Dynasty (AD 557-581) and the Song Dynasty (AD 960-1279). The principal Buddha is modelled as a young image of simple and sincere in Qinzhou.

In the cave visitors will enjoy a clay Buddha modelled in the Northern Zhou Dynasty. Details are as follows.

Type: It is a small chaitya arched niche open to the cliff face. A square pedestal throne is built on the main wall.

Sculpture: A seated Buddha survives on the main wall.

The Buddha on the main wall bears a polished low topknot, and the square face is carved with the white hair between the brows (urnalaksana), the arched brows sweeping above gently opened almond eyes inlaid with stone beads, the high nose flanked by pendulous ears, and mustached. He is robed in an inner vest covering the left shoulder and armpits, an upper garment that completely covers his body, with U-shaped collar falling to the chest, the lappet of the robe resting on the left arm and down to the left knee. His left hand rests on knee, and the right hand in a gesture of preaching. He sits in dhyanasana on the square throne. Partial face is the restoration of the Song Dynasty. There were several small broken holes in the chest and right wrist, with a circular aureole painted in relief behind him.

Extension and Elaboration

The principal Buddha is identical with that in Cave 60, both are young images of round and full in Qinzhou.

第 54 窟

第54窟位于西崖下部,开凿于西魏(公元535年—公元556年),北周(公元557年—公元581年)重修。

该窟有三身泥塑造像,左右壁上部各绘两身飞天,左右壁及顶部十九则墨书题记。

形制:该窟是圆拱形、敞口龛。正壁设有一方形基座,左右壁各一莲台。

造像:正壁塑一坐佛,左右壁各一胁侍菩萨,共计三身。

正壁佛,磨光低肉髻,面形方圆,弯眉平目,黑色琉璃眼珠,高鼻大耳,长颈窄肩。着通肩袈裟。左手抚膝,右手施无畏印。结跏趺坐于方形台座上。身后绘多重同心圆项光和莲瓣形身光,饰有忍冬纹、火焰纹。

左右壁菩萨,均束发戴冠,上有摩尼宝珠,余发披肩。面形长方,弯眉细目,高鼻大耳,长颈窄肩。内着僧祇支,外着交领衣,束腰系带打结。双足残失,立于莲台上。身后项光上有多重同心圆、忍冬纹和联珠纹。其中左壁菩萨,左手掩袖置于腹部,右手持

第二章 麦积山石窟汉英解说词

Cave 54

Cave 54 is located at the lower part of the western cliff. It was originally dug in the Western Wei Dynasty (AD 535-556) and repaired in the Northern Zhou Dynasty (AD 557-581).

In the cave visitors will enjoy three clay sculptures, two flying apsaras painted above each of the side walls, 19 inscriptions with a brush on each of the flanking walls and the ceiling. Details are as follows.

Type: It is a chaitya arched niche open to the cliff face. A square pedestal throne is built on the main wall and a lotus base on each of the side walls.

Sculptures: A seated Buddha occupies the main wall, and an attendant bodhisattva stands on each of the side walls. There are three figures in all.

The Buddha on the main wall wears a polished low topknot, the round and square face is carved with the arched brows, eyes inlaid with black glaze beads looking straight ahead, the high nose flanked by pendulous ears, long neck and narrow shoulders. He is robed in an upper garment that completely covers his body, with U-shaped collar falling to the chest, the lappet of the robe resting on the left arm and down to the left knee. His left hand rests on knee, and his right hand in the abhaya mudra. He sits in dhyanasana on the square throne. There is a circular aureole composed of multi-tiered concentric circles and a lotus petal-shaped mandorla adorned with motifs of honeysuckle and flame behind him.

The hair of the bodhisattvas on each of the side walls is gathered in topknots encircled by the diadems decorated with a cintamanand and falling down the shoulders. The long square face is carved with arched brows sweeping above gently opened almond eyes, high

莲蕾于胸部。右壁菩萨,双手举覆莲于胸前。

壁画:左右壁靠上位置各有两身飞天,衣带向上飘扬,细节模糊不辨。

题记:左右壁及顶部留有十九则墨书题记。

引申与拓展

该窟与第60窟相似,主佛身体西魏原作,头部北周补塑。左壁菩萨头部也为北周补塑,浮雕手法简洁明快,宛如石雕。

nose flanked by pendulous ears, long neck and narrow shoulders. They are robed in the inner vests covering the left shoulder and armpits, outer garments with a crossing collar, a band tied at the waist falling in a knot. They stand on the lotus platforms with feet missing. There are circular aureoles composed of multi-tiered concentric circles adorned with motifs of honeysuckle and the linked-pearl behind them. Among them, the left hand of the bodhisattva on the left wall is placed on the abdomen concealing in the sleeve, and the right hand is lifted to the chest holding a lotus bud. The right-wall bodhisattva holds a upside-down lotus to the chest in both hands.

Paintings: Two flying apsaras followed by the swirl of their trailing scarves are painted above each of the side walls, and we can't make out the details.

Inscriptions: Visitors have left 19 inscriptions with a brush on each of the flanking walls and the ceiling.

Extension and Elaboration

The cave is similar to that in Cave 60, and the body of the principal Buddha is the original works of the Western Wei Dynasty and the head is the restoration of the Northern Zhou Dynasty. The head of the bodhisattva on the left wall is also the restoration of the Northern Zhou Dynasty, and the technique in relief is simple and smooth, seems like the stone carving.

第 55 窟

第55窟位于西崖下部,开凿于北周(公元557年—公元581年)。主佛的形象突出了西北民族强健的体魄,既表现了"曹衣出水、轻纱透体"的风格,又深化了人体美的内涵。

该窟内有三身泥塑造像,一身石刻佛像。

形制:该窟是平面长方形、圆拱顶、敞口龛,窟前部塌毁。正壁设一长方形基座。

造像:正壁塑一坐佛,左侧塑一菩萨。左壁塑一菩萨,右壁石雕一立佛,共计四身。

正壁佛,头已失。内着红边蓝色僧祇支,胸前打结垂带自然下垂,外着袒右袈裟,绘有赭红色田相格。衣褶细密,具有流动感。左手置于腹部握衣角,右手施无畏印,手指残。结跏趺坐于长方形基座上,下摆垂于座前,线条流畅。

正壁左侧、左壁菩萨,低平发髻,余发披肩。肩部各有一圆形佩饰,颈戴项圈,腕饰环。内着僧祇支,帛带自肩绕臂下垂。下着高腰长裙,腰间系带,两侧垂有环形饰物,衣纹均为垂直雕刻形式。左手置腹前,右手垂于腿侧提圆形玉璧,双足穿云头履,立于

Cave 55

Cave 55 is located at the lower part of the western cliff. It was dug in the Northern Zhou Dynasty (AD 557-581). The principal Buddha accentuates the strong physique of the northwest nation, which not only shows the style of "the robe of the figure clings tightly to the body and limbs, as if he has just emerged from the water. For the drapery is almost total disappearance of the robe, leaving the contour of the body exposed." , and deepens the connotation of beauty of human body.

In the cave visitors will enjoy three clay sculptures, and a Buddha of stone stele carving. Details are as follows.

Type: It is a plane rectangular niche open to the cliff face with the chaitya arched ceiling, and the front of the cave has fallen away. A rectangle pedestal throne is built on the main wall.

Sculptures: A seated Buddha occupies the main wall, and an attendant bodhisattva stands on the left. A bodhisattva also stands on the left wall, and the right wall contains a standing Buddha of stone stele carving. There are four figures in all.

The Buddha on the main wall is headless. He is robed in a blue inner vest with red hem covering the left shoulder and armpits, a band tied at the chest falling in a knot, the outer robe adorned with reddish-brown "paddy-field design" thrown over the left shoulder or the upper throwing a strong diagonal across the body, leaving the right side of the body and shoulder bare. The folds of garments are densely modelled with a strong rhythmic movement. The left hand is put at the abdomen holding the corner of the robe, while the right hand in the abhaya mudra with fingers broken. He is seated in dhyanasana on the rectangle throne with the hem covering in front in smooth lines.

The bodhisattvas on the left of the main wall and the left wall wear low topknots, leaving the rest hair cascading over their shoulders. There are circular ornaments on each shoulders,

半圆形莲台上。

右壁石雕佛,头部已失,腹部微凸。内着僧祇支,外着双领下垂袈裟。腿部均有"U"形衣纹。左手说法印,右臂前伸,手已残。跣足立于方形覆莲座上,四角各雕一蹲狮,面朝外。

引申与拓展

该窟右壁石雕立佛布局和位置与龛内其他造像不协调,可能从他处移入。

with the collars around the necks and rings around the wrists. They are robed in the inner vests (samkaksika) covering the left shoulder and armpits, the long broad scarves cover the shoulders and hang down through the armpits. The high-waisted dresses are on their lower bodies with the bands tied at the waists, the circular pendent hanging on either side. The draperies are carved in vertical lines. The left hands are placed on the abdomens, the right hands hang down beside the thighs carrying the round jades, they stand on the semicircular lotus bases in cloud head shoes.

The Buddha of stone stele carving on the right wall is also headless, with slightly swelling abdomen. He is robed in an inner vest(samkaksika) covering the left shoulder and armpits, an upper garment that completely covers his body, with U-shaped collar falling to the chest, the lappet of the robe resting on the left arm and down to the left knee. The drapery of the legs hangs in "U" shaped folds. His left hand is in gesture of preaching (Vitarka mudra), the right arm is stretched forward with the hand damaged. He stands on the square base of upsid-down lotus-petal, supported by a crouching lion at each of the four corners with its head looking outward.

Extension and Elaboration

The layout and location of the standing Buddha of stone stele carving on the right wall are incompatible with other sculptures in the niche, might have been moved in from other place.

第 58 窟

第58窟位于西崖东下部,东邻第173窟,西邻第57窟。开凿于宋代(公元960年—公元1279年),明代(公元1368年—公元1644年)重修。该窟"水月观音"自在地坐在台座上,凝视着月亮在水中的倒影。

该窟内有三身泥塑造像,一身石刻佛像,明代绘于左右壁的花草、树木、流水图案,左壁一则刻画题记。

形制:该窟是平面圆拱形、敞口龛,顶部与第175窟连通。正壁前一山形基座,可见莲叶、流水图案。基座后建一面立体"T"形木骨泥塑假山。假山造型复杂,顶部中间和两侧有兽头,施色赭石、石绿颜料。右壁前塑一不规则山石状高坛基。左右壁浮塑层叠的山石,泉水呈旋涡状流出。

造像:正壁塑一身水月观音,右壁塑一身供养人,共计两身。

水月观音,束高发髻,戴花冠。长圆丰满的面容带着沉思的表情,兼有女性和男性的特征。眉间有白毫相,双眼俯视。颈上有三道阴刻线,项圈饰有三个吊坠。上着僧祇支,下系长裙,有沥粉堆积的花卉、祥云纹饰。披帛带覆盖双肩下垂于腹前,缠绕两圈后垂

Cave 58

Cave 58 is located at the lower east part of the western cliff, adjacent to Cave 173 in the east and Cave 57 in the west. It was initially dug in the Song Dynasty (AD 960-1279) and rebuilt in the Ming Dynasty (AD 1368-1644). The Water-Moon Guanyin in the cave is seated in royal ease on the pedestal contemplating the reflection of the moon in the water.

In the cave visitors will enjoy three clay sculptures, a Buddha of stone stele carving, motifs of flowers, trees, flowing water painted in the Ming Dynasty on the left and right walls, an inscription carved on the left wall. Details are as follows.

Type: It is a plane chaitya arched niche open to the cliff face. The ceiling is connected with Cave 175. The main wall contains a mountain-shaped pedestal, motifs of lotus leaves and flowing water are decipherable. Behind it stands a T-shaped rockery of clay modelled on a wooden armature in the round, which is in complex modelling with beast heads on the center of the ceiling and both sides, colouring in the ochre-colored and a bluish grey tint pigmens. A high irregular rock-shaped base is set on the right wall. The layered hillstones are modelled in relief on each of the side walls, with the spring water flowing in whirlpool.

Sculptures: A Water-Moon Guanyin occupies the main wall, a donor stands on the right wall. There are two figures in all.

The Water-Moon Guanyin bears a high topknot adorned with a corolla. The oval and full face with a contemplative expression that embodies both male and female characteristics, carved with the white hair between the brows(urnalaksana) and downcast eyes. The neck is adorned with three incised lines, three pendants hanging from a heavy collar around it. She is robed in an inner vest (samkaksika) covering the left shoulder and armpits, a long dress on the lower body decorated with the patterns of flowers and clouds. The technique of embossed painting and gilding craft was used here. The broad scarf comes over the

于双腿外侧。自在坐于长方形高腰岩石基座上,左腿下垂,左足踩于莲花上。右膝弯曲,右足踏在基座上。左臂抚台座,右臂轻放于屈膝之上。

右壁供养人,头戴六梁冠,面容清秀,留胡须。内着交领窄袖衣,外着交领长袍,衣着上有沥粉堆积的花卉纹饰。足穿云头履立于坛基上。

壁画:明代于左右壁绘少许竹叶、花草、树木、流水等,施色为石绿、赭红。

题记:左壁上刻画一则题记。

引申与拓展

观音菩萨有33个不同形象的法身,其中化作观水中月影状的称水月观音。而此种左脚垂在莲花上,右臂优雅地放在屈膝之上的"御前坐"姿则出自《妙法莲华经观世音菩萨普门品》。经中讲述善财童子往普陀洛迦山参访佛法,见观音道场于"岩谷之中,泉流萦映"。坐于山岩之上、观水中之月的自在惬意观音形象即由此衍生,因而此造型的观音造像亦有"水月观音"之名。

shoulders and down to the abdomen in two loops and down beside each thigh. She is seated in royal ease on the high waisted rockwork pedestal, the left leg is pendent with the left foot resting upon a lotus blossom, the right knee is bent, with that foot resting on the base on which the figure is seated, the left arm hangs down and the hand touches the base, the right arm extends resting on the right knee.

The donor on the right wall wears a crown adorned with six beams, the delicately carved face, bearded. His upper garment is of a collar folded across in front and tight sleeves, a long outer gown with a crossing collar decorated with motifs of flowers. The technique of embossed painting and gilding craft was used here. He stands on the base in cloud head shoes.

Paintings: There are a few motifs of bamboo leaves, flowers, trees, flowing water painted in the Ming Dynasty on the left and right walls, colouring in a stone green, and a reddish-brown.

Inscription: There is a carved inscription left by visitors on the left wall.

Extension and Elaboration

Avalokiteshvara has thirty-three different image dharmakayas, among which the one who admires the reflection of the moon in the water is called the Water-Moon Guanyin. The seated posture in royal ease of the iconography, with the left foot pendent upon a lotus blossom, the right leg gracefully raised supporting the right arm on the knee, is based on *The Lotus Sutra Guanyin Bomun Goods* where Avatamsuka or Guanyin resided on Mount Potalaka where the young pilgrim Sudhana visited him. He found Guanyin seated on the rocky shores of the grotto "Sound of the Waves" appreciating the reflection of the moon in the water. In due course this specific form of Guanyin became better known as the Water-Moon Guanyin.

第 59 窟

第59窟位于西崖下部,开凿于宋代(公元960年—公元1279年),是一座题记龛,存有一则书写于公元1035年的摩崖墨书题记《麦积山应乾寺重修东西两阁佛像施主舍钱记》。

该窟内有一则书写于摩崖上的公元1035年的题记。

形制:该窟是一个平面横长方形、摩崖浅龛,高2.5米、宽2.56米、深0.25米。

题记:这是一篇毛笔书写的黑色题记,现存1200多字。记载了当时应乾寺主持僧人慧珍与来自山西太原的信徒王秀等人,向附近区域信徒募捐钱重新装修一些麦积山洞窟,还有木材、铁钉、麻布等具体物品。

第二章 麦积山石窟汉英解说词

Cave 59

Cave 59 is located in the lower part of the western cliff and was dug in the Song Dynasty (AD 960-1279). It is a niche containing a dated inscription *A Record of Donors Who Raised Funds to Repair and Redecorate the Images in the Two Side Halls of Yingqian Temple at Maijishan of* AD1035 written on the cliff face with a brush.

Visitors can read a dated inscription of AD1035 written on the cliff face with a brush. Details are as follows.

Type: It is a plane horizontal rectangular shallow niche open to the cliff face, with 2.50 meters high, 2.56 meters wide, 0.25 meters deep.

Inscription: This is an inscription which has been written on the cliff face with a brush, running over 1200 characters. It clearly records that Huizhen, the host of the Yingqian Monastery, and Wang Xiu, a worshipper from Taiyuan, Shanxi Province, who raised money from the nearby area to redecorate some caves at Maijishan and other specific items such as woods, nails, linen cloth.

引申与拓展

从《麦积山应乾寺重修东西两阁佛像施主舍钱记》中我们可以看到，来自不同地方的施主姓名和钱数，寺院的主持僧人惠珍是被皇帝赏赐予紫色袈裟的僧人。这是对其在佛学方面取得较高水平僧人的褒奖，也是对所在寺院的认可。

尽管公元1027年发生了灾难性的地震，但之后还能挖掘新窟，并在公元1035年对造像进行了大量的维修和重塑，说明麦积山再次处于繁荣状态。

Extension and Elaboration

From the content of *A Record of Donors Who Raised Funds to Repair and Redecorate the Images in the Two Side Halls of Yingqian Temple at Maijishan* we can see the names and amounts of money given by donors from different places, we also notice that the monk Huizhen, the head of the monastery, was awarded purple robe by the emperor. It is a praise for him who has achieved a higher level in Buddhism, and also the recognition of his monastery. Despite the disastrous earthquake in AD 1027, new caves were able to be excavated in the following years, in AD1035 a large number of sculptures were repaired and remodelled, indicating that Maijishan was in a prosperous state again.

第 60 窟

第60窟位于西崖下层,东邻第62窟,西邻第94窟。开凿于西魏(公元535年—公元556年),隋代(公元581年—公元618年)重修。造像精致、精确和甜美的五官与公元675年的龙门石窟卢舍那大佛相似,主佛为俊美的北方青年形象。

该窟内有三尊头部隋代重塑的造像。

形制:该窟是平面方形、平拱顶敞口龛。

造像:正壁塑一坐佛二胁侍菩萨,共三身造像。身躯均为西魏原作,头部隋代补塑。

正壁主佛,低平肉髻,面形丰满圆润,弯眉细眼,大耳垂肩。目光慈祥,微露笑意,显出内心的平和与安宁。内着僧祇支,外着双领下垂袈裟。右手施无畏印,左手抚膝。结跏趺坐于基座上,下摆垂于地面。身后彩绘圆形头光和莲瓣形身光。

左右侧胁侍菩萨,戴花冠,方圆脸,略带冥想沉思和平静的笑意。五官精致而自然。立于圆台上,身后彩绘同心圆头光。其中左侧菩萨双目微合。内着圆领衣,外着宽领大袖交领衣,下着长裙。肩部有圆形饰物。双手拢袖于胸前。右侧菩萨戴桃形项圈。内着僧祇支,天衣覆肩下垂,下着长裙。右手举莲蕾于胸前,左手握火焰

第二章 麦积山石窟汉英解说词

Cave 60

Cave 60 is located in the lower layer of the western cliff, adjacent to Cave 62 in the east and Cave 94 in the west. It was originally dug in the Western Wei Dynasty (AD 535-556) and repaired in the Sui Dynasty (AD 581-618). The exquisite, precise and sweet features of sculptures are similar to that of the great Vairocana at Longmen Grottoes in AD 675, and the principal Buddha is a handsome youth image in the north.

In the cave visitors will enjoy three sculptures with their heads remodelled in the Sui Dynasty. Details are as follows.

Type: It is a flat square niche open to the cliff face with a flat vault ceiling.

Sculptures: The main wall contains a seated Buddha flanked by two bodhisattvas. There are three figures in all. Their bodies are original works of the Western Wei Dynasty, and their heads were remodelled in the Sui Dynasty.

The principal Buddha on the main wall bears a low flat topknot, the full round face carved with arched brows sweeping above gently opened almond eyes and flanked by pendulous ears. His kind eyes are in a slightly smiling, showing inner mild and calm. He is robed in an inner vest covering the left shoulder and armpits, with a band tied at the chest falling in a knot, an upper garment that completely covers his body, with U-shaped collar falling to the chest, the lappet of the robe resting on the left arm. His right hand is in the abhaya mudra, and his left hand rests on knee. He sits in dhyanasana on the throne with the hem falling to the ground. There is a coloured circular aureole and a lotus petal-shaped mandorla behind him.

The attendant bodhisattvas on the left and right wear corollas, the square round faces with a serene and tranquil slightly smiling. The features are delicate and natural. Standing on the circular platforms, they are backed by coloured aureoles composed of concentric circles.

宝珠于腿前。

引申与拓展

  该窟匠师将主佛塑造为秦州本地质朴善良的青年形象，既刻画出圣洁温和的性格，又掩不住青春的活力与稚气，体现出神性与人性完美结合的世俗性特征。

  他们把对世俗生活的理解、对人间美的追求，融入令人神往的宗教艺术形象当中，使似乎不相融合的两者结为一体。

Among them, the left-hand bodhisattva keeps her eyes half closed. She wears an inner robe with a roll collar, an outer garment of a collar folded across in front with long loose sleeves, and a long dress on the lower body. There are circular ornaments on the shoulders. The hands are placed on the chest concealing in the sleeves. The right-hand bodhisattva is decorated with a peach-shaped collar round the neck. She is robed in an inner vest covering the left shoulder and armpits, the outer shawl covers both shoulders and down, and a long dress on the lower body. Her right hand is raised to the chest holding a lotus bud, with a flaming pearl in the left hand in front of the leg.

Extension and Elaboration

The principal Buddha is modelled as a simple and kind youth image of Qinzhou in the hands of craftsmen here, which not only depicts the holy and gentle character, but also shows the vitality and childishness of youth, reflecting the secular characteristics of the perfect combination of divinity and human nature.

They integrate their understanding of secular life and the pursuit of human beauty into the fascinating religious artistic images, making the two presumably incompatible into one.

第 62 窟

第62窟位于西崖下部,开凿于北周(公元557年—公元581年),是北周洞窟中保存最完好而又未经后代重修的洞窟。

该窟是北周典型的帐形龛,有十二身泥塑造像,两则刻画于甬道壁面和窟门上方的题记。

形制:该窟是平面方形、四角攒尖顶窟。窟高1.84米、宽1.7米、进深1.7米。前壁开方形甬道,顶部及四壁角各雕凿半圆形石胎泥塑帐杆。地面四周凿"凹"字形低坛基,正、左、右壁各开一圆拱形浅龛。

造像:正、左、右三龛内各塑一坐佛,每龛外各塑二胁侍菩萨,壁门两侧各塑一弟子,窟门外左侧残存一力士,共计十二身。

正壁佛,高0.92米。磨光低平肉髻,面形方圆,双眼微启下视。内着僧祇支,中着对襟衣并胸前系带下垂,外着袒右袈裟。褶纹密集,衣摆呈两瓣式垂覆座前。结跏趺坐于台座上,右手施无畏印,左手施与愿印。

正壁左右侧菩萨,高约1.1米,头戴宝冠。方圆脸,颈戴桃形

Cave 62

Cave 62 is located in the lower part of the western cliff, excavated in the Northern Zhou Dynasty (AD 557-581), is the best preserved cave in the Northern Zhou Dynasty and has not been repaired by later generations.

Visitors will enjoy the typical tent-shaped niche of the Northern Zhou Dynasty, 12 clay sculptures, and two inscriptions carved on the wall of the passage and above the door. Details are as follows.

Type: It is a flat square niche with the "dome of heaven" ceiling, with 1.84 meters high, 1.7 meters wide and 1.7 meters deep. There is a square passage on the front wall. The semicircular tent poles in clay plaster over a core of rock are carved on the ceiling and four corners of walls. A low concave base is cut around the ground, and a shallow chaitya arched recess is excavated on each of the main wall and the side walls.

Sculptures: There is a niche cut into the main wall and each of the side walls, each containing a seated Buddha flanked by an attendant bodhisattva outside the niche, and a disciple stands on each side of the door, and on the left of the door remains a dvarapala. There are 12 figures in all.

The Buddha on the main wall is 0.92 meters high. He wears a polished low flat topknot, the round face with downcast eyes slightly open. He is robed in an inner vest covering the left shoulder and armpits, a straight-collar garment is worn over the vest with a band tied at the chest falling in a knot, the outer robe thrown over the left shoulder or the upper throwing a strong diagonal across the body, leaving the right side of the body and shoulder bare. With the drapery falling in heavy folds, the hem covers the throne in two large petals. He sits in dhyanasana on the throne, his right hand in the abhaya mudra, and his left hand in the varada mudra.

项圈。斜披络腋，下穿翻边长裙。帔帛自双肩垂至腹前绕臂下垂。串珠状璎珞自双肩垂至小腿。身体微扭跣足立于坛基上。其中左侧菩萨左手掌心朝外举于肩前，右手握火焰宝珠置于腹部。右侧菩萨左手抚胸，右手呈托举状于腹部。

左右壁佛和菩萨五官、形体与正壁佛和菩萨相似。其中两佛双手施禅定印。左壁一菩萨左手托钵，右手中指下指。右壁一位菩萨右手握莲花置于胸前。

壁门两侧弟子，均高0.94米。内着僧祇支，外着双领下垂袈裟。左侧弟子左手掌心向内抚于腹前，右手掌心向外置于胸前。右侧弟子左手贴于腿侧，右手抚于胸前。

门外左侧力士，怒目圆睁，颈骨隆起。上身袒露，下着腰系带长裙。手势同于右侧弟子。

题记：甬道壁面和窟门上方刻画两则题记。

引申与拓展

该窟三壁开三龛，供三佛，外侧左右各一菩萨侍立，这种布局让进入室内的信徒觉得似乎主佛两侧各有两位胁持菩萨。其中一位内敛，另一位衣着华丽、身体微扭与第43窟菩萨相同。

Two flanking bodhisattvas on the main wall are about 1.1 meters high with a crown. They have the square faces, the peach-shaped collar round the necks. They are dressed in the upper throwing a strong diagonal across the body, leaving the right side of the body and shoulder bare, and their lower bodies in the long dresses with revers at the waist. The broad scarves hang from the shoulders and down to the lower abdomens then up through the armpits and down again. A string of beads-like garland hangs from the shoulders and down to the shins. They stand on the bases' barefoot with the slightly swaying curves of the bodies. Among which the bodhisattva on the left raises her left hand to the shoulder with palm outward, and the right hand is placed to the abdomen holding the flaming pearl. The bodhisattva on the right puts her left hand on her chest, while placing her right hand to the abdomen in a pose of supporting.

The Buddhas and bodhisattvas in flanking niches are similar in features and size to those of the Buddha and bodhisattvas on the main wall. Among which two Buddhas perform their hands in dhyana mudra. A bodhisattva on the left wall holds a bowl in her left hand, with her middle finger pointing it. A bodhisattva on the right wall places her right hand to the chest holding a lotus flower.

The disciple on each side of the door is 0.94 meters high. They are robed in the inner vests covering the left shoulder and armpits, an upper garments that completely cover their bodies, with U-shaped collar falling to the chest, the corner of the robe resting on the left arm. The disciple on the left puts the left hand on the abdomen with the palm inward, and the right hand is raised to the chest level with the palm outward. The disciple on the right clings his left hand to the thigh, and his right hand on the chest.

The dvarapala on the left outside the door has eyes round open in fury attitude with bulging neck bones. The upper body is exposed, and the lower body wears a long dress with a sash tied at the waist. The gesture is the same as the disciple on the right.

Inscriptions: There are two inscriptions carved by visitors on the wall of the passage and above the door.

Extension and Elaboration

The layout of a niche cut into each on the main wall and two side walls, each containing a seated Buddha flanked by an attendant bodhisattva outside the niche makes the worshippers entering the cave feel as if there are two attendant bodhisattvas on each side of the principal Buddha. Among which one is restrained, the other is richly dressed and the slightly swaying curves of the body is identical with that in Cave 43.

第 69 窟

第69窟位于西崖下部,与西面第169窟为双窟。两窟之间塑双龙交尾,上面影塑一尊坐佛。开凿于北魏(公元386年—公元534年),是麦积山石窟几组双窟形制之一。

该窟体现了麦积山双窟特征,窟内有三尊造像。

形制:该窟为平面方形、平拱顶。

造像:正壁塑一坐佛,左右各塑一身菩萨立像,共三身造像。

正壁佛,磨光高肉髻,面相丰满圆润,弯眉细目,嘴角上翘。着圆领通肩袈裟。双手施禅定印。结跏趺坐于台座上,衣摆呈三瓣式下垂。后绘同心圆头光,带状和火焰纹身光。

左右侧菩萨,戴宝冠,五官清秀。斜披络腋,天衣覆肩起翘。下身长裙衣纹呈对称"U"形或者层状分布,裙摆上形成水波纹的衣褶。跣足立于莲台上。其中左菩萨左手托莲蕾于腹前,右手拈花于胸前;右菩萨左手举于胸前,右手提净瓶于腹前。

Cave 69

Cave 69 is located in the lower part of the western cliff, and it is a pair cave with Cave 169 to the west. Between the two caves there is a pair of dragons with heads and tails twisting together, with above a seated Buddha modelled in relief on the cliff face. Built in the Northern Wei Dynasty (AD 386-534), it is one of several groups of pair caves at Maijishan.

In the cave visitors will enjoy the characteristics of pair caves at Maijishan, and three sculptures. Details are as follows.

Type: It is a flat square niche open to the cliff face with a flat vault ceiling.

Sculptures: The main wall holds a seated Buddha flanked by a standing bodhisattva on the left and the right. There are three figures in all.

The Buddha on the main wall bears a polished high topknot, the full and round face carved with arched brows sweeping above gently opened almond eyes, and the corners of the mouth upwards. He is robed in an upper garment that completely covers his body and hangs in heavy folds round his shoulders. The two hands are in dhyana mudra. He is seated in dhyanasana on the throne with the hem falling in three large lotus petals. There is an aureole composed of concentric circle and mandorla adorned with belt-shaped and flaming motifs.

The attendant bodhisattvas on the left and the right wear coronets with delicately modelled features. They are robed in the upper throwing a strong diagonal across the body, leaving the right side of the body and shoulder bare, the outer shawls cover both shoulders and up at the elbows. The draperies of their lower dresses are arranged in symmetrical U-shape or layers with the wavy folds on the hems. They stand on the lotus platforms barefoot. Among them, the bodhisattva on the left holds a lotus bud in front of the abdomen, and the right hand is raised on the chest holding a flower. The right-hand bodhisattva lifts the left hand to the chest, and the right hand hangs down to the abdomen holding a vase.

引申与拓展

　　该窟与第169窟形制和规模一致,但造像稍有差异。第69窟塑禅定坐像,第169窟塑交脚弥勒菩萨,均配置有胁侍菩萨。这种明确以双窟组合出现,但造像内容却不同的样式,在国内石窟寺双窟中并不多见,这可能与当时盛行的信仰有关。

Extension and Elaboration

Cave 69 and Cave 169 are identical in type and size, but slightly different in sculptures. Cave 69 contains a seated Buddha in meditation, while a Maitreya as a bodhisattva in cross-ankled pose occupies Cave 169, both are flanked by attendant bodhisattvas on the left and the right. The two caves are excavated in the group of pair caves, but the content of the figures are different, which is rare among that in China. This is presumbably related to the prevailing belief at the time.

第72窟

第72窟位于西崖中层,开凿于北魏(公元386年—公元534年)。造像手法熟练和自信,是典型的六世纪风格。

该窟内有四尊造像。

形制:该窟是平面方形、平顶窟。正、左、右三壁各开一个圆拱形龛。

造像:正、左、右三龛各塑一坐佛,正壁左侧存一胁侍菩萨立像,共记四尊像。

三尊佛大致相同,磨光高肉髻,五官清秀。细目下视,腹部隆起。上身内着僧祇支,外着双领下垂袈裟。结跏趺坐于台座上,袈裟下摆呈"八"字覆于台座前。正壁佛双手施禅定印,左右壁佛右手抚膝,左手握衣角。

正壁左侧菩萨,束双丫式发髻,挺胸鼓腹。双手握花于胸前。帛带覆肩下垂到地面,肩部各有一圆形饰物。下着长裙。

Cave 72

Cave 72 is located in the middle tier of the western cliff and was dug in the Northern Wei Dynasty (AD 386-534). Its style of image-making is masterly and confident, which is typical of the sixth century style.

In the cave visitors will enjoy four sculptures. Details are as follows.

Type: It is a flat square niche with a flat ceiling. A chaitya arched recess is cut into each of the main wall, the left wall and the right wall.

Sculptures: A seated Buddha occupies a recess cut into each of the main wall, the left wall and the right wall, and a standing attendant bodhisattva on the left of the main wall. There are four figures in all.

Three Buddhas are almost identical, with polished high topknots, delicately modelled features, their almond eyes gently opened and downcast, and bulging abdomens. They are robed in inner vests covering the left shoulder and armpits, upper garments that completely cover the bodies, with U-shaped collar falling to the chest, the corner of the rob resting on the left arm. They sit in dhyanasana on the thrones with the hems covering in two large lotus petals. The two hands of the Buddha on the main wall are in dhyana mudra. The right hands of the Buddhas on the left and the right walls rest on knees, and their left hands holding the corner of the robes.

The hair of the bodhisattva on the left of the main wall is braided and looped up on either side of her head, with squared shoulders and slightly swelling abdomen. Her two hands are raised to the chest holding a flower. The broad scarf hangs from the shoulders and falls to the ground, each shoulder decorated with a circular ornament. The lower body wears a long dress.

引申与拓展

　　该窟佛像上身着短外袍,肚子上的肉折痕袒露无遗。这种奇怪的造型在第64窟的佛像中也可以看到,为抽象的、颇具灵性的造像增添了一种稍微不协调的现实主义音符。坐佛像胸前刻着闪光珠宝也很特别。

Extension and Elaboration

The Buddhas here are robed in short outer robes, leaving their folding of the flesh over the stomach exposed. This strange modelling can also be seen in the Buddha in Cave 64, adding a slightly incongruous realism note to the abstract, rather spiritual sculpture. It is also very special that a flaming pearl is engraved on the chest of a seated Buddha.

第 74 窟

第74窟位于西崖中下部,开凿于后秦(公元415年—公元470年),北魏(公元386年—公元534年)、明代(公元1368年—公元1644年)重修。其造像风格古朴雄健,受外来雕塑艺术的影响,是麦积山最具代表性的早期洞窟。其洞窟布局、佛像和壁画风格与第78窟非常相似,几乎是同时期开凿的双窟形式。

该窟具有麦积山石窟早期洞窟的特点,造像十一身,窟顶残存千佛壁画。

形制:该窟是平面长方形、穹隆顶、敞口大龛。高4.6米、宽4.45米、深2.45米。窟内正、左、右三壁环列有方形高坛基,正壁上方左右两侧各凿一圆拱形小龛,这是麦积山石窟早期窟龛所具有的典型特征。

造像:窟内正、左、右三壁前,分别塑过去、现在、未来三佛像。正壁佛两侧各一身胁侍菩萨,正壁上方左右小龛各塑三身菩萨组合,共存塑像十一身,大多为木骨泥塑。

正壁主佛高2.86米,头部明代重塑,制作粗糙与身体极不协调。发髻高圆,方脸,眼睛鼓圆,挺胸敛腹。内穿僧祇支,外着袒右袈裟。粗细相间的阴刻衣纹在膝盖前自然下垂,衣摆呈两瓣式垂覆座前。左臂屈肘前伸,左手握拳。右手施无畏印,手指残损。身后有莲瓣形大背光。形体高大雄健,造像古朴,神情威严,明显受

Cave 74

Cave 74 is located in the middle and lower part of the western cliff, and was originally dug in the Later Qin Dynasty (AD 415-470), and repaired in the Northern Wei Dynasty (AD 386-534) and the Ming Dynasty (AD 1368-1644). Its style of image-making is simple and vigorous under a foreign sculptural art, is the most representative early cave at Maijishan. Its layout, style of images of Buddhas and paintings are very similar to Cave 78, almost a pair cave dug at the same period.

Visitors will enjoy the characteristics of the early caves at Maijishan, 11 sculptures and paintings of the Thousand Buddhas on the ceiling. Details are as follows.

Type: It is a large plane rectangular open niche on the cliff face with the "dome of heaven" ceiling. It is 4.6 meters high, 4.45 meters wide and 2.45 meters deep. A high square base of a stone pedestal is set in a circle on each of the main wall and the side walls. A small chaitya arched recess is cut above each end of the main wall. This is the typical feature of the early caves at Maijishan.

Sculptures: Three Buddhas, a representation of the past, the present and future Buddhas are modelled on the main wall and the side walls respectively. The Buddha on the main wall is flanked by an attendant bodhisattva on each side, and each recess above each end of the main wall contains a group of three bodhisattvas. There are 11 figures in all, with mostly of clay modelled on a wooden armature.

The principal Buddha on the main wall is 2.86 meters high. The head restored in the Ming Dynasty is very crudely made and discordant to the body. He wears high round topknot, the square face with bulging eyes, keeping shoulders squared and stomach flat. He is robed in an inner vest covering the left shoulder and armpits, the outer garment thrown over the left shoulder or the upper throwing a strong diagonal across the body, leaving the right side of the body and shoulder bare. The drapery made in incised lines of thick and thin cascades over his knees, covering the throne in two large petals. He lifts his left arm to the chest level

西域犍陀罗地区造像风格的影响。

两侧胁侍菩萨高2.62米，保存相对完好。躯体修长，头戴兽面纹花冠。耳戴长条形耳坠，颈戴项圈。上身袒露，披巾覆左肩，衣褶紧贴着身体。一手拈花于胸前，一手提净瓶。单薄的衣裙紧贴体躯。

左右小耳龛各塑交脚菩萨和思维菩萨。交脚菩萨同样是坐在高坐具上，两脚下垂并在脚腕处交叉，双手在胸部前后相叠作转法轮印。思维菩萨的形象是一个菩萨装的人物坐在一个高坐具上，头偏于右侧并以右手相托，同时右腿翘在左腿上，表现出一种思考问题的状态。

左右壁佛整体形象和正壁佛相同，但高度略小，以此来表示对释迦牟尼佛的崇敬。双手做禅定印。右壁佛头顶水波纹高肉髻，左壁佛头毁。

壁画：窟顶部分残存一小部分壁画，表层的千佛是六世纪中期重绘的，在千佛的底层，还保存有五世纪末期的壁画，但模糊不清，难以辨别具体的内容。

引申与拓展

该窟和临近的第78窟在洞窟大小、形制及造像内容和风格完全相同，很有可能是同时期开凿，由同一组工匠塑作。在云冈石窟由北魏皇室开凿的石窟中也存在这种情况，就是同时开凿两个洞窟，为皇帝和皇太后祈福，学者们将这种情况称为"双窟"。

在洞窟后壁左右两侧的角部，各开凿一个小龛，在佛教石窟考古术语中称为"耳龛"。在耳龛中分别供奉交脚菩萨和思维菩萨。这种形式在早期洞窟中普遍存在，如第51窟、第74窟、第78窟等。据学者研究，这种开窟形式可能是来自犍陀罗（今巴基斯坦一带）地区。

with a clenched fist, and his right hand in the abhaya mudra with fingers damaged. There is a large lotus-petalled mandorla behind him. The Buddha is of considerable and vigorous size, simple conceived and in dignified attitude, which was obviously carved under the influence of the style of image-making in the Gandhara region of the Western Regions.

The two flanking attendant bodhisattvas are 2.62 meters high, relatively well preserved. They are slender and long-legged, bearing the high crowns with a small beast head image. They are decorated with a long ear pendants and a collar round the necks. The upper bodies are exposed, with scarves covering the left shoulder, and the draperies melted into the bodies. One hand is raised to the chest holding a flower, with a vase in the other hand. They are thinly clad, with the lower garments melting against the legs.

A small recess cut above each end of the main wall contains a cross-ankled bodhisattva and a bodhisattva in pensive pose. The former figure sits on a high seat with legs pendent and crossed at the ankles and hands in the dharma-takra-mudra. The latter figure as a bodhisattva also sits on a high seat with the fingers of the right hand gently touching the cheek, with head bent to the right, one leg pendent, the right leg crossed over the left, in a pensive pose.

The whole image of Buddhas on each of the side walls is identical with that of the Buddha on the main wall, but by making them slightly smaller to show the reverence for Sakyamun, with hands in dhyana mudra. The right-hand Buddha wears a high topknot with water wavy, while the head of the left-hand Buddha appears to be missing.

Paintings: A small part remains on the ceiling of the cave, with the Thousand Buddhas repainted in the mid-sixth century on the surface, below which we can still see that of the late fifth century, but it was too damaged to make out the specific content.

Extension and Elaboration

The size, type, content of image-making and style in the cave are identical with that in adjacent Cave 78. They might have been dug at the same time and modelled by the same group of craftsmen. This practice also appears in the Yungang Grottoes cut by the royal family of the Northern Wei Dynasty, where two caves were excavated at the same time to pray for the emperor and the empress dowager, which is referred to as "pair caves" by scholars.

A small recess cut above each end of the main wall is called "side niche" in the archaeological term of the Buddhist caves, each containing a cross-ankled bodhisattva and a bodhisattva in pensive pose, which appears common in early caves, such as Cave 51, Cave 74 and Cave 78. According to scholars, this excavation may have come from the areas of Gandhara (now Pakistan).

第76窟

第76窟位于西崖中下部，开凿于北魏公元502年，和第115窟年代相当。该窟佛座存有墨书开窟题记。

该窟可体现麦积山早期洞窟的特征，二十身造像和最完整的飞天藻井壁画，佛座和供养人身旁有六则墨书题记。

形制：该窟是平面方形、平顶敞口小型窟。窟高1.3米、宽1.15米、深1.2米。窟内有小龛共十四个：正壁上部开左右两小龛，左右二壁各开六小龛。正壁前塑有长方形基座，左右壁前塑有半圆形台。

造像：正壁塑一坐佛，左右壁各立一身胁侍菩萨和三身供养人，十四个小龛内有影塑坐佛十一身，共计造像二十身。

主佛磨光高肉髻，面型长方，双耳垂肩，嘴角上扬。坐姿挺拔，身着圆领袈裟，双手施禅定印。粗细相间的阴刻线衣纹在膝盖前自然下垂，衣摆呈三花瓣式垂覆座前。

左右菩萨大小、体貌和衣饰基本相同，唯姿势有所区别。头戴宝冠，耳饰，颈戴项圈。斜披络腋，下着长裙。披帛穿肘于左右侧

Cave 76

Cave 76 is located in the middle and lower part of the western cliff, and was dug in AD 502 of the Northern Wei Dynasty, of same dateable to Cave 115. It contains an inscription of the excavating on the throne of the Buddha with a brush.

Visitors will enjoy the features of early caves at Maijishan, 20 sculptures and the most complete paintings of flying apsaras on the coffered ceiling, and six inscriptions on the throne of the Buddha and beside the donors with a brush. Details are as follows.

Type: It is a small flat square open niche on the cliff face with a flat ceiling. It is 1.3 meters high, 1.15 meters wide and 1.2 meters deep. There are 14 small recesses in all, with two cut above each end of the main wall and six above each end of the side walls. A rectangular throne is set at the front of the main wall, and a semicircular platform at the front of each side walls.

Sculptures: The main wall retains a seated Buddha, an attendant bodhisattva and three donors stand on each of the side walls, and 14 small recesses contain 11 seated Buddhas in relief. There are 20 figures in all.

The principal Buddha bears a polished high topknot, the square face flanked by pendulous ears, with the corners of the mouth upwards. He wears a robe with a roll collar seated in stiff pose, with hands in dhyana mudra. The drapery made in incised lines of thick and thin cascades over his knees, covering the throne in three large lotus petals.

The size, appearance and dress of bodhisattvas on each side are identical, only in different posture. They wear the crowns, earrings, the collar round the necks. They are robed in the upper throwing a strong diagonal across the body, leaving the right side of the body and

飘扬,跣足立于较高的莲台上。左菩萨左手下垂拈披巾,右手置于腹前拈花蕾。右菩萨身体微向左倾斜,左手握莲蕾于胸前,右手掌心向外,屈指贴于胯部。

正壁小龛影塑小佛面部特征和主佛相似。袈裟分圆领、袒右式、双领下垂三种。正壁左侧供养人均为男性,戴冠,低圆髻,着交领宽袖袍。右侧均为女性,上着交领宽袖上衣,下着裙,双手合于腹前。左壁外侧供养人与正壁女供养人装束大致相同。右壁内侧女供养人结三瓣高髻,双手垂隐于袖中。

壁画:在壁面和顶部残存两平方米隋代(公元581年—公元618年)重绘壁画,色彩鲜明如新。窟顶正中绘圆莲,周围绘飞天绕莲,各种形态的莲苞、花瓣等似散落的花瓣雨在飞天之间飘飘落落。清代有"无云花自雨"的诗句,所指的就是这种场景。左右壁下方绘供养比丘和供养人,其中一中心人物着红色袈裟,拱手而

第76窟"花雨飞天"壁画

shoulder bare and a lower garment. The scarves coming from shoulders hang down coil in loops at the arms fluttering in the wind on each side, and they stand on the higher lotus platforms barefoot. The left hand of the bodhisattva on the left hangs down holding a scarf, and the right hand is raised to the chest holding a flower bud. With slightly swaying curve of the body to the left, the right-hand bodhisattva lifts the left hand to the chest holding a flower bud, and she puts the right hand beside the hip with bent fingers and outward palm.

The facial features of the small Buddhas in relief in the small recesses on the main wall are similar to that of the principal Buddha. Their robs are divided into three kinds: a rob with a roll collar, a garment thrown over the left shoulder or the upper throwing a strong diagonal across the body, leaving the right side of the body and shoulder bare and a rob covering the body, with U-shaped collar falling to the chest, the corner of the robe resting on the left arm. Donors on the left of the main wall are all male wearing the crowns, the low topknots, who are dressed in the robes with long loose sleeves and a collar folded across in front. Those on the right are all female wearing the dresses with long loose sleeves and a collar folded across in front, and the lower skirts with palms pressed together at the abdomens. The costume of the donors on the outer left wall is almost identical with that of female figures on the main wall. The female donor on the inner right wall wears a tall topknot adorned with three lotus petals, concealing her clasped hands in sleeves.

Paintings: Two square-meters paintings repainted in the Sui Dynasty (AD 581-618) survive on the walls and the ceiling, they have retained their pristine freshness of colour. The ceiling is beautifully decorated with angels flying round a central lotus, various forms of lotus buds and petals lie scattered like falling rain between the flying apsaras. The verse "Even without clouds, the rain will fall from the flowers." in the Qing Dynasty depicts the very scene. Monks as worshippers and donors are painted on the lower part of each side walls, among which a central figure in red robe stands with the right hand into a fist and the left hand held straight against the fist, an attendant holds a parasol over the head of the central figure.

Inscriptions: There are six inscriptions left by visitors in the cave. Visitors might have written dedications and roughly scratched their names on the throne of the Buddha or beside the donors with a brush. Among which one of them on the front of the throne records the excavating at Maijishan by an important figure's wife, but characters of the title and name of the figure are barely legible. Others beside the donors are dedications with names or dates by monks.

Extension and Elaboration

The seated Buddhas modelled in relief appear in the cave. Visitors can refer to the part of Thousand Buddhass modelled in relief in Cave 4 (Pavilion of Scattered Flowers) for the

立，一名侍从为其撑起宽大的华盖。

题记：该窟残存六则题记。佛座正面、供养人旁身旁有墨书题记、留名。其中在佛座正面有一则题记，记录一个重要人物的妻子在麦积山开凿洞窟。但是人物的称号和姓名文字模糊不清。供养人旁有五则僧人供养的题名。

引申与拓展

该窟出现影塑坐佛，关于影塑造像的具体制作过程请参考第4窟散花楼中的影塑千佛部分。

供养人是麦积山雕塑和壁画主题之一，该窟供养人像较多。主要是当地官员乡绅、出家僧尼、世俗信徒等开窟造像时，在洞窟里塑上或画上自己和家族亲眷、部下属僚以及侍从奴仆的肖像。该窟供养人形象较小，站在菩萨身后不明显的位置。人物都穿着天水本地民族的服饰，是研究北魏服饰的重要资料。供养人出资开凿石窟或是参加佛教活动，都需要聘请僧人作为导师，指导自己的学习或是实践。导师一般都站在供养人队列的最前面，在壁面上绘制的身穿红色袈裟的僧人应该是导师中比较重要的一个。

more specific production process.

The donor image is one of the themes of sculptures and paintings at Maijishan, and the cave contains more donor images. They are mainly local officials, gentries, monks and nuns, and secular worshippers have portraits of themselves, their relatives, subordinates and servants painted or modelled in the caves. The size of donors here is rather small, standing in no obvious position behind the bodhisattvas. They wear the local dress of Tianshui, which is an important data for studying the costume of the Northern Wei Dynasty. When donors give patronage to excavations or participate in Buddhist activities, they need to hire monks as mentors to guide their study or practice. The mentors generally stand at the front of the group of donors, and the monk in red robe in the painting here should be a more important one.

第78窟

第78窟位于西崖中下部,开凿于后秦(公元384年—公元417年),北魏(公元386年—公元534年·)重修。该窟是北魏早期具有代表性的洞窟,造像具有典型的早期外来风格。其洞窟布局、佛像和壁画风格与第74窟非常相似,几乎是同时期开凿的双窟形式。

该窟类似草原游牧民族毡帐的石窟,有十一尊木骨泥塑造像,两则供养人身份的墨书题记。

形制:该窟是平面长方形、穹隆顶、敞口大龛。正壁和左右壁前有倒凹字形高基座,宽4.6米、高4.5米、深2.8米,正壁上方左右两侧各开凿一个小龛。

造像:正、左、右三壁各塑结跏趺坐佛一身,正壁佛两侧各塑一胁侍菩萨立像。正壁两侧上方的圆拱形小龛内,塑交脚菩萨和思维菩萨,菩萨两侧又有二胁侍菩萨,共计十一身木骨泥塑造像。

正壁佛高3米,躯体粗壮。水波纹高肉髻,面形方圆,高鼻大眼,薄唇棱角分明,下巴微翘,大耳垂肩。内穿僧祇支,外着袒右袈裟。袈裟衣纹凸起,褶纹密集,在膝盖前自然下垂,衣摆呈两瓣式垂覆座前。右手施无畏印,左手惨毁,结跏趺坐于基座上。

Cave 78

Cave 78 is located in the middle and lower part of the western cliff, and was originally dug in the Later Qin Dynasty (AD384-417) and repaired by the Northern Wei Dynasty (AD 386-534). It is the representative cave of the early Northern Wei Dynasty, and the sculptures show a typical early foreign style. Its layout, style of images of Buddhas and paintings are very similar to Cave 74, almost a pair cave dug at the same period.

In the cave visitors will enjoy the niche similar to the tents of the nomads on the grassland, 11 figures of clay modelled on a wooden armature, and two inscriptions containing the identity of the donors with a brush. Details are as follows.

Type: It is a large plane rectangular open niche on the cliff face with the "dome of heaven" ceiling. A high base of a stone pedestal in upside-down concave shape is set on each of the main wall and the side walls. It is 4.6 meters wide, 4.5 meters high and 2.8 meters deep. A small recess is cut above each end of the main wall.

Sculptures: A Buddha sits in dhyanasana on the main wall and each of the side walls, among which the Buddha on the main wall is flanked by a standing attendant bodhisattva on each side. A small chaitya arched recess cut above each end of the main wall contains a cross-ankled bodhisattva and a bodhisattva in pensive pose, each is flanked by an attendant bodhisattva. There are 11 figures of clay modelled on a wooden armature.

The Buddha on the main wall is 3.0 meters high and of stalwart build. He bears a high topknot with water wavy, the round face with high nose and big eyes, a thin slips with the delicate curve of the mouth, slightly pointed chin and flanked by pendulous ears. He is robed in an inner vest covering the left shoulder and armpits, the outer robe thrown over the left shoulder or the upper throwing a strong diagonal across the body, leaving the right side of the body and shoulder bare. The drapery in raised lines falling in heavy folds cascades over his knees, covering the throne in two large petals. He sits in dhyanasana on

左侧佛整体形象和正壁佛相同,但形体略小,以此来表示对释迦牟尼佛的崇敬。佛头部略低,目光俯视,双手施禅定印。右侧的佛已经破坏,只保留一点残迹。

左右侧胁侍菩萨下半身部分残损。高冠,袒裸上身,下着长裙。体态浑厚,塑像曾重塑、妆銮。左菩萨斜披络腋,左手握莲花于胸部。右菩萨披天衣,左手上举于胸前。

左右小耳龛各塑交脚菩萨和思维菩萨。

壁画:窟内左侧佛座的垂直面上,保存有北朝(公元386年—公元581年)供养人形象的壁画。这些供养人都是男性,头戴黑色的帽子,身穿交领上衣,下穿黑色的裤子。双手在胸前持一莲花恭敬向佛,每个供养人旁边都有墨书题记以标明其身份。

题记:供养人画像旁各有墨书题记一则,书写供养者籍贯、姓名,其中一则中有"仇池镇"字样。

引申与拓展

该窟和临近的第74窟在洞窟大小、形制及造像内容和风格完全相同,是一组双窟。窟内主要内容为三佛信仰,泥塑高大、庄严、肃穆,体现出麦积山石窟早期彪悍雄健的艺术风格。正壁小龛的布局位置不符合中原地区民众对建筑的审美,有研究者认为,这种小龛的形式是来源于犍陀罗地区,是佛教文化通过丝绸之路交流的见证。

左右两侧胁侍菩萨分属于不同的时代,左侧菩萨为最初的作

the high base of a stone pedestal with his right hand in the abhaya mudra, and his left hand damaged.

The overall image of the Buddha on the left is identical with that of the Buddha on the main wall, but the size is slightly smaller to express the reverence for Sakyamun. He lowers his head slightly with downcast eyes, hands in dhyana mudra. The Buddha on the right has been destroyed, leaving only a few traces.

The lower bodies of the attendant bodhisattvas on each side have been partially damaged. They wear high crowns, and the upper bodies are bare and the lower bodies are dressed in the long dresses. With solid bodies, the figures were restored and redecorated. The bodhisattva on the left is dressed in the upper throwing a strong diagonal across the body, leaving the right side of the body and shoulder bare, the left hand is raised to the chest level holding a lotus flower. The outer shawl covers both shoulders of the right-hand bodhisattva, with the left hand lifted to the chest.

A small recess cut above each end of the main wall contains a cross-ankled bodhisattva and a bodhisattva in pensive pose. Visitors can refer to Cave 74 for a detailed introduction.

Paintings: Images of the donors in the Northern Dynasty (AD 386-581) are painted on the vertical surface of the throne of the Buddha on the left. They are all male, wearing black hats, upper garments with a collar folded across in front and black trousers. Their hands are raised to the chest level holding a lotus flower towards the Buddha, and an inscription is written on each side of them with a brush to indicate their identities.

Inscription: An inscription left with a brush on each side of the portrait of the donors, recording their native places and names, one of which scratched the characters "Chou Chizhen".

Extension and Elaboration

The size, type, content of image-making and style in the cave are identical with those in adjacent Cave 74, they are pair caves. The belief of three Buddhas are main contents, and the sculptures modelled in clay are tall, dignified and solemn, reflecting the early tough and vigorous artistic style of Maijishan Caves. The layout of a small recess cut above each end on the main wall does not conform to the aesthetic appreciation of architecture in the Central Plains. Some researchers believe that it might have come from the Gandhara areas and is a witness of the communications of Buddhist cultures through the Silk Road.

品，面相神情服饰等有浓厚的犍陀罗地区特点，可惜大部分表层的泥质剥落。右侧的是七世纪初期的作品，据推测是最初的菩萨遭破坏后，七世纪初期补塑了这尊造像。和五世纪的左菩萨对比，可以明显看出不同时代的信众对佛教造像审美的不同，这也是佛教中国化的一种反映。

The attendant bodhisattvas on each side are works of different times. The left-hand bodhisattva is the original works, her face, attitude and costume bear strong Gandhara characteristics, but most thin skin of clay plaster has peeled away. The right-hand bodhisattva is the works of the early 17th century, which was presumably the restoration made in the seventh century after the destruction of the original works. Compared with the left-hand figure in the fifth century, we can clearly see that worshippers in different times have different aesthetics of Buddhist image-makings, which is also a reflection of the sinicization of Buddhism.

第 80 窟

第80窟位于西崖中下部最东端,开凿于北魏(公元386年—公元534年),北周(公元557年—公元581年)重修,是佛教造像从域外雕塑艺术向中原雕塑艺术转型时期的代表性洞窟。

该窟体现了麦积山石窟初期洞窟建筑特点,内有十八身造像。

形制:该窟是平面方形、平顶,洞窟前部因地震坍塌,现在只剩下后壁部分和两壁佛龛的一小部分。高2.48米、宽2.98米、残深1.35米。正壁前筑一石胎泥塑"工"字形佛座,佛左右侧壁面上下各开二小龛。左右两壁各开一龛,内塑一半圆形覆莲台。

造像:窟内正壁一坐佛,正壁左右侧上层小龛内各塑一坐佛,下层小龛内各塑释迦多宝两佛并坐,下方两侧各影塑三身供养人。左右壁内侧各塑一身胁侍菩萨。右壁龛内贴三尊影塑小坐佛,共计十八身。

正壁佛破坏严重,头部十七世纪重修,制作粗糙,和原有的造像风格完全不一致。佛像磨光高肉髻,内着僧祇支,外着双领下垂式袈裟。右手作无畏印,左手抚膝,结跏趺坐。

两侧菩萨保存较好,身后有身光,头戴花冠,面庞方圆,双目

Cave 80

Cave 80 is located at the easternmost end of the middle and lower part in the western cliff. It was originally dug in the Northern Wei Dynasty (AD 386-534) and repaired in the Northern Zhou Dynasty (AD 557-581). It is a representative cave in the transformation period of Buddhist image-making from a foreign sculptural art into that of the Central Plains.

Visitors in the cave will enjoy the early cave building at Maijishan, and 18 sculptures. Details are as follows.

Type: It is a flat square niche with a flat ceiling, the front has fallen away by the earthquakes, leaving only the rear part and a small part of the recesses into two side walls. The height is 2.48 meters, the width is 2.98 meters, and the residual depth is 1.35 meters. An I-shaped throne built up in clay plaster over a core of rock is set in front of the main wall, and two small recesses in two tiers cut above each end of the main wall, and a small recess cut into each side walls containing a semi-circular upsid-down lotus throne.

Sculptures: The cave contains a seated Buddha on the main wall, a seated Buddha in the upper recess cut into above each end of the main wall, and Sakyamuni and Prabhutaratna sharing the throne in the lower recess, below which are three moulded donors on each side. An attendant bodhisattva is made on each inner side walls. Three small seated Buddhas in relief applied to the wall of the recess into the right wall. There are 18 figures in all.

The Buddha on the main wall is badly damaged, the head restored in the 17th century and very crudely made, is completely inconsistent with the original style of image-making. With a high polished topknot, he wears an inner vest covering the left shoulder and armpits, an upper garment that completely covers his body, with U-shaped collar falling to the chest. He sits in dhyanasana on a throne with his right hand in the abhaya mudra, and his left hand rests on knee.

细长,嘴角含有笑意。袒露上身,左肩斜披络腋,下穿羊肠裙,裙子紧裹腿,裙纹为突起的圆弧形。帔巾从双肩搭下穿肘飘动外扬,赤足立于莲台上。左手下垂持瓶,右手拈花蕾于胸前。

正壁下层小龛内各塑释迦多宝两佛并坐,下方有影塑的男性供养人形象。头戴笼冠,身穿圆领长袍,双手合拢于腹前而立,体量较大。

壁画:正壁中部尚存北魏早期身光左右缘小火焰纹的痕迹。其上的边缘被北周赭石色的颜料覆盖。正壁左右侧小龛内外及右壁龛内侧小佛后壁面上尚见北魏早期用色较为淡雅的火焰纹、忍冬纹、联珠纹等。

引申与拓展

该窟是麦积山石窟开凿历史上北魏早期向中期过渡的典型洞窟,这一历史阶段出现多个类似洞窟,如第100窟、第128窟、第148窟。其洞窟建筑、造像题材内容、造像风格等和早期的第74窟、第78窟相比,更趋向于中原地区的文化因素。

二佛并坐依据《法华经·见宝塔品》第十一章,讲述释迦牟尼佛在讲经的时候,一位来自遥远的过去的多宝佛乘坐宝塔从空中降落下来,并邀请释迦牟尼佛和自己坐在一起,用这种办法来对释迦牟尼的讲经活动进行支持和肯定。

The bodhisattva on each side is well preserved, backed by mandorlas, wearing the high crowns, the square faces carved with long brows sweeping above gently opened almond eyes, taking a smile on lips. Their upper bodies are bare, with the upper throwing a strong diagonal across the body, leaving the right side of the body and shoulder bare, the lower sheath dresses melting against the legs with drapery in raised rippling curves. The scarves coming from shoulders coil in loops at the arms fluttering in the wind on each side, and they stand on the lotus platform. The left hand hangs down holding a vase, while the right hand is raised to the chest holding a lotus bud.

Sakyamuni and Prabhutaratna sharing the throne are modelled in the lower recess on the main wall, below which are three male moulded donors on each side. They wear the cage crowns, the garments with a roll collar, standing with clasped hands to the abdomen level. They are larger in size.

Paintings: Traces of small flame motifs on each border of the mandorla in early Northern Wei Dynasty remain in the center of the main wall. Its outer border was covered by the ochre-colored pigment of the Northern Zhou Dynasty. Motifs of flame, honeysuckle and the linked-pearl painted in light colour of the early Northern Wei Dynasty are visible in inner and outer of the recess above each end of the main wall and the inner wall behind the small Buddha of the niche cut into the right wall.

Extension and Elaboration

The cave is typical of the transformation period from early to the middle of the Northern Wei Dynasty in the excavation history at Maijishan, a number of similar caves, such as Cave 100, Cave 128 and Cave 148 appeared at this period. Compared to early caves of Cave 74 and Cave 78, their architectures, subjects, contents and style of image-making tend to carry more of the cultural elements of the central plains area.

Two Buddhas sharing a throne is a represerntation of *the Apparition of the Stupa,* Chapter XI of the *Lotus*, which describes when Sakyamuni was preaching, Prabhutaratna, a Buddha of the remote past, landed from a stupa rose out of the earth and moved aside to make room for Sakyamuni on his throne to support and affirm his preaching of the *Lotus*.

第 85 窟

第85窟位于西崖中层西面,东邻第170窟,西邻第84窟。开凿于北魏(公元386年—公元534年)。该窟是麦积山三佛龛之一,正壁左侧菩萨的露齿微笑表现极具感染力。

该窟有八身泥塑造像,左壁弟子和右壁菩萨头光内各留有一则刻画题记。

形制:该窟为平面方形、平顶窟。前壁有长方形甬道。正、左、右三壁设低坛基并各有一台座。窟内四壁上方塑二层小坛台。

造像:正、左、右三壁各塑一身坐佛,正壁佛左右侧各塑一身胁侍菩萨,左壁左侧塑一身菩萨右侧塑一身弟子,右壁左侧塑一身弟子,共计八身。

正、左、右壁三佛,磨光高肉髻,方圆脸,双目下视,长颈削肩。内着交领衣,胸前系带,外着双领下垂袈裟。左臂屈肘前伸,手部残毁。右手施无畏印,五指已毁。结跏趺坐于台座上,下摆垂于台座前。身后绘不同色彩的同心圆圆形项光,浮塑莲瓣形身光,外缘为火焰纹。其中左右壁二佛,高肉髻,瘦长脸,体躯扁平。双手作禅定印。

Cave 85

Cave 85 is located at the west side of the middle tier in the western cliff, adjacent to Cave 170 in the east and Cave 84 in the west. It was excavated in the Northern Wei Dynasty (AD 386-534). It is one of the three Buddha niches at Maijishan, and the representation of the bodhisattva who smiles broadly on the left of the main wall is contagious.

In the cave visitors will admire eight clay sculptures, two carved inscriptions on the aureoles behind each of the disciple on the left wall and the bodhisattva on the right wall. Details are as follows.

Type: It is a flat square niche with a flat ceiling. There is a passage on the front wall. A low base is cut on each of the main wall and two flanking walls, over each of which a pedestal is set. Two-tier ledges are built above the four walls.

Sculptures: A seated Buddha occupies each of the main wall and two side walls. On the main wall stands an attendant bodhisattva on either side, a bodhisattva on the left and a disciple on the right on the left wall, a disciple on the left of the right wall. There are eight figures in all.

The three Buddhas on the main wall and the two side walls wear polished high topknots, the square and round faces flanked by downcast eyes, with long necks and narrow shoulders. They are robed in inner robs of collars folded across in front, with a sash tied at the chests, upper garments that completely cover their bodies, with U-shaped collar falling to the chest, the lappet of the robe resting on the left arm and down to the left knee. Their left arms are stretched forward with hands broken, while the right hands in the abhaya mudras with fingers damaged. They sit in dhyanasana on the thrones with the hems covering in front. There are circular aureoles composed of concentric circles in different colours, and lotus-petal shaped mandorlas with the motif of flames on the outer rims in relief behind them. Among them, two Buddhas on the left and right walls have high topknots, the long-skinning faces, and the flat bodies. Their two hands are in dhyana mudra.

正壁左右侧菩萨，束高发髻，戴花冠，面容清瘦，细颈削肩。服饰华丽。颈戴项圈并下坠有桃形饰物。内着僧祇支，外披天衣。帛带搭肩绕臂向外飘扬下垂，由谷穗和花饰组成的粗大璎珞，于腹前十字穿环后分垂于两腿处，经身后上绕。下着长裙，跣足立于坛基上，头后有浮塑的莲瓣形项光。其中左侧菩萨，露齿微笑。左手置于腹部，右手抚胸。右侧菩萨，左手持桃形玉璧于胸前，右手握莲蕾垂于腿侧。

　　左壁左侧菩萨、右侧弟子，内着僧祇支，外着双领下垂袈裟。头后有浮塑的莲瓣形项光。其中左侧菩萨，自腹下均已残毁。束扇形髻，露齿微笑，细颈削肩。双手合十于胸前。右侧弟子，身材修长，瘦长脸，双目下视。左臂置于腹部，手已失，右手握莲蕾于胸前。

　　右壁左侧弟子，双目深凹，颧骨突出，身材修长。衣着、项光同于左壁右侧弟子。左手提净瓶于腹部，右手抚胸。

　　题记：该窟左壁弟子和右壁菩萨头光内各留有一则刻画题记。

引申与拓展

　　不同于麦积山其他微笑作品所表现出的内敛、含蓄、会心，该窟正壁左侧菩萨露齿微笑。她笑眯了眼，小嘴张开，露出一排整齐的牙齿。喜悦之情溢于面庞，让人不禁感叹，开心真的会感染。

The bodhisattvas on either side of the main wall wear high topknots carved by corollas, the skinny faces, the thin necks and narrow shoulders. They are abundantly robed. The peach-shaped pendants hang from the collar round the necks. They are robed in the inner vests covering the left shoulder and armpits, the outer shawls cover both shoulders. The scarves come from shoulders and hang down through the armpits fluttering in the wind on each side, the heavy garlands composed of millet ears and flowers dip down to the abdomens to cross the ring and into the hollow between the legs to sweep up again pointing to the shoulders. With long dresses on the lower bodies, they stand on the bases barefoot backed by the lotus-petal shaped aureoles. Among which the left-side bodhisattva grins. The left hand is placed on the abdomen, and the right hand on the chest. The right-side bodhisattva holds a peach-shaped jade in her left hand on the chest, and the right hand hangs down beside the thigh holding a lotus bud.

The bodhisattva on the left and the disciple on the right of the left wall are in the inner vests covering the left shoulder and armpits, the upper garments that completely cover their bodies, with U-shaped collar falling to the chests, the lappet of the robe resting on the left arm and down to the left knee. There are lotus-petal shaped aureoles in belief behind them. Among them, below the lower abdomen of the left-side bodhisattva has broken. She has a fan-shaped high topknot, grinning, thin neck and narrow shoulders. Her palms are pressed together at the chest. The right-side disciple is slender and long-legged, with the long-skinning face and downcast eyes. The left arm is placed at the abdomen with hand lost, and the right hand is lifted to the chest holding a lotus bud.

The left-hand disciple on the left wall has sunken eyes, bulging cheeks, slender and long-legged. His clothing and aureole are identical with those of the disciple on the right of the left wall. The left hand is placed on the abdomen holding a vase, and the right hand on the chest.

Inscriptions: There are two carved inscriptions left by visitors on the aureoles behind each of the disciple on the left wall and the bodhisattva on the right wall.

Extension and Elaboration

Different from the introverted, implicit and understanding shown by other smiling works at Maijishan, the bodhisattva on the left of the main wall grins. She smiles with squinted eyes and her mouth open, revealing a neat row of teeth. The representation of joy on the face lets a person can not help but sigh that happiness is really infectious.

第90窟

第90窟位于西崖中部,开凿于后秦(公元384年—公元417年),北魏(公元386年—公元534年)、宋代(公元960年—公元1279年)重修,为麦积山早期三佛窟。该窟重绘壁画和改塑造像痕迹明显。

该窟内有五身宋代重塑造像,正壁右侧着胡服供养人壁画,正壁两侧四则墨书题记。

形制:该窟为平面方形、平顶敞口龛,高3.23米、宽3.58米、残深2.49米。龛内三壁前凿"凹"字形高坛基。

造像:窟内正壁塑一坐佛二弟子,左右壁各塑一坐佛,共五身造像,均为宋代重塑。

正壁佛高1.65米,头顶为低平肉髻,有肉髻珠,面部呈椭圆形,脖颈处刻有三道曲纹。胸部袒露,内着僧祇支,外披双领下垂袈裟。褶纹呈阶梯式下垂到座前,衣摆呈圆弧状。右手上举至胸前作说法印,左手抚膝,结跏趺坐于圆形莲台上。身后圆形头光内绘四身坐佛和莲瓣形身光。

左侧弟子迦叶高1.8米,面容苍老但身躯健壮。内穿交领衫,外披双领下垂袈裟,上有田字方格。双手相握拱于胸前,脚穿

Cave 90

Cave 90 is located in the middle part of the western cliff. It was originally dug in the later Qin Dynasty (AD 384-417), and repaired in the Northern Wei Dynasty (AD 386-534) and the Song Dynasty (AD 960-1279). Is the early Three Buddhas caves at Maijishan. The traces of repainted paintings and remodelled sculptures are obvious.

Visitors will enjoy five sculptures remodelled in the Song Dynasty, paintings of donors in the dress of the ancient minority nationality-Hu on the right of the main wall, and four inscriptions with a brush on both sides of the main wall. Details are as follows.

Type: It is a flat square open niche on the cliff face with flat ceiling, 3.23 meters high, 3.58 meters wide and a depth of 2.49 meters. A high concave throne is cut on each front of the main wall, the left wall and the right wall.

Sculptures: A seated Buddha flanked by two disciples are modelled on the main wall, a seated Buddha on each of the side walls. There are five figures in all, which were all remodelled in the Song Dynasty.

The Buddha on the main wall is 1.65 meters high, with a low flat topknot, a bead between the ushnisha and the bottom hair, the oval face with three incised lines to the neck. With upper body bare, he is robed in an inner vest covering the left shoulder and armpits, an upper garment that completely covers his body, with U-shaped collar falling to the chest, the lappet of the robe resting on the left arm. The drapery cascades over the throne in layered symmetrical folds ending in rippling curves at the hem. He sits in dhyanasana on a circular lotus throne, with his right hand in gesture of preaching, and his left hand rests on knee. There is a circular aureole adorned with four seated Buddhas, and a lotus-petal shaped mandorla in relief behind him.

尖头履，站于半圆形台基上。右侧弟子阿难为青年形象，高1.78米，椭圆面形。内穿僧祇支，外披双领下垂袈裟。双手合十于胸前，脚穿圆头履，站于半圆形台基上。二弟子身后均有圆形头光，由五个同心圆组成。

左右两壁佛和正壁的佛基本形象大致相同。

壁画：正壁右侧绘着胡服的供养人画像，面部色彩脱落，形象模糊。身穿深色交领短袍，腰束带，脚穿乌皮靴站立。佛身光画火焰纹、千佛、忍冬花纹、卷草等。

题记：四则墨书题记分别写于正壁两侧。

引申与拓展

该窟有非常明显的两次修复，第一次主要重绘壁画，第二次对塑像进行了整体重塑。从遗迹判断，该洞窟内原作应为三佛二菩萨，在这个洞窟中我们能看到的是十至十一世纪改塑的三佛二弟子，但是在弟子身后两侧，我们还可以看到菩萨的飘带，并且其色彩、风格等和弟子形象完全不同，所以推测最初在正壁佛的两侧塑作的应该是菩萨形象。

The disciple Kasyapa on the left is 1.8 meters high, an elder image but with a strong body. He wears an inner garment with a collar folded across in front and an upper garment that completely covers his body, with U-shaped collar falling to the chest, the lappet of the robe resting on the left arm which is adorned with coloured "paddy-field design". He stands on a semicircular platform, with the right hand into a fist and the left hand held straight against the fist in shoes with pointed toe. While the right-hand disciple Ananda is a young figure, 1.78 meters tall, the oval-shaped face. He is robed in an inner vest covering the left shoulder and armpits, and an upper garment that completely covers his body, with U-shaped collar falling to the chest, the lappet of the robe resting on the left arm. His palms are pressed together at the chest, standing on a semicircular platform in shoes with round toe. There is a circular aureole behind each of them, composed of five concentric circles.

The basic image of the Buddha on each side walls is identical with that of the Buddha on the main wall.

Paintings: Figures of donors in the dress of the ancient minority nationality-Hu are painted on the right of the main wall, their facial colours have fallen away, and the images are blurred. They wear the dark short coats with a collar folded across in front, a sash tied round the waist, standing in dark leather boots. The mandorla behind the Buddha is decorated with motifs of flam, the Thousand Buddhas, honeysuckle and curly grass.

Inscriptions: There are four inscriptions left by visitors with a brush on both sides of the main wall.

Extension and Elaboration

We can see two very obvious refurbishments in the cave, the paintings were mainly repainted by the first restoration, and the sculptures were remodelled completely by the second one. Judging from the remains of the cave, the original works should be three Buddhas and two bodhisattvas, what we can see here is a group of three Buddhas and two disciples remodelled in the 10th to 11th century, but on both sides behind the disciples we can see traces of the ribbons of the bodhisattvas which are completely different in colouring and style with that of disciples, so presumably that the original image on each side of the Buddha should be a bodhisattva.

第 92 窟

第92窟位于西崖中下部,开凿于北魏(公元386年—公元534年)。雕塑和绘画风格呈现出北魏晚期秀骨清像的特征。

该窟内有三尊泥塑造像,三尊影塑小坐佛像,正壁左侧和左壁菩萨,右侧七身供养人画像,前壁左侧一尊小坐佛画像和窟顶两身飞天。

形制:该窟是平面方形、平顶窟。正壁建一"工"字形台座,正、左、右三壁壁前凿低坛基,正壁主佛两侧壁面各砌两层小坛台。

造像:正壁一身坐佛,主佛两侧两层小坛台存影塑坐佛三身。左壁右侧立一身胁侍菩萨,右壁左侧塑一身弟子,共计六身。

正壁佛,磨光高肉髻,秀骨清像。内着僧祇支,外着双领下垂袈裟。双臂前举,双手已残失。结跏趺坐于"工"字形台座上,下摆呈两瓣垂覆于座前。身后彩绘同心圆项光和浮塑莲瓣形身光。

左壁菩萨和右壁弟子,与主佛同相,立于坛基上。身后彩绘同心圆项光。其中左壁菩萨内着立领衣,外着对襟宽袖袍。披帛搭肩

第二章 麦积山石窟汉英解说词

Cave 92

Cave 92 is located in the middle and lower part of the western cliff and was dug in the Northern Wei Dynasty (AD 386-534). The style of the sculptures and paintings show the characteristics of long and slender figure and delicately modelled features in the late Northern Wei Dynasty.

Visitors will enjoy three scultures modelled in clay, three small seated Buddhas in relief, seven donors painted on the left of the main wall and the right of the bodhisattva on the left wall, a small seated Buddha on the left of the front wall, and two flying apsaras decorated on the ceiling. Details are as follows.

Type: It is a flat square niche with a flat ceiling. An I-shaped throne is set on the main wall, a low base is cut around the ground in front of the main wall and the side walls, and two-tier ledges are built on each side of the principal Buddha of the main wall.

Sculptures: A seated Buddha is modelled on the main wall, three small seated Buddhas in relief rest on two-tier ledges built on each side of the principal Buddha. An attendant bodhisattva stands on the right of the left wall, and a disciple on the left of the right wall. There are six figures in all.

The Buddha on the main wall bears a polished high topknot, with long and slender figure and delicately modelled features. He is robed in an inner vest covering the left shoulder and armpits, an upper garment that completely covers his body, with U-shaped collar falling to the chest, the lappet of the robe resting on the left arm. The two arms are raised in front with the hands missing. He sits in dhyanasana on the I-shaped throne with the hem covering the throne in two large lotus petals. There is a circular aureole composed of coloured concentric circles and a lotus petal-shaped mandorla in belief behind him.

下垂到腿侧。右手胸前托供物，左手垂于腿侧。右壁弟子着装与主佛相同。左手胸前托供物，右手垂于腿侧。影塑小坐佛着装也与主佛相同。右手施无畏印，左手持衣角于胸前。

壁画：壁画烟熏严重，但人物轮廓依稀可辨。正壁左侧和左壁菩萨，右侧七身供养人画像，前壁左侧一身小坐佛画像和窟顶两身飞天。

引申与拓展

尽管此窟前壁大半坍毁，内部也因侵蚀而严重受损，但一些北魏晚期窟龛和造像特征仍然存在。该窟形制与第115窟相似，均在正壁佛两侧壁面两层小坛台上贴影塑小坐佛。造像均秀骨清像，其精雕细琢的面孔仍然保持着坚定、庄严和内敛。

The bodhisattva on the left wall and the disciple on the right wall seem to be very similar to that of the principal Buddha in appearance, standing on the platforms. There are circular aureoles composed of coloured concentric circles behind them. Among them the bodhisattva on the left wall wears an inner garment with a stand collar, an outer robe with long loose sleeves and a parallel collar. The scarf covers both shoulders and falls down beside the thighs. The right hand is raised to the chest holding up an offering, and the left hand hangs down beside the thigh. The disciple on the right wall is dressed in the same way as the principal Buddha. The left hand is raised to the chest holding up an offering, and the right hand hangs down beside the thigh. The robs of the small seated Buddhas in relief are also identical with that of the principal Buddha. Their right hands perform the abhaya mudra, and their left hands are put on the chest holding the corner of robs.

Paintings: The paintings are badly smokedarkened, but the contour of the figures is slightly decipherable. We can still see seven donors painted on the left of the main wall and the right of the bodhisattva on the left wall, a small seated Buddha on the left of the front wall, and two flying apsaras decorated on the ceiling.

Extension and Elaboration

Although most of the front wall of the cave collapsed and the interior was severely damaged by erosion, some characteristics of caves and sculptures in the late Northern Wei Dynasty still survive. The type of the cave is similar to Cave 115, which applies small seated Buddhas in relief to the walls on two-tier ledges built on each side of the principal Buddha. The images are all in long and slender figure and delicately modelled features, and their finely made faces remain firm, solemn, and reserved.

第93窟

第93窟位于西崖中部,东邻第165窟,西邻第96窟。开凿于北魏(公元386年—公元534年),宋代(公元960年—公元1279年)重修。窟外壁面对称开凿小龛的形式在麦积山比较特殊。

该窟内有三尊泥塑造像,三十六尊影塑佛、菩萨、供养人像。

形制:该窟是平面方形、平顶窟。正壁建一长方形台座,正、左、右三壁两侧壁面各砌五层小坛台。

造像:正壁宋代重塑一尊坐佛,左右壁各立一身弟子。正、左、右三壁两侧五层小坛台存影塑佛、菩萨、供养人像三十六身,共计三十九身。

正壁佛,磨光低肉髻。内着僧祇支,外着双领下垂袈裟。结跏趺坐于长方形高台座上,双手施禅定印。

左壁弟子,头失。着交领僧衣。双手拱于胸前,穿靴立于莲台上。右壁弟子,衣着与主佛相同。双臂拱举于胸前,双手残失。穿靴立于莲台上。身后绘莲瓣形身光。

影塑佛像五官均相似,结跏趺坐或站立,着圆领通肩袈裟或袒右袈裟,大多施禅定印。影塑菩萨为交脚和思惟菩萨的形象,衣饰

Cave 93

Cave 93 is located in the middle part of the western cliff, adjacent to Cave 165 in the east and Cave 96 in the west. It was originally dug in the Northern Wei Dynasty (AD 386-534) and repaired in the Song Dynasty (AD 960-1279). The excavation of the small niches on the exterior cliff face of the cave in symmetrical is quite unusual at Maijishan.

Visitors will enjoy three sculptures modelled in clay, and 36 Buddhas, bodhisattvas and donors in relief. Details are as follows.

Type: It is a flat square niche with a flat ceiling. A rectangle throne is set on the main wall, five-tier ledges are built on each side of the main wall and two flanking walls.

Sculptures: A seated Buddha is remodelled in the Song Dynasty on the main wall, and a disciple stands on each side of the left and the right walls. 39 Buddhas, bodhisattvas and donors in relief rest on five-tier ledges built on each side of of the main wall and two flanking walls. There are 39 figures in all.

The Buddha on the main wall bears a polished low topknot. He is robed in an inner vest covering the left shoulder and armpits, an upper garment that completely covers his body, with U-shaped collar falling to the chest, the lappet of the robe resting on the left arm. He is seated in dhyanasana on a high rectangular throne with two hands in dhyana mudra.

The head of the disciple on the left wall has disappeared. He is dressed in a gown of a collar folded across in front. With the right hand into a fist and the left hand held straight against the fist on the chest, he stands on the lotus platform in boots. The rob of the disciple on the right wall is identical with that of the principal Buddha. The two arms are raised to the chest with the hands missing, standing on the lotus platform in boots. There is a lotus petal-shaped mandorla behind him.

基本相同。影塑供养人分为男性供养人和女性供养人，着圆领衣或交领衣。

引申与拓展

该窟造像题材多样化，有一佛二菩萨、交脚菩萨和思惟菩萨及二胁侍菩萨、千佛等。无论是洞窟形制、壁面布局、泥塑小坛台和造像题材与第76窟、第86窟、第89窟、第114窟、第115窟和第156窟有强烈的共性。

The features of the Buddhas in relief are similar, they either sit in dhyanasana or stand, either dressed in upper garments that completely cover the bodies and hang in heavy folds round the shoulders or in outer robes thrown over the left shoulder or the upper throwing a strong diagonal across the body, leaving the right side of the body and shoulder bare, most of them with two hands in dhyana mudra. The images of bodhisattvas in relief are the cross-ankled bodhisattva and the bodhisattva in pensive pose, with their robs almost identical. The figures of donors are male or female, in the robes either with a roll collar or a crossing collar.

Extension and Elaboration

The themes of the sculptures in the cave are diverse, including a Buddha flanked by an attendant bodhisattva, a cross-ankled bodhisattva and a bodhisattva in pensive pose flanked by an attendant bodhisattva and the Thousand Buddhass. The type of the cave, the layout on the walls, the little ledges cut in clay and the theme of image-making bear strong similarities with Cave 76, Cave 86, Cave 89, Cave 114, Cave 115 and Cave 156.

第 94 窟

第94窟位于西崖中部，东邻第60窟，西邻第191窟。开凿于北周（公元557年—公元581年）。该窟是麦积山受山体渗水严重的洞窟。

该窟内有五身造像。

形制：该窟是马蹄形、敞口、穹隆顶窟。

造像：正壁一尊坐佛，左、右壁各立一身弟子和一身菩萨，共计五身。

正壁佛，低平肉髻，面形圆润。内着僧祇支，外着双领下垂袈裟。双手施禅定印。结跏趺坐于台座上，下摆呈两瓣下垂。

左右壁弟子，衣着与主佛相同。其中左壁弟子，圆脸厚唇，面带微笑，体格敦实。左手下垂置于腹侧，右手似乎轻轻地指着衣领。跣足而立。身后绘多层同心圆项光。右壁弟子，圆脸突额。左手置于腹前，右手自然下垂于腿侧。穿履而立。

左右壁菩萨，戴花冠，面形圆润。上身袒露，下着长裙。颈戴项圈，帛带自双肩下垂至双膝再上卷至肘部下垂。跣足而立。其中左壁菩萨，右肩斜披粗大璎珞，提在左手，右手下垂置于腹部。右壁菩萨，肩部有圆形饰物，左手抚肩，右手下垂置于腿侧。

Cave 94

Cave 94 is located in the middle part of the western cliff, adjacent to Cave 60 in the east and Cave 191 in the west. It was dug in the Northern Zhou Dynasty (AD 557-581). It is a cave that is badly damaged by moisture seeping down within the friable rock.

In the cave visitors will enjoy five sculptures. Details are as follows.

Type: It is a horseshoe-shaped open niche with the "dome of heaven" ceiling.

Sculptures: A seated Buddha is modelled on the main wall, and a disciple and a bodhisattva stand on each side of the left and the right walls. There are five figures in all.

The Buddha on the main wall wears a low topknot with the round face. He is robed in an inner vest covering the left shoulder and armpits, an upper garment that completely covers his body, with U-shaped collar falling to the chest, the lappet of the robe resting on the left arm. With two hands in dhyana mudra, he is seated in dhyanasana on a throne with the hem of the robe falling in two large petals.

The robs of the disciple on the left and the right walls are identical with that of the principal Buddha. Among them the left-hand disciple has the round face and thick lips, with a smiling and a solid body. The left hand hangs down on the ventral side, and the right hand seems to be lightly fingering the collar of his robe. He stands barefoot. There is a circular aureole composed of multi-tiered concentric circles behind him. The right-hand disciple has the round face with the protruding forehead. The left hand is put in front of the abdomen, and the right hand falls down naturally beside the thigh. He stands in shoes.

The bodhisattvas on the left and right walls wear crowns with the round and full faces.

引申与拓展

该窟布局在麦积山最早的一佛二菩萨模式基础上增加到五像，左右壁各增塑一身弟子。增设的弟子形体小于菩萨，以突出主佛。作为佛的贴身侍从，二弟子在一定意义上代表了普通人，为高高在上的神界增添了一抹人间情感，从而拉近了与崇拜者心理距离。

Their upper bodies are bare, with the long dresses on their lower bodies. They are decorated with collars around the necks, their scarfs hanging in a loop from both shoulders and down to knees and up to the elbows and down again, standing barefoot. Among which a heavy garland of the left-hand bodhisattva hangs in a loop from the right shoulder, which is held in her left hand, and the right hand is put in front of the abdomen. The right-hand bodhisattva, each shoulder decorated with a circular ornament, the left hand is put on the shoulder, while the right hand drooping beside the thigh.

Extension and Elaboration

The layout of the cave is increased to five figures on the basis of the earliest pattern of a Buddha flanked by two bodhisattvas at Maijishan, adding a disciple on each side of the left and right walls. The additional disciples are smaller than the neighbouring bodhisattvas in size to emphasize the principal Buddha. As the personal attendants of the Buddha, the two disciples represents ordinary people in a sense, adding a touch of human emotion to the superior divine world, thus narrowing the psychological distance with the worshippers.

第 98 窟 西崖大佛

第98窟位于西崖中部，开凿于北魏（公元386年—公元534年），宋代（公元960年—公元1279年）重修。因三尊摩崖高浮雕像，也被称为"西崖大佛"，是麦积山石窟两组摩崖大佛造像之一。虽然形体略小于第13窟"东崖大佛"，但是造像年代却早了近一百年。

该窟为麦积山石窟另一组，一佛二菩萨石胎泥塑造像洞窟，直接在崖面上雕凿的大型造像。

形制：该窟是摩崖龛，高14米、宽10米、深1米。

造像：摩崖石胎泥塑一佛二菩萨，共计三身。宋代修复了造像泥层。

主佛高12米，螺髻，有肉髻珠，面形丰满，眉间白毫相。内着僧祇支，腰间束带，外着通肩袈裟。左臂屈肘前伸，手已残。右手自然下垂握袈裟衣角。两眼平视，赤足立于悬空云头上。

左侧菩萨高7.7米。外敷泥均已脱落，仅残存裙裾，石胎外露，可见木桩孔眼及木桩架。右侧菩萨高8米，头戴宝冠，长披发。方圆脸，佩戴项圈。内穿僧祇支，下系长裙。肩搭帔帛，胸前垂挂长璎珞至膝。左手提挑形物于腹侧，右手于胸前持莲蕾，赤足立于悬空云朵上。

Cave 98

Cave 98 is located in the middle part of the western cliff, and was initially excavated in the Northern Wei Dynasty (AD 386-534) and repaired in the Song Dynasty (AD 960-1279). It is also called "Great Triad on the Western Cliff" for the three colossal figures modelled in high relief on the cliff face. It is one of the two groups of colossal figures carved on the cliff face at Maijishan. Although their size is slightly smaller than that of Cave 13 (Great Triad on the Eastern Cliff), but the dating of image-making is nearly a hundred years earlier.

Visitors can enjoy another group of figures at Maijishan more closely, with a Buddha flanked by two bodhisattvas built up in clay plaster over a core of rock, and the three colossal figures carved on the cliff face. Details are as follows.

Type: It is an open niche on the cliff face, with 14 meters high, 10 meters wide, 1 meter deep.

Sculptures: A Buddha flanked by two bodhisattvas are built up in clay plaster over a core of rock. There are three figures in all. The thin skin of clay plaster was restored in the Song Dynasty.

The principal Buddha is 12 meters high with a spiral-shaped topknot, a bead between the bun and the bottom hair, and the full face is carved with the white hair between the brows. He wears an inner vest covering the left shoulder and armpits, a sash tied round the waist, an upper garment that completely covers his body and hangs in heavy folds round his shoulders. His left arm is elevated to the chest level with the hand damaged. The right hand hangs down naturally holding the corner of the rob. With eyes looking straight ahead, he stands barefoot on the suspended cloud heads.

The bodhisattva on the left is 7.7 meters high. All her thin skin of clay plaster has peeled away, leaving the hems, the core of rock exposed, and the pile holes and wooden armature are visible. The bodhisattva on the right is 8.0 meters high, with the hair gathered high encircled by a diadem and falling down the back. The round face is carved with a collar round the neck. She is robed in an inner vest covering the left shoulder and armpits, and

第98窟西崖大佛远景

引申与拓展

　　该窟和第13窟是麦积山两组摩崖大佛造像，直接在崖面上雕凿的大型造像。体量都比较大，采用的艺术手法多种多样，可以是高浮雕，也可以是浅浮雕或线刻。限于崖面，内容基本上都是一佛二菩萨的组合。

the lower body in a long dress. The scarf covers both shoulders, and the long garland hangs from the shoulders and down to the knees. The left hand is placed to the abdomen holding a peach-shaped object, and the right hand is elevated to the chest level holding a lotus bud, who stands barefoot on the suspended cloud heads.

Extension and Elaboration

Cave 98 and Cave 13 are two groups of colossal figures carved on the cliff face at Maijishan, the colossal figures carved on the cliff face. The size is relatively larger, and a variety of artistic techniques are adopted, either in high relief, or shallow relief or line carving. Limited to the cliff surface, the content of cliff carvings is basically a group of a Buddha flanked by two bodhisattvas.

第100窟

第100窟位于西崖西上区,开凿于北魏(公元386年—公元534年)。为麦积山重要早期洞窟中的三佛龛,造像留有多次整修痕迹。

该窟内有五身泥塑造像,三十八身影塑造像。留在右壁佛项光内和左壁佛座正面的四则刻画和墨书题记。

形制:该窟是平面方形、平顶窟。前壁开门,正壁低坛基上设一个"工"字形台座,左右二壁各作一个三重半圆形莲台,左右两壁各开一大龛。四壁和左右壁大龛内均开有小龛,现存三十二个。

造像:窟内正壁和左右壁龛内各塑一坐佛,左右二壁前各站立一菩萨,四壁和左右壁大龛内三十二个小龛,内贴三十八身影塑坐佛和菩萨,共计四十三身。

正壁和左右壁龛三佛,低平肉髻,圆脸。着双领下垂袈裟,结跏趺坐于台座上。其中正壁佛双手胸前结智拳印,左右壁龛佛双手结禅定印。

左右壁菩萨姿势和特征相同,一个是另一个的镜像。戴三珠

Cave 100

Cave 100 is located in the upper west part of the western cliff, and it was dug in the Northern Wei Dynasty (AD 386-534). It is the important early three Buddhas niches at Maijishan, and the sculptures remain many traces of refurbishment.

In the cave visitors will enjoy five sculptures modelled in clay, 38 figures in relief. Four inscriptions are carved or written with a brush in the aureole of the Buddha on the right wall and on the front of the throne of the Buddha on the left wall. Details are as follows.

Type: It is a flat square niche with a flat ceiling. There is a door on the front wall, an I-shaped throne is set on the low base of the main wall. A three-tier semicircular lotus platform is built on two flanking walls into which a large niche is cut. A recess is carved into each of the four walls and large ones on the left and right walls, now remaining 32.

Sculptures: A seated Buddha occupies the main wall and the niche into the left and right walls, a bodhisattva standing on each side of the flanking walls, 38 seated Buddhas and bodhisattvas in relief are inserted into 32 recesses which are cut into each of the four walls and two large niches on the left and right walls. There are 43 figures in all.

Three Buddhas on the main wall and the niche into the left and right walls bear low topknots with the round faces. They are robed in upper garments that completely cover their bodies, with U-shaped collars falling to the chests, the lappet of the robes resting on the left arms. They sit in dhyanasana on the thrones. Among them the Buddha on the main wall performs the vajra mudra (Fist of Wisdom) on the chest, while those into the niche on the left and right walls are in dhyana mudra.

The postures and characteristics of two bodhisattvas on each of the side walls are identical,

冠，长发披肩。圆脸长颈，身材修长。上身袒露，戴桃形项圈、臂串和手镯。左肩斜披络腋，下穿羊肠裙，裙子紧裹腿，裙纹为突起的圆弧形。帔巾从双肩搭下穿肘飘动外扬，身体微扭，赤足立于莲台上。其中左壁菩萨左手下垂持净瓶，右手拈花于胸前。右壁菩萨姿势相反。

影塑坐佛均结跏趺坐，分别着圆领通肩袈裟或袒右袈裟，双手结禅定印。影塑菩萨分为思惟菩萨、交脚菩萨和胁侍菩萨。

壁画：绘画大多脱落，左右壁大龛窟顶依稀可辨数身飞天和比丘。

题记：右壁佛项光内和左壁佛座前留有四则刻画和墨书题记。

引申与拓展

该窟布局与第128窟相同。两侧壁上部各一小龛，内塑一佛。前壁门上方两小龛，内塑一佛或一佛二菩萨。

one is a mirror image of the other. They wear three bead-shaped crowns with long hair trailing over shoulders. Their faces are round and necks are long, they are slender and long-legged. Their upper bodies are bare, decorated with peach-shaped collars, arm strings and bracelets. They are dressed in the upper throwing a strong diagonal across the body, leaving the right side of the body and shoulder bare, the lower sheath dresses melting against the legs with drapery in raised rippling curves. The scarves coming from shoulders coil in loops at the arms fluttering in the wind on each side, they stand on the lotus platforms with the slightly swaying curves of their bodies. Among them the left hand of the bodhisattva on the left wall hangs down holding a vase, while the right hand is raised to the chest holding a lotus. The posture of the right-hand bodhisattva is opposite.

All the Buddhas in relief are seated in dhyanasana, either robed in upper garments with a roll collar that completely cover their bodies and hangs in heavy folds round their shoulders or the outer robes thrown over the left shoulder or the upper throwing a strong diagonal across the body, leaving the right side of the body and shoulder bare. Their two hands perform the dhyana mudra. Bodhisattvas in relief fall into cross-ankled bodhisattvas, bodhisattvas in pensive pose and attendant bodhisattvas.

Paintings: Most paintings have fallen away, and several flying apsaras and bhikkhus on the ceilings of the two large niches on the left and right walls are vaguely discernible.

Inscriptions: There are four inscriptions carved or written with a brush left by the visitors in the aureole of the Buddha on the right wall and on the front of the throne of the Buddha on the left wall.

Extension and Elaboration

The layout in the cave is the same as that in Cave 128. A niche containing a Buddha is carved on either side of the flanking walls. Two niches containing a Buddha or a Buddha flanked by two bodhisattvas cut above the door on the front wall.

第101窟

第101窟位于西崖西上区,开凿于北魏(公元386年—公元534年)。

该窟内有六尊泥塑造像,窟顶大圆莲壁画,三则留在正壁右侧、左壁右侧和左壁佛身光内的刻画题记。

形制:该窟是平面方形、平顶窟。正、左、右三壁前设方形台座,地面凿低坛基。

造像:窟内现存正壁塑一佛及二胁侍菩萨,左壁一交脚菩萨,右壁一坐佛和一胁侍菩萨,共计六身。

正壁佛和右壁佛,旋涡纹高肉髻,面相丰圆。内着僧祇支,衣带胸前打结下垂,外着双领下垂袈裟。双手已毁,结跏趺坐于台座上,下摆分三片覆盖座前。

左、右侧弟子,衣着与主佛相同。双手合十于胸前,穿履向佛而立。其中左侧弟子束螺形发髻,双手已毁。右侧弟子,光头,身后浮塑莲瓣形身光。

左壁交脚菩萨,束扇形高髻,面容圆润,细颈削肩。颈戴宽桃

Cave 101

Cave 101 is located on the upper west part of the western cliff, and was dug in the Western Wei Dynasty (AD 535-556).

Visitors in this cave can appreciate six clay sculptures, paintings of large circular lotus on the ceiling, three inscriptions carved on the right of the main wall, in mandorlas on the right of the left wall and the Buddha on the left wall. Details are as follows.

Type: It is a flat square niche with the flat ceiling. A square throne is set on each of the main wall and two side walls, and a low base is cut around the ground.

Sculptures: A Buddha flanked by two attendant bodhisattvas are modelled on the main wall, a cross-ankled bodhisattva on the left wall, a seated Buddha and an attendant bodhisattva on the right wall. There are six figures in all.

The Buddhas on the main and the right walls bear the spiral-shaped high topknots with the full faces. They are robed in inner vests covering the left shoulder and armpits, with a band tied at the chest and falling, the upper garments that completely cover their bodies, with U-shaped collar falling to the chest, the lappet of the robes resting on the left arm. With two hands lost, they sit in dhyanasana on the thrones with hem covering the thrones in three large lotus petals.

The clothing of the disciples on either side is identical with that of the principal Buddha. With palms pressed together at the chests, they stand in shoes turning to the Buddha. Among them the left-hand disciple wears a spiral-shaped topknot with both hands damaged. The right-hand disciple is bald-headed backed by a lotus petal-shaped mandorla

形项圈。内着交领衫，衣带腹前打结下垂。下着贴体长裙。身后浮塑莲瓣形身光。双臂伸于胸前，双手惨毁。右壁胁侍菩萨，五官和体格与交脚菩萨相似。外着宽袖长袍，下着长裙。帛带自肩部下垂于膝部交叉，再上卷搭于双臂下垂。左臂上举，右臂置于腹前，双手均残。

壁画：窟顶绘大圆莲，四角绘一朵小圆莲，交替出现数身飞天。

题记：正壁右侧、左壁右侧和左壁佛身光内留有三则刻画题记，其中两则留于公元937年和公元1201年。

引申与拓展

该窟菩萨服饰、头部和头饰的表现方式与第93窟和第121窟侍从像相似，可能出自同一雕塑师之手。

in relief.

The cross-ankled bodhisattva on the left wall wears a high fan-shaped topknot, the round and full face with thin neck and narrow shoulders. A broad peach-shaped collar is decorated around the neck. He is robed in an inner garment with a collar folded across in front, with a band tied at the abdomen and falling in a knot, the lower body in a long dress melting the body. There is a lotus petal-shaped mandorla in relief behind him. The two arms are placed to the chest with both hands broken. The features and physique of the attendant bodhisattva on the right wall are similar to those of the cross-ankled bodhisattva. She is dressed in an outer robe with long and loose sleeves, a long dress on the lower body. The scarf comes over the shoulders and down to cross at the knees, then up rest on the arms and down naturally. The left arm is lifted, and the right arm is put at the abdomen with both hands damaged.

Paintings: A large circular lotus is painted on the ceiling, a small round lotus at four corners with the alternation of several flying apsaras.

Inscriptions: There are three carved inscriptions left by the visitors on the right of the main wall, in mandorlas on the right of the left wall and the Buddha on the left wall. Among which two are of AD 937 and AD1201.

Extension and Elaboration

The costume, treatment of the head and headdress in the cave are similar to those attendant images in Cave 93 and Cave 12l, and may have been modelled by the same sculptor.

第102窟

第102窟位于西崖西上区,开凿于西魏(公元535年—公元556年)。该窟维摩诘为俊俏的青年形象。

该窟内有五尊泥塑造像。

形制:该窟是平面方形、四角攒尖顶。高2.9米、宽2.88米、进深2.75米。圆拱形窟门,正壁和左壁前有台座,窟内地面凿低坛基。

造像:窟内正壁塑一佛及二胁侍菩萨,左壁维摩诘及右侧弟子,共计五身。

正壁佛,高1.2米。旋涡纹高肉髻,面相丰圆,脸部有贴金痕迹。内着僧祇支,腰间系带,外着双领下垂袈裟。右手无畏印,左手与愿印,结跏趺坐于台座,下摆分两片覆盖座前。

左右侧菩萨,中分式发髻,头戴花冠,圆脸。帛带自肩部下垂于腹前穿环交叉后上绕穿肘自然垂下。左侧菩萨内着交领衫,胸前系带,下着裙。左手下垂腿侧提玉环,右手置于胸前。右侧菩萨内着尖领衣,外着交领宽袖长袍。左手置于腹前,右手下垂腿侧提桃

Cave 102

Cave 102 is located on the upper west part of the western cliff, and was dug in the Western Wei Dynasty (AD 535-556). Vimalakirti in the cave is a handsome youth image.

Visitors in this cave can appreciate five clay sculptures. Details are as follows.

Type: It is a flat square niche with the "dome of heaven" ceiling. It is 2.9 meters high, 2.88 meters wide and 2.75 meters deep. With a chaitya arched door, a throne is set on each of the main wall and the left wall, and a low base is cut around the ground.

Sculptures: A Buddha flanked by two attendant bodhisattvas are modelled on the main wall, and Vimalakirti and his disciple on the right are made on the left wall. There are five figures in all.

The Buddha on the main wall is 1.2 meters high, with a spiral-shaped high topknot, the full face covered with traces of gilding. He is robed in an inner vest covering the left shoulder and armpits, with a band tied at the waist, an upper garment that completely covers his body, with U-shaped collar falling to the chest, the lappet of the robe resting on the left arm. With his right hand in the abhaya mudra, and his left hand in the varada mudra, he sits in dhyanasana on the throne with hem covering the throne in two large lotus petals.

Two flanking bodhisattvas bear the topknots parted down the middle, with the crowns and the round faces. The scarves come over the shoulders and down to pass through a ring over the lower abdomens, then up through the elbows and down naturally. The bodhisattva on the left wears an inner garment with a collar folded across in front, with a band tied at the chest, a dress on the lower body. The left hand hangs down beside the thigh holding a jade

形玉璧。

左壁维摩诘，高0.96米。头戴卷荷帽，长圆脸，目视前方。内着圆领衫，胸前系带打结，外着宽博外衣。左手抚膝，袖口反卷至上臂。右臂屈举于胸前，手已毁。结跏趺坐于台座，衣摆分两片，卷云状垂于台座前。

右侧弟子，头部已残，残高0.75米。内着僧祇支，外着袒右袈裟。左手掩于衣袖中，右手提净瓶。足已失。

引申与拓展

该窟维摩诘和第123窟同为青年形象，但衣着不同。第123窟维摩诘着汉服，而该窟杂糅了胡汉服装与北魏晚期以来流行的褒衣博带式佛装。

ring, and the right hand is placed to the chest. The bodhisattva on the right is robed in a pointed-collar garment, an outer crossed-collar robe with loose sleeves. The left hand is lifted to the abdomen, and the right hand hangs down beside the thigh holding a peach-shaped jade.

Vimalakirti on the left wall is 0.96 meters high. He wears a hat with rolled brim, the oval face with eyes looking ahead. He is robed in an inner garment with a circular collar, a band tied at the chest falling in a knot, and a loose gown with wide girdle. His left hand rests on knee with sleeve rolled up to the upper arm. His right arm is raised over the chest with hand destroyed. He sits in dhyanasana on the throne with hem covering the throne in two large curly clouds.

The disciple on the right with the head broken is 0.75 meters high. He bears an inner vest covering the left shoulder and armpits, the outer robe thrown over the left shoulder or the upper throwing a strong diagonal across the body, leaving the right side of the body and shoulder bare. Concealing the left hand in the sleeve, he holds a vase in his right hand. The feet have disappeared.

Extension and Elaboration

Vimalakirti in the cave and in Cave 123 are both young images, but in different clothing. In Cave 123 he is in Han costume while here he has mixed Hu-Han clothing and the loose gown with wide girdle popular since the late Northern Wei Dynasty.

第105窟

第105窟位于西崖西上区,开凿于西魏(公元535年—公元556年),宋代(公元960年—公元1279年)重修。该窟是麦积山又一个常见三佛龛中主佛缺失的例子。该三佛窟中出现了弟子形象。

该窟内有八身泥塑造像,窟顶十三排千佛绘画。

形制:该窟是平面方形、平顶。正、左、右三壁各开一圆拱形浅龛并各设一个台座。

造像:正壁主佛已失,左右两侧各塑一身弟子。左右壁各塑一佛二菩萨,共计八身。

正壁左右侧弟子,内穿僧祇支,外着袒右袈裟。其中左侧弟子,光头圆脸,双手胸前托钵,穿云头履立于圆莲台上。右侧弟子,浓眉高鼻,额头布满皱纹,跣足立于圆莲台上。

左右壁佛,宋代重修。低肉髻,面形方圆。内穿僧祇支,外着双领下垂袈裟。结跏趺坐于台座上,下摆分两片垂覆于座前。

左壁二菩萨,束发髻,面形方圆,颈戴桃形项圈。上穿僧祇支,帔帛搭肩自然下垂,下着长裙。左手持玉环自然下垂,右手置于胸前。立于圆莲台上。右壁二菩萨,左手惨毁,右手下垂提净

Cave 105

Cave 105 is located on the upper west part of the western cliff. It was originally dug in the Western Wei Dynasty (AD 535-556) and repaired in the Song Dynasty (AD 960-1279). It is another example of the usual three Buddhas niches at Maijishan with the loss of the principal Buddha. The image of the disciples appears in this three Buddhas cave.

Visitors can appreciate eight clay sculptures, paintings of 13 rows of the Thousand Buddhass on the ceiling. Details are as follows.

Type: It is a flat square niche with a flat ceiling. A chaitya arched shallow niche is cut into each of the main wall and two flanking walls, in which a throne is set respectively.

Sculptures: The principal Buddha on the main wall has disappeared, only a disciple standing on his either side. A Buddha flanked by two bodhisattvas are modelled on the left and the right walls. There are eight figures in all.

The disciples on the left and right of the main wall are robed in inner vests covering the left shoulder and armpits, the outer robes thrown over the left shoulder or the upper throwing a strong diagonal across the bodies leaving the right side of the body and shoulder bare. Among them, the left-hand disciple has a bald head and the round face, his two hands are raised to the chest holding a bowl, standing on the circular lotus platform in cloud head shoes. The right-hand disciple wears thick brows and high nose, with wrinkled forehead, standing on the circular lotus platform barefoot.

The Buddhas on the left and right walls are remodelled in the Song Dynasty. They wear low topkonts and the square faces. They are robed in inner vests covering the left shoulder and armpits, upper garments that completely cover the bodies, with U-shaped collar falling to the chests, the lappet of the robes resting on the left arm and down to the left knee. They sit

瓶，或左手垂于身侧，右手持莲蕾于腹前。

壁画：窟顶绘十三排千佛，形象基本可辨。

引申与拓展

该窟虽然主佛缺失，但两身弟子和第92窟一样出现在主佛两侧，侍立在旁。

in dhyanasana on the thrones with the hem covering in two large lotus petals.

The two bodhisattvas on the left wall bear topknots and the round faces, with peach-shaped collars around the necks. They are dressed in inner vests covering the left shoulder and armpits, their broad scarves come over the shoulders and down naturally, with their lower bodies on long dresses. The left hands hang down naturally holding a jade ring, and the right hands placed on the chests, standing on the circular lotus platforms. The left hand of the two bodhisattvas on the right wall has broken, and the right hand hangs down holding a vase. Or the left hand falls down beside the thigh, the right hand is put on the abdomen holding a lotus bud.

Paintings: 13 rows of the Thousand Buddhass are painted on the ceiling, and the images are almost discernible.

Extension and Elaboration

Although the loss of the principal Buddha in the cave, the two disciples stand in attendance on his either side, the same as that in Cave 92.

第112窟

第112窟位于西崖西上部,开凿于北魏(公元386年—公元534年),是麦积山又一个常见三佛龛中主佛缺失的例子。

该窟内有四身泥塑造像,八身影塑小造像,窟顶和四角圆莲及绕莲飞行的飞天绘画,留在左壁龛内和主佛身光周围的五则刻画和墨书题记。

形制:该窟是平面方形平顶龛。正、左、右三壁各开一个浅圆拱形龛并设台座,左右壁与前壁转角处各有一莲台。

造像:正壁龛内主佛已失。左右壁龛各塑一坐佛。左右壁与前壁转角处各塑一站立力士。八身影塑造像分别贴于壁面、龛内、龛柱上。其中五身坐佛于正壁上部、左、右壁龛柱上、左壁龛内、前壁上方,左壁龛内一身供养人和一身供养菩萨,右壁龛内一身立像,共计十二身造像。

左右壁佛,磨光高肉髻,面形长方。内穿僧祇支,外着双领下垂袈裟。双手施禅定印。结跏趺坐于长方形台座上,下摆层叠垂覆于座前。

第二章 麦积山石窟汉英解说词

Cave 112

Cave 112 is located in the upper west part of the western cliff and was dug in the Northern Wei Dynasty (AD 386-534). It is another example of the usual three Buddhas niches at Maijishan with the loss of the principal Buddha.

Visitors will enjoy four clay sculptures, eight small Buddhas modelled in relief, circular lotuses painted on the ceiling and at the four corners surrounded by flying apsaras, and five inscriptions carved or written with a brush in the niche on the left wall and around the mandorla of the principal Buddha. Details are as follows.

Type: It is a flat square niche with flat ceiling. A shallow chaitya arched bay is carved into the main wall and each of the flanking walls in which a throne is set respectively. There is a lotus platform built at the corner between the niches of each flanking walls and the front wall.

Sculptures: The principal Buddha in the niche on the main wall has lost. A seated Buddha is modelled in each niche into the side walls. A dvarapala stands at the corners between the niches of each flanking walls and the front wall. Eight small images in relief are applied respectively to the walls, in the niches and columns of the niches. Among which five seated Buddhas above the main wall, to the columns of the niches on the left and the right walls, in the niche on the left, and above the front wall, a donor and a votive bodhisattva in the niche into the left wall, and a standing figure in the niche into the right wall. There are 12 figures in all.

The Buddhas on the left and right walls bear polished high topknots and the rectangle faces. They are robed in inner vests covering the left shoulder and armpits, upper garments that completely cover the bodies, with U-shaped collar falling to the chests, the lappet of

左右壁与前壁转角处力士，束低发髻，眼窝深陷，怒目圆睁，颈部肌肉凸起，表情凶悍。帛带搭肩自然下垂。上身袒露，腰系长裙，束带打结下垂并配有玉璧。跨步立于莲台上。其中左力士，张口，双手残缺。右力士，双臂屈肘上举紧握拳，双唇紧闭。

壁画：窟顶中心和四角绘圆莲，周围飞天环绕。

题记：左壁龛内和主佛身光周围留有五则墨书和刻画题记。

引申与拓展

该窟内一对力士站在左右壁与前壁转角处。右力士用他高举的手臂和凶悍的表情威胁着任何胆敢越过他右边门槛的信仰敌人。护法成双出现在洞窟门口作为守门神似乎是麦积山最早的圆塑造像。我们在第4窟、第112窟和第154窟都可以找到更多例子。

the robes resting on the left arm and down to the left knee. Their two hands are in dhyana mudra. They sit in dhyanasana on the rectangle thrones with the hem cascading them in large folded loops.

The dvarapalas at the corners between the niches of each flanking walls and the front wall wear their hair in low ushnishas right on the top, the sunken eyes are round open in fury attitude, with bulging muscles on the necks and fierce expressions. Their broad scarves hang over the shoulders and down naturally. Their upper bodies are bare, the waists are wrapped with long dresses, a band tied around the waists falling in a knot decorated with a jade. They stand on the lotus platforms at a stride. Among which the left-hand dvarapala keeps his mouth open, with two hands missing. The two arms of the right-hand dvarapala are lifted over the head with clenched fists, leaving lips closed.

Paintings: The circular lotuses are painted in the center of the ceiling and at the four corners surrounded by flying apsaras.

Inscriptions: There are five inscriptions carved or written with a brush in the niche into the left wall and around the mandorla of the principal Buddha.

Extension and Elaboration

A pair of dvarapalas stand at the corners between the niches of each flanking walls and the front wall. The right-hand dvarapala threatens any enemy of the faith who dares to cross the threshold to his right with his raised arm and fierce expression. The guardian appears in pair at the gate of the cave as the dvarapalas, seems to be the earliest sculptures in the round at Maijishan. We can find more examples in Cave 4, Cave 112 and Cave 154.

第114窟

第114窟位于西崖西上区,东邻第115窟,西邻第179窟。开凿于北魏(公元386年—公元534年),是麦积山现存十一个三佛窟之一。

该窟内有五身泥塑造像、二十身影塑造像,窟顶圆莲图案,留在正壁佛身光内、左壁龛楣和右壁龛内的十二则刻画或者墨书题记。

形制:该窟是平面方形、平顶窟,前壁坍塌。正壁砌长方形基座。左右两壁凿浅方拱龛并各设台座。窟内正、左、右三壁设小坛台。

造像:正壁塑一身坐佛。左右壁龛内各塑一身坐佛,龛外各立一身菩萨。正壁两侧两层坛台上贴塑十身造像,左右壁坛台上各贴四身或三身坐佛。左右壁龛楣上方残存两身或者一身影塑飞天,共计二十五身。

正壁佛,磨光高肉髻,长方面形,宽额瘦颊,高鼻大耳。内着交领衣,外着通肩袈裟。施说法印。结跏趺坐于长方形台座上,下摆覆于台座上。身后浮塑莲瓣形身光,上方残存两身影塑飞天。

第二章　麦积山石窟汉英解说词

Cave 114

Cave 114 is located in the upper west part of the western cliff, adjacent to Cave 115 in the east and Cave 179 in the west. It was dug in the Northern Wei Dynasty (AD 386-534), and is one of the 11 three Buddhas caves survived at Maijishan.

In the cave visitors can appreciate five clay sculptures, 20 figures in relief, the motif of circular lotus on the ceiling, 12 carved inscriptions or with a brush left on the mandorla behind the Buddha on the main wall, on the lintel above the niche into the left wall and in the niche into the right wall. Details are as follows.

Type: It is a flat square niche with the flat ceiling, and the front wall has fallen away. A rectangular throne is built on the main wall. A shallow square arched recess is cut into each of the two flanking walls and each with a pedestal. There are little ledges on each of the main wall and two flanking walls.

Sculptures: A seated Buddha occupies the main wall. A seated Buddha is modelled in each niche into the side walls, outside which a bodhisattva stands. Ten sculptures in relief rest on the two-tier ledges on either side of the main wall, four or three seated Buddhas in relief are applied on the little ledges of the left and right walls. Two flying apsaras or a flying apsara in relief remain above the lintels of each niche into the flanking walls. There are 25 figures in all.

The Buddha on the main wall has a polished high topknot with the long face, wide forehead and thin cheeks, the high nose flanked by pendulous ears. He is robed in an inner garment of collar folded across in front and an outer garment that completely covers his body and hangs in heavy folds round his shoulders. With two hands in gesture of preaching, he sits with legs tightly locked in a yogic pose on a rectangle throne with the hem covering. There is a lotus petal-shaped mandorla in relief behind him, above which remain two flying

两侧两层坛台上对称影塑思惟菩萨和交脚菩萨，下面对称各二佛并坐。

左右壁龛佛，外貌和神态与正壁佛相似。施禅定印，结跏趺坐于台座上。上部影塑千佛。其中左壁龛佛着通肩袈裟，龛楣上方残存两身影塑无头飞天。右壁龛佛内着僧祇支，外着袒右袈裟。龛楣上方残存一身影塑无头飞天。

左壁龛右侧菩萨和右壁龛左侧菩萨，面形长圆，面带微笑。头戴三珠宝冠，颈饰宽项圈，袒胸露臂。斜披络腋，帛带披肩绕臂飘扬。下着长裙，跣足立于莲台上。身后浮塑莲瓣形背光，上贴四身或三身影塑坐佛。其中左壁龛右侧菩萨左手拈飘带，右手执莲蕾。右壁龛左侧菩萨手势相反。

壁画：窟顶绘有圆莲图案，左侧有一身飞天形象。

题记：正壁佛身光内、左壁龛楣和右壁龛内留有十二则刻画或者墨书题记。

引申与拓展

该窟三壁两龛，正壁一佛，两侧壁龛内各一佛。与第100窟属于同一时期。

apsaras in relief. The bodhisattva in pensive pose and the bodhisattva with ankles crossed in relief are applied symmetrically on two-tier ledges of both sides, below which two Buddhas symmetrically share the same throne.

The appearances and expressions of the Buddhas in the niches into the flanking walls are similar to those of the Buddha on the main wall. With two hands in dhyana mudra, they sit with legs tightly locked in a yogic pose on the thrones. The Thousand Buddhass in relief are applied above. Among which the Buddha in the niche on the left wall is dressed in a garment that completely covers his body and hangs in heavy folds round his shoulders. Two headless flying apsaras in relief remain above its lintel. The Buddha in the niche on the right wall is robed in an inner vest covering the left shoulder and armpits, the outer robe thrown over the left shoulder or the upper throwing a strong diagonal across the body, leaving the right side of the body and shoulder bare. A headless flying apsara in relief survives above its lintel.

The right-side bodhisattva in the niche into the left wall and the left-side bodhisattva in the niche into the right wall have the long round faces with a smile. They bear the crowns adorned with a pearl on three sides, the broad collars around the necks, with the chests and arms exposed. They are dressed in the upper throwing a strong diagonal across the bodies, leaving the right side of the body and shoulder bare, the scarves come from shoulders and down through the armpits fluttering in the wind on each side. Wearing long dresses on their lower bodies, they stand on the lotus platforms barefoot. There are the lotus petal-shaped mandorlas in relief behind them, above which four or three seated Buddhas in relief are applied. Among them the right-side bodhisattva in the niche into the left wall holds a ribbon in the left hand, and a lotus bud in the right hand. The left-side bodhisattva in the niche into the right wall performs the opposite gesture.

Paintings: The ceiling is painted with a circular lotus pattern, and on the left there is an image of a flying apsara.

Inscriptions: There are 12 inscriptions carved or with a brush left by visitors on the mandorla behind the Buddha on the main wall, on the lintel above the niche on the left wall and in the niche on the right wall.

Extension and Elaboration

The cave contains three walls and two niches, a Buddha on the main wall and a Buddha in each niche into the two side walls. It belongs to the same period as Cave 100.

第115窟

第115窟位于西崖西上部,开凿于北魏(公元386年—公元534年)。保留麦积山石窟中最早也是唯一有确切纪年的开窟题记,对确定麦积山石窟一些相同洞窟的年代提供证据。

该窟内有三身泥塑造像,六身影塑小坐佛,窟壁佛教因缘故事和窟顶盘龙飞天,主尊佛座上麦积山最早的一则墨书题记。

形制:该窟是平面方形平顶龛,窟高1.07米、宽1.06米、进深1.3米。地面正、左、右三壁前凿低坛基,左、右壁上部各有两层低坛台。正壁前有长方形台座,左、右壁前各有一圆形莲台。

造像:正壁塑一身坐佛,左、右壁各塑一站立菩萨,左右壁上部泥塑小坛台上贴影塑六身小坐佛,共计九身造像。

主尊佛高0.62米,旋涡状高肉髻,面形方圆,双耳下垂。内穿僧祇支,外穿袒右袈裟。右手作说法印,左手施与愿印,结跏趺坐于长方形"工"字形高座上。身后浮塑莲瓣形身光。

左右壁二胁侍菩萨高0.71米,面形长方,双目平视。戴三珠宝冠,斜披络腋,下穿羊肠裙。跣足立于半圆形坛台上,右手拈莲蕾于胸前,左手贴壁下垂。左壁菩萨左手提净瓶,而右壁菩萨左手握

第二章　麦积山石窟汉英解说词

Cave 115

Cave 115 is located in the upper west part of the western cliff, and was dug in the Northern Wei Dynasty (AD 386-534). It contains the earliest and unique dated inscription for the excavating of cave shrine at Maijishan, which offers evidence for dating of some identical caves at Maijishan.

Visitors will enjoy three clay sculptures, six small seated Buddhas modelled in relief, Buddhist karmic stories painted on the walls and the coiling dragon on the ceiling, and an earliest dated inscription with a brush on the throne of the principal Buddha at Maijishan. Details are as follows.

Type: It is a flat square niche with flat ceiling with 1.07 meters high, 1.06 meters wide and 1.3 meter deep. A low base is cut around the ground in front of the main wall and the side walls, two-tier ledges are built above each of the left wall and the right wall. A rectangle throne is set in front of the main wall and a circular lotus platform in front of the left and right walls.

Sculptures: A seated Buddha is modelled on the main wall, a standing bodhisattva on each of the side walls, and six small seated Buddhas in relief rest on the little ledges above each of the left wall and the right wall. There are nine figures in all.

The principal Buddha is 0.62 meters high, the hair and ushnisha arranged in whirlpool, the round face flanked by pendulous ears. He wears an inner vest covering the left shoulder and armpits, the outer robe thrown over the left shoulder or the upper throwing a strong diagonal across the body, leaving the right side of the body and shoulder bare. The Buddha sits in dhyanasana on the "I-shaped" high square throne, his right hand in the vitarka mudra, and his left hand in the varada mudra. There is a lotus petal-shaped mandorla in relief behind him.

飘带。身光中可见莲花纹和忍冬纹。

六身影塑小坐佛,模制,均高0.2米,皆施禅定印。根据衣饰分两种:一为着圆领通肩袈裟;一为内穿交领衣,外穿垂领式袈裟,右手从衣领处伸出。第二种影塑佛又见于第76窟,说明二窟为同时期所开。

壁画:该窟是早期装饰最丰富的洞窟之一。窟壁绘僧人坐禅、诵经、婆罗门、羽人等内容,表现某种佛教因缘故事。窟顶中心绘摩尼宝珠、盘龙,周围飞天环绕。

题记:该窟主佛座上墨书题记十三行、一百九十余字,为景明三年(公元502年)九月十五日上邽镇张元伯在此开窟造像的发愿文。

引申与拓展

根据发愿文的内容,其所造的造像具有明显的菩萨大乘特点,并且有强烈的神生兜率、信仰弥勒的思想,反映了这一时期麦积山石窟造像的特点和思想内涵。

The two attendant bodhisattvas on each of the side walls are 0.71 meters high, the square face with eyes looking straight ahead. They wear the crowns adorned with a pearl on three sides, with the upper throwing a strong diagonal across the bodies, leaving the right side of the body and shoulder bare, the lower sheath dresses melting against the bodies. They stand on the semicircular platforms barefoot, with right hands raised to the chest level holding a lotus bud, and the left hands flung back against the wall. The left-wall bodhisattva holds a vase in the left hand, and the right-wall bodhisattva grasps a ribbon in the left hand. The motifs of flame and and honeysuckle are visible in the mandorlas behind them.

Six small seated Buddhas in relief are made in moulds, with an average height of 0.2 meters, and hands in dhyana mudra. They are divided into two kinds according to their clothing, some robed in the upper garments with a roll collar that completely covers their bodies and hangs in heavy folds round their shoulders, and others are dressed in inner robes of necklines folded across in front, and the right shoulder of the outer robes hangs directly down to the wrist of the right hand, completely covering the right arm, the right hand outstretches from the long loose collar. The second type of Buddha figures in relief is also found in Cave 76, indicating that the two caves were excavated in the same period.

Paintings: It is one of the most richly decorated of the early caves. The walls are painted with the monks sitting in meditation, chanting sutras, Brahmins and divines with wings, presenting some kind of Buddhist karmic stories. The ceiling is decorated with a cintamanand, a coiling dragon in the center surrounded by flying apsaras.

Inscription: There is an inscription with a brush on the throne of the principal Buddha, running to 13 lines and over 190 characters, dated to September 15th in the third year of Jingming corresponding to AD 502, a dedication for the cave excavatings and image makings there by Zhang Yuanbo of Shanggui Township.

Extension and Elaboration

The content of the dedication indicates that the sculptures he made here bear obvious characteristics of the Bodhisattva Mahayana, and there is a strong thought of Maitreya Ascension to Tusita Heaven and faith in Maitreya, reflecting the characteristics and ideological connotations of the sculptures at Maijishan Caves during this period.

第117窟

第117窟位于西崖西上部,开凿于北魏(公元386年—公元534年),宋代(公元960年—公元1279年)重修。正壁原石雕坐佛像是麦积山石窟为数不多的雕刻精品,多次在国内展示。

该窟内有两身泥塑造像,窟顶大圆莲及绕莲飞行的飞天绘画。

形制:该窟是平面方形平顶龛。左右两壁各设一台座。

造像:正壁原一身西魏石刻主佛造像已移至文物库房。左右壁龛各塑一宋代重修坐佛,共计两身造像。

左右壁佛,头部惨毁,双肩浑圆。内穿僧祇支,外着双领下垂袈裟。袒胸露腹,衣带于腹前打结下垂。双手施智拳印。结跏趺坐于方形台座上,下摆呈半圆形垂覆于座前。身后存北魏原作莲瓣形身光。

壁画:窟顶中心绘大圆莲,周围飞天环绕。

Cave 117

Cave 117 is located in the upper west part of the western cliff, and it was originally dug in the Northern Wei Dynasty (AD 386-534) and repaired in the Song Dynasty (AD 960-1279). The original stone seated Buddha on the main wall is one of the rare elaborate carvings at Maijishan Caves, which has been displayed in China for many times.

Visitors will enjoy two clay sculptures, a large circular lotus painted on the ceiling surrounded by flying apsaras. Details are as follows.

Type: It is a flat square niche with flat ceiling. A throne is set on each of the flanking walls.
Sculptures: A stone carving image of the principal Buddha on the main wall has been moved to the cultural relics warehouse. A seated Buddha restored in the Song Dynasty is modelled on either side of the left and the right walls. There are two figures in all.

The heads of the Buddhas on the left and right walls have been damaged, who have round shoulders. They are robed in inner vests covering the left shoulder and armpits, upper garments that completely cover the bodies, with U-shaped collar falling to the chests, the lappet of the robes resting on the left arm and down to the left knee. Their chests and abdomens are bare, with a band tied at the abdomens falling in a knot. The two hands perform the vajra mudras on the chests. They sit in dhyanasana on the square thrones with the hem covering in semicircle folded loops. There are original lotus petal-shaped mandorlas painted in the Northern Wei Dynasty behind them.

Paintings: The ceiling is decorated with a large circular lotus in the center surrounded by flying apsaras.

引申与拓展

该窟正壁原石雕坐佛已移至文物库房巡展。虽然雕像的大部分身光残缺，但佛像的主体保存极为完好。涡旋纹高发髻，面部圆润饱满，细眉双目下视。衣着与左右壁佛相同。左手施与愿印，右臂置于胸前，右手残失。结跏趺坐在须弥座上，下摆呈多重褶皱如瀑布般覆盖座前，石绿、土红和黑色痕迹尚存。石雕佛座刻有公元984年和公元1283年的题记。右侧尚有浮塑右手持香炉和左手提花瓶做礼拜的弟子一身。

Extension and Elaboration

The original stone image of seated Buddha on the main wall has been moved to the cultural relics warehouse for itinerant exhibition. Although most part of the mandorla is broken off, the main body of the Buddha is extremely well preserved. He bears a spiral-shaped topknot with the round and full face, the arched browns sweeping above downcast eyes. His rob is identical with that of the Buddhas on the left and right walls. With his left hand in the varada mudra, the right arm raised to the chest with the hand missing, he sits in dhyanasana on the Sumeru throne with the hem cascading it in layered folds, traces of stone green, reddish-brown and black survive. There are two inscriptions carved on the throne from AD 984 and AD 1283. There is a worshipping disciple modelled in relief on the right carrying an incense-burner in his right hand and vase in his left hand.

第121窟

第121窟位于西崖西上部,开凿于北魏(公元386年—公元534年),宋代(公元960年—公元1279年)重修。该窟讨人喜欢的菩萨与弟子组像为麦积山世俗化造像的经典之作。

该窟内有十九身北魏原作、宋代修复和重塑的造像。

形制:该窟为平面方形、覆斗顶。窟高2.53米、宽2.36米、进深2.13米。前有方形甬道,窟内正、左、右三壁各开一圆拱龛,其中正壁龛内两侧塑小坛台。窟内地面作低坛基。

造像:正壁龛内塑一佛二弟子,两侧坛台上现存八身悬塑弟子(左五右三),龛外左右侧各塑一弟子。左右壁龛内各塑一身菩萨,龛外两侧各塑一身菩萨。前壁左右两侧各塑一身力士。其中正壁主佛及前壁左右二力士,头部为宋代重塑。左右二壁菩萨原为坐佛,宋代改塑为菩萨,其余为原作,共计十九身。

正壁龛内佛,高1.47米。头部以及上身部分为宋代重修,袈裟下摆为原作。低平肉髻,方面大耳。内着僧祇支,外着双领下垂袈裟。结跏趺坐于方台上,下摆搭于座前呈三瓣式下垂。右手施无畏印,左手拢袖抚膝。身后绘头光和身光。台座左右侧弟子,高0.75

Cave 121

Cave 121 is located in the upper west part of the western cliff. It was originally dug in the Northern Wei Dynasty (AD 386-534) and repaired in the Song Dynasty (AD 960-1279). The delightful groups of bodhisattvas and disciples are the classic work of the secular sculptures at Maijishan.

Visitors can appreciate 19 original works of the Northern Wei Dynasty, restorations and remodellings of the Song Dynasty. Details are as follows.

Type: It is a flat square niche with the upside-down *dou* ceiling, is 2.53 meters high, 2.36 meters wide and 2.13 meters deep. There is a square passage on the front wall, a chaitya arched bay is carved into the main wall and each of the flanking walls, among which a ledge is set on each side of the central niche. A low base is cut around the ground.

Sculptures: A Buddha flanked by two disciples occupies the niche into the main wall, eight disciples modelled in relief rest on each of its flanking ledges (five to the left and three to the right), and a disciple stands outside each side. A bodhisattva sits in each of the right and left niches with a bodhisattva standing outside the right and left sides. A dvarapala stands on either side of the front wall. Among them, the heads of the principal Buddha and two dvarapalas were remade in the Song Dynasty. The original seated Buddhas in the right and left niches were remodelled into bodhisattvas in the Song Dynasty. The rests are unrestored work. There are 19 figures in all.

The Buddha in the niche into the main wall is 1.47 meters high. The head and the upper part of the body were remodelled in the Song Dynasty, the hem of the robe is the original works. He has a low flat topknot, the square face flanked by pendulous ears. He is robed in an inner vest covering the left shoulder and armpits, an upper garment that completely covers his body, with U-shaped collar falling to the chest, the lappet of the robe resting on

米左右。左侧弟子左手拢袖于腰部，右手立掌于胸前。右侧弟子双手已残。小坛台上弟子均着厚重宽大的袈裟，不同相貌和神情，俯视着坐佛，身体弯曲成弧形。

正壁龛外两侧两组菩萨弟子像最引人注目。弟子双手合十，内着僧祇支，下着长裙，外穿宽博大衣。左弟子螺旋发髻。菩萨束扇形高髻，身材修长。身穿褒衣博带式上衣，下着长裙。天衣覆盖双肩。帛带自肩部下垂于膝部交叉，再上卷搭于双臂。足穿云头履而立。左侧菩萨右手置于腹前，左手屈于腹部。右侧菩萨左手持莲蕾于腹部，右手举于胸前，手指已残。菩萨与弟子头靠头，清秀俊美，面带笑意，似在窃窃私语，分享快乐。

左右壁龛内菩萨，高1.45米左右。原作和重修部分同于正壁龛内佛。顶作中分高发髻，颈部戴项链。结跏趺坐于台座上。其中左壁菩萨内着交领长袍，腰部系带，绕两臂下搭至膝部。左臂屈肘于腹前，左手已毁。右手施无畏印。右壁菩萨内着僧祇支，外着双领下垂袈裟，下摆分两片垂于台座前。左手施与愿印，右手施说法印。

前壁两侧二力士头部宋代重修。左力士袒上身，下着裙，披巾覆肩于胫部交叉后搭于双臂。左手持金刚杵立于脚下，右手提风带。右力士着交领宽袖上衣，下着长裙，外穿护身铠甲。双手拢袖垂于胯部。

the left arm. He is seated in dhyanasana on the throne with the hem covering it in three large petals. His right hand is in the abhaya mudra, and his left hand concealing in the sleeve rests on knee. He is backed by aureole and mandorla. The disciple on either side of the throne is about 0.75 meters high. The left-hand disciple conceals his left hand in sleeve at the waist, and his right hand is raised to the chest with fingers upward. Both hands of the right-hand disciple are damaged. The disciples on the little ledges wear the heavy loose robes with different features and expressions, looking down the seated Buddha, their bodies curved into an arc.

The two groups of bodhisattvas and disciples outside both sides of the niche into the main wall are the most striking. With clasped hands, the disciples are dressed in the inner vests covering the left shoulder and armpits, the long skirts on the lower bodies, with loose and broad overcoats worn above. The disciple on the left bears a spiral-shaped topknot. With fan-shaped high topknots and slender figures, the bodhisattvas are robed in the loose gowns with wide girdle and the long skirts on the lower bodies. Their outer shawls cover both shoulders. Their broad scarves hang over the shoulders and down to cross at the knees and up again rest on the arms. They stand in cloud head shoes. The left-hand bodhisattva places the right hand in front of the abdomen, and her left hand over the abdomen. The right-hand bodhisattva puts her left hand on the abdomen holding a lotus bud, and raises her right hand in front of the chest, with fingers mutilated. The bodhisattvas and disciples lean their heads towards each other, and they are beautiful and with smiles, they seem to be whispering and share joys.

The bodhisattvas in each of the right and left niches are about 1.45 meters high. The original and restored parts are identical with that of the Buddha in the niche on the main wall. They wear the high topknots parted down the middle with a collar round the neck. They are seated in dhyanasana on the thrones. Among which the left-niche bodhisattva is dressed in a long garment of a collar folded across in front tied at the waist with a sash, which rests on the arms and down to knees. The left arm is raised to the abdomen with hand destroyed. His right hand is in the abhaya mudra. The right-niche bodhisattva is robed in an inner vest covering the left shoulder and armpits, an upper garment that completely covers the body, with U-shaped collar falling to the chest, the lappet of the robe resting on the left arm, with the hem covering the throne in two large petals. The right hand is in the abhaya mudra, and the left hand in the varada mudra.

The heads of the two dvarapalas on either side of the front wall were remodelled in the Song Dynasty. With the upper body bare, the left-hand dvarapala wears a long dress on the lower body, the long broad scarf covers the shoulders and down to cross at the shins and up rests on the arms. His left hand holds a vajra at the feet, his right hand is placed beside the thigh holding a band. The right-hand dvarapala is dressed in an upper garment of a collar folded across in front and long loose sleeves, a long dress on the lower body, the protective armor worn above them. The hands concealing in the sleeves are placed on the hips.

引申与拓展

麦积山石窟北魏晚期造像不断呈现出生动活泼的表现形式。流行三佛主题,并配置以菩萨、弟子、比丘、比丘尼和力士或天王造像。该窟是很有代表性的洞窟。窟内菩萨与比丘、比丘尼肩和头靠拢在一起,他们的微笑仿佛在分享聆听佛说法的喜悦,又仿佛是人间的一对亲密朋友在窃窃私语。苏立文先生在其著作《麦积山石窟寺》❶中称两组菩萨弟子像是"麦积山所有洞窟中最富有想象力和最迷人的造像",并选择右侧组合为其著作封面,以此可以看出作者对该组造像的喜爱。

第121窟菩萨(左壁)

---

❶ SULLIVAN, M. Cave Temples of Maichishan [M]. London:Faber & Faber, 1969:27.

Extension and Elaboration

The vivid and lively representations of sculptures continue to appear in the late Northern Wei Dynasty at Maijishan. The popular theme is three Buddhas flanked by bodhisattvas, disciples, bhikkhus, bhikkhunis, and dvarapalas or heavenly kings. This cave is of very representative. The bodhisattvas and bhikkhus and bhikkhunis lean their shoulders and heads towards each other with their smiles, they seem to share the joy of listening to the Buddha's preaching, and also seem to be whispering just as a pair of close friends do. Mr. Sullivan describes the two groups of bodhisattvas and disciples as "the most imaginative and charming figures in all the caves" in *The Cave Temples of Maichi Mountain* (1969: 27), and chooses the pair on the right for the cover of his book, which indicates the writer's fondness for this group of figures.

第122窟

第122窟位于西崖西上层,开凿于北魏(公元386年—公元534年)。为麦积山重要早期洞窟中的三佛龛。

该窟内有八身泥塑造像,小坛台上四十四身影塑坐佛。

形制:该窟是平面方形、平顶窟。地面有低坛基。正、左、右壁前各设一台座。正壁和左壁上方各砌六层小坛台,右壁上方开七层小坛台。

造像:窟内正、左、右三壁各塑一坐佛。正壁左右两侧各立一身菩萨和一身弟子,左壁右侧和右壁左侧各一身菩萨,前壁左侧一身后塑弟子。三壁小坛台上贴影塑坐佛:正壁十三身、左壁十六身、右壁十五身,共计五十二身。

正壁和左右壁三佛,头部宋代重塑。中分式水波纹低肉髻,方面大耳,弯眉细目。内着僧祇支,外着双领下垂袈裟。结跏趺坐于长方形台座上,下摆呈三瓣覆盖座前。左手抚膝,右手施无畏印。身后浮塑莲瓣形头身光。

正壁左侧菩萨和右侧弟子,衣着与三佛相同。身体微扭,身后

Cave 122

Cave 122 is located at the upper west tier of the western cliff. It was dug in the Northern Wei Dynasty (AD 386-534). It is the important early three Buddhas niches at Maijishan.

In the cave visitors will enjoy eight sculptures modelled in clay, 44 seated Buddhas in relief on little ledges. Details are as follows.

Type: It is a flat square niche with a flat ceiling. A low base is cut around the ground. A pedestal throne is cut into each of the main wall and two flanking walls. Six-tier ledges are built above each of the main wall and the left wall, with seven-tier ledges above the right wall.

Sculptures: A seated Buddha occupies each of the main wall and two side walls. On the main wall stands a bodhisattva on the left and a disciple on the right, a bodhisattva on each of the right of the left wall and on the left of the right wall, a later restored disciple on the left of the front wall. Seated Buddhas in relief are inserted on little ledges into each of the three walls: 13 on the main wall, 16 on the left wall, 15 on the right wall. There are 52 figures in all.

The heads of three Buddhas on the main wall and the two side walls were remodelled in the Song Dynasty. They bear low topknots with water wavy parted down the middle, the square faces flanked by pendulous ears, with arched brows sweeping above gently opened almond eyes. They are robed in inner vests covering the left shoulder and armpits, upper garments that completely cover their bodies, with U-shaped collar falling to the chest, the lappet of the robe resting on the left arm and down to the left knee. They sit in dhyanasana on the rectangle thrones with the hems covering in three petals. Their left hands rest on knees, and the right hands in the abhaya mudras. There are lotus-petal shaped aureoles and mandorlas in relief behind them.

浮塑莲瓣形头身光。其中左侧菩萨，螺旋高发髻，面容清瘦，颈戴宽项圈。双手交合在胸前，右膝提起。右侧弟子，光头，面容清秀圆润。左手胸前持宝瓶，右手掩袖下垂。

左壁右侧和右壁左侧菩萨，高髻已残，戴项圈。内着僧祇支，下着长裙。帔帛于胸前交叉后再上卷搭于双臂，戴莲朵及鼓形璎珞。跣足立于坛基上，身后浮塑莲瓣形火焰纹身光。其中右侧菩萨，左臂前伸，左手残损。右手持宝石于胸前。左侧菩萨，左手持净瓶于髋部，右手持莲蕾于胸前。

前壁左侧弟子，光头，高鼻深目。内着僧祇支，外着袒右袈裟。左手腹前提帛带，右手持净瓶于腿侧。

小坛台上四十四身影塑坐佛，磨光高肉髻。衣着与三佛相似。左手握衣角垂于腹部，右手施无畏印。

引申与拓展

该窟正壁和右壁拐角处站立一组菩萨弟子组合，它们是正壁佛和右壁佛的侍从。因身体微扭，看起来似乎在相互交流。这组菩萨弟子组合与邻近的第121窟非常相似，均属于六世纪中期作品。

The dresses of the bodhisattva on the left and the disciple on the right of the main wall are identical with that of the three Buddhas. With the slightly swaying curves of their bodies, they are backed by lotus-petal shaped aureoles and mandorlas in relief. Among them the left-hand bodhisattva wears a high spiral-shaped topknot, the thin face is adorned with a broad collar around the neck. Two hands are raised in front of the chest with fingers crossed, the right knee is lifted. The right-hand disciple, bald with the delicately and fully made face. The left hand is put on the chest holding a vase, the right hand hangs down concealing in the sleeve.

The topknots of the bodhisattva on the right of the left wall and the left of the right wall are broken with collars around the necks. They are robed in inner vests covering the left shoulder and armpits, the long dresses on the lower bodies. Their broad scarves come over the shoulders and fall down to cross at the chests and up again rest on the arms, with heavy garlands composed of lotus flowers and drum-shaped motif hanging from the shoulders. They stand on the bases' barefoot backed by lotus-petal shaped mandorlas of flame motifs in relief. Among them, the left arm of the right-hand bodhisattva is lifted forward with the hand damaged, and the right hand holding a jewel to the chest level. The left hand of the bodhisattva on the left hangs down on the hip carrying a vase, and holding a lotus bud in the right hand on the chest level.

The disciple on the left of the front wall is bald, with high nose and sunken eyes. He is robed in an inner vest covering the left shoulder and armpits, the outer robe thrown over the left shoulder or the upper throwing a strong diagonal across the body, leaving the right side of the body and shoulder bare. His left hand is put on the abdomen with a ribbon passing between the fingers, while her right hand hangs down beside the thigh holding a vase.

44 seated Buddhas in relief on little ledges have polished high topknots. Their robs are identical with that of the three Buddhas. The left hands are put at the abdomens holding the corner of the robs, and the right hands perform the abhaya mudras.

Extension and Elaboration

A pair of a bodhisattva and a disciple standing at the corner between the main and the right walls in the cave, they are actually the attendants of the Buddha on the main wall and the Buddha on the right wall. With the slightly swaying curves of their bodies, they seem to be communicating with each other. This group of the bodhisattva and the disciple is very similar to that in the adjacent Cave 121, and both belongs to the work of the mid-sixth century.

第123窟

第123窟位于西崖西上层,开凿于西魏(公元535年—公元556年)。该洞窟是西魏造像保存最完整的窟龛之一,没有后塑或重绘的迹象。以塑像的形式表现《维摩诘经》,这是麦积山石窟"维摩诘变"的特点。而将世俗人物作为胁侍,充分体现了麦积山北朝晚期造像的世俗化特点。

该窟内有九尊木骨泥塑造像,正右壁面刻十则题记。

形制:该窟为平顶方形窟,高2.5米、宽2.34米、进深2.36米。地面四周凿高宽各0.3米的低坛基,正、左、右壁各开一圆拱形浅龛。左右壁龛前的坛基上做长方形佛座。

造像:正壁龛内塑一佛二菩萨,左壁龛内塑维摩诘,右壁龛内塑文殊菩萨,龛外里侧塑二弟子,外侧塑男女二侍者(童男、童女),共九身木骨泥塑造像,均为六世纪原作。

正壁坐佛生动秀美。头顶磨光高肉髻,双目下视,面部圆润,身躯微微前倾。穿双领下垂袈裟,下摆呈"八"字形垂至座前。右手施无畏印,左手施与愿印。背后残留白色项光和身光痕迹。

左右菩萨清秀、苗条。束高发髻,身穿交领宽袖服饰,下穿齐胸长裙。外披天衣,帔帛自双肩垂下,肩部各有一圆形饰物。一手自然下垂,一手置于腹部,脚蹬云头履而立。

Cave 123

Cave 123 is located at the upper west tier of the western cliff. It was dug in the Western Wei Dynasty (AD 535-556). It is one of the most intact niches containing sculptures of the Western Wei Dynasty, which shows no evidence of later restoration or repainting. The represertation of the *Vimalakirti Sutra* in the form of sculptures is a characteristic of "the Vimalakirti Sutra Illustration" at Maijishan Caves. The secular figures modelled as attendants fully reflect the secularization characteristic of image-making in the late Northern Dynasty at Maijishan.

Visitors will enjoy nine figures of clay modelled on a wooden armature, and ten inscriptions carved on each of the main and right walls. Details are as follows.

Type: It is a square niche with a flat ceiling, 2.5 meters high, 2.34 meters wide and 2.36 meters deep. A low base of 0.3 meters for each height and width is cut around the ground, a shallow chaitya arched recess is excavated on each of the main wall and the side walls. A long throne is set on the base in front of each recess of the side walls.

Sculptures: A seated Buddha occupies a recess cut into the main wall flanked by a bodhisattva outside of each side, Vimalakirti and Manjushri sit in their own recess into the left wall and the right wall, a disciple stands outside of each inner walls, and an attendant (a boy and a girl) outside of each outer walls. There are nine figures of clay modelled on a wooden armature in all, which appear to be unrestored work of the sixth century.

The seated Buddha on the main wall is life-like and graceful. He bears a polished high topknot, the round face with downcast eyes, the body is slightly frontal. He is dressed in an upper garment that completely covers his body, with U-shaped collar falling to the chest, the lappet of the robe resting on the left arm, of which the hem cascades over his knees, covering the throne in two large lotus petals. His right hand is in the abhaya mudra, and his left hand in the varada mudra. White traces remain on the aureole and mandorla behind him.

右壁弟子迦叶高鼻深目,面相清苦,作思考状。左壁弟子阿难面形饱满圆润,憨厚可爱。均双手拢袖于胸前。

左壁维摩诘,顶束半圆形小髻,着对襟外衣。左手抚膝,右手举于胸际,塑造了一位六世纪知识分子的形象。

右壁文殊菩萨,头戴方形冠,外披天衣。头部略微前倾,双眼下视,表现得非常谦恭。左手掩袖置于膝上,右手举于胸前。

左右壁童男童女像均高 1.14 米。神情淳朴自然,生活气息浓厚。其服饰属于中国西北少数民族风格。童男头戴圆毡帽,身穿圆领窄袖长袍,双手拢袖置于胸前,脚穿尖头靴。童女头梳双丫髻,内穿圆领长袖衣,外着背带长裙,露出鞋尖。一手置胸前,一手下垂。

题记:该窟残存十则题记。访客在正、右壁面刻题记、留名。

第123窟童男童女

The bodhisattvas on each side are delicate and slender. With the high topknots, they wear the dress with long loose sleeves and a collar folded across in front, and the breast-high dresses. The outer shawls cover both shoulders, and the broad scarves hang from the shoulders, each shoulder decorated with a circular ornament. One hand hangs down naturally, and the other is placed on the abdomen. They stand in cloud head shoes.

The disciple Kasyapa on the right wall has a high nose and sunken eyes, the bitter face with a pensive expression. The disciple Ananda on the left wall bears a full, rounded face, and is simple-minded and lovely. All of them raise hands to the chests level concealing the clasped hands in the sleeves.

Vimalakirti on the left wall bears a small semi-circular topknot, and an overcoat with a parallel collar. His left hand rests on knee, and his right hand is raised to the chest level. The image is of a sixth-century intellectual.

Manjushri on the right wall wears a square crown, with the outer shawl covering both shoulders. Her head is slightly frontal with downcast eyes, showing great modesty. Her left hand rests on knee concealing in the sleeve, and the right hand is raised to the chest.

The boy and the girl on each side walls are 1.14 meters high, with a simple and natural expressions, and in the richness of their lives. The style of their costume is that of the northwest minorities of China. With a circular felt hat, the boy is dressed in a long coat with a roll collar and close-fitting sleeves in which he conceals his clasped hands, standing in shoes with pointed toe. The hair of the girl is braided and looped up on either side of her head, she wears a dress with long loose sleeves and a roll collar, and a high-waisted skirt held up by shoulder straps, leaving the toes of her shoes. One hand is placed to the chest and the other hangs down.

Inscriptions: There are ten inscriptions left by visitors in the cave. Visitors might have carved dedications and their names on each of the main and right walls.

Extension and Elaboration

The unusual and attractive youthful attendants in the cave are little boy and girl scarcely in their teens. The iconographic scheme is simple, they are of plain and natural expressions, revealing a higher artistic level. The costume truly reflects the cultural characteristics of the daily life in the northwest minorities of China, showing the characteristics of folklorization, secularization and localization at Maijishan Caves.

引申与拓展

  该窟独特的、引人注目的年轻侍从是刚刚十几岁的童男童女。造型简练，神情纯朴自然，具有较高的艺术水平。服饰真实反映了西北少数民族日常生活的文化特点，体现出麦积山石窟民俗化、世俗化、本土化特点。

  维摩诘是自魏晋以来北朝至隋唐盛行不衰的佛教艺术题材之一。《维摩诘经》描述了维摩诘是一位明心见性者，在释迦牟尼住世时，示现居士身来教化众生。维摩诘为弘扬大乘佛教义理示疾，释迦牟尼遣众弟子去探望，其座下十四位大弟子（包括两位菩萨）都声称不堪胜任，最后才由文殊菩萨出面去探病。维摩诘和文殊菩萨佛法辩论成为"维摩经变"的主要表现形式。不同于第4窟（散花楼）隔龛对坐式和第133窟同龛并坐式，该窟采用隔佛对坐式。此窟维摩诘作青年型，面貌清俊，眯眼微笑，与常见的手执羽扇"清羸示病之容，隐几忘言之状"的老者型不同。

Vimalakirti is one of the prevalent Buddhist art themes since the Wei and Jin dynasties until the Sui and Tang dynasties. *Vimalakirti Sutra* describes Vimalakirti was an enlightened being manifesting as a layman in order to teach living beings during the time of Shakyamuni. One time, he expediently "manifested" being sick so that people would gather around him while he expounded the Prajnaparamita teaching of non-duality. Shakyamuni asked his 14 senior disciples (including two bodhisattvas) to go visit this layman. They were all afraid to go and visit him. Finally, Manjushri went to see him. The theological disputation between Vimalakirti and Manjushri has become the main version of the representation of "the Vimalakirti Sutra Illustration". Unlike the version of the pair seated in their own niche at each end, turning towards each other in Cave 4 (Pavilion of Scattered Flowers) and the version of the pair sharing the same throne in Cave 133, the version of the pair separated widely, each on his own throne, with Shakyamuni seated on a higher throne between them is illustrated in the cave. Here Vimalakirti is a young image of handsome face, smiling with squinting eyes, which is totally different from what had created the old prototype with holding his fan in one hand "well-defined and emaciated features that plainly show his feigned illness, and which shows him leaning upon a table".

第126窟

第126窟位于西崖西上层,开凿于北魏(公元386年—公元534年)。该窟主尊胁侍造像排列不对称,弟子阿难单独出现。

该窟内有五身泥塑造像,四壁上三十四身影塑造像,前、右壁墨书题记三则。

形制:该窟是平面方形、平顶窟。地面有低坛基。正壁设一方形基座。正壁左右两侧和左右两壁各砌两个两层半圆形坛台。

造像:窟内正壁塑一坐佛,左右两侧各一身菩萨和一身弟子。左右两壁各塑一身力士。四壁上贴三十四身影塑小坐佛、菩萨、供养人、飞天立像,共计三十九身。

正壁佛,高肉髻,方脸大耳,弯眉细目,目视前方,挺胸收腹。面部被烟熏呈黑色。内着僧祇支,外着袒右袈裟。结跏趺坐于方形台座上,下摆呈三瓣覆盖座前。双手残损。身后浮塑莲瓣形身光。

正壁左侧菩萨和右侧弟子,面形长圆。内着僧祇支,外着双领

Cave 126

Cave 126 is located at the upper west tier of the western cliff. It was dug in the Northern Wei Dynasty (AD 386-534). The arrangement of attendants of the principal Buddha is asymmetrical, and the disciple Ananda appears alone.

In the cave visitors will enjoy five sculptures modelled in clay, 34 figures in relief on four walls, and three inscriptions with a brush on the front and right walls. Details are as follows.

Type: It is a flat square niche with a flat ceiling. A low base is cut around the ground. A square pedestal throne is built on the main wall. There are two two-tier semicircular platforms on each side of the main wall and two flanking walls.

Sculptures: The main wall contains a seated Buddha flanked by a bodhisattva and a disciple on either side. A dvarapala is modelled on each of the left and the right walls. Four walls are covered with 34 figures of small seated Buddhas, standing bodhisattvas, donors and flying apsaras in belief. There are 39 figures in all.

The Buddha on the main wall bears a high topknot, the square face flanked by pendulous ears, with arched brows sweeping above gently opened almond eyes, looking straight ahead, keeping shoulders squared and stomach flat. The face is smokedarkened into black. He is robed in an inner vest covering the left shoulder and armpits, the outer robe thrown over the left shoulder or the upper throwing a strong diagonal across the body, leaving the right side of the body and shoulder bare. He sits in dhyanasana on the square throne with the hem covering in three petals. His two hands are damaged. There is a lotus-petal shaped mandorla in relief behind him.

The bodhisattva on the left and the disciple on the right of the main wall have long

下垂袈裟，下摆呈三片式。下着长裙，下摆呈燕尾形。身后均浮塑圆形项光。其中左侧菩萨，束扇形高发髻。双手胸前合十，双脚残损。右侧弟子，弯眉细眼。左手掌心向外置于胸前，右手掩袖置于腹前，穿鞋而立。

左右壁力士，束锥状发髻，怒目圆睁，眉眼上扬，颈部肌肉突起。面部烟熏严重，跣足而立。其中左壁力士，张口。内穿双领宽袖长袍，外穿铠甲。左手掩袖置于胯侧，右手置于腹前。右壁力士，闭口。内着僧祇支，下着长裙。帛带自双肩下垂至腹前交叉后上绕穿肘自然垂下。右手握拳于胸部，左臂置于腹部，手已失。身后浮塑桃形项光。

四壁上贴三十四身影塑小坐佛、菩萨、供养人、飞天立像。大部分头部已失，只有两身飞天保存完整。

题记：前、右壁留有墨书题记三则。

引申与拓展

该窟造像排列形式独特，正壁坐佛的一侧为弟子阿难，另一侧为菩萨。这种布局与第122窟相同。

and round faces. They are robed in inner vests covering the left shoulder and armpits, upper garments that completely cover their bodies, with U-shaped collar falling to the chests, the lappet of the robes resting on the left arm, the hems in three petals. Their lower bodies are dressed in long dresses with swallow tail-shaped hems. There are circular aureoles in relief behind them. Among which the left-hand bodhisattva has a fan-shaped high topknot. Her palms are pressed together at the chest, with feet damaged. The right-hand disciple is carved with arched brows sweeping above gently opened almond eyes. The left hand is placed in front of the chest with palm outward, the right hand at the abdomen concealing in the sleeve, standing in shoes.

The dvarapalas on either side walls bear cone-shaped ushnishas, raised brows and eyes round open in fury attitude, with bulging muscles on the necks. Their faces are badly smokedarkened, they stand barefoot. Among which the left-hand dvarapala keeps his mouth open. He is dressed in an inner crossed-collar robe with loose sleeves, and an outer armor. The left hand is put beside the hip concealing in the sleeve, and the right hand rests at the abdomen. The right-hand dvarapala leaves lips closed. He is robed in an inner vest covering the left shoulder and armpits, a long dress on the lower body. The broad scarf comes over the shoulders and down to cross the abdomen, then up through the elbow and down naturally. The right hand is raised to the chest in a fist, and the left arm placed at the abdomen with hand missing. There is a peach-shaped aureole in relief behind him.

Four walls are decorated with 34 figures of small seated Buddhas, standing bodhisattvas, donors and flying apsaras in belief. Most of the heads have disappeared, only two flying apsaras remain intact.

Inscriptions: There are three inscriptions with a brush left by the visitors on the front and the right walls.

Extension and Elaboration

The arrangement of sculptures in the cave is unique. On one side of the seated Buddha on the main wall is the disciple Ananda, and the bodhisattva is on the other side. This layout is identical with that in Cave 122.

第127窟

第127窟位于西崖西上部。开凿于北魏（公元386年—公元534年），宋代（公元960年—公元1279年）和元代（公元1271年—公元1368年）重修，是麦积山石窟壁画最丰富的洞窟。

该窟内有三身石雕像和九身泥塑造像，四壁、藻井顶及四披的北魏原作经变画和本生故事画，七则刻画或墨书于正壁龛内外、左壁龛内和窟中央佛座的题记。

形制：该窟是平面横长方形、四面坡式盝顶窟。窟高3.95米、宽8.6米、深5米。正、左、右壁各开一圆拱形浅龛并设台座，窟中央塑一高台座。

造像：正壁龛内置石雕一坐佛二胁侍菩萨，左右壁龛内各塑一坐佛二胁侍菩萨，窟中央宋塑一坐佛元塑二胁侍菩萨，共计十二身。

正壁龛内石雕佛，高1.4米，旋涡纹高肉髻，面形长圆，大耳垂肩。内着僧祇支，腰间系带作结下垂，外穿双领下垂袈裟。左手与愿印，右手施无畏印。结跏趺坐于须弥座上，衣摆呈三花瓣式垂于座前。佛后圆形头光和莲瓣形身光同为整块灰岩大理石雕成。头

第二章　麦积山石窟汉英解说词

Cave 127

Cave 127 is located on the upper west part of the western cliff. It was originally dug in the Northern Wei Dynasty (AD 386-534) and repaired in the Song Dynasty (AD 960-1279) and the Yuan Dynasty (AD 1271-1368). It contains the most abundant paintings at Maijishan Caves.

In the cave visitors will enjoy three stone carvings and nine clay sculptures, the original paintings of sutra illustrations and jataka tales in the Northern Wei Dynasty painted on the four walls, the coffered ceiling and its four sloping sides, seven inscriptions carved or with a brush inside and outside the niche into the main wall, inside the niche on the left wall and on the throne in the center of the cave. Details are as follows.

Type: It is a horizontal rectangular cave with tent-style ceiling and four sloping sides, 3.95 meters high, 8.6 meters wide, and 5 meters deep. A chaitya arched bay holding a throne is carved into the main wall and each of the flanking walls, a high throne is set in the center of the cave.

Sculptures: A seated Buddha flanked by two attendant bodhisattvas carved in stone occupy the niche into the main wall, on each of the side walls contains a seated Buddha flanked ocaupies by two attendant bodhisattvas in clay, the center of the cave holds a clay seated Buddha of the Song Dynasty and two clay attendant bodhisattvas of the Song Dynasty on each side. There are 12 figures in all.

The stone Buddha in the bay into the main wall is 1.03 meters high, bearing a spiral-shaped topknot, the oval face flanked by pendulous ears. He is robed in an inner vest covering the left shoulder and armpits, with a sash tied round the waist falling in a knot, an upper garment that completely covers his body, with U-shaped collar falling to the chest, the corner of the rob resting on the left arm. His right hand is in the abhaya mudra, and his left hand in the varada mudra. He sits with legs tightly locked in a yogic pose on

光中从内向外有浮雕莲瓣、缠枝莲花、十二伎乐天各一圈，上部正中刻一小坐佛。伎乐天以小坐佛为轴心左右对称，相向飞行。飞天姿态各异，手或提飘带或托供品，多数手持乐器。身光左右两侧有浮雕散花飞天及供养飞天各四身、一身双手合十的弟子。

左右二胁侍石雕菩萨，身高1.08米，造像风格相同：五梁冠，余发披肩。颈戴桃形项圈，胸佩璎珞。帔帛自双肩下垂，于腹前穿圆璧，后又向两侧分开上卷，或搭于双臂，或系于腰际。内着僧祇支，下穿长裙。一手屈二指举于胸际，一手提桃形璧置于腹侧，跣足立圆台上。后有桃形项光。

左右两壁龛佛，头部和上身均经宋代重修，面圆体胖，结跏趺坐于长方形台座上。内着僧祇支，外披通肩袈裟，原作衣摆呈八字形下垂座前。两佛手势略有不同，左壁龛佛左手与愿印，右手施无畏印。右壁龛佛双手施禅定印，手指残损。

两壁龛内四身胁侍菩萨为北魏晚期"秀骨清像"的代表作品。其中左壁龛二菩萨均束发戴冠，余发披肩。胸佩项圈，下坠花饰，腕戴环。上身半袒微前倾，下着长裙，并束带作结下垂。天衣覆盖双肩。帔帛沿两胸下垂，在膝前交叉上卷，或搭于双臂（左侧菩萨），或一端提在手中，一端搭于肩头（右侧菩萨），跣足立于半圆台上。左侧菩萨左手示礼，右手托盘，内盛供物。右侧菩萨左手示礼，右手提巾带。右壁龛菩萨亦为同一风格。

窟中央宋塑佛高2.5米，低平螺髻，有肉髻珠，面形方圆，袒胸。内着僧祇支，外披通肩袈裟。左手抚膝，右臂屈肘向前，手已失。结跏趺坐于须弥座上，下摆呈半圆形垂于座前。左右胁侍菩萨，身高均2.32米，面形方圆，戴尖顶冠。体躯壮实，下穿长裙，腰间系带下垂，上身袒露。肩搭帔帛绕双肩下垂。两臂屈肘向前，跣足立于圆台上。

a Sumeru throne, the hem covering the throne in three large lotus petals. The circular aureole and lotus petal-shaped mandorla behind him is carved from the same block. The aureole is carved in a scroll with several bands: lotus petals round the lotus at the center, interlocking lotus stalk on secondary band, the outer band of 12 celestial musicians, at the topmost of which is a small seated Buddha. Those musicians take the small seated Buddha as the axis, two on each side, flying toward each other. They are in different postures, either holding ribbons or offerings in their hands, mostly carrying instruments. On each side of the Buddha's mandorla are four flying apsaras scattering flowers and votive flying apsaras modelled in relief, a disciple with palms pressed together at the chest.

The two stone attendant bodhisattvas on each side with 1.08 meters tall, are similar in style of image making: a crown adorned with five beams, the rest hair cascading over their shoulders. With a peach-shaped collar round the neck, a heavy garland of jewels hangs from the shoulders. The broad scarves hanging over the shoulders and down to pass through a large ring over the lower abdomen then up again, either resting on the arms or tied at the waist. They wear the inner vests covering the left shoulder and armpits, and the long dresses on the lower bodies. With one hand is raised to the chest, leaving two fingers bent, and the other holding a peach-shaped jade beside the thigh, they stand on the circular platforms barefoot backed by peach-shaped aureoles.

The head and upper body of the Buddha in each of the side bays were restored in the Song Dynasty, the round faces and plump bodies, sitting with the legs tightly locked in a yogic pose on the rectangle thrones. They are robed in the inner vests covering the left shoulder and armpits, an upper garments that completely cover their bodies and hang in heavy folds round their shoulders, the original hem cascades over the thrones in two large lotus petals. The two Buddhas are slightly different in gestures, the right hand of the Buddha in the left bay is in the abhaya mudra, and his left hand in the varada mudra. The two hands of the Buddha in the right bay are in dhyana mudra with fingers damaged.

The four attendant bodhisattvas in the two flanking bays are representative work of the late Northern Wei Dynasty, which are "long and slender figure and delicately modelled features". Among them, the hair of two bodhisattvas in the left bay is gathered high encircled by the diadems and falling down the shoulders. A pendant adorned with a flower pattern hangs from a heavy collar round the necks, wrist rings on the arms. Their upper bodies are partially bare with a slightly frontal, the long dresses on the lower bodies with a band tied at the waist falling in a knot. Their outer shawls cover both shoulders. Their broad scarves hang over the shoulders and down to cross at the knees and up again, either resting on the arms (left bodhisattva), or holding one end in the hand and the other hanging on the shoulder (right bodisattva), they stand on the semi-circular platforms barefoot. The left-hand bodhisattva curves the left hand upward towards the Buddha, and his right hand holds a tray containing an offering. The right-hand bodhisattva bends the left hand upward towards the Buddha, and his right hand is raised with a ribbon passing between the fingers. The style of the two bodhisattvas in the right bay is identical to that in the left bay.

壁画：该窟壁画内容最丰富，保存最完整。四壁、窟顶藻井及四披均绘壁画，主要为经变画和本生故事画。正壁画涅槃经变，左壁画维摩诘经变，右壁画西方净土变，前壁上部画七佛，下部甬道左侧画地域变，右侧画十善十恶图。窟顶藻井绘帝释天，正、左、右披绘萨埵那太子本生故事，前披绘睒子本生故事。

涅槃经变位于正壁上部。纵2.2米，横8.22米，略有残损。中间绘一佛、二菩萨，左右有山水树木，为释迦说法图。其左侧绘释迦涅槃前最后一次说法和涅槃的情形。右侧绘八王争舍利，车马人物，姿态各异，争战激烈，气势磅礴，下部还有宏大的进军行列。

维摩诘经变位于左壁上部。纵2.3米，横4.48米，略有残损。画面充分展示了《维摩诘所说经·问疾品》所描绘的场面：左侧维摩诘端坐于须弥座上，镇定自若，右侧文殊率众菩萨、声闻及诸天人徐徐而来。画面还描绘了《维摩诘所说经·方便品》中的国王、大臣和《维摩诘所说经·香积品》中的吉祥天女形象，天女清秀洒脱。规模宏大壮观，是早期经变画中的优秀作品。

西方净土变位于右壁上部。画面高1.63米，长4.55米，是我国石窟寺中现存时代最早、规模最大、内容最完备的一幅净土变。画面正中一佛结跏趺坐于须弥座上，后有宝盖殿堂，前设高台栏杆，旁及树木城墙，墙上有角楼。佛左右分列二菩萨，再两边各有弟子两身、比丘十身恭身侍立。座前正中置鼓一面，旁各一伎乐击鼓，再两旁各有一伎乐，戴花蔓冠，内穿紧身小袄，外套广袖衫。下穿曳地长裙，腰部系带，舒袖起舞。再向两侧又各有四身伎乐手持乐器演奏，乐器有笙、箫、鼓、竽及箜篌等。画面左侧城外七宝莲池畔，有十余位僧众人等朝佛走来。左侧城外大树旁有比丘和女供养人各十余身，亦朝佛而来。

七佛图位于前壁上部。画面高1.47米，长8.22米。七佛平列，

The Buddha of the Song Dynasty sit in the center of the cave is 2.5 meters high, with a low flat spiral-shaped topknot, a bead between the bun and the bottom hair, the round face, bare chested. He is robed in an inner vest covering the left shoulder and armpits, an upper garment that completely covers his body and hangs in heavy folds round his shoulders. His left hand rests on knee, and his right arm raised to the chest level with hand disappeared. He sits with legs tightly locked in a yogic pose on a Sumeru throne, the hem covering the throne in semicircle arched lines. The two flanking bodhisattvas are 2.32 meters tall, with the square faces and steeple crowns. With solid bodies, they are robed in the long dresses on the lower bodies with a sash tied round the waist falling in a knot, leaving upper bodies bare. Their broad scarves hang over the shoulders and down, and two arms are raised up, they stand on the round platforms barefoot.

Paintings: The paintings in the cave are of the richest in contents and the most well-preserved. They are painted on the four walls and the coffered ceiling and its four sloping sides, mainly are sutra illustrations and jataka tales. Nirvana Sutra Illustration on the main wall, Vimalakirti Sutra Illustration on the left wall, Illustration to the Pure Land on the right wall, the Seven Buddhas on the upper front wall, Ballads and Stories from Hell on the left and Ten Good Deeds or Ten Evil Deeds on the right of the passage on the lower front wall. Sakra-devanam-Indra on the coffered ceiling, the Jataka of Prince Mahasattva on each of the main, the left and right sloping sides, and the Jataka of Syamaka on the front sloping side.

Nirvana Sutra Illustration painted on the upper part of the main wall. Vertical 2.2 meters, horizontal 8.22 meters, slightly damaged. A Buddha attended by two bodhisattvas are painted in the center, on either side of them there are mountain landscapes and trees, which is the scene of Sakyamuni's preaching. On the left of the wall is a scene of Sakyamuni's last preaching before nirvana and the situation of his nirvana. On the right of the wall illustrates the eight kings who fought for Buddha's remains, horses and carriages, groups of people in different attitudes, fierce battles, magnificent, and on the lower part we can see the grand marching procession.

Vimalakirti Sutra Illustration painted on the upper part of the left wall. Vertical 2.3 meters, horizontal 4.48 meters, slightly damaged. The picture bears inscriptions about the story of *Vimalakirti-Nirdesa-Sutra:Bodhisattva ManJusri Visiting the Sick Vimalakirti*: On the left Vimalakirti is seated straight on the Sumeru pedestal calmly, while on the right Manjusri followed by bodhisattvas, sravakas and divines sweep forward towards Vimalakirti. The painting also depicts the king and ministers in *Vimalakirti-Nirdesa-Sutra: Convenience* and the Pelden Lhamo in *Vimalakirti-Nirdesa-Sutra: Heaped Fragrance*, who is elegant and graceful. With grand and spectacular scale, it is an excellent work of early sutra paintings.

Illustration to the Pure Land painted on the upper part of the right wall. The painting is 1.63 meters high and 4.55 meters long. It is the earliest, the largest and the most complete content of illustration to the pure land survived in cave temples in China. In the center a Buddha sits with legs tightly locked in a yogic pose on a Sumeru throne. Behind him stands a hall decorated with a canopy over, the terraces with stone carvings are built in front of the hall, on either side are trees and city wall with corner towers. The Buddha is flanked by two

结跏趺坐于须弥座上。其左右各有二胁侍菩萨或弟子，立于圆莲座上，躯体修长，仪态潇洒。再左右又各绘供养比丘数身，身穿各色袈裟，或手托供品，或笼袖而立。衣饰、佛座、宝盖、身光等，多用青、绿加墨色描绘。

地狱变及战骑图位于前壁下部。面积约14平方米。左侧绘地狱变中的"善报"，阎罗宫殿楼阁因被熏黑隐约可辨，两条墨书榜题清晰："此人行十善得参道时""诸天罗汉迎去时"。右侧绘地狱变中的"恶报"，烟熏严重，隐约可见鬼差数身，其他内容不辨，墨书榜题可辨识者两条："此人生时好□□当堕刀山地狱""此生时好□□□□令人截臂地狱"。左侧下部绘战骑图，画中的飞天随风飞舞，骑士戴胄披甲，跨一匹着甲红马，纵横驰骋。

帝释天位于窟顶正中长方形藻井内。纵1.32米，横4.68米。帝释天身穿袍服，端坐于四龙云车之上，前有飞天导引，后有仙人、羽人乘龙护送。上有华盖，旌幡飘扬，旁有诸天相随。色彩灰暗，铁线描清晰，晕染的石青、石绿尚且鲜艳。其内容一说为东王公巡游。

睒子本生故事画位于窟顶前披。披面呈梯形，上底边长4.61米，下底边长7.35米，高1.3米，为长卷式佛本生故事画。现存画面以迦夷国国王狩猎、拜见盲夫妇、帝释天施药、睒子复生为主要情节。国王及侍从们纵马奔驰在深山旷野之间，鸟兽惊慌四散，极富生活情趣。草庐前，国王寻找盲夫妇，门外端坐的盲夫妇似急切地盼望儿子回来，国王似告知睒子不幸中箭的经过。

穆天子拜见西王母位于窟顶梯形后披。上底边长4.75米，下底边长7.35米，高1.28米，已剥落过半。据《穆天子传》所述，穆天子乘八骏马车西行，途经玉山宝地，在瑶池拜见了西王母。此画

standing bodhisattvas, and two disciples and other ten bhikkhus. A drum is placed in the middle of the front seat, with a musician beating on either side, and another musician on both sides with hair encircled by a flower vine, the inner dresses clinging tightly to the upper bodies, and the outer garments with long loose sleeves. Their lower bodies wear the long dresses sweeping to the floor, with a sash tied at the waist, they dance spreading their long loose sleeves. On either side bears four more seated musician playing musical instruments whose instruments include *sheng* (bamboo organ), pan-pipes, drum, *Yu* (a wind instrument) and *konghou* (an ancient plucked stringed instrument). On the left side of the painting is the bank of the Seven Treasure Lotus Pond outside the city, more than ten monks sweep forward towards the Buddha. On the left side of the picture, by the big tree outside the city, more than ten bhikkhus and female donors also sweep forward towards the Buddha.

The Seven Buddhas are painted on the front wall above entrance. The height of the painting is 1.47 meters and the length is 8.22 meters. Seven Buddhas are arranged in a row and sit with legs tightly locked in a yogic pose on the Sumeru throne. They are flanked by two attendant bodhisattvas or disciples, standing on the round lotus platforms, they are slender and long-legged, and in natural manners. They are also attended by several votive bhikkhus wearing a variety of coloured robes, either holding the offerings in their hands, or standing with his clasped hands concealed in their close-fitting sleeves. The ornaments of robes, Buddha' thrones, canopies and halos, etc., are chiefly painted in a bluish grey tint, green and black.

Ballads and Stories from Hell and Hunting Scene painted on the lower part of the front wall. They cover an area about fourteen square meters. On the left of the painting describes "rewards" of Ballads and Stories from Hell, the smokedarkened traces of Yama's palace and pavilions are subtly discernible. Two inscriptions written on it with a brush are not all lost: "When this person practices the ten good deeds, he will gain enlightment.". "He will be welcomed by arhats". On the right of the painting depicts "punishments" of Ballads and Stories from Hell, badly smokedarkened, several godlings or demons are slightly decipherable, other contents are illegible, two inscriptions with a brush are visible: "This person who is addicated to □□in his previous lives will be put into the Hell of Swords after death.". "This person who is addicated to □□□□in his previous lives will be put into the Hell of Cutting Arms after death." On the lower left bears the hunting scene, in which flying apsaras are dancing with the wind, warriors in helmets and armours riding a red horse in armour, which is at a full gallop.

Sakra-devanam-Indra painted on the central rectangle cassion ceiling. Its vertical side is 1.32 meters, and a horizontal side is 4.68 meters. Wearing a robe, Indra sits on a carriage drawn by four dragons flying among the clouds, with flying apsaras accompanying him, and escorted by celestials and winged figures riding on dragons flying among the clouds. The carriage is surmounted by a canopy, with banners and streamers fluttering in the wind, followed by Gods. The colouring is gray, the fine-drawn lines are clearly visible, and traces of the faint dyed bluish grey tint and a deep emerald green are still bright. The content is said to be the carriage carries East Maharaja through the sky.

所绘周穆王身穿袍服,在重臣们的簇拥下,由东向西而来。上有伞盖,旁及山水树木。迎面站着几个身穿长衫的人,由西向东而来,其中一人手牵红马,一说为西王母迎接穆天子的情景。

萨埵那太子舍身饲虎位于窟顶左右梯形披。左右披梯形大小一样,上底长1.34米,下底长3.8米,高1.1米。画面以摩诃罗陀国三位王子"出游"、三王子萨埵"饲虎"、向国王"报信"等情节为主线,用连环画的形式,将故事绘制在左右二披之内。右披绘山林间悬崖下蹲伏大小老虎两组,每组八只。其中一组在老虎中间三王子的形骸隐约可见,是为舍身饲虎。左披以城郭殿宇为主,间绘人物活动。城郭庄严,殿宇巍峨。城门之外,一边有数人牵马徐步而行,另一边有两人乘马飞奔而来。城内宫殿外,有国王闻报昏厥在地的情节。画面以半鸟瞰的透视法,描绘出宏伟壮丽的城郭建筑。该组建筑的形式及结构是研究北朝时期王宫建筑形式的重要实物材料。

题记:正壁龛内外、左壁龛内和窟中央佛座有七则刻画或墨书题记。

The Painting to the Jataka of Syamaka is painted on the front sloping side of the cassion ceiling. It is trapezoidal with the upper of 4.61 meters, the bottom of 7.35 meters, and the height of 1.3 meters, which is a scroll of the Painting to the Jataka of Buddha. Main plots consist of the king of Kashi hunting, visiting blind couple, Indra giving medicine, the resurrection of Syamaka. The king and his attendants rode the horses at a gallop in the mountains and the wilderness, leaving birds and animals scattered in panic, and full of interest of life. In front of the cottage, the king looked for the blind couple. The blind couple sitting straight outside the door were eager for their son's return. The king seemed to telling them that Syamaka had been unlucky to be hit by an arrow.

King Mu Visiting the Queen Mother of the West is drawn on the back sloping side of the cassion ceiling. It is trapezoidal with the upper of 4.75 meters, the bottom of 7.35 meters, and the height of 1.28 meters, half of which have peeled away. According to *the Biography of King Mu*, King Mu took a carriage drawn by eight horses for his western expedition, passing through the holy land Jade Mountain, and visited the Queen Mother of the West at the Yao Pond. Here wearing a robe, King Mu moves forward from east to west surrounded by his important ministers. The carriage is surmounted by a canopy, on either side are mountains, rivers and trees. On the other side stand several figures in long gowns, moving forward from west to east, one of them leading a red horse by the halter, which is said to be the scene of Queen Mother of the West welcoming King Mu.

The Jataka of the Starving Tigress is painted on the left and right trapezoidal sloping sides of the cassion ceiling. They are identical in size with the upper of 1.34 meters, the bottom of 3.8 meters, and the height of 1.1 meters. The picture emphasizes the plots of the "travelling" of the three princes in Mahabharata, the third prince Mahasattva "offering himself to a starving tigress" and the "reporting the bad news" to the king. In the form of a series of pictures portraits the story on the left and right sloping sides of the cassion ceiling. Two groups of tigers of different sizes crouching under the cliffs in the mountains are painted on the left sloping side, each of eight tigers. The remaining skeleton of the third prince Mahasattva among the tigers is barely visible, this is the scene of Mahasattva offering himself to a starving tigress. The left sloping side is dominated by tower walls and gate, the palace buildings, between which character activities are painted. The tower walls and gate are solemn, and the palace is mighty. Outside the tower gate, on one side several people walked slowly leading their horses by the bridles, and on the other side two people came on galloping horses. Inside the town outside the palace there is a scene that the king fainted on the ground at the bad news. The painting depicts the magnificent architecture of the town in half-bird's-eye perspective. The form and structure of this group of buildings are important physical image materials to study the architectural form of palace buildings in the Northern Dynasties.

Inscriptions: There are seven inscriptions carved or with a brush left by the visitors inside and outside the main bay, in the bay on the left and on the throne in the center of the cave.

引申与拓展

该窟壁画主要由经变画和本生故事画两部分组成。以绘画的形式呈现佛经教义和释迦牟尼佛前世的故事。佛经中讲到释迦牟尼在没有成佛之前有多次转生,有时转生为人,有时转生为动物。佛常用本生故事来阐释因缘果报、轮回转世等概念,强调一些重要的道德价值观。

窟内原存一块《法生造像碑》,现藏文物库房。通高43厘米,宽37厘米,厚6厘米。右下角残损。方额。上刻一列五个小浅龛,各龛高、宽、深分别为8厘米、5厘米、1厘米,内各刻一尊浮雕坐佛。碑文12行,每行12字,约140字,是麦积山现存最早的石刻造像记,刻于北魏景明至熙平年间(公元503年—公元516年)。

碑文记录一位来自"洛阳刘姓沙弥法生在麦积崖,请良匠造龛一所"。碑面的"大魏"等文字是极其珍贵的文物资料,为麦积山石窟的分期断代提供了依据。郭沫若、吴作人、马衡、谢国桢、叶恭绰、冯国瑞、丁希农、邓宝珊等名人先后在碑之拓本上题跋,对于考证造像碑亦有重要价值。

Extension and Elaboration

The paintings in the cave are mainly composed of two parts: sutra illustrations and jataka stories. The doctrines in Buddhist sutras and Sakyamuni Buddha's previous life stories are presented in the form of paintings. Buddhist sutras depict earlier incarnations of the being who would become Siddhartha Gautama, the future Buddha—sometimes as an animal, sometimes as a human. The Buddha himself used jataka stories to explain concepts like gamma and rebirth and to emphasise the importance of certain moral values.

The Stone Tablet of Monk Fasheng was originally preserved in the cave, which has been moved to the storehouse now. It is 4.3 meters high, 3.7 meters wide and 0.6 meters deep. The lower right corner is broken. The top part of the tablet is square with five small recesses carved in a row, each of 0.8 meters high, 0.5 meters wide and 0.1 meters deep, into which contains a seated Buddha in relief. There are 12 lines, each of twelve characters and about 140 words. It is the earliest stone carving inscription preserved at Maijishan, the date is between Jingming under the reign of Emperor Xuanwu and Xiping of the reign of Emperor Xiaoming in the Northern Wei Dynasty (AD 503-516).

The stone tablet records that a Luoyang novice monk Fasheng with surname of Liu invited the skilled craftsmen to excavate a cave at Maijishan. The "Dawei" and other characters on the tablet are extremely precious cultural relics, which provide the evidence for the periodic dating of Maijishan Caves. Guo Moruo, Wu Zuoren, Ma Heng, Xie Guozhen, Ye Gongchuo, Feng Guorui, Ding Xinong, Deng Baoshan, etc. have inscribed preface and postscript on the rubbing of the tablet. It is also of great value to verify the monument.

第128窟

第128窟位于西崖中部,西邻第98窟。开凿于北魏(公元386年—公元534年),宋代(公元960年—公元1279年)重修。该窟是常见的三佛龛,是麦积山石窟开凿历史上北魏早期向中期过渡的典型洞窟。

该窟内有七身泥塑造像,二十四身影塑造像以及两则留在右壁龛左右侧的刻画题记。

形制:该窟是平面方形、平顶窟。前壁开门。正、左、右三壁凿低坛基。正壁上设一个"工"字形台座。左右两壁各开一圆拱形大龛,龛内也各设一个"工"字形台座。四壁和左右壁大龛内凿三十七个小龛:正壁两侧各三个三层小龛,左右壁龛内两侧各两个两层小龛,左壁上方三小龛,右壁上方六小龛,前壁上方七个两层小龛。左壁右侧、右壁左侧和前壁两侧各作一个半圆形莲台。

造像:窟内正壁和左右壁龛内各塑一坐佛,左右二壁前和前壁两侧各站立一胁侍菩萨。四壁和左右壁大龛内三十七个小龛内塑二十四身影塑坐佛和菩萨,共计三十一身。

正壁和左右壁龛三佛,高肉髻,长方脸,蓄八字胡须。内着僧祇支,外着袒右袈裟。双手施禅定印,结跏趺坐于"工"字形台座

Cave 128

Cave 128 is located in the middle part of the western cliff, adjacent to Cave 98 in the west. It was originally dug in the Northern Wei Dynasty (AD 386-534) and repaired in the Song Dynasty (AD 960-1279). It is the usual three Buddhas niches, is typical of the transformation period from early to the middle of the Northern Wei Dynasty in the excavation history at Maijishan.

In the cave visitors will enjoy seven sculptures modelled in clay, 24 figures in relief. Two inscriptions are carved on either side of the niche into the right wall. Details are as follows.

Type: It is a flat square niche with a flat ceiling. There is a door on the front wall. A low base is cut on the main wall and two side walls. An I-shaped throne is set on the main wall. A large chaitya arched niche is carved on each of the side walls, in which an I-shaped throne is built. 37 recesses are carved into each of the four walls and large ones on the left and right walls: three recesses of three tiers on each side of the main wall, two recesses of two tiers in each large niches into the left and right walls, three recesses above the left wall, six recesses above the right wall, seven recesses of two tiers above the front wall. A semicircular lotus platform is built on the right of the left wall, the left of the right wall and the two sides of the front wall.

Sculptures: A seated Buddha occupies the main wall and the niche in the left and right walls, an attendant bodhisattva standing on each side of the flanking walls and the front wall. 24 seated Buddhas and bodhisattvas in relief are inserted into 37 recesses cut into each of the four walls and two large niches into the left and right walls. There are 31 figures in all.

Three Buddhas on the main wall and the niche into the left and right walls bear high topknots with the rectangle faces, moustached. They are robed in inner vests covering the left shoulder and armpits, the outer robes thrown over the left shoulder or the upper

上。其中左右壁龛佛身后彩绘圆形项光和莲瓣形身光。

左右壁菩萨，戴宝冠，方圆脸，蓄八字胡须。上身袒露，戴桃形项圈、臂串和手镯。左肩斜披络腋，下穿羊肠裙，裙子紧裹体。帔巾从双肩搭下穿肘下垂掷到墙上。赤足立于半圆形莲台上。身后浮塑莲瓣形身光。其中左壁右侧菩萨左手靠墙自然下垂，右手持莲蕾于胸前。右壁左侧菩萨左手持莲蕾于胸前，右手自然下垂提净瓶。

小龛内坐佛，五官、手印和坐姿与主佛相同，分别着圆领通肩袈裟或袒右袈裟。菩萨分为思惟菩萨和胁侍菩萨。

题记：右壁龛左右侧留有两则刻画题记。

引申与拓展

该窟布局与第100窟相同，均为平顶方形窟，左右壁开龛，四壁及龛内两侧开小龛。右壁左侧菩萨，身躯修长，右手提净瓶。这身造像比第100窟的制作更精美，头部更圆润饱满，衣裙贴体，衣纹线条呈阶梯式。

throwing a strong diagonal across the body, leaving the right side of the body and shoulder bare. With two hands in dhyana mudra, they sit in dhyanasana on the I-shaped thrones. Among them there are coloured circular aureoles and lotus petal-shaped mandorlas behind the Buddhas on the left and right walls.

The bodhisattvas on each of the side walls wear coronets with round faces, moustached. Their upper bodies are bare, decorated with peach-shaped collars, arm strings and bracelets. They are dressed in the upper throwing a strong diagonal across the body, leaving the right side of the body and shoulder bare, the lower sheath dresses melting against the bodies. The scarves come from shoulders and through the armpits flung against the walls, they stand on the semicircle lotus platforms barefoot. There are lotus petal-shaped mandorlas in relief behind them. Among them the left hand of the bodhisattva on the right of the left wall hangs down naturally against the wall, and the right hand is raised to the chest holding a lotus bud. The left hand of the bodhisattva on the left of the right wall is lifted to the chest holding a lotus bud, and the right hand falls down naturally holding a vase.

Features, mudras and sitting postures of the seated Buddhas in the recesses are identical to those of the principal Buddha, they are robed either in upper garments with a roll collar that completely cover their bodies and hang in heavy folds round their shoulders or the outer robes thrown over the left shoulder or the upper throwing a strong diagonal across the body, leaving the right side of the body and shoulder bare. Bodhisattvas are bodhisattvas in pensive pose and attendant bodhisattvas.

Inscriptions: There are two carved inscriptions left by the visitors on either side of the niche on the right.

Extension and Elaboration

The layout in the cave is the same as that in Cave 100. Both belong to the flat square niche with a flat ceiling. A large niche is carved on either side of the flanking walls. Recesses are cut into each of the four walls and two large niches on the left and right walls. The left-hand bodhisattva on the right wall is slender and long-legged, holding a vase in her right hand. The figure is more delicately modelled than that in Cave 100, the head is much rounder and fuller, the dress melting into the body, and the lines of the drapery hang in layered symmetrical folds.

第133窟 万佛洞

第133窟位于西崖中部，因龛间墙壁影塑佛像加上碑刻佛像数量过万而被称为"万佛洞"，又因保存十八块石刻造像碑被称为"碑洞"，王仁裕在《玉堂闲话》中称之为"万菩萨堂"。开凿于北魏（公元386年—公元534年），五代（公元907年—公元960年）、宋代（公元960年—公元1279年）、元代（公元1271年—公元1368年）重修。该窟是麦积山石窟内部空间最大、造像最多，且内容最丰富、最具代表性和艺术性的最重要洞窟之一。

该窟内有十五个龛，二十七尊泥塑像、一千余尊影塑千佛像，十八块造像碑，窟顶及各龛内残存北魏原作壁画，内容为中国传统神话题材，碑上和窟内刻画或墨书七十四则题记，门楣悬挂一牌匾。

形制：该窟为方楣平顶，前部平面为横长方形享堂，后开竖长方形左右二室，前部右侧凿覆斗形藻井。周壁上下两层开十五佛龛。窟内存十八块石刻造像碑。

造像：窟内有泥塑二十七尊，其中前室正中塑大小立像各一尊，前壁门左右侧各塑一身菩萨，十五个佛龛内各有一佛或一佛二菩萨。一千余身壁面影塑千佛，三千八百多身造像碑中的浮雕小千佛。

前室正中有宋代塑大小立像各一尊。大佛，高3.5米，螺髻，中有肉髻珠，方面大耳。内着僧祇支，外披双领下垂袈裟，衣纹宽

Cave 133

Cave 133 is located on the middle part of the western cliff, also known as "Cave of a Myriad Buddhas" for the amount of Buddhas made in moulds applied to lower walls among niches and carved Buddhas in the tablets is more than ten thousand and "Cave of the Steles" for 18 stone steles surviving, it was also called "Ten Thousand Bodhisattva Hall " by the poet Wang Renyu of the Tang Dynasty in his work *Idle Tales of the Jade Hall*. It was originally dug in the Northern Wei Dynasty (AD 386-534) and repaired in the Five Dynasties (AD 907-960), the Song Dynasty (AD 960-1279) and the Yuan Dynasty (AD 1271-1368). It is one of the caves with the largest interior space, and the most sculptures of abundant content, as well as the most representative and most important art at Maijishan.

Visitors will enjoy 15 niches, 27 sculptures modelled in clay, more than 1,000 Thousand Buddhas in moulds, 18 stone steles, and the original paintings of the Northern Wei Dynasty on the ceiling and inside the niches containing the theme of traditional Chinese mythology, 74 carved inscriptions or with a brush on the stelae and inside the caves, and a plaque above the lintel of the door. Details are as follows.

Type: It is a cave with a square lintel and a flat ceiling. The entrance chamber of horizontal rectangular lies at its front, and two shafts of vertical rectangular are carved at its rear. The flat-topped ceiling with sloping sides in the form of an upside-down *dou* is cut on the right of the front. 15 recesses of double tiers holding seated Buddha figures are excavated into walls around the cave. There are 18 stone stelae in the cave.

Sculptures: The cave contains 27 sculptures modelled in clay, among which a tall figure and a small figure stand in the middle of the entrance chamber, a bodhisattva on each side of the entrance door, in each of 15 niches remain a Buddha or a Buddha flanked by two bodhisattvas. There are more than 1,000 Thousand Buddhas made in moulds applied to lower walls, over three thousand eight hundred small Thousand Buddhas figures carved in relief in the stone stelae.

A tall figure and a small figure modelled in the Song Dynasty stand in the middle of the entrance chamber. The tall Buddha is 3.5 meters high, spiral-shaped topknot, a bead between the bun and the bottom hair, the square face flanked by pendulous ears. The

博厚重。胸部袒露,上身微前倾,低头俯视。双臂屈肘前伸,左手掌心向上,右手掌心向下置于小像头顶,赤足立于圆台上,神态含蓄慈祥。小像立于大佛右前方,高1.44米,旋涡纹发髻,方圆脸。着袒右袈裟,双手合十,头略低俯,跣足立圆台上,是一天真憨厚少年形象。这组造塑展现了释迦牟尼和儿子罗睺罗相见时的复杂情感。

前壁门两侧各塑一宋元代的菩萨,均束高发髻,面部方圆。左侧菩萨立像,左肩斜披络腋,下穿贴身长裙。双手合十,跣足立圆台上。右侧菩萨坐像,着紧身窄袖短衫,结跏趺坐于高莲台座上。

十五个佛龛内各有一佛或一佛二菩萨。这里主要介绍第3龛、第9龛和第11龛。

第3龛佛与胁侍菩萨:佛高0.82米,佛两侧侍立菩萨。佛与菩萨均细颈削肩,体躯修长,为典型的"秀骨清像"。优美潇洒,保存完好,色彩犹存。佛作高肉髻,结跏趺坐,外披双领下垂袈裟,衣角搭于左臂,衣摆呈三花瓣式垂覆座前。右菩萨束高髻,左菩萨发髻已失,面形长方。身穿交领宽袖上衣,下穿长裙腰系带。帔帛绕双臂飘扬下垂,足蹬云头履(云头已失)。

第9龛弟子阿难:俗称"小沙弥",位于龛内佛座下右侧龛底台座上,圆塑。高0.87米,光头,面容清俊,面带微笑,身林匀称。内着僧祇支,外穿宽大的双领下垂袈裟,衣角搭于左臂。左手牵衣角下垂,右手屈肘举于胸际,手已失。衣摆落地呈喇叭形,衣纹为

Buddha wears an inner vest covering the left shoulder and armpits and an outer garment that completely covers his body, with U-shaped collar falling to the chest, the corner of the robe resting on the left arm with broad and heavy draperies. With bare-chested, the upper body slightly leans forward, leaving his head lower and looking downward. His two hands are extended downward, with the left palm up, while his right hand extends over the head of the small figure with palm down, standing on a circular platform barefoot, with implicit and kind expressions. The small figure standing on the right of the tall Buddha, is 1.44 meters high with a spiral-shaped topknot, a square and round face. He is dressed in the outer robe thrown over the left shoulder or the upper throwing a strong diagonal across the body, leaving the right side of the body and shoulder bare. His palms are pressed together at the chest with slightly lowered head, and he stands on the round platform barefoot respectfully. It is an innocent and simple-minded youthmage. This group of figures shows Sakyamuni's complex father-son affection when he meets his son Rahula.

A bodhisattva made in the Song and Yuan dynasties on each side of the entrance door. They bear the tall topknots and the round faces. The bodhisattva on the left in standing posture is dressed in the upper throwing a strong diagonal across the body, leaving the right side of the body and shoulder bare, the lower sheath dress melting against the body. Her palms are pressed together at the chest, standing on the round platform barefoot. The right-hand bodhisattva in seated posture wears a short tight-fitting gown with close-fitting sleeves, sitting in dhyanasana on a high lotus pedestal.

A Buddha or a Buddha flanked by two bodhisattvas occupies each of 15 niches, we will mainly introduce Niche 3, Niche 6 and Niche 11.

Buddha and attendant bodhisattvas in Niche 3: The Buddha is 0.82 meters high flanked by two standing bodhisattvas. Both the Buddha and the bodhisattvas are in general typical style of "long and slender figure and delicately modelled features", with long thin necks and narrow shoulders, tall, slender and long-legged. They are elegantly and naturally made, well preserved, and traces of colour remain. The Buddha bears a high topknot, sits in the pose of the left leg lying over the right leg. He is robed in an upper garment that completely covers his body, with U-shaped collar falling to the chest, the corner of the robe resting on the left arm, and the hem cascades over his knees, covering the throne in three large lotus petals. The right-hand bodhisattva has high topknot, and the left-hand bodhisattva lost her topknot, with rectangular faces. Their upper garments are of a collar folded across in front and long loose sleeves, their long dresses on the lower bodies with a sash tied at the waist. The scarves coming from shoulders hang down through the armpits fluttering in the wind on each side, their boots embroidered with cloud heads (The cloud heads have disappeared.).

Disciple Ananda in Niche 9: commonly known as the "Little Novice", stands on the base at the bottom of the right side niche beneath the throne of the principal Buddha on the main wall, modelled in the round. He is 0.87 meters high, bald, delicately modelled face, smiling, beautifully proportioned. He is robed in an inner vest covering the left shoulder and

稀疏的阴刻压线，是一天真聪慧少年形象。

第11龛龛楣释迦灵鹫山说法图：悬塑，高0.43米，宽2米。塑有山峦及树木。释迦结跏而坐，袈裟裹膝，在山间为跪听的弟子说法，其旁禅窟有僧禅修。上部左右角二天人起舞。造像头多失，唯右上角飞天最完整，高0.2米，长圆面形，发髻高耸，身穿广袖交领束腰长袍。两手胸前相叠，双腿后翘，帔帛、裙裾一同向身后飘扬，具有强烈的动感。

造像碑：窟内十八块北朝（公元439年—公元581年）石雕造像碑，除10号雕佛传故事外，其他多雕千佛。这里主要介绍1号造像碑、10号造像碑、11号造像碑和16号造像碑。

1号造像碑：北魏（公元386年—公元534年），俗称"千佛碑"。通高1.81米，宽0.59米，厚0.12米。四面雕像，石质坚细，是石刻中的精品。圆拱碑额雕释迦佛灵鹫山说法。上部边缘雕莲瓣饰纹，左右两侧下部内收以突出所雕山形。正面和背面内容大致相同，即各雕一释迦结跏坐浅龛，手作说法印，佛左右各立一菩萨、一弟子。正面龛雕一结跏而坐的小佛，左侧山峦中一走兽。碑身四面雕数排敷彩千佛，共一千三百一十二身，旁有墨书供养人姓名等内容榜题小字，现多已漫漶，是现存造像数量最多的石碑。

10号造像碑：北魏（公元386年—公元534年），又称"佛传碑"，是以释迦牟尼生平事迹为主要内容的碑刻。通高1.37米，宽0.72～0.8米，厚0.1米。圆额，正面分上、中、下三栏，各栏正中各雕一浅龛，龛外两侧设1～2个小格，每格内刻1～3个故事情

armpits, and an outer garment that completely covers his body, with U-shaped collar falling to the chest, the corner of the robe resting on the left arm. His left hand falls, holding the corner of his robe, and his right hand is raised to the chest with hand disappeared. The hem cascades over the ground in the shape of a trumpet, and the drapery in scattered engraving lines. The innocent and intelligent image is scarcely in his teen.

The Preaching of Sakyamuni on the Vulture Peak carved on the lintel in Niche 11: modelled in relief, 0.43 meters high, 2 meters wide. We can just discern a mountainous landscape and flowering trees. Sakyamuni sits with legs tightly locked, with the hem covering over both legs, preaching for his kneeling disciples in the mountains, and on the right a monk meditates in the cave. Above, on the corners of left and right are two dancing flying apsaras. The heads of most sculptures have disappeared. Only the flying apsaras on the upper right corner is intact, with 0.2 meters high, long round face, the high-domed ushnisha, dressed in a waist robe of long loose sleeves and a collar folded across in front. With clasped hands in front of the chest, her two legs bent backwards to the curve of the vault followed by the swirl of the trailing scarves and hems, with a strong rhythmic movement.

Stone Steles: There are 18 stone steles of the Northern Dynasty (AD 439-581), except Stele 10 has the life story of Buddha, others carved Thousands Buddhas. We mainly introduce Stele 1, Stele 10, Stele 11 and Stele 16.

Stele 1: It was erected in the Northern Wei Dynasty (AD 386-534), commonly known as "the Stele of the Thousand Buddhass", with 1.81 meters high, 0.59 meters wide, 0.12 meters thick. The images are carved on four sides, the stone is solid and fine, it is an elaborate work of stone carvings. It is crowned with the Preaching of Sakyamuni on the Vulture Peak. The upper edge of the lintel is decorated with motif of lotus petals, while the mountains are subtly accentuated by receding the lower part of the two sides. The contents of the front and the back are almost identical, each containing Shakyamuni attended by a standing bodhisattva and a disciple on either side, he sits with the legs tightly locked in a yogic pose in a shallow niche, his hands in gesture of preaching. A small Buddha sits with the legs tightly locked in a yogic pose in the front niche, a beast on the left side of the mountains. Several rows of coloured Thousand Buddhas are engraved on the front, the back and the two sides of the stele, there are 1,312 Buddhas in all. Some donors have roughly scratched their names with a brush beside the Buddhas, most of them are illegible now. The most sculptures survive in the stele.

Stele 10: It was erected in the Northern Wei Dynasty (AD 386-534), also known as "Stele of Biography of Buddha", its main content consists of scenes from the life and former lives of the historical Buddha, with 1.37 meters high, 0.72-0.8 meters wide and 0.1 meters thick. With round lintel, the front of the stele is divided into upper, middle and lower three columns, a recess is carved in the center of each column, outside of which one panel or two panels are cut on either side, each engraved with one or three story plots. Except the high relief carvings, those in plastic form also appear. With abundant content and vivid plots, it is the finest work in art of stone stele carvings.

节。除高浮雕外，还出现透雕。内容丰富，情节生动，是石刻造像碑艺术的珍品。

上栏：正中为圆拱浅龛，内刻释迦、多宝二佛并坐。龛左右龛柱上凤鸟做回首反顾状，莲瓣龛楣上有小佛七身。左上格刻"树下思维"和"阿育王施土"，分别表现菩萨成道前在菩提树下思维的情形和古印度阿育王小时候出于对佛的崇敬，双手捧土代面，敬献于佛，佛预言他将来做转轮圣王的故事。左下格雕"佛入涅槃"，表现释迦牟尼在拘尸那迦双树下涅槃的情景。右侧一格雕"断发出家"，表现悉达多太子舍弃富贵，甘愿清苦，夜半逾城出走，进入深山寻师求道。画幅雕山峦丛林，太子坐在山石上持刀断发，上部有两身飞天，右下部五身站像，当为净饭王从亲族中挑选出来陪伴太子的五人。

中栏：正中为楼阁式浅龛，龛内雕一交脚菩萨及二胁侍菩萨，表现将于后世继承释迦佛位为未来佛的弥勒菩萨住在兜率天院内的情景。左上格刻"乘象入胎"，表现佛母摩耶夫人梦见菩萨乘六牙白象前来投胎的故事；左下格刻"降魔成道"，生动地表现了释迦降魔成道的故事内容。右上格刻"树下诞生"和"九龙灌顶"，表现释迦牟尼于农历四月初八日在蓝毗尼园诞生、沐浴的情景；右下格刻"燃灯授记"，正中偏右刻倚坐式燃灯佛，儒童五体投地，布发掩泥，身后有一持花女子站立，是买花献佛的情节。

下栏：正中浅龛内刻释迦成道后在王舍城说法的情景。释迦结跏趺坐于须弥座上，左右各一胁侍菩萨，侧身向佛侍立。龛楣，三个小巧玲珑的化生童子游戏其间。左右两侧有八角龛柱，柱头上

Upper Column: In the topmost center is a panel, in which Shakyamuni and Prabhutaratna share the same throne. The pair of large phoenixes perch on either side of the column in the panel looking backward, and seven small Buddhas are engraved on the lintel decorated with motif of lotus petals. "Meditating under a Tree" and "Offering of a Handful of Dust by Ashoka to Buddha in His Previous Birth" are carved in the upper left panel (upper), they respectively show the scenes that Shakyamuni as a young bodhisattva meditated under a bodhi tree before his enlightenment and the story of the ancient Indian King Ashoka, out of reverence for the Buddha, held a bowl of soil to replace the flour with his hands and offered it to the Buddha. The Buddha gave him an assurance of future attainment of a Chakravartin King. "The Parinirvana of the Buddha" is rendered in the upper left panel (lower), depicting the scene of Buddha's nirvana between the twin sala trees in Kusinagara. "Renunciation of the Head Hair and Going forth into Homelessness" is shown in the upper right panel, it depicts that Prince Siddhartha abandoned his royal life, willing to live in poverty, he rode a horse across the city of Viravastu at midnight and went into the mountains to practice dukkaracariya seeking hermits and enlightenment. The Prince is sitting on the rock holding a knife to cut off his own hair in a mountainous landscape and flowering trees, there are two flying apsaras on the upper part, and five standing figures on the right lower part, which might have been the five disciples selected by King Suddhone from lineages to accompany the Prince.

Middle Column: A bodhisattva with legs pendent and ankles crossed flanked by an attendant bodhisattva occupies the central panel in pavilion style. It shows that Maitreya who, while now still a bodhisattva, will inherit Sakyamuni and come to rule the world in the next kalpa. Here he appears as the present Lord of the Tusita Heaven. "Gautama Entering the Embryo as a White Elephant" is cut in the upper left panel, it describes that the Buddha's mother, Queen Mahamaya dreamed that a white elephant with six tusks entered her right side, which was interpreted to mean that she had conceived a child who would become either a world ruler or a Buddha. The lower left panel is engraved with "Gautama Defeating Mara and Attaining the Enlightenment" is vividly depicted in the lower left panel. The upper right panel is carved with "Gautama Being Born under a Tree" and "Nine Dragons Bathing Gautama as a Baby", showing that Sakyamuni was born on the eighth day of April of the lunar calendar in the Lumbini Garden, and nine dragons sprayed water to bathe the baby Buddha at his birth. The lower right panel "Dipamkara Giving Sumedha Assurance of Future Attainment of Buddhahood", Dipamkara is seated with both legs pendent on a high throne in the center on the right, Sumedha prostrates himself before him, offering his hair for the Buddha to walk upon. A maid with a bunch of flowers in her hands is standing behind Sumedha. It illustrates the incident of the pilgrimage of a boy named Sumedha buying a bunch of fowers and throwing the flowers over the Buddha's head.

Lower Column: In the central panel is engraved with the scene that Sakyamuni devoted himself to the preaching of Buddhism in Rajgir after he himself achieved enlightenment. Shakyamuni sits with the legs tightly locked in a yogic pose on a Sumeru throne, flanked by a standing attendant bodhisattva turning to the Buddha. Three little lotus boys are playing

各一胡跪供养菩萨，柱础下各一足踏夜叉、头顶柱础的托重力士。龛内上部左右两角各一凤鸟，相向而鸣。龛外左右两侧下部各一阙门，门内各天王两身、相向蹲伏的雄狮两头。左上部刻"文殊问疾"，维摩身穿襦袍，手执麈尾，踞坐于方台之上，文殊坐对面，似凝神恭听。右上方刻"初转法轮"，亦称"鹿野苑初转法轮"，释迦佛结跏而坐，座前左右各一卧鹿，回首翘望，左上角有四身飞天自天而降，表现释迦成佛后第一次说法。

11号造像碑：西魏（公元535年—公元556年）。位于前室前壁东侧。方额。高1.84米，宽0.87米，厚0.13米。分上、中、下三栏。上下两栏各刻千佛三排，下栏栏边又刻小千佛一排，共计六十七身。中栏分左、中、右三格。中格，佛帐式浅龛。龛楣并排存七身莲花化生，外上部又并排刻莲蕾、罗汉头像。龛左右为莲花龛柱，柱外垂挂硕大璎珞各一串。龛内刻一佛、二菩萨。佛后有莲瓣形背光，顶作高肉髻，手作说法印，结跏趺坐。身穿双领下垂袈裟，衣摆覆座，褶纹规整而繁密。胁侍菩萨，束发戴冠，肩搭帔帛，下着长裙腰系带，一手拈花，一手下垂，立于覆莲台座上。台座下各刻一蹲狮，翘首反顾，其下一排九身小千佛。左右两格，上各刻飞天上下两身，均作回首反顾状，衣带飘扬。下各雕一圆拱尖楣浅龛，内刻结跏趺坐佛，佛着双领下垂袈裟。低头俯视，神情专注。

16号造像碑：西魏（公元535年—公元556年）。位于前室前壁西侧。方额。高1.8米，宽0.9米，厚0.1米。正面造像，分上下两栏。上栏，中间上部开一竖长方形浅龛，内刻三坐佛。下部刻五坐佛。龛外左右两侧各刻两个方楣龛，上部两龛内二佛并坐，龛楣饰帷幔。下部两龛上部左右角雕宝相花，其中左下龛雕一佛、

in the lotus flowers carved on the lintel of the panel. On either side of the panel there is an octagonal pilaster, on which a votive bodhisattva in the hun way of kneeling with right knee on the ground and left knee up on top of the pilaster, supported by an atlantid on his hands with one foot resting on a yaksha. A pair of large phoenixes that hover on either side of the Buddha's head, chirping towards each other. In the bottom left and right corners cut two tower-shaped panels containing two guardians and two lions crouching towards each other. Upper left engraved "Bodhisattva Manjusri Visiting the Sick Vimalakirti", we can seen that Manjusri and Vimalakirti share the same throne, turning towards each other. The latter wears a robe, holding his fan in his right hand, leaning upon a table, while the bodhisattva seems to be gazing and listening. "First Setting in Motion the Wheel of Dharma", also known as "First Setting in Motion the Wheel of Dharma in Deer Park" in upper right panel, here Sakyamuni sits with the legs crossed and the bottom of the feet under the buttocks, a deer is crouching on each side of the front of the throne, turning their heads around, four flying apsarases are diving headlong down in the upper left corner, it describes the scene of Sakyamun's first preaching after the Enlightenment.

Stele 11: It was erected in the Western Wei Dynasty (AD 535-556), stands on the east side of the front wall of the entrance chamber. With square lintel, it is 1.84 meters high, 0.87 meters wide, 0.13 meters thick. It is divided into three columns: upper, middle and lower. The upper and lower columns are engraved with three rows of Thousand Buddhass, and at the edge of the lower column is carved with a row of small Thousand Buddhass, there are 67 figures in all. The middle column consists of left, middle and right panels. The central panel is a tent-style recess, a group of seven lotus boys in a row on the lintel survive, and the heads of Arhat adorned with lotus buds are carved in a row on the outer upper part. A lotus pilaster on either side of the panel hangs an exceptionally heavy jewelled garland. The panel holds a Buddha flanked by two bodhisattvas. There is a lotus-shaped halo behind the Buddha, he has a high topknot, his hands in gesture of preaching, he sits in the pose of the left leg lying over the right leg. He is robed in an upper garment that completely covers his body, with U-shaped collar falling to the chest, the corner of the rob resting on the left arm, and the hem cascades over his knees, with the symetrical and heavy folds. The hair of the attendant bodhisattvas is gathered high encircled by the diadems, their scarves come over the shoulders, the long dresses on the lower bodies with a band tied on the waist, with one hand raised holding a lotus flower, and the other hanging down, stand on upside-down lotus platforms. Below which a crouching lion is carved on either side with the heads turning around, and there is a row of nine small Thousand Buddhass underneath. On either side are panels depicting two flying apsaras with one above the other, diving headlong down followed by the swirl of their trailing scarves (upper). While each of the lower panels holds a chaitya arched recess with pointed lintel containing a seated Buddha with the legs tightly locked in a yogic pose. He is robed in an upper garment that completely covers his body, with U-shaped collar falling to the chest, the corner of the rob resting on the left arm. He lowers his head, and looking down with rapt expression.

Stele 16: It was erected in the Western Wei Dynasty (AD 535-556), located on the west of the front wall of the entrance chamber. With square lintel, it is 1.8 meters high, 0.9 meters wide,

二菩萨,右下龛雕一佛、二弟子。本栏下部又有坐佛两排,每排七身。下栏,宫殿式圆拱浅龛。龛楣及龛柱饰帷幔,上刻宝珠七颗,其左右各雕一口衔大璎珞蟠龙,龙头外侧又各刻飞天一身,相向飞行。龛内雕三坐佛,中间为倚坐式佛,两侧佛侧身面向主佛,结跏趺坐于通长须弥座两侧。三佛均内着僧祇支,外披双领下垂袈裟。龛外左右下部各雕一天王立于蹲狮背上。本栏下部又刻小坐佛两排,每排七身。

壁画:窟内壁画大部剥落,残存于窟顶及各龛内北魏原作壁画,内容为中国传统神话题材。有千佛、弟子、飞天等,以及龙、凤、鱼、莲花、忍冬、云水纹及火焰纹等图案。窟顶右前方藻井内较完整绘千佛及忍冬,窟顶左侧残存壁画绘有乘龙、骑

第133窟16号造像碑

0.1 meters thick. The sculptures on the front are divided into two columns: upper and lower. In upper column a vertical rectangular recess is cut on the upper part of the center containing three seated Buddhas, and five seated Buddhas on its lower. Outside which on either side are two niches with square lintels, the upper depicting two Buddhas sharing the same throne above the canopy (upper right), and the lower decorated with lotus flowers at the upper left and right corners, among which a Buddha attended by two bodhisattvas (lower left), a Buddha meditating between two disciples (lower right). At the bottom of the upper column there are also two rows of the seated Buddhas, seven on each. In the lower column a palace-style chaitya arched recess is cut, adorned with canopies on the lintel and pilasters crowned by seven pearls, a dragon head with a heavy jewel in its mouth on either side, and on outer side two flying apsaras flying towards each other. It shows two Buddhas sharing a throne, a third Buddha seated with both legs pendent on a higher dais between them. The two flanking Buddhas sit with the legs tightly locked in a yogic pose on the inseperate lotus Sumeru thrones, turning to the central figure. All three Buddhas are robed in the inner vests covering the left shoulder and armpits, the upper garments that completely cover their bodes, with U-shaped collar falling to the chest, the corner of the rob resting on the left arm. Outside the recess a dvarapala standing on the back of a crouching lion is carved at the lower part on each side. Another two rows of the seated Buddhas, seven on each, appear at the bottom of the lower column.

Paintings: Most paintings have peeled away in many places, only the original works of the Northern Wei Dynasty survive on the ceiling and inside the niches containing the theme of traditional Chinese mythology. They are adorned with figures of the Thousand Buddhass, disciples, flying apsaras, etc., as well as motifs of dragons, phoenixes, fish, lotus, honeysuckles, clouds and water and flame. The Thousand Buddhass and honeysuckles are painted completely on the caisson ceiling in the right front, the remainings on the left side of the ceiling are heavenly beings riding on dragons, tigers, phoenixes, flower scattering flying apsaras, and winged figures striding forward, etc.

Inscriptions: There are 74 carved inscriptions or with a brush of different dynasties left by visitors on the steles and inside the cave.

Plaque: The wooden frame is embedded in the inner side of the door. Above its lintel hangs the wooden horizontal board inscribed with "Elysium Hall" engraved in the 41st year of Wanli in the Ming Dynasty (AD 1613).

Extension and Elaboration

Wang Renyu (AD 880-956), also known by his courtesy name Denian, was a native of Tianshui.

虎、跨凤的诸天仆乘、散花飞天，又有肩生羽翼、大步流星奔驰的羽人等。

题记：碑上和窟内刻画或墨书七十四则不同朝代的访客参观题记。

牌匾：窟门内侧嵌置木门框，门楣前悬明万历四十一年（公元1613年）木制牌匾一块，题曰"极乐堂"。

引申与拓展

王仁裕（公元880年—公元956年），字德辇，天水人也。后仕蜀为翰林学士，有《西江集》。根据历史文献记载，公元911年，王仁裕曾登临该窟，并写诗对洞窟内的造像、碑刻、空间等大加赞叹。他写道："由西阁悬梯而上，其间千房万屋。缘空蹑虚，登之者不敢回顾。将及绝顶，有万菩萨堂，凿石而成，广若今之大殿。其雕梁画栱，绣栋云楣，并就石而成，万躯菩萨，列于一堂。"时前唐末辛未年，登此留题，于今三十九载矣。

He later served as a Hanlin scholar in Shu (AD 907-925), and compiled a collection of poems called *The Collection of Xi River*. According to historical documents, Wang Renyu ascended the cave in AD 911 and wrote an inscription in the cave praising the sculptures, stone steles, and space of the cave highly. He wrote, "When you went up the hanging ladder of the West Pavilion, you could see many grottoes and because the hanging ladder was high up in the air, some ladder climbers afraid of high places dared not look back. Near the summit, there is the Hall of Ten Thousand Bodhisattvas, which was built by chiseling rocks and is as wide as the today's hall. Its carved and embroidered beams and painted arches were all carved out of stone. Ten thousand Bodhisattva statues are arranged in a large room. It was in the year of Xinwei (AD 911) after the Tang Dynasty, I came here to write a poem as a souvenir, so it is 39 years from then.

Readers can compare the English version of the poem from *The Cave Temples of Maichi Mountain* by Michael Sullivan, 1969: 34.

"Ascending a hanging ladder from the Western Alcove, there are on the way a thousand rooms and a myriad chambers; the edge is unprotected, and from it one steps on to air; in climbing none dares look over his shoulder. Climbing to the very top one discovers a Hall of a Myriad Bodhisattvas excavated in the rock, more spacious than any of the great halls of ancient and modern times. Carved beams and painted struts, carved ceiling ridges and lintels with relief carving of clouds, all were excavated from the living rock. In a hall are aligned a myriad figures of bodhisattvas." The interval of 39 years which elapsed between Wang Renyu's visit and the writing of this description.

第135窟 天堂洞

第135窟位于西崖东上部,王仁裕在《玉堂闲话》中称之为"天堂",俗称"天堂洞"。开凿于北魏(公元386年—公元534年),北周(公元557年—公元581年)、宋代(公元960年—公元1279年)重修。该窟是西崖最高的洞窟,存有麦积山最大的单体石雕造像。

该窟内有北魏、北周和宋代十五身泥塑和石雕像,正壁上部涅槃经变画,二十八则在基座、壁面的刻画或墨书题记。

形制:该窟为平面横长方形、平顶。窟高4.65米、宽8.84米、深4.71米。前壁正中开方形甬道,窟内正、左、右三壁原各开一个圆拱形浅龛,北周在正壁龛两侧各增开一个圆拱形深龛。窟门之上凿通三个明窗可让更多光线照进洞窟。

造像:窟内正壁中龛和左壁龛内塑一佛二菩萨,其他三龛造像均有残缺。正壁左右侧龛内分别塑二坐佛和一佛一菩萨,右壁龛内塑一佛一菩萨。窟中央左侧石雕一佛二菩萨立像,共计十五身。

正壁中龛和左壁龛内一佛二菩萨造像风格大致相同。两佛磨光高肉髻,长圆面形,身躯前倾。上身内着僧祇支,外着双领下垂袈裟。左手施与愿印,右手施无畏印,结跏趺坐于长方形台座之

Cave 135　Hall of Heaven

Cave 135 is located in the upper east part of the western cliff, and it is commonly known as "Hall of Heaven" for being called "Heaven" by the poet Wang Renyu of the Tang Dynasty in his work *Idle Tales of the Jade Hall*. It was originally dug in the Northern Wei Dynasty (AD 386-534) and repaired in the Northern Zhou Dynasty (AD 557-581) and the Song Dynasty (AD 960-1279). It is the highest cave in the western cliff which contains the largest single stone carving at Maijishan.

Visitors will enjoy 15 clay sculptures and stone carvings of the Northern Wei, the Northern Zhou and the Song dynasties, paintings of the Nirvana Sutra Illustration on the upper part of the main wall, and 28 inscriptions carved or with a brush on the seats and the walls. Details are as follows.

Type: It is a plane horizontal rectangle niche with a flat ceiling. It is 4.65 meters high, 8.84 meters wide and 4.71 meters deep. A square passage is cut in the center of the front wall, a chaitya arched shallow bay is originally carved into the main wall and each of the flanking walls, a chaitya arched deep bay into each of the main wall was added in the Northern Zhou Dynasty. Three windows were cut above the door, admitting more light into the cave.

Sculptures: A Buddha flanked by two bodhisattvas are modelled in the central niche of the main wall and the niche on the left wall, sculptures in other three niches are incomplete. Two seated Buddhas or a Buddha attended by a bodhisattva in each of the side niches of the main wall respectively, and a Buddha and a bodhisattva in the niche into the right wall. On the left in the center of the hall stands a stone Buddha flanked by two bodhisattvas. There are 15 figures in all.

The style of a Buddha flanked by two bodhisattvas in each niche into the main wall and the niche into the left wall is almost identical. Two Buddhas bear the polished high topknots, the round faces, in a frontal pose. They are robed in the inner vests covering the left shoulder and armpits, the upper garments that completely cover the bodies, with U-shaped collar falling to the chest, the corner of the rob resting on the left arm. With their right

上。袈裟下摆呈"八"字重叠覆于台座前,身后绘有莲瓣形项光及身光。

四身胁侍菩萨,顶束扇形高髻,面形消瘦,体躯扁平前倾侧向主佛。身着交领衣,披帛自双肩下垂。足穿云头履而立,头后项光为多重同心圆。其中正壁中龛左侧菩萨左手下垂提桃形玉璧,右手携帛带抚于胸前。右侧菩萨左手拈花抚胸,右手下垂提帛带。左壁龛菩萨左手提桃形法器于腹前,右手举于胸前。

正壁左侧龛内主佛和左侧小坐佛塑于北周。双手施禅定印,结跏趺坐于方形台座之上。主佛的衣摆呈三瓣下垂覆盖座前。正壁右侧龛宋代佛,螺髻,手势和坐姿同于正壁左侧龛内主佛。其左侧宋代菩萨,双手于胸前上下交叠,跣足而立。右壁龛宋代佛,螺髻,左手抚膝,右手无畏印,结跏趺坐于长方形座上。左侧胁侍菩萨,左手置于胸前,右手下垂于腿侧。

窟中央左侧石雕一佛二菩萨北魏石雕立像,是天堂洞的杰出造像。主佛高1.9米,旋涡纹高肉髻,面形方圆。内着僧祇支,胸前系带作结下垂,外着双领下垂袈裟。衣纹褶皱线条流畅、轻薄贴体。左手施与愿印,右手无畏印(手已残),赤足站立在圆形仰覆莲台上。

左右胁侍菩萨,头均残失,均高约1.3米,颈饰花式宽项圈,腕戴环。上身坦露,下着长裙。帛带与璎珞自双肩下垂至腹前穿环交叉后上绕搭臂自然垂下。右手拈花上举于胸前,左手置于腹部,跣足立于圆形仰覆莲台上。左侧菩萨提桃形法器,右侧菩萨提圆形玉璧。

壁画:墙壁上的画面脱落严重,但残存的均为六世纪初作品。正壁上方存涅槃经变画,由三部分组成。中间为释迦说法图,右侧绘八王争舍利,其左侧主题模糊无法确定。

hands in the abhaya mudra, and their left hands in the varada mudra, they sit in dhyanasana on the rectangular thrones. The hem covers the thrones in two large lotus petals. There are lotus petal-shaped aureoles and mandorlas behind them.

Four attendant bodhisattvas have the high fan-shaped topknots, the thin faces, the flat frontal bodies turning to the principal Buddhas. Dressed in outer garments with a crossing collar, their scarves hang from the shoulders. They stand in cloud head shoes backed by aureoles composed of multi-tiered concentric circles. Among them, the bodhisattva on the left in the central niche of the main wall holds a peach-shaped jade to the abdomen level in her left hand, and her right hand is raised on the chest holding a ribbon. The bodhisattva on the right puts the left hand on the chest carrying a flower, and her right hand is placed to the abdomen level holding a ribbon. The bodhisattva in the niche into the left wall holds a peach-shaped object to the abdomen level in her left hand, and her right hand is lifted to the chest level.

The principal Buddha and the small Buddha on his left occupy the niche on the left of the main wall are modelled in the Northern Zhou Dynasty. With hands in dhyana mudra, they sit with the legs tightly locked in a yogic pose on the square thrones. The hem of the principal Buddha covers the throne in three large lotus petals. The Buddha in the niche on the right of the main wall modelled in the Song Dynasty bears a spiral-shaped topknot, whose gesture and sitting posture are the same as the principal Buddha in the niche on the left of the main wall. The bodhisattva on his left made in the Song Dynasty lifts the two hands to the chest, her palms with fingers extended and touching each other, standing barefoot. The Buddha in the niche into the right wall made in the Song Dynasty has a spiral-shaped topknot, his left hand rests on knee, and his right hand is in the abhaya mudra, sitting in dhyanasana on the rectangular throne. The attendant bodhisattva on his left places the left hand to the chest, and the right hand hanging down beside the thigh.

On the left in the center of the hall stands a stone Buddha flanked by two bodhisattvas carved in the Northern Wei Dynasty are the outstanding sculpturs of the Hall of Heaven. The principal Buddha is 1.9 meters high, with a high spiral-shaped topknot and the square face. He is robed in an inner vest covering the left shoulder and armpits, with a band tied at the chest falling in a knot, an upper garment that completely covers his body, with U-shaped collar falling to the chest, the lappet of the robe resting on the left arm. The folds of the drapery are cut in smooth and flat lines, thinly clad and melting into the body. With his left hand in the varada mudra and the right hand in the abhaya mudra, which has damaged, he stands on a circular double-reverse lotus platform barefoot.

The heads of the two attendant bodhisattvas on each side have disappeared. They are about 1.3 meters high, decorated with the broad flower-shaped collars round the necks and the wrist rings on the arms. With upper bodies bare, their lower bodies are robed in the long dresses. The broad scarves and jewelled garlands come over the shoulders and down to pass through a ring over the lower abdomen, then up resting on arms and down naturally. Holding a lotus flower to the chest level in their right hands, and their left hands are placed

第135窟八王争舍利壁画（局部）

中间说法图中画一佛二菩萨，为释迦说法的情景。佛和二菩萨头部均残失。佛着通肩袈裟。双手结禅定印，结跏趺坐于"工"字形台座上，袈裟下摆呈两瓣下垂覆盖座前。身后有身光。两侧菩萨饰品和衣着与石雕菩萨大致相同。左手举于肩前，跣足立于覆莲台上。其右侧八王争舍利，色彩模糊，主要情节尚可辨认。壁面右侧绘一长方形祭坛，坛上放置八个装舍利的宝瓶。左侧有手持兵器武士策马争斗场面。

题记：在基座、壁面留有二十八则刻画或墨书游客题记。

引申与拓展

该窟正壁上部的涅槃经变场景，几乎与第127窟相同。

to the abdomen level, they stand on double-reverse lotus platforms barefoot. The left-hand bodhisattva carries a peach-shaped object, and the right-hand figure holds a circular jade.

Paintings: Pictures on the walls have fallen away badly, but what remains is the works of early sixth-century. Above the main wall we can see the Nirvana Sutra Illustration, composed of three parts. The scene of Sakyamuni's preaching is painted in the center, on its right illustrates the eight kings who fought for Buddha's remains, the topic on its left is too blur to be made out.

A Buddha attended by two bodhisattvas on either side are painted in the center, which is the scene of Sakyamuni's preaching. Each head of the Buddha and two bodhisattvas has disappeared. The Buddha is robed in an upper garment that completely covers his body and hangs in heavy folds round his shoulders. With two hands in dhyana mudra, he sits with legs tightly locked in a yogic pose on an "I-shaped" throne, the hem covering the throne in two large lotus petals. There is a mandorla behind him. The ornaments and clothing of two flanking bodhisattvas are almost identical with that of stone bodhisattvas. Their left hands are raised to the shoulder level, they stand on the upside-down lotus platforms. The colour of the eight kings who fought for sacred relics of the Buddha on its right is indistinct, but we can still make out the main plots. A rectangular altar is painted on the right of the picture, on which eight vases containg the sacred relics of the Buddha are placed. On its left, there is a scene of the warriors armed with weapons fighting on horses.

Inscriptions: There are 28 inscriptions carved or with a brush on the seats and the walls left by visitors.

Extension and Elaboration

The scene of the Nirvana Sutra Illustration on the upper part of the main wall is almost identical with that of Cave 127, visitors can compare their differences.

In AD 911 the poet Wang Renyu of the Tang Dynasty entered the Hall of Heaven, he described his climb experience in his collection *Idle Tales of the Jade Hall*. "Above this room, there is a niche called heaven. With a single wooden ladder in the air, you can climb along it. When we arrived at this place, none of the ten thousand people dared to climb it. When you look down from here, the mountains are like low towers. Wang Renyu was the only one who could get up there alone. And he inscribed on the west wall of the heaven."

Michael Sullivan described the hazards of Wang Renyu climbing the Hall of Heaven in *The Cave Temples of Maichi Mountain*, 1969: 40. "by climbing up a single ladder. Not one in a thousand has the nerve for this climb. Looking down from this position we see the mass of

公元911年，五代时期文学家王仁裕进入天堂洞，在其《玉堂闲话》中这样描述攀登体验："自此室之上，更有一龛，谓之天堂。空中倚一独梯，攀缘而上。至此则万中无一人敢登者。于此下顾，其群山皆如培楼。王仁裕时，独能登之。仍题诗于天堂石壁上。"

迈克尔·苏立文在其书中描述王仁裕登天堂洞的危险性时，提到王仁裕从六个角度"万仞梯、白云齐、群山小、落日低、人少到、鹤频栖"描写麦积山巍峨险峻的自然景观。

王仁裕小诗《题麦积山天堂》摘录如下。

题麦积山天堂

蹑尽悬空万仞梯，
等闲身共白云齐。
檐前下视群山小，
堂上平分落日低。
绝顶路危人少到，
古岩松健鹤频栖。
天边为要留名姓，
拂石殷勤手自题。

mountains like a low bank." In AD 911 the brave poet Wang Renyu climbed up to it alone and left a poem on its west wall.

The poem *Written on the Wall in the Hall of Heaven at Maijishan* by Wang Renyu is as follows. The poet describes the towering and precipitous natural landscape of Maijishan from six angles, "the high ladder hanging in the air, as high as the white clouds, small mountains, low sunset, few people, and frequent cranes".

Written on the Wall in the Hall of Heaven at Maijishan
Ascending to the end of the high ladder hanging in the air,
I am already as high as the white clouds.
When I look down under the eaves of the "heaven", the mountains have become short and small,
the "heaven" is as low as the setting sun.
The top of the cliff is rarely reached because of the perilous ladder,
cranes are often attracted by strong green pines from ancient rocks.
The purpose of my arriving at the sky is to leave my name here,
so I gently wipe the rock and affectionately write my own poem here.

Readers can compare another version of the poem in *The Cave Temples of Maichi Mountain* by Michael Sullivan, 1969: 40.
I have climbed the full length of the myriad-fathom ladder suspended over space,
Making my idle body the co-equal of the white clouds.
Beyond the caves and far below how small the mountains!
From the hall the level rays of the setting sun seem low;
At the peak the road is perilous; few men can reach so far.
On the aged cliff the pines are sturdy, the cranes there love to dwell.
I would leave my name in this distant place beyond the horizon,
So, dusting the rocks, I diligently inscribe these words.

第136窟

第136窟位于西崖东上部,开凿于北周(公元557—公元581年),宋代(公元960年—公元1279年)重修。两尊菩萨和主佛一样结跏趺坐于莲花座上。

该窟内有精美的十一世纪的三身造像,三座"工字形"高仰覆莲座,一则刻画于正壁左侧的题记。

形制:该窟平面方形、四角攒尖顶,高3.06米、宽3.1米、深3.1米。正、左、右三壁有十一世纪制作的"工"字形高莲花座,两层仰莲,边缘装饰花卉。

造像:窟内正壁塑十一世纪一佛、左、右壁塑二菩萨,共三尊造像,都坐在束腰高仰莲坐上。

佛高1.1米,螺纹发髻,有圆形肉髻珠,方圆脸,双眼微启。内着僧祇支,腰部束带打结下垂,外着袈裟为双领下垂式。双手施禅定印,结跏趺坐,袈裟下摆平放在莲花台上面。佛后绘圆形头光,由两圈白色和橘黄色同心圆组成。

左右壁菩萨高度均为1.1米,姿态基本相同。束高发髻,戴头巾,其状如高耸的莲花,方圆脸。项戴三、四道串珠项饰,结跏趺

第二章 麦积山石窟汉英解说词

Cave 136

Cave 136 is located on the upper east part of the western cliff, and was initially excavated in the Northern Zhou Dynasty (AD 557-581), and repaired in the Song Dynasty (AD 960-1279). The two bodhisattvas are seated in dhyanasana on lotus thrones like that of the principal Buddha.

Visitors can enjoy three exquisite sculptures of the 11th century, three high I-shaped double reverse lotus thrones, and an inscription carved on the left of the main wall. Details are as follows.

Type: It is a flat square niche with the "dome of heaven" ceiling, is 3.06 meters high, 3.1 meters wide, 3.1 meters deep. A high I-shaped lotus throne made in the 11th century is set on each of the main wall and the side walls, with two tiers of upturned lotus petals, and the borders decorated with flowers.

Sculptures: A Buddha of the 11th century remains on the main wall, and two bodhisattvas on each of the side walls. There are three figures in all, which are all seated on the high I-shaped upturned lotus thrones.

The Buddha is 1.1 meters high, the hair and ushnisha arranged in tight curls, a circular bead between the bun and the bottom hair, the round face with eyes slightly open. He is robed in an inner vest covering the left shoulder and armpits, a band tied around the waist falling in a knot, an upper garment that completely covers his body, with U-shaped collar falling to the chest, the lappet of the robe resting on the left arm. With two hands in dhyana mudra, he is seated with legs tightly locked in a yogic pose, the hem of the robe resting over the lotus throne. There is a circular aureole behind him, composed of two concentric circles in white and orange.

坐于莲花座上。袈裟的着装形式与佛基本相同。左壁菩萨双手施禅定印，右壁菩萨双手相握于腹前。右壁菩萨可见三层同心圆头光和椭圆形身光。

题记：正壁左侧有一条十七世纪的题记，文字不全，是一位来自凉州（武威）的僧人到这里拜访时留下的。

引申与拓展

常见的麦积山石窟菩萨为站姿，但我们前面也见到坐姿的交脚菩萨和思维菩萨。该窟两尊菩萨结跏趺坐于须弥座上，须弥座介绍可参考第25窟。这是佛教认为最安稳、宁定的一种坐姿，所以，以这种坐姿出现的菩萨造像，给人的感觉都是比较庄严的。

该窟菩萨五官、头巾、着装、手势与第165窟菩萨基本相同。

The bodhisattva on each side walls is 1.1 meters high, and their attitudes are basically identical. They bear the high topknots tucked by the hairscarves like a towering lotus, the round faces. Three or four strings of pearls hang from a heavy collar round the necks, they sit with legs tightly locked in a yogic pose on the lotus thrones. The way they are dressed is almost the same with that of the Buddha. The hands of the bodhisattva on the left are in dhyana mudra, and the right-hand figure rest two hands at the abdomen with the left hand into a fist and the right hand held straight against the fist. An aureole composed of three layers of concentric circles and an oval mandorla behind her are visible. The two attendant bodhisattvas on the side walls are 2.4 meters high, the high topknot.

Inscription: There is an inscription of the 17th century carved on the left of the main wall, with some characters missing. It was left by a monk from Liangzhou (Wuwei) when he visited here.

Extension and Elaboration

Bodhisattvas at Maijishan are common in standing posture, but we have also seen the seated cross-ankled bodhisattva and the bodhisattva in pensive pose. The two bodhisattvas in the cave are seated in dhyanasana on the lotus Sumeru throne, which you can consult more information in Cave 25. This is the most stable and peaceful seated position in Buddhism, so the bodhisattva appearing in this pose gives a more solemn impression.

The facial features, headscarves, clothes and gestures of the bodhisattvas in the cave are basically the same as those of the bodhisattvas in Cave 165. Readers can compare the similarities and differences.

第139窟

第139窟位于西崖东上部,开凿于北魏(公元386年—公元534年)。整个窟被香火熏黑,壁画均脱落。

该窟内有五身泥塑造像。

形制:该窟是平面方形、平顶窟。前壁有方形甬道,地面凿低坛基。正壁砌长方形基座。

造像:正壁塑一身坐佛,右侧一身弟子。左壁塑一身菩萨、一身力士。右壁塑一身力士,共计五身。

正壁佛,磨光高肉髻,方脸,眉间白毫相。内着交领衣,外着双领下垂袈裟。左手抚膝,右臂置于胸前,手已残。结跏趺坐于长方形基座上,袈裟下摆呈两片弧形覆盖于座前。

右侧弟子,高鼻细目,嘴角上扬。内着僧祇支,外着双领下垂袈裟。双手合十置于胸前,穿靴立于低坛台上。

左壁菩萨,半圆形高发髻,方面,眉间有白毫相。颈戴圆形项圈并坠有花饰和璎珞。上身袒露,肩部有圆形佩饰。帛带与璎珞自双肩下垂于腹前交叉后绕搭双肘自然垂下,璎珞由串珠、珊瑚、玉

Cave 139

Cave 139 is located at the upper east part of the western cliff, and was excavated in the Northern Wei Dynasty (AD 386-534). The whole cave was smokedarkened by incenses, and all the paintings have fallen away.

In the cave visitors will enjoy five clay sculptures. Details are as follows.

Type: It is a flat square niche with a flat ceiling. There is a square passage on the front wall. A low base is cut around the ground. A rectangle throne is set on the main wall.

Sculptures: A seated Buddha is modelled in clay with a disciple on his right on the main wall. The left wall holds a bodhisattva and a dvarapala. A dvarapala occupies the right wall. There are five figures in all.

The Buddha on the main wall has a polished high topknot, and the square face is carved with the white hair between the brows. He is dressed in an inner robe with a crossing collar, an outer garment that completely covers his body, with U-shaped collar falling to the chest, the corner of the robe resting on the left arm with broad and heavy draperies. His left hand rests on knee, and the right arm is raised to the chest with the hand destroyed. He sits in dhyanasana on the rectangular throne with the hem covering it in two curved petals.

The disciple on the right has a high nose flanked by gently opened almond eyes, with the corners of the mouth upwards. He is robed in an inner vest covering the left shoulder and armpits, an outer garment that completely covers his body, with U-shaped collar falling to the chest, the lappet of the robe resting on the left arm. With palms pressed together at the chest, he stands on the low platform in boots.

璧等组成。腰带佩饰玉璧。左手施无畏印，右手持莲于腹部。下着长裙，跣足立于坛基上。

左右壁力士，额头有皱纹，凸目圆睁。塌鼻，鼻孔外翻。上身袒露，下着长裙并腰间系带作结。天衣覆肩，立于低坛台上，双足残失。其中左壁力士，双腿叉开，身体略向左斜倾。低平球形发髻，粗眉倒竖，面颊凹陷，络腮胡须，歪嘴，颈部肌肉凸起。双臂残失。右壁力士，身体向右斜倾。扇形高发髻，弯眉凸颊，张口。天衣自肩头从腹前垂下后上绕，一端搭于右臂，一端自然下垂。左前臂残失，右手握拳至胸部。

引申与拓展

该窟左壁力士，双腿跨开站立，身体呈"S"形向窟门方向倾斜。此种站姿具有明显的动感，与第142窟前壁左侧力士相似。

The bodhisattva on the left wall bears a high semi-circular topknot, and the square face is carved with the white hair between the brows. There is a circular collar around the neck with pendents of flowers and wreaths. The upper body is exposed, and there are circular ornaments on the shoulders. Both scarf and garland of jewels hang from the shoulders and down to cross at the abdomen and up rest on the arms and down again naturally, the latter is composed of strings of pearls, corals and jades. The sash is adorned with a jade. The left hand is in the abhaya mudra, and the right hand is placed on the abdomen holding a lotus. With a long dress on the lower body, she stands on the platform barefoot.

The dvarapalas on either side walls get wrinkles on the foreheads, the bulging eyes are round open in fury attitude. They are snub-nosed, their nostrils face upward. With exposed upper bodies, their lower bodies are robed in long dress with a band tied at the waists falling in a knot. Their outer shawls cover both shoulders, they stand on the low platforms with feet missing. Among them, the dvarapala on the left wall stands with his legs wide open, with the slightly swaying curve of the body towards the left. He bears a low flat spherical topknot, inverted broad brows, sunken cheeks, bearded, slanting mouth, swelling muscles on the neck, with both arms lost. The dvarapala on the right wall sways the slightly curve of the body towards the right. He has a high fan-shaped topknot, arched brows and raised cheeks, keeping his mouth open. The outer shawl covers both shoulders and down to cross at the abdomen, one end resting on the right arm and the other down naturally. With the left forearm missing, the right hand is lifted to the chest in a fist.

Extension and Elaboration

With the slightly swaying curve of the body towards the door, the dvarapala on the left wall stands with his legs wide apart. This standing posture carries an obvious rhythmic movement, similar to the dvarapala on the left of the front wall in Cave 142.

第140窟

第140窟位于西崖东上部,开凿于北魏(公元386年—公元534年)。窟顶存麦积山唯一北周(公元557年—公元581年)飞天与佛塔组合壁画。

该窟内有八身泥塑造像,窟顶飞天佛塔图,十一则留在正、左、右壁和窟顶的刻画或墨书题记。

形制:该窟是平面方形、平顶窟。前壁有长方形圆拱顶甬道,地面凿低坛基,三壁前各砌"工"字形台座。

造像:正、左、右壁各塑一坐佛,主佛两侧各一立胁侍菩萨,左壁佛左侧一胁侍菩萨,右壁佛左、右两侧各一胁侍菩萨,共计八身。

正、左、右壁坐佛,造像风格基本相同,只是主佛体量略大于两侧佛。均内着僧祇支,衣带胸下打结,外着双领下垂袈裟。结跏趺坐于基座上,下摆分三片呈圆弧状垂于座前。身后浮塑莲瓣形项身光。身光外侧作火焰纹,项光由忍冬纹、多重同心圆、放射状条纹组成。其中主佛双臂前伸,双手已失。项光左、右下方各有一胡跪供养弟子。主佛和右壁佛磨光高肉髻,长方面形,弯眉高鼻,

Cave 140

Cave 140 is located at the upper east part of the western cliff, and was excavated in the Northern Wei Dynasty (AD 386-534). The ceiling contains the only mural of a combination of flying apsaras and a stupa painted in the Northern Zhou Dynasty (AD 557-581) at Maijishan.

In the cave visitors can enjoy eight clay sculptures, the image combination of flying apsaras and a stupa on the ceiling, 11 inscriptions carved or with a brush left on the main wall, two side walls and the ceiling. Details are as follows.

Type: It is a flat square niche with a flat ceiling. There is a rectangle passage with the chaitya arched ceiling on the front wall. A low base is cut around the ground. An I-shaped rectangle throne is set on each of the main wall and two flanking walls.

Sculptures: A seated Buddha is modelled on each of the main wall and two side walls, with an attendant bodhisattva on either side of the principal Buddha, an attendant bodhisattva on the left of the Buddha on the left wall, an attendant bodhisattva on each side of the Buddha on the right wall. There are eight figures in all.

The style of the seated Buddhas on each of the main wall and two side walls is basically the same, only the size of the principal Buddha is slightly larger than the two flanking Buddhas. They are robed in the inner vests covering the left shoulder and armpits, a sash tied round the waists, the outer garments that completely cover their bodies, with U-shaped collar falling to the chest, the lappet of the robe resting on the left arm. They are seated with legs tightly locked in a yogic pose on the thrones with the hems covering in three large circular arcs. There are lotus petal-shaped aureoles and mandorlas in relief behind them, with flaming motif on the outer rim of the mandorlas, the aureoles are composed of honeysuckle patterns, multi-tiered concentric circles and radioactive stripes. Among them, the arms of the principal Buddha are raised forward with

小嘴，宽肩。左壁佛头已失。右壁佛左手提衣角下垂，右手施无畏印。

正壁左右侧菩萨，颈部戴项圈坠璎珞。上身袒露，帛带自双肩下垂至腹前交叉上绕穿肘自然下垂，长璎珞于腹下交叉上绕，有串珠、玉璧等饰物。右手提桃形法器于腹前，左臂残失。下系长裙，腰带悬玉璧。立于低坛基上，身后有多重同心圆项光。其中左侧菩萨高发髻，右侧菩萨头已失。

左壁左侧菩萨，高发髻，双手捧供品于胸前。内着僧祇支，外着双领下垂袈裟。右膝微屈站立。

右壁左侧菩萨，头已失，左手提桃形法器于腹前。右臂及右手残，双足残失。

右侧菩萨，高发髻，双手合十置于胸前。衣着与左壁左侧菩萨相同。屈左膝站立。

壁画：窟顶正中绘有圆莲，下方有一佛塔，飞天从两侧绕飞。

题记：游客在正、左、右壁和窟顶留下十一则刻画或墨书题记。

引申与拓展

在正、右壁之间地面角落有一接近于圆形的孔洞通此窟下方的第154窟，左壁内侧有一长方形圆拱顶的孔洞通第141窟。

hands lost. There is a votive disciple in the hun way of kneeling with right knee on the ground and left knee up is modelled in rerief below either side of the aureole. Both the principal Buddha and the right-wall Buddha bear polished high topknots, the long and square faces carved with arched brows, high noses and small mouths, broad shoulders. The left-wall Buddha has lost his head. The left hand of the right-wall Buddha hangs down holding the corner of the robe, and the right hand is in the abhaya mudra.

The bodhisattvas on either side of the main wall bear the collars around the necks with pendents of wreaths. Their upper bodies are exposed, their scarves hang from the shoulders and down to cross at the abdomens and up through the armpits and down again naturally, their long garlands of jewels cross below the abdomens and up, which are composed of strings of pearls, jades and other ornaments. Their right hands are placed to the abdomen level carrying the peach-shaped objects, and their left arms are missing. Their lower bodies are robed in long dresses with the sashes adorned with jades. They stand on the low platforms backed by circular aureoles composed of multi-tiered concentric circles. Among them, the left-side bodhisattva has a high topknot, and the right-side bodhisattva is headless.

The left-side bodhisattva on the left wall wears a high topknot with hands holding the offering on the chest. She is robed in an inner vest covering the left shoulder and armpits, an outer garment that completely covers the body, with U-shaped collar falling to the chest, the lappet of the robe resting on the left arm. She stands with the right knee slightly bent.

The left-side bodhisattva on the right wall is headless, and the right hand is placed to the abdomen level holding a peach-shaped object. She has lost her right arm, right hand and feet. The right-side bodhisattva has a high topknot, with palms pressed together at the chest. The robe is identical with that of the left-side bodhisattva on the left wall. She stands with the left knee slightly bent.

Paintings: A circular lotus is painted on the center of the ceiling, below is a stupa with the flying apsaras around from both sides.

Inscriptions: There are 11 inscriptions carved or with a brush left by visitors on the main wall, two side walls and the ceiling.

Extension and Elaboration

In the corner of the ground between the main and right walls, there is a nearly circular hole leading to Cave 154 just below the cave, and a rectangular arched hole in the inner side of the left wall passing through Cave 141.

第141窟

第141窟位于西崖东上部,西邻第140窟,开凿于北周(公元557年—公元581年)。该洞窟内现存造像为北周原作,单薄贴体的衣着风格受到当时绘画形式的影响。

该窟为北周的典型帐形洞窟,七尊木骨泥塑造像,窟顶藻井绘卷云纹图案,正壁和右壁龛内四则刻画或墨书题记。

形制:该窟为平面方形、覆斗顶,宽3.08米、高2.68米、进深2.8米,洞窟保存完整。窟前壁有方形甬道,窟内各个壁面与窟顶相接处均雕刻半圆形帐杆、帐柱。窟顶正中凿方形藻井,内雕一凸起的圆形莲花。正壁开一圆拱尖楣大龛,左右壁各开凿一字排开的三个略小佛龛,形成七佛的布局。

造像:窟内正壁龛内一坐佛,龛外两侧各一身胁侍菩萨,左、右壁各龛残存两佛,共七身木骨泥塑造像。

正壁佛高1.34米。头顶有低平肉髻,躯体浑圆。上身着僧祇支,胸下系带,外披双领下垂袈裟,单薄贴体。双臂前伸、双手已经残损。结跏趺坐,下摆分两片覆盖座前。佛身后绘有莲花瓣形头光和身光,其上绘制火焰纹、莲华、忍冬纹图案。

第二章 麦积山石窟汉英解说词

Cave 141

Cave 141 is located on the upper east part of the western cliff, to its west is the Cave 140, excavated in the Northern Zhou Dynasty (AD 557-581). The surviving sculptures are the original works of the Northern Zhou Dynasty, the style of thinly clad and melting into the body influenced by the paintings at the time.

Visitors will enjoy the typical tent-shaped cave of the Northern Zhou Dynasty, seven figures of clay modelled on a wooden armature, the motif of curly cloud painted on the coffered ceiling, and four engraved inscriptions or with a brush on the main wall and in the niche into the right wall. Details are as follows.

Type: It is a flat square niche with the upside-down *dou* ceiling, is 3.08 meters wide, 2.68 meters high, 2.80 meters deep, and it is well-preserved. There is a square passage on the front wall, the semi-circular tent poles, and tent columns are carved at the junction between the ceiling and four corners. A square coffered ceiling is cut in the center of the ceiling containing a raised circular lotus flower. A chaitya arched recess with a pointed lintel is cut into the main wall, and three slightly smaller niches in a row into each side wall, reaching a layout of the seven Buddhas.

Sculptures: A seated Buddha occupies a niche cut into the main wall, outside which a bodhisattva stands on each side, two Buddhas remain in each niches into each of the side walls. There are seven figures of clay modelled on a wooden armature in all.

The Buddha on the main wall is 1.34 meters high. He bears a low topknot, the body is round and full. He is robed in an inner vest covering the left shoulder and armpits, a sash tied at the chest, an upper garment that completely covers his body, with U-shaped collar falling to the chest, the lappet of the robe resting on the left arm, which is thinly clad and melting in the body. The arms are stretched out in front with hands damaged. He is seated

两侧胁侍菩萨头顶束高发髻,戴装饰着花瓣头冠,长圆脸,五官清秀,颈戴项圈,帔帛从双肩下垂至膝部上卷。下穿翻边长裙,跣足立于莲台上。

左右壁各龛内佛整体形象与正壁佛相同,只是高度略小。

壁画:窟顶藻井绘有卷云纹图案,为北周原作。多以赭红、石绿为主。

题记:访客在正壁和右壁龛内四则刻画或墨书题记。

引申与拓展

由于该窟与第140窟距离太近,两个洞窟之间的石壁厚度只有10厘米。第140窟开凿时间早于该窟,所以该窟在开凿的时候就挖了直通第140窟的一个洞口。

曹仲达是六世纪著名的画家,他绘制的人物形象躯体饱满圆润,衣服单薄,衣纹贴体,犹如刚从水中出来一般。当时的佛教雕塑也受到这种绘画形式的影响,而该窟就是比较典型的例子。

in dhyanasana with hem covering the throne in two large petals. There is a lotus petal-shaped aureole and mandorla behind him, painted with the motifs of flame, lotus flower, and honeysuckle.

The attendant bodhisattva on each side bears a high topknot, a crown decorated with flower petals, the long round face with delicately modelled features. They are decorated with the collar round the necks, their broad scarves come over the shoulders and fall down to the knees and up again. The lower bodies wear the long dresses with revers at the waist, standing on the lotus platforms barefoot.

The overall image of the Buddha in each niche into both side walls is identical with that of the Buddha on the main wall, only slightly smaller.

Paintings: The motif of curly cloud painted on the coffered ceiling is the original works of the Northern Zhou Dynasty, chiefly in a reddish-brown and a bluish grey tint.

Inscriptions: There are four inscriptions engraved or with a brush left by the visitors on the main wall and in the niche into the right wall.

Extension and Elaboration

Because the cave is too close to its neighboring Cave 140, the rock between them is only about 0.1 meters. Cave 140 was excavated earlier than this cave, so a hole leading to Cave 140 directly was hollowed out at its excavation.

Cao Zhongda, a famous painter of the sixth century, painted the figures with full, rounded bodies, which are thinly clad and the draperies melting into the bodies, as if emerging from the water. Buddhist sculptures of the time were also influenced by this form of painting, and the cave is a typical example.

第142窟

第142窟位于西崖东上部,开凿于北魏(公元386年—公元534年)。造像均秀骨清像,褒衣博带,为典型的汉民族风格。正壁左右两角上方分别塑猴头、象头,是麦积山石窟北魏造像中仅存的动物形象。壁面影塑母子供养人像,是麦积山所有供养人影塑造像中唯一由工匠单独制作的。

该窟内有八身泥塑造像,五十五身影塑造像。

形制:该窟为平面方形、平顶。高2.15米、宽2.03米、进深2.54米。前壁有长方形甬道。窟内地面凿"凹"字形低坛基。正、左、右三壁壁面各砌小坛台,正壁两侧现存四层,左壁右侧现存六层,右壁两侧现存四层。

造像:窟内正壁塑一佛二菩萨,左右两角上方分别塑猴头、象头及其他塑像。左壁塑一身坐佛和其右侧一身弟子。右壁塑交脚菩萨和其左侧胁侍菩萨。三壁小坛台上贴影塑佛、菩萨、弟子、女供养人。前壁左侧存一力士,共计六十三身造像。

正壁佛,高1.56米。磨光高肉髻,面形方圆。细颈端肩。内着僧祇支,衣带胸前打结下垂,外着双领下垂袈装,衣角搭左前臂后垂覆至左膝。右手施无畏印,左手施与愿印,结跏趺坐于"工"字形台座上,下摆呈四瓣覆盖座前。身后浮塑莲瓣形身光。

Cave 142

Cave 142 is located in the upper east part of the western cliff, and excavated in the Northern Wei Dynasty (AD 386-534). All the sculptures are in the typical style of the Han nationality, with long and slender figure and delicately modelled features, they are robed in the loose gowns with wide girdle. The heads of a monkey and an elephant built above each angle of the main wall are the only surviving animal images of the Northern Wei Dynasty at Maijishan. The mother and her son applied on the wall is the unique figure modelled by the craftsmen alone among all the donor images in relief at Maijishan.

Visitors can enjoy eight clay sculptures and 55 figures made in moulds. Details are as follows.

Type: It is a flat square niche with the flat ceiling, and is 2.15 meters high, 2.03 meters wide and 2.54 meters deep. There is a rectangle passage on the front wall. A low concave base is cut around the ground. Little ledges are built on each of the three walls, four tiers on either side of the main wall, six tiers on the right of the left wall, and four tiers on either side of the right wall.

Sculptures: There is a Buddha flanked by two bodhisattvas on the main wall, the heads of a monkey and an elephant as well as other figures are modelled above each angle. The left wall holds a seated Buddha and his disciple on the right. A cross-ankled bodhisattva and his attendant bodhisattva on the left occupy the right wall. Figures of Buddhas, bodhisattvas, disciples, female donors modelled in relief rest on each ledges of the three walls. A dvarapala stands on the left of the front wall. There are 63 figures in all.

The Buddha on the main wall is 1.56 meters high. He wears a polished high topknot and the square face, with a thin neck and squared shoulders. He is robed in an inner vest covering the left shoulder and armpits, a band tied at the chest falling in a knot, an upper garment that completely covers his body, with U-shaped collar falling to the chest, the lappet of the robe resting on the left forearm and down to the left knee. With the right hand in the abhaya mudra, and the left hand in the varada mudra, he sits in dhyanasana

正壁左右侧胁侍菩萨，束发髻，面形长圆，细颈削肩。天衣覆盖双肩。上着僧祇支，下着长裙，衣带腹前打结下垂。身体略前倾，跣足立于圆莲台上。身后浮塑桃形头光，内彩绘同心圆。其中左侧菩萨高1.02米，胸前佩戴璎珞。左手持净瓶于腹前，右臂微屈于胸前，右手残毁。右侧菩萨高1.16米。左手上举齐肩，托一尊饰莲瓣形背光的影塑坐佛。右手置于胸前，作执物状。

正壁两侧四层小坛台上贴影塑佛、菩萨、弟子、女供养人等。其中左右两角上方动物形象表现大象、猴的佛本生故事。右侧第二层上贴一组影塑母子供养人像，母亲头戴笼冠，上身着宽袍，下身着裙。右手持莲花形油灯，左手拉一身着裲裆衫的男童。

左壁佛，高1.42米。面部神态、衣着和手势同正壁佛。袈裟下摆呈"八"字形垂覆于座前。右侧弟子，高0.92米。身着宽博交领袈裟，左手举于胸前作捻花状。右手掩袖于腹前，跣足立于圆形莲台上。后有浮塑桃形项光，中间彩绘同心圆。弟子身后六层小坛台上贴影塑佛、菩萨、弟子。

右壁交脚菩萨，高1.51米。高发髻，方面大耳，细颈端肩。颈饰桃形项圈，天衣覆肩。胸前璎珞垂至膝前交叉后搭臂下垂。内着偏衫，下着贴体长裙，裙带腹部打结后下垂，帛带搭肩下垂至胫搭臂下垂至地面。左手伸至胸前握帛带，右手作无畏印。交脚坐于"工"字形台座上。身后浮塑同心圆形项光、莲瓣形身光。左侧菩萨，高0.98米，束高发髻，面形方中带圆，弯眉细目。内着偏衫，下着长裙，外着双领下垂袈裟。双手托举一罐于胸前。跣足立于圆形莲台上。身后浮塑同心圆形项光、桃形身光。两侧四层小坛台贴影塑佛、菩萨、弟子、女供养人。

前壁左侧力士，高0.64米。束发髻，面形方正，突目阔口，粗颈端肩。上身袒露，下着长裙。天衣覆肩垂至腹前交叉，一端搭于

on the I-shaped throne with the hem covering it in four large petals. There is a lotus petal-shaped mandorla in relief behind him.

The attendant bodhisattva on each side of the main wall wears topknots and oval faces, with thin necks and narrow shoulders. Their outer shawls cover both shoulders. They are dressed in the inner vests covering the left shoulder and armpits, the long dresses on the lower bodies, a band tied at the abdomens falling in a knot. With slightly frontal, they stand on the circular lotus platforms barefoot. There are peach-shaped aureoles in relief composed of coloured concentric circles behind them. Among them the bodhisattva on the left is 1.02 meters high, a heavy garland of jewels hangs from the shoulders. She puts her left hand to the abdomen holding a vase, and the right arm is raised to the chest with the hand destroyed. The right-hand figure is 1.16 meters high. She lifts her left hand to the shoulder level, supporting a seated Buddha in relief decorated with lotus petal-shaped mandorla. Her right hand is in front of the chest holding a certain object.

Figures of Buddhas, bodhisattvas, disciples, female donors modelled in relief rest on each four-tier ledges on either side of the main wall. Among which the animal images modelled above each angle illustrate the jataka storie of the Buddha about monkeys and elephants. A group of mother and her son in relief are applied on the second tier on the right, the mother is robed in a cage crown, a loose gown on the upper body, and a long dress on the lower body. Her right hand holds a lotus-shaped oil lamp, pulling a boy in a thick vest by the left hand.

The Buddha on the left wall is 1.42 meters high. His facial expression, clothing and gestures are identical with those of the Buddha on the main wall. The hem of the robe covers the throne in two large petals. The disciple on the right is 0.92 meters tall. Dressed in a loose gown with a collar folded across in front, he puts his left hand to the chest twisting a flower. With the right hand raised to the abdomen concealing in the sleeve, he stands on the circular lotus platform barefoot. There is a peach-shaped aureole in relief behind him composed of the coloured concentric circles. Figures of Buddhas, bodhisattvas, disciples modelled in relief rest on the six-tier ledges behind him.

The cross-ankled bodhisattva on the right wall is 1.51 meters high. She bears a high topknot, the square face flanked by pendulous ears with thin neck and squared shoulders. A peach-shaped collar is decorated around the neck, the outer shawl covers both shoulders. A heavy garland of jewels hangs from the shoulders and down to cross at the knees and up rests on the arms and down again. She is dressed in an inner gown draped slantingly over the left shoulder, a long dress on the lower body melting into the body, with a band tied at the abdomen falling in a knot. The long broad scarf covers the shoulders and down to cross at the shins and up rests on the arms and down again to the ground. The left hand is stretched to the chest holding a ribbon, and the right hand in the abhaya mudra. She sits on the I-shaped throne with ankles crossed. There is a circular aureole composed of concentric circles and a lotus-petal shaped mandorla behind her. The bodhisattva on her left is 0.98

右臂,一端下垂至脚面。身体呈"S"形弯曲,跣足立于圆形莲台之上。

引申与拓展

该窟内主尊造像四周壁面影塑佛、菩萨、弟子、供养人的做法普遍见于麦积山北魏晚期窟龛中,是当时法华造像思想在时间和空间上的三世与十方诸佛的图像表现。通过经文可知,壁面影塑造像系表现幻化而成的无数菩萨供养十方诸佛、弟子礼拜佛、佛说法、母子供养人持物供佛等场景。

meters high, with a high topknot, a pear-shaped face carved with arched brows sweeping above gently opened almond eyes. She is dressed in an inner gown draped slantingly over the left shoulder, a long dress on the lower body, an upper garment that completely covers her body, with U-shaped collar falling to the chest, the corner of the robe resting on the left arm. Holding a jar in front of the chest with both hands, she stands on the circular lotus platform barefoot. There is a circular aureole composed of concentric circles and a peach-shaped mandorla behind her. Figures of Buddhas, bodhisattvas, disciples, female donors modelled in relief rest on the four-tier ledges of either side.

The dvarapala on the left of the front wall is 0.64 meters high. He wears a topknot, the square face with bulging eyes and a wide mouth, broad neck and squared shoulders. With upper body bare, he is robed in a long dress on the lower body. The outer shawl covers both shoulders and down to cross at the abdomen, one end resting on the right arm and the other down to the feet. With the slightly swaying curve of his body, he stands on the circular lotus platform barefoot.

Extension and Elaboration

The practice of making Buddhas, bodhisattvas, disciples, female donors in moulds and applied around the walls of each principal figures commonly appears in the caves of the late Northern Wei Dynasty at Maijishan. It is the iconographical representation of the thought of the image-makings in the *Lotus* at that time, the Buddhas of Past, Present and Future in time and the Buddhas of the Ten Quarters in space. In the sutra, the figures in relief applied on the walls illustrate the scenes of innumerable replicas of bodhisattvas making offerings to the Buddhas of the Ten Quarters, the disciples worshipping the Buddhas, the Preaching of the Buddhas, the donor images of mothers and their children making offerings to the Buddhas by holding objects.

第146窟

第146窟位于西崖东上部,开凿于西魏(公元535年—公元556年)。该窟是麦积山西魏佛"女相化"的另一个例子。

该窟内有两身泥塑造像。

形制:该窟大部分残损,仅存正壁及右壁。正壁开一浅龛,内设长方形基座。

造像:正壁龛塑一身坐佛,龛外右侧一身菩萨,共计两身。

正壁龛佛,磨光高肉髻,椭圆脸面带笑容,细颈削肩。内着僧祇支,外着双领下垂袈裟。右手施无畏印,左手施与愿印。结跏趺坐于基座上,右足显露在外,下摆分三片覆盖于台座之前。身后隐约可见圆形项光及身光痕迹。

右侧菩萨,高发髻,面形清瘦。肩部有圆形配饰。内着圆领衣,外着交领衣衫,腰间束带。帛带自两肩垂下在腹部交叉后上绕至两臂再自然下垂。左手掩袖下垂,右手举于肩前掌心向外持莲蕾。跣足立于低坛基上。身后可见项光及莲蕾纹饰。

Cave 146

Cave 146 is located at the upper east part of the western cliff. It was dug in the Western Wei Dynasty (AD 535-556). It is another example of the Buddhas with "Feminine Appearance" modelled in the Western Wei Dynasty at Maijishan.

In the cave visitors can enjoy two clay sculptures. Details are as follows.

Type: Much of the cave is damaged, leaving only the main wall and the right wall. A shallow niche is cut into the main wall, in which a rectangle throne is set.

Sculptures: A seated Buddha occupies the niche into the main wall, outside which stands a bodhisattva on the right. There are two figures in all.

The Buddha in the niche cut into the main wall has a polished high topknot, an oval face with a smile, thin neck and narrow shoulders. He is robed in an inner vest covering the left shoulder and armpits, an outer garment that completely covers his body, with U-shaped collar falling to the chest, the corner of the robe resting on the left arm. His right hand is in the abhaya mudra and his left hand in the varada mudra. He is seated in a pose of deep yogic meditation, the legs tightly locked, the sole of the right foot uppermost on the throne, with the hem covering in three large petals. Traces of the circular aureole and mandorla are faintly visible behind him.

The bodhisattva on the right side has a high topknot, the thin face. There are circular ornaments on the shoulders. She is dressed in an inner robe with a roll collar, an outer garment of a crossing collar with a sash tied at the waist. The scarf hangs from the shoulders and down to cross at the abdomen and up through the armpits and down again naturally. With the left hand hangs down concealing in the sleeve, and her right hand is raised to

引申与拓展

该窟主佛外貌、微笑、手印以及瀑布般的下摆与第44窟、第22窟和第20窟主佛相同。

第146窟佛像

the shoulder holding a lotus bud with the palm outward. She stands on the low platform barefoot, the aureole and the motif of lotus bud are decipherable behind her.

Extension and Elaboration

The appearance, smiling, mudra and the waterfall-like hem of the principal Buddha in the cave are identical with those in Cave 44, Cave 22 and Cave 20.

第147窟

第147窟位于西崖东上部,开凿于北魏(公元386年—公元534年)。主佛具有北魏晚期秀骨清像的典型特征。

该窟内有一身泥塑造像。

形制:该窟大部分已坍塌,仅存正壁及右壁一小部分。正壁开一浅龛,内设长方形基座。

造像:正壁龛内塑一坐佛。

正壁龛内佛,螺发高肉髻,面容清秀,弯眉细目,高鼻大耳,面带笑意。内着僧祇支,胸下系带,外着双领下垂袈裟。右手施无畏印,左手施与愿印,手指均残毁。结跏趺坐于基座上,右足显露在外,下摆呈两瓣折叠下垂覆盖座前。身后残存火焰纹背光痕迹。

Cave 147

Cave 147 is located at the upper east part of the western cliff. It was dug in the Northern Wei Dynasty (AD 386-534). The principal Buddha shows the typical characteristics of long and slender figure and delicately modelled features in the late Northern Wei Dynasty.

In the cave visitors can enjoy a clay sculpture. Details are as follows.

Type: Much of the cave has fallen away, leaving only the main wall and a small part of the right wall. A shallow niche is cut on the main wall, in which a rectangle throne is set.

Sculpture: A seated Buddha occupies the niche cut into the main wall. There is only a figure in all.

The Buddha in the niche into the main wall has a spiral-shaped topknot, the delicately modelled features carved with arched brows sweeping above gently opened almond eyes, the high nose flanked by pendulous ears, with a smile. He is robed in the inner vest covering the left shoulder and armpits, a sash tied at the chest, the outer garment that completely covers his body, with U-shaped collar falling to the chest, the lappet of the robe resting on the left arm. His right hand is in the abhaya mudra, and his left hand in the varada mudra, with all the fingers destroyed. He is seated in a pose of deep yogic meditation, the legs tightly locked, the sole of the right foot uppermost on the throne with the hem covering in two large folded petals. Traces of the aureole painted with flaming motif are visible behind him.

引申与拓展

该窟主佛的衣摆如瀑布般垂于座前,右腿部分袈裟衣褶呈莲花瓣形,右足部从层层叠叠的衣摆中露出。造型独特,新颖别致,极具美感。

第147窟主佛

Extension and Elaboration

The hem of the principal Buddha cascades over the throne, the drapery of the rob on the right leg falls in lotus petals, and the sole of the right foot uppermost over the layered folds. It is modelled in unique and very novel, carrying a sense of aesthetic movement.

第148窟

第148窟位于西崖东上部，东邻第177窟，西上邻第159窟、西下邻第160窟。开凿于北魏（公元386年—公元534年），是麦积山另一个北魏早期向中期过渡的洞窟。

该窟内有一身泥塑造像，二十二身影塑造像。

形制：该窟为平面方形、平顶窟，前部坍塌。正壁设方形基座，两侧各凿三个三层小龛。右壁存一圆拱大龛，龛内左侧凿一两层小龛，龛上方凿三个小龛。

造像：正壁塑一坐佛，两侧上层小龛各贴交脚菩萨和思维菩萨及二胁侍菩萨。

两佛并坐分别贴于正壁中、下层小龛，右壁大龛内左侧下龛及上部三个小龛，共计二十三身。

正壁佛，磨光高肉髻，高鼻方面，大眼大耳，宽肩挺身，沉思状。内着方格纹及花瓣图案僧祇支，外着袒右袈裟，袈裟紧裹身体。双手施禅定印，结跏趺坐于方形基座上。身后有浮塑莲瓣身光内有火焰纹、联珠纹、小坐佛、忍冬纹，主要色彩有石青、石绿、赭石等。

第二章 麦积山石窟汉英解说词

Cave 148

Cave 148 is located at the upper east part of the western cliff, adjacent to Cave 177 in the east and Cave 159 in the upper west and Cave 160 in the lower west. It was dug in the Northern Wei Dynasty (AD 386-534), is another transitional cave from early to the middle of the Northern Wei Dynasty at Maijishan.

In the cave visitors will enjoy a sculpture modelled in clay, and 22 figures in relief. Details are as follows.

Type: It is a flat square niche with a flat ceiling, and the front has fallen away. A square throne is set on the main wall, with three three-tier recesses on its either side. A large chaitya arched niche survives on the right wall, with a two-tier recess carved on its left and three recesses in a row above it.

Sculptures: A seated Buddha occupies the main wall, the cross-ankled bodhisattva and the bodhisattva in pensive pose flanked by their own attendant bodhisattvas are inserted in the upper recess on either side of the main wall. Two Buddhas sharing the same throne are applied separately in the middle and lower recesses on the main wall, in the lower recess on the left in the large niche into the right wall and three recesses above it. There are 23 figures in all.

The Buddha on the main wall bears a polished high topknot, a tall nose on the square face flanked by a pair of big eyes and pendulous ears, broad shoulders and stiff body, with a meditative expression. He is robed in an inner vest with motifs of checks and flower petals covering the left shoulder and armpits, the outer robe thrown over the left shoulder or the upper throwing a strong diagonal across the body, leaving the right side of the body and shoulder bare, which melts against the body. With two hands in dhyana mudra, he sits in dhyanasana on the square throne. There is a lotus petal-shaped mandorla adorned

第148窟主佛

正壁上部左右小龛各塑思惟菩萨和思维菩萨。交脚菩萨两脚下垂并在脚腕处交叉，双手作转法轮印。思维菩萨头偏于右侧并以右手相托，同时右腿翘在左腿上，表现出一种思考问题的状态。均束发戴冠，上身袒露，下系贴体长裙，坐于束帛座上。身后浮塑莲瓣形火焰纹背光。左右两胁侍菩萨，跣足立于半圆形莲台上。

影塑二佛并坐，均高圆肉髻，面形方圆。结跏趺坐，施禅定印。左侧佛着袒右袈裟，右侧佛着通肩袈裟。二佛项光均为多重同心圆。

引申与拓展

该窟与第80窟、第100窟、第128窟均为麦积山石窟开凿历史上北魏早期向中期过渡的典型洞窟。

with motifs of flame, the linked-pearl, small seated Buddhas and honeysuckle behind him, chiefly in a bluish grey tint, a stone green, and a reddish-brown.

The upper recess cut into either side on the main wall contains a cross-ankled bodhisattva and a bodhisattva in pensive pose. The former figure sits with legs pendent and crossed at the ankles, and hands in the dharma-takra-mudra. The latter figure as a bodhisattva also sits with the fingers of the right hand gently touching the cheek, head bent to the right, one leg pendent, the right leg crossed over the left, in a pensive pose. Their hair is gathered high encircled by the diadems, and their upper bodies are bare, their lower bodies are robed in long dresses melting against bodies, sitting on the waist drum-shaped thrones with a ribbon tied at the waist. There is a lotus petal-shaped mandorla in relief with flame motif behind them. Their own attendant bodhisattvas on either side stand on the semicircular lotus platforms barefoot.

Two Buddhas sharing the same throne in relief bear high and circular topknots with the square faces. With two hands in dhyana mudra, they sit in dhyanasana on the thrones. The left-side Buddha wears the robe thrown over the left shoulder or the upper throwing a strong diagonal across the body, leaving the right side of the body and shoulder bare, the right-side Buddha is in garment that completely covers his body and hangs in heavy folds round the shoulders. There are aureoles composed of multi-tiered concentric circles behind them.

Extension and Elaboration

The cave together with Cave 80, Cave 100 and Cave 128 are all typical of the transformation period from early to the middle of the Northern Wei Dynasty in the excavation history at Maijishan.

第155窟

第155窟位于西崖东中部,开凿于北魏(公元386年—公元534年),是麦积山又一处常见的三佛龛。主佛两侧出现弟子阿难和迦叶形象,是保存较好的具有北魏早期向中期过渡特征的窟龛。

该窟内有装饰精美的龛楣和龛柱,六身泥塑造像,五十八身影塑造像。

形制:该窟是平面方形、平顶。高2.11米、宽2.51米、深2.12米。前壁开有方形甬道。地面有低坛基。正、左、右壁前各开一尖楣圆拱龛。正壁龛内两侧各凿有两层小坛台,龛外两侧各开凿三层小龛。左右壁龛上方各开六小龛和八小龛。前壁上方开九小龛,两侧各塑三层小坛台。

造像:窟内正、左、右壁龛内各塑一佛,正壁龛外左侧一身胁侍菩萨,左壁龛外右侧、右壁龛外左侧各一身弟子。正壁龛内两侧两层坛台,上层贴三身坐佛,下层左侧贴四身坐佛,右贴三身交脚菩萨。其龛楣上部贴一佛二菩萨,龛楣外两侧贴七身飞天。柱基下各有一身托柱力士。左上方耳龛内分别贴思惟菩萨及二胁侍菩萨。左壁上方现存六个小龛,五身坐佛。右壁上方现存八个小龛,

Cave 155

Cave 155 is located in the middle east part of the western cliff, and excavated in the Northern Wei Dynasty (AD 386-534). It is another usual three Buddhas niches at Maijishan, the disciple images of Ananda and Kasyapa appear on either side of the principal Buddha. It is a well-preserved cave with transitional characteristics from the early to the middle of the Northern Wei Dynasty.

Visitors can appreciate the beautifully decorated lintel and column of the niche, six clay sculptures, and 58 figures made in moulds. Details are as follows.

Type: It is a flat square niche with a flat ceiling, and is 2.11 meters high, 2.51 meters wide and 2.12 meters deep. There is a square passage on the front wall. A low base is cut around the ground. A chaitya arched recess with a pointed lintel is cut into each of the main wall and two flanking walls. Two-tier ledges are built on each side of the niche cut into the main wall, outside which are three-tier bays on either side. There are six bays and eight bays above each niche into the left wall and the right wall. Above the front wall contains nine bays, with three-tier ledges on each side.

Sculptures: A Buddha occupies each niche into the main wall and two side walls, outside which stands a bodhisattva on the left of the main wall, a disciple on the right outside the niche into the left wall and on the left outside the niche into the right wall respectively. Three seated Buddhas on the upper tier, four seated Buddhas on the left, and three bodhisattvas with ankles crossed on the right of the lower tier are applied on two-tier ledges on each side of the niche into the main wall. Its lintel is decorated with a Buddha flanked by two bodhisattvas in relief, outside which seven flying apsaras are applied on both sides. Under the column base, each has an atlantid supporting the column on his upraised hands. A small recess above each end of the main wall containing a bodhisattva in pensive pose flanked by an attendant bodhisattva. There are six bays holding five seated Buddhas above the niche into the left wall, and eight bays of two seated Buddhas above the niche into

两身坐佛。前壁上部现存九个小龛，龛内各一身坐佛，左右三层坛台上贴十四身坐佛，共计六十四身。

正壁佛，高0.79米。磨光高肉髻，面形方圆。内着僧祇支，外着袒右袈裟。左手置于腹部握袈裟衣角。右臂前举，右手已残失。结跏趺坐于"工"字形台座上。身后绘多重同心圆项光及莲瓣形身光。左侧胁侍菩萨高1.07米，身体表面风化严重。头戴高冠，上身袒露，披帛搭肩绕臂。左手自然下垂握帛带，右手持莲蕾于胸前。下系贴身长裙，跣足立于半圆形莲台上。身后绘圆形项光及莲瓣形身光。

左右壁佛，体格小于主佛。发髻、面部表情、坐姿、项光和身光与主佛相似。身着通肩袈裟。双手施禅定印。左壁右侧、右壁左侧弟子，面形瘦削，高鼻深目。外着袒右袈裟，袈裟衣角自右肩下垂至腹部搭左臂下垂。左手握衣角置于腹部，右手持莲蕾置于胸前，立于莲台上。

五十八身影塑造像中坐佛、飞天、供养菩萨造像轻薄、庄重和飘逸，更加注重用线条突出人物的立体感和动感。

引申与拓展

该窟正壁两侧出现弟子阿难和迦叶形象，这种新的组合对麦积山之后的造像影响很大。造像形体修长，服饰略显厚重，衣纹稀疏而简洁显示出受绘画风格的影响。

the right wall. Nine bays above the front wall of each containing a seated Buddha, and 14 seated Buddhas rest on three-tier ledges on each side. There are 64 figures in all.

The Buddha on the main wall is 0.79 meters high. He bears a polished high topknot and the square face. He is robed in an inner vest covering the left shoulder and armpits, the outer robe thrown over the left shoulder or the upper throwing a strong diagonal across the body, leaving the right side of the body and shoulder bare. The left hand is placed on the abdomen holding the corner of the robe. The right arm is raised in front with the hand missing. He sits in dhyanasana on the I-shaped throne. There is a circular aureole composed of multi-tiered concentric circles and a lotus petal-shaped mandorla behind him. The bodhisattva on the left is 1.07 meters, with the surface of her body badly weathered. With a high crown, her upper body is bare, and the scarf comes from shoulders and hangs down through the armpits. She puts down her left hand naturally holding a ribbon, and the right hand is lifted to the chest holding a lotus bud. Her lower body wears a long dress melting to the body, and she stands on a semi-circular lotus platform barefoot backed by an aureole composed of multi-tiered concentric circles and a lotus petal-shaped mandorla.

The Buddhas on the left and right walls are smaller in size than the principal Buddha. Their hair styles, facial expressions, sitting postures, aureoles and mandorlas are similar to those of the principal Buddha. They are robed in upper garments that completely cover their bodies and hang in heavy folds round their shoulders. Their two hands are in dhyana mudra. The disciples on the right of the left wall and on the left of the right wall have thin faces with high noses and deep eyes. They wear the outer robes thrown over the left shoulder or the upper throwing a strong diagonal across the body, leaving the right side of the body and shoulder bare, with its corner dropping down from the right shoulder to the abdomen and up resting on the left arm and down again. They stand on the lotus platforms, their left hands are placed on the abdomens holding the corner of the robes, and their right hands are lifted to the chests holding the lotus buds.

Among 58 figures in relief, the seated Buddhas, flying apsaras and votive bodhisattvas are lightly, solemnly and elegantly modelled, pay more attention to the lines to emphasize the three-dimensional and dynamic senses of images.

Extension and Elaboration

The disciples Ananda and Kasyapa appear on both sides of the main wall, and this new group of disciple images has a great influence on the later image-makings at Maijishan. The figures are long and slender with slightly heavy costumes, and the drapery is loose and simple under the influence of painting style.

第162窟

第162窟位于西崖东上部,东邻第160窟,西邻第154窟。开凿于北魏(公元386年—公元534年),为另一个麦积山重要早期洞窟中的三佛龛。

该窟内有三身泥塑造像、四身影塑造像,顶部绘两身飞天。

形制:该窟是平面方形、平顶。前壁开有方形甬道,正、左、右三壁砌通长基座。

造像:正、左、右三壁各塑一身坐佛。主佛左上方和右壁佛左上方各贴一身影塑立佛,主佛左下方和左壁佛右下方各贴一身影塑立菩萨,共计七身。

正、左、右壁坐佛,造像风格基本相同,只是主佛体量略大于两侧佛。均内着僧祇支,衣带胸下打结,外着双领下垂袈裟。上身微前倾,结跏趺坐于基座上,下摆分两片呈圆弧状垂于座前。身后浮塑莲瓣形身光,外缘有较宽火焰纹,内侧为条带纹,项光为多重同心圆组成,可见石青、石绿、赭红等色。其中主佛和左壁佛磨光高肉髻,瘦长脸,双目下视,细颈削肩。右壁佛头已失。主佛右手无畏印,左手施与愿印。左、右壁佛,双手施禅定印。

Cave 162

Cave 162 is located at the upper east tier of the western cliff, adjacent to Cave 160 in the east and Cave 154 in the west. It was dug in the Northern Wei Dynasty (AD 386-534), is another important early three Buddhas niche at Maijishan.

In the cave visitors can enjoy three sculptures modelled in clay, four figures in relief, and two flying apsaras painted on the ceiling. Details are as follows.

Type: It is a flat square niche with a flat ceiling. There is a square passage on the front wall. An inseperate pedestal is cut on each of the main wall and two flanking walls.

Sculptures: A seated Buddha occupies each of the main wall and two side walls. A standing Buddha in relief is applied above each of the left of the principal Buddha and the left of the Buddha on the right wall, and a standing bodhisattva in relief is applied below each of the left of the principal Buddha and the right of the Buddha on the left wall. There are seven figures in all.

The style of the seated Buddhas on each of the main wall and two side walls is basically the same, only the size of the principal Buddha is slightly larger than the two flanking Buddhas. They are robed in the inner vests covering the left shoulder and armpits, a sash tied at the chests, the outer garments that completely cover their bodies, with U-shaped collar falling to the chest, the lappet of the robe resting on the left arm. With the suggestion of a sweeping forward movement of the upper bodies, they are seated with legs tightly locked in a yogic pose on the thrones with the hems covering in two large circular arcs. There are lotus petal-shaped mandorlas in relief behind them, with flaming motif on the outer borders and stripes on the inner rims, the aureoles composed of multi-tiered concentric circles, colouring in a bluish grey tint, a stone green, and a reddish-brown. Among them, both the

主佛左上方和右壁佛左上方影塑立佛，均面带微笑。内着僧祇支，外着双领下垂袈裟。右手施无畏印，左手于腹部提衣角。内着长裙，跣足立于圆形莲台之上。后绘莲瓣形身光，外缘为火焰纹，项光为多重同心圆组成。

主佛左下方和左壁佛右下方影塑立菩萨，头均已失。上着交领衣，下系裙。天衣覆肩，帛带自双肩垂下至腹前交叉再上绕至左前臂后自然垂下。左手拢袖置于腹侧，右手于胸前持花。身后绘圆形项光。

壁画：顶部残存两身飞天，形象清秀飘逸。线条不受拘束，在飞腾中不断变化。

引申与拓展

该窟影塑佛立像曾在国内巡展。嘴唇上扬，露出愉快的微笑，很有感染力。

principal Buddha and the left-wall Buddha bear the polished high topknots, the long-skinning faces carved by downcast eyes, thin necks and narrow shoulders. The right-wall Buddha has lost his head. The right hand of the principal Buddha performs the abhaya mudra, and the left hand in the varada mudra. The two hands of the Buddha on each side walls are in dhyana mudra.

Both of the standing Buddhas in relief above the left of the principal Buddha and the left of the Buddha on the right wall are smiling. They are robed in the inner vests covering the left shoulder and armpits, the outer garments that completely cover their bodies, with U-shaped collar falling to the chest, the lappet of the robe resting on the left arm. Their right hands are in the abhaya mudra, and their left hands are placed on the abdomens holding the corner of the robs. Their lower bodies wear the long dresses, they stand on the semi-circular lotus platforms barefoot, backed by the lotus petal-shaped mandorlas with flaming motifs on the outer borders, the aureoles composed of multi-tiered concentric circles.

Both of the standing bodhisattvas in relief below the left of the principal Buddha and the right of the Buddha on the left wall are headless. They are robed in upper garments of a crossing collar and lower long dresses. The outer shawls cover both shoulders, their scarves hang from the shoulders and down to cross at the abdomens and up resting on the left forearms and down again naturally. The left hands concealing in the sleeves are placed on the abdomens, and their right hands are lifted to the chests holding a flower. There are circular aureoles behind them.

Paintings: Two flying apsaras survive on the ceiling, whose images are delicate and elegant modelled. The lines are unrestrained, soaring in constant chang.

Extension and Elaboration

The standing Buddha in relief in the cave has taken part in the itinerant exhibition in China, with lips pursed up in a pleasant smile, is very contagious.

第163窟

第163窟位于西崖东上部,东邻第149窟,西邻第164窟。开凿于北魏(公元386年—公元534年),是麦积山三佛龛中另一处弥勒造型为服饰华丽的交脚菩萨。

该窟内有五身泥塑造像,六十四身影塑造像,七则留在右壁供养人像前和左壁下方的墨书题记。

形制:该窟是平面方形、平顶窟,前壁坍塌。地面凿低坛基,正、左、右壁各砌一"工"字形台座。正壁两侧各开三层小龛,左壁上方现存六个小龛,右侧有三层、左侧四层小坛台。右壁上方开七个小龛,右侧凿四层、左侧两层小坛台。前壁左侧上方残存三个小龛。左壁右侧和右壁左侧各砌一圆形莲台。

造像:正、左、右三壁各塑一坐佛,左、右壁各立一胁侍菩萨。六十四身影塑造像分别贴于壁面和小龛内:正壁二十二身,左壁十三身,右壁二十五身,前壁四身。造像组合包括三佛、一佛二菩萨、二佛并坐、千佛等,共计六十九身。

正壁佛,旋涡纹高肉髻,方脸,弯眉细眼,高鼻大耳。内着僧祇支,腰间束带并作结,外着双领下垂袈裟。右手施无畏印,左手

Cave 163

Cave 163 is located at the upper east tier of the western cliff, adjacent to Cave 149 in the east and Cave 164 in the west. It was dug in the Northern Wei Dynasty (AD 386-534), is another image of Maitreya pictured as a bodhisattva dressed in gorgeous jewels and garment in the cross-ankled pose in three Buddha niches at Maijishan.

In the cave visitors can enjoy five clay sculptures, 64 figures in relief, and seven inscriptions with a brush left in front of the donor painted on the right wall and below the left wall. Details are as follows.

Type: It is a flat square niche with a flat ceiling, and the front wall has fallen away. A low base is cut around the ground. An I-shaped throne is carved on each of the main wall and two flanking walls. Three-tier bays are built on each side of the main wall, six bays above the left wall with three-tier ledges on the right and four-tier ledges on the left. There are seven bays above the right wall with four-tier ledges on the right and two-tier ledges on the left. Above the left on the front wall contains three bays. A circular lotus platform is set on the right of the left wall and the left of the right wall.

Sculptures: A seated Buddha is modelled on each of the main wall and two side walls, and an attendant bodhisattva stands on each of the side walls. 64 figures in relief are applied on the walls and in the bays: 22 on the main wall, 13 on the left wall, 25 on the right wall, and four on the front wall. The groups of sculptures include three Buddhas, a Buddha flanked by two bodhisattvas, two Buddhas sharing the same throne, the Thousand Buddhass and so on. There are 69 figures in all.

The principal Buddha on the main wall bears a spiral-shaped topknot, the square face carved with arched brows sweeping above gently opened almond eyes, the high nose flanked by pendulous ears. He is robed in the inner vest covering the left shoulder and armpits, a

施与愿印。右脚心朝上外露，结跏趺坐于长方形台座之上，袈裟下摆分四瓣垂于座下。身后浮塑多重同心圆项光和莲瓣形身光，由火焰纹、忍冬纹、条带纹组成。

左壁交脚弥勒菩萨，束高髻戴冠，长发披肩。长圆脸，弯眉细眼，高鼻小嘴。颈戴桃形项圈坠有突起圆形饰物。上身袒露，帛带自双肩下垂至胸部相交垂下，下系翻腰长裙。双臂及膝下已残失，交脚姿势坐于"工"字形台座上。身后浮塑项光和身光与主佛相同。

右壁佛，五官与正壁佛相似。内着僧祇支，外着袒右袈裟。衣着单薄贴体。双臂屈肘，双手已毁，倚坐于"工"字形台座上。身后浮塑项光和身光与主佛相同。

左右壁胁侍菩萨，精美生动。面形方圆，细眼面带微笑。颈戴桃形项圈坠有突起圆形饰物。上身袒露，斜披络腋，天衣覆肩。帛带自双肩垂于腹际相交上绕搭臂向身后飘扬。下系长裙，跣足立于莲台上。身后浮塑项光和身光与主佛相同。其中左壁菩萨戴花蔓冠，宽发辫。左手持莲于胸前，右手提桃形玉璧于腿侧。右壁菩萨束发髻。左手端桃形物品于腹前，右手提净瓶于腿侧。

六十四身影塑造像中有十二身坐佛、二十三身胁侍菩萨、八身交脚供养菩萨和十四身胡跪供养菩萨。

题记：右壁供养人像前和左壁下方留有七则墨书题记。

sash tied round the waist and falling in a knot, the outer garment that completely covers his body, with U-shaped collar falling to the chest, the lappet of the robe resting on the left arm. His right hand is in the abhaya mudra, and his left hand in the varada mudra. He is seated in a pose of deep yogic meditation, the legs tightly locked, the sole of the right foot uppermost on the rectangle throne with the hem covering in four large petals. There is an aureole in relief adorned with multi-tiered concentric circles and a lotus petal-shaped mandorla composed of motifs of flame, honeysuckle and stripes behind him.

The Maitreya as a bodhisattva in the cross-ankled pose on the left wall has the hair gathered high encircled by a diadem and falling down the back. The long round face carved with arched brows sweeping above gently opened almond eyes, the high nose flanked by pendulous ears, wearing a peach-shaped collar around the neck with bulging circular pendents. The upper body is bare, the scarf hangs from the shoulders and down to cross at the chest and down again, a long dress on the lower body with revers at the waist. With two arms and the knees below lost, he sits in the cross-ankled pose on an I-shaped throne. The aureole and mandorla in relief behind him are identical with those of the principal Buddha.

The Buddha on the right wall resembles the principal Buddha in the features. He is robed in an inner vest covering the left shoulder and armpits, the outer robe thrown over the left shoulder or the upper throwing a strong diagonal across the body, leaving the right side of the body and shoulder bare. He is thinly clad and the drapery melting into the body. The arms are raised with hands destroyed, he is seated with legs pendent on an I-shaped throne. The aureole and mandorla in relief behind him are identical with those of the principal Buddha.

The attendant bodhisattvas on each of the side walls are delicately and vividly modelled. Their square round faces are carved with gently opened almond eyes with a smile. They bear the peach-shaped collars around the neck with bulging circular pendents. Their upper bodies are bare, the upper throwing a strong diagonal across the bodies, leaving the right side of the body and shoulder bare, the outer shawls cover both shoulders. Their scarves coming from shoulders hang down to cross at the abdomens and up resting on the arms fluttering in the wind on each side. They are robed in long dresses on the lower bodies, stand on the lotus platforms barefoot. The aureole and mandorla in relief behind them are identical with those of the principal Buddha. Among them, the left-wall bodhisattva has the wide braids encircled by a flower vine crown. The left hand is raised on the chest holding a lotus, and the right hand hangs down beside the thigh carrying a peach-shaped jade. The right-wall bodhisattva wears a topknot. The left hand is placed at the abdomen holding a peach-shaped object, and the right hand hangs down beside the thigh carrying a vase.

Among the 64 figures in relief there are 12 seated Buddhas, 23 attendant bodhisattvas, eight cross-ankled votive bodhisattvas and 14 of those in the hun way of kneeling with right knee on the ground and left knee up.

Inscriptions: There are seven inscriptions with a brush left by visitors in front of the donor painted on the right wall and below the left wall.

引申与拓展

该窟形制与第19窟和第149窟相同。三壁三佛，正壁耳龛内皆贴有造像，包括释迦、多宝二佛并坐、一佛二菩萨或千佛等。

弥勒佛在中国的佛教徒中很受欢迎，被认为是接替释迦牟尼的未来佛，住在兜率宫。弥勒造型主要有两种：一为佛装，梳发髻，着袈裟，多为站姿或交脚坐姿；另一为菩萨装，戴宝冠，服饰华丽，坐姿为交脚式。交脚菩萨坐姿是魏晋南北朝造像中最受欢迎的，这是其在兜率宫为度化仙界说法时的形象。

Extension and Elaboration

The type of the cave is identical with that in Cave 19 and Cave 149. A Buddha is modelled on each of the main wall and the side walls, sculptues in relief are applied in the recess cut above each end of the main wall, containing Shakyamuni and Prabhutaratna sharing the same throne, a Buddha flanked by two bodhisattvas or the Thousand Buddhass.

Buddha Maitreya enjoys high popularity among Buddhists in China. He is regarded as a Buddha of the Future to succeed Shakyamuni, living in the palace of Tushita. Maitreya is modelled mainly in two types: one is pictured as Buddha wearing topknot in a kaṣaya robe, would usually be standing or sitting (cross-legged, with legs down or cross-ankled). The other is as a bodhisattva wearing a coronet dressed in gorgeous jewels and garment, with a cross-ankled sitting pose. The bodhisattva with a cross-ankled sitting pose is the most popular among his statues of the Wei, Jin, Southern and Northern Dynasties. It is the image when he preaches to celestials in palace of Tushita Heaven.

第165窟

第165窟位于西崖中下层,开凿于后秦(公元384年—公元417年),重修于北魏(公元386年—公元534年)和宋代(公元960年—公元1279年)。该窟造像布局新颖,菩萨坐在正壁主尊位置,两侧各立一位供养人。造像泥质纯朴自然,艺术风格写实洗练,是宋代泥塑的代表作品。两身供养人形象堪称宋代人物塑像的典范。

该窟内有五尊宋代重塑造像,残损的五世纪原作束帛座和身光,身光上的火焰纹和彩绘伎乐,留在左壁菩萨项光和右侧供养人裙子的两则墨书题记。

形制:该窟是平面横长方形、略带弧形窟顶、敞口大龛,宽4.6米、深2.48米、高3.85米。前部坍塌,整体保存完整。正壁残存一束帛座。

造像:正壁塑一坐菩萨和二女供养人立像,左右壁各立一胁侍菩萨。共五身泥塑造像,均没有上彩,呈现出自然的土黄色。

正壁菩萨高2.1米,梳发戴冠,长发披肩。面型丰腴,眉间生有白毫相,双目下视。腰间束带做结,外披双领袈裟。衣纹简练写实贴体,结跏趺坐于束帛座上。身后莲花瓣形头光和身光中绘制火焰纹。

左右两侧女供养人也高2.1米,高髻花冠。椭圆脸,眼角上

第二章　麦积山石窟汉英解说词

Cave 165

Cave 165 is located on the middle and lower part of the western cliff, and was originally excavated in the Later Qin Dynasty (AD 384-417) and repaired in the Northern Wei Dynasty (AD 386-534) and the Song Dynasty (AD 960-1279). The layout of the sculptures is novel, a bodhisattva flanked by a standing donor occupies the principal position on the main wall. The plaster being pure and natural, the sculptures are the representative works of clay figures in the Song Dynasty with a realistic and simple artistic style. The image of two donors is considered to be a model of figure sculptures in the Song Dynasty.

Visitors in this cave can appreciate five figures remodelled in the Song Dynasty, traces of damaged original works of the waist drum-shaped throne with a ribbon tied at the waist and the mandorlas in the fifth century, the flame motif and colored celestial musicians painted in the mandorlas behind the figures, and two inscriptions left with a brush in the aureole behind the bodhisattva on the left wall and on the dress of the donor on the right. Details are as follows.

Type: It is a large horizontal rectangle open niche with a slightly curved ceiling, with 4.6 meters wide, 2.48 meters deep, 3.85 meters high. The front has fallen away, the whole cave is intact. A damaged waist drum-shaped throne with a ribbon tied at the waist survives on the main wall.

Sculptures: A seated bodhisattva flanked by a female standing donor, and a standing attendant bodhisattva on each side walls. There are five clay sculptures in all, uncoloured, showing a natural earthy yellow colour.

The bodhisattva on the main wall is 2.1 meters high, the hair gathered high encircled by a diadem and falling down the back. The full face is carved with the white hair between the brows and downcast eyes. He wears an upper garment that completely covers his body, with U-shaped collar falling to the chest, the lappet of the robe resting on the left arm, with a sash tied round the waist falling in a knot. He is seated in dhyanasana on the waist drum-shaped throne with a ribbon tied at the waist, the drapery being simple and realistic and melting into the body. There is a lotus petal-shaped aureole and mandorla painted with the flame motif behind him.

翘，小嘴。着当时世俗女式服装，外着交领长衣，右边腰中系带，长裙盖足露脚尖，衣纹线条呈阶梯式。右手握拳上举，左手下垂。为当时上层社会年轻贵妇的真实写照。

左右两壁胁侍菩萨身高2.4米，束高发髻，戴头巾，其状如高耸的莲花。五官与二女供养人相同。斜披络腋，外披双领下垂袈裟。双手轻轻相交叠于腹前，赤足站立于莲台之上。身后绘制莲花瓣形头光和身光。

壁画：大体无存，仅有三身身光着青绿火焰纹可辨。另外，在左壁菩萨身光顶部隐约可以看出数身彩绘伎乐。

题记：左壁菩萨项光和右侧供养人裙子留有两则墨书题记，内容是公元1196年4月8日某人到这里游览的记录。从断续的文字可知，此人多次来到麦积山石窟。

引申与拓展

早期供养人像表现为窟龛的辅助和较为次要的位置。隋唐之后由于统治者和社会风气的影响，石窟中的供养人形象增大，甚至逐渐超过了主佛的高度。第165窟就是该风潮的代表。该窟两身供养人像高2.1米，与正壁菩萨相同。两身供养人的造型、服饰基本相同，与两壁菩萨塑像五官也非常接近，显然是出于同一风格的工匠之手。间接显示出供养人在佛教石窟造像中的地位提高了，供养人的艺术形象开始发展成石窟艺术中的重要组成部分。

该窟菩萨五官、头巾、着装、手势与第136窟菩萨基本相同。读者可比较异同。

The female donor on each side is also 2.1 meters high, with a high topknot and a crown. The oval face is carved with slimed eyes and four-flap mouth. They wear secular female costumes of the time, the long dresses of a collar folded across in front, a sash tied at the right waists, covering the feet leaving the toes, the lines of the drapery hangs in layered symmetrical folds. Their right hands are raised in a fist, and the left hands hang down. They are a true portrayal of young noble ladies of local upper class at that time.

The two attendant bodhisattvas on the side walls are 2.4 meters high, the high topknots tucked by the hairscarves like a towering lotus. Their features are identical with that of two female donors. They are robed in the upper throwing a strong diagonal across the bodies, leaving the right side of the body and shoulder bare, the upper garments that completely cover the bodies, with U-shaped collar falling to the chest, the lappet of the robe resting on the left arm. With hands holding together to the abdomen level, they stand on the lotus platforms barefoot. They are backed by lotus petal-shaped aureoles and mandorlas.

Paintings: With much has disappeared, we can only see three mandorlas with lime green flame motif. In addition, several colored celestial musicians are vaguely visible on top of the mandorla behind the bodhisattva on the left wall.

Inscriptions: There are two inscriptions with a brush left by the visitors in the aureole on the left wall and on the dress of the donor on the right. The first one records that a certain person visited here on April the eighth, AD 1196. We can see from the intermittent characters that this person had been here several times.

Extension and Elaboration

The images of donors are a representation of auxiliary in caves and niches, they are often arranged in the secondary place in the early days. Under the influence of the rulers and social customs after the Sui and Tang dynasties, the size of donors in caves was larger and even gradually exceeded the height of the principal Buddha. Cave 165 is a representative of this trend. The two donors here are 2.1 meters high, the same as the bodhisattva on the main wall. Their modeling and clothing are identical with each other, and even with the same features of two bodhisattvas on side walls, apparently by the same style of craftsmen. This indirectly shows that the status of the donors has increased in image makings of Buddhist caves, and their artistic images begin to develop into an important part of cave art.

The facial features, headscarves, clothes and gestures of the bodhisattvas in the cave are basically the same as those of the bodhisattvas in Cave 136. Readers can compare the similarities and differences.

第168窟

第168位于东崖中层,第3窟东侧。开凿于北周(公元557年—公元581年),窟廊道上和崖面上有宋代以后的一些摩崖题刻和碑刻,是反映麦积山石窟历史发展的重要历史文献资料。

该窟正壁上有四幅摩崖题刻和镶嵌在北侧和东侧壁面上的五块碑刻。

形制:该窟是在崖壁上凿出的从地面通往第3窟的斜梯廊道。

题记:正壁上刻四幅摩崖题刻。

碑刻:北侧和东侧壁面镶嵌五块碑刻,分别是《麦积山开除常住地粮碑》《胡安游麦积山次泰谿甘公韵碑》《李筵登麦积岩小憩二绝碑》《冯惟讷游麦积山四首碑》《甘茹重游麦积山六首与乐山胡公同赋碑》等。

1.《麦积山开除常住地粮碑》

此碑立于该窟梯道口。明崇祯十五年(1642年)立,通高1.21米、宽0.7米、厚0.22米。碑首方形,正中竖列阴刻双钩篆书"大明"二字。碑面左右边框线刻连续忍冬纹图案。首题"麦积山开除

第二章 麦积山石窟汉英解说词 425

Cave 168

Cave 168 is located in the middle part of the eastern cliff, on the east side of Cave 3. Built in the Northern Zhou Dynasty (AD 557-581), there are some inscriptions carved on the cliff face on the corridor and stone tablets inserted in the walls from the Song Dynasty, which are important historical documentations reflecting the historical development of Maijishan Caves.

Visitors in this cave can appreciate four inscriptions carved on the cliff face on the main wall and five stone tablets inserted in the north and east walls. Details are as follows.

Type: It is a ramp passage cut on the cliff face leading to Cave 3 from the ground.

Inscriptions: There are four inscriptions carved on the cliff face on the main wall.
Stone Tablets: There are five stone tablets inserted in the north and east walls. They are *the Stone Tablet on Exemption from the Regular Grain Tribute for Monks in Maijishan, the Stone Tablet of Hu An's Poems on Visiting Maijishan Writing According to Gan Ru's Poems' Rhyming Words, the Stone Tablet of Li Ting's Poems on Climbing the Maiji Rock on April 15th in the First Year (AD 1567) of the Longqing period, and Composing Two Poems During a Short Rest, the Stone Tablet of Feng Weine's Four Poems on Touring Mount Maiji, the Stone Tablet of Gan Ru's Six Poems on Revisiting Maijishan Composed Together with Hugong from Leshan*. The entire texts read as follows.

1. *The Stone Tablet on Exemption from the Regular Grain Tribute for Monks in Maiji Mountain*

This tablet is located at the stair entrance of the cave. It was erected in the 15th year of Emperor Chongzhen in the Ming Dynasty (AD 1642), with 1.21 meters high, 0.7 meters wide and 0.22 meters thick. The head of the tablet is square, in the middle of which are engraved with two characters "Da Ming" in vertical incised double hook seal. A continuous honeysuckle motif is carved on the raised borders of its either side. The title *The Tablet on*

常住地粮碑",碑文楷书十八行,满行三十字,保存完好,字迹清晰。尾题"崇祯十五年九月十五日庚午举人姚隆远撰",后列本寺僧人十多人名号,是关于麦积山石窟开凿的又一碑刻文献,具有一定的参考价值。碑文如下。

按《广舆记》称,麦积山为秦地林泉之冠。其古寺系历代敕建者,有碑碣可考。自姚秦至今,一千三百余年,香火不绝。林壑幽峭,松桧阴森,有瀑布泻出崖苍之间,天然奇景也。杜甫、李师中俱有题咏,志云:何谷无兰芷,何渊无蛟龙。麦积累产灵芝,圣灯贝光,照耀林谷。洵一方名胜,可与五岳竞高矣。旧设常住田三百二十亩,皆瘠薄,山阴寒陡礀,春回暑际,霜落秋前,所出不过燕麦、小荞等。寥寥山僧,多食野菜资生。杜诗云:"野寺残僧少。"山田硗确,故僧突不黔耳。各处常住地原不入粮额,独此寺香火田,乡愚侵占不遂,妄告增粮二石九斗五升。僧输不前,逃窜过半。兼兵荒重困之后,牛种无出,地全荒芜。佃户已填沟壑,而催租者尚打寺门不休。致法堂前草深一丈,良可惜也。幸巡道范老公祖征寇住寺,见寺僧菜色未苏,问及香火之资,僧人能信泣诉前因。公慨然曰:"寺田几何,追呼不免,此地方官之羞也。"即准诉察免。又幸州守毛公神明慈谅,具有佛种者,欣然愿藉是作一大姻缘是,申请开除,详文及剀切恳至。蒙批:"荒粮如议开豁,仍谕里老不得混催此缴。"由是名刹中兴,僧行安生矣。窃念山地数亩,得其税不足以裨国储,贻其害遂足以累山灵。范、毛二公,信是三世诸佛,现宰官身护法者乎?理宜勒名,以志二公之德不朽。如再有乡愚妄讦,及里老混催诈骗者,本寺僧请官重治不贷。范公讳学颜,山西万泉县人,辛酉乡进

Exemption from the Regular Grain Tribute for Monks in Maijishan is written on the topmost of the body, the inscription runs for 18 lines in regular script, a full line of 30 characters, well preserved and clearly legible. On the 15th day of the ninth month in the 15th year of the reign of Emperor Chongzhen in the Qing Dynasty (AD 1642), the scholar Yao Longyun wrote this on the bottom of the tablet, and the names of more than ten monks in the Ruiyin Temple were engraved there. It is another literary of stone tablets about Maijishan Caves, bearing relatively high referential value. The entire text reads as follows.

According to the *Guangyuji*, the Maijishan is the crown of forests and springs in the land of Qin. There are tablets available for verification regarding the successive imperial decrees for the construction of this ancient temple. From the Later Qin Dynasty (AD 383-417) to the present, for more than 1,300 years, the incense has never ceased. The woods and valleys are steep and secluded, with dark and eerie pine and cypress trees. There is also a waterfall cascading between the cliffs, creating a natural marvel. Both Du Fu and Li Shizhong have poems about the Maijishan. as expressed by the line: In which valley there are no orchids blooming, in which abyss there are no dragons dwelling? In the Maijishan Ganoderma lucidum were produced continuously. The sacred lamp shines, illuminating the forest and valley with holy pearl-like lights. Truly, it is a renowned scenic spot comparable to the Five Great Mountains in China (Taishan Mountain in Shandong, Hengshan Mountain in Hunan, Huashan Mountain in Shaanxi, Hengshan Mountain in Shanxi and Songshan Mountain in Henan). In the past, there were 320 mus of permanent fields, but they were all barren and thin. The mountain area was cold and steep, with cliffs. In spring, summer, and autumn, the produce was limited to oats, buckwheat, and the like. The few mountain monks mostly relied on wild vegetables for sustenance. In Du Fu's poem, it is said, "There are few remaining monks in the wild temple." The mountain fields are rocky and rough, causing the monks to suffer. The designated permanent residences in various places were originally not included in the grain quota. However, due to the failed attempts by ignorant villagers to occupy the fields intended for offering and support purposes by this temple, they falsely accused, resulting an increase of two shis, nine dous, and five shengs in the grain quota of this temple. The temple monks lost the lawsuit, and more than half of them fled. After the devastation of war, there were no cattle to raise, and the land was completely barren. The tenant farmers had to fill the ditches themselves, while the rent collectors incessantly knocked on the temple doors. As a result, the grass in front of the Dharma Hall grew one zhang thick (approximately three meters), a great pity indeed. Fortunately, Fan Xueyan, who was on his tour as an official, happened to be staying at the temple due to the military situation. Upon noticing that the monks' living conditions were not ideal, he inquired about the financial resources for the temple. The monk Nengxin tearfully explained the reasons behind their situation. Fan, with a deep sigh, said, "How can such fertile land be left uncultivated? This is a shame on the local officials." Upon hearing the case, it was immediately granted exemption from investigation. Fortunately, Governor Mao Fengguan, known for his divine wisdom and compassion, possessed qualities in line with the teachings of Buddhism. He gladly offered to facilitate this significant opportunity for a positive connection. Therefore, he submitted a detailed and earnest request for exemption from the regular grain tribute for monks in Maijishan, accompanied by a meticulously crafted letter. Such an official document was received, which states, "Regarding the distribution of surplus grain, it is advised not to rush the village head in handling it. This matter should be properly resolved." With the revival of this renowned Buddhist Temple, the monks can live a peaceful life. However, I have a personal thought. Although the temple owns several acres of mountain land, the tax revenue generated is insufficient to support the national treasury, and it poses a threat to the surrounding mountains and forests. Could Venerable Fan and Venerable Mao be the

士。毛公讳凤冠，四川富顺县人，丁卯乡进士。崇祯十五年九月十五日庚午，举人姚隆运撰。

2.《胡安游麦积山次泰谿甘公韵碑》

按《明诗纪事》：嘉靖朝已签，胡安，字仁夫，余姚人。嘉靖甲辰进士，累官苑马寺卿。有《趋庭集》。

一入招提境，能令长昼添。
俯临渭水曲，遥数陇山尖。
爱树才留榻，成诗辄捻髯。
幽栖无所好，濡滞复何嫌。
蜂房成户牖，斗绝复孤悬。
颇胜楼观日，还期剑倚天。
含恨非宿约，坐食亦前缘。
无异匡庐上，晴峰散紫烟。
珠玉忽盈手，翩翩艺苑雄。
客来尊上绿，僧起日初红。
陇蜀驱驰后，蕃戎指授中。
伊吾欲鸣剑，感事忆臧宫。
云消初见洞，风满自开扉。
曲迳人稀到，悬崖鸟倦飞。
暂当挹晴霁，聊复临玄微。
尘鞅今如此，何由早息机？
珠林有奇赏，色界本来澄。
鸟韵和禅磬，岚光杂佛灯。
门临千树杪，身上五云层。

reincarnations of the three Buddhas, entrusted with the task of protecting the temple as government officials? It would be appropriate to record their names to commemorate their enduring virtues. If there are any ignorant individuals who make baseless accusations or village leaders who engage in fraud and extortion, the monks of this temple earnestly request that the authorities take decisive action and not tolerate such behavior. Fan, whose courtesy name is Xueyan, was a native of Wanquan County in Shanxi Province. He achieved the position of Juren (—a successful candidate in the imperial examinations at the provincial level in the Ming and Qing dynasties) in the Xinyou year. Mao, whose courtesy name is Fengguan, came from Fushun County in Sichuan Province. He achieved the position of Juren in the Dingmao year. On the 15th day of the ninth month in the fifteenth year of the Chongzhen reign (AD 1642), the scholar Yao Longyun wrote this.

2. The Stone Tablet of Hu An's Poems on Visiting Maijishan Writing According to Gan Ru's Poems' Rhyming Words

According to the sixth part (of the Jiajing reign of the Ming Dynasty) of *Ming Shi Ji Shi*, Hu An, courtesy name Renfu, was from Yuyao. He passed the imperial examination in AD 1544 in the Jiajing reign. He held various official positions, including the magistrate of Pasturage Office. He authored *Quting Collection*.

As I enter the tranquil temple ground, Daylight seems to lengthen all around.
Below me lies the winding Wei River's bend, Distantly count the peaks of Longshan Mountains.
I love the trees here and often linger by. Composing poems, stroking my beard with sighs.
In this peaceful retreat, I've nothing to demand, Even when it rains, I bear no complaints.
A beehive turned into a household with windows and doors. Steep and perilous, yet still remaining isolated and alone.
It outdoes the viewing platform on a sunny day. And I aspire to wield my sword like the protagonist in *Tianlong Babu*.
I bear no grudges against my past lodging. But I reap the fruits of my previous karma.
Like ascending to Kuanglu Mountain (the Lu Mountain in Jiangxi Province). Watching misty peaks scatter in purple haze.
With precious objects filling up one's hands, one becomes a master in elegant artistry.
As guests arrive, they drink from green cups, while the monk's robe is dyed red by the morning sun.
After traveling through Long and Shu regions, one receives guidance from the barbarians.
Yearning to draw the sword, one recalls the Zang Gong a general in the East Han Dynasty amid sincere emotions.
As clouds dissipate, the cave comes into sight; with the wind blowing, the door opens wide.
Along winding paths there are few passersby; tired birds fly above cliffside.
For now, let's enjoy this clear weather and explore the mysterious and subtle.
With the dust of this world as it is, how can we find peace?
The forest offers unique scenery, originally clear and limpid.
The rhythm of birds blends with the sound of Zen bells, while the misty light mingles with Buddhist lanterns.
The entrance gate stands before a thousand trees and the body reaches five layers of cloud.
Occasionally, when conversing with the abbot, I am humbled by his serene wisdom.
Passing through the scenic beauty of Gansu, this mountain stands supreme.

偶及乘除语，萧然愧老僧。
度陇观形胜，今为第一山。
勒摹前代姓，谈笑古人颜。
坐卧浑忘暑，登临始觉闲。
丹梯分手处，谁与再登攀。

3.《李筵隆庆元年四月望日登麦积岩小憩二绝碑》

上尽诸天喜未还，归来无力济民艰。
回首陇麦连云起，但愿登场似此山。
万佛千佛洞几崇，不知佛在此心中。
老僧指点云霄上，回首乾坤一笑空。

邺郡西野李筵题。

4.《冯惟讷游麦积山四首碑》

山川雄且都，法界盛规模。
陇蜀屯灵气，乾坤辟壮图。
天垂云幄近，月照相轮孤。
相像昙花现，西来启觉途。
疏山开净土，镂玉写金仙。
翠蔼连三积，空香隐四禅。
莲宫长曜日，桂栋欲浮天。
不入沈灰劫，灵光独曒然。
鹫岭横西极，祇园复在兹。
孤标拔地起，万象入云危。
月殿金枝秀，霜林锦树披。
经过未辞数，猿鹤久相期。

Capturing the essence of our forefathers, we engage in joyful conversation with ancient figures.
Sitting or lying down, we forget about the heat; Climbing to the top, we finally feel at peace.
On the path where the red ladder divides, who else will ascend with me again?

3. *The Stone Tablet of Li Ting's Poems on Climbing the Maijishan on April 15th in the First Year (AD 1567) of the Longqing period, and Composing Two Poems During a Short Rest*

Exhausting all the joys of the heavens yet powerless to ease the people's hardship upon return.
Looking back, clouds shroud the Long Mountain.
I hope to ascend the stage like this mountain.
In the cave of countless Buddhas, so majestic and sublime, who knows where the Buddha truly resides—perhaps within one's own heart.
The old monk points to the sky, and looking back upon the universe with a smile, nothingness prevails.

By Li Ting from Yejun of the Henan Province

4. *The Stone Tablet of Feng Weine's Four Poems on Touring Maijishan*

The mountains and rivers are majestic and magnificent, and the scale of the Dharma realm is prosperous.
The spiritual energy of Long and Shu is gathered here, creating a vast and impressive landscape.
The sky hangs low like a curtain of clouds, while the moon shines alone like a solitary wheel.
These sights resemble the appearance of a blooming "Tan Hua" (night-blooming cereus), revealing a path to enlightenment from the west.
Clearing the mountain to open up new land, and carving jade to depict golden immortals.
Verdant canopy accumulates three folds, empty fragrance conceals four meditations.
The lotus palace enjoys long days of radiance, the elegant hall is about to float into the sky.
Not succumbing to the age of darkness, its spiritual light shines alone.
Crossing the Egret Ridge at its western extreme, The Zhiyuan Garden once more in sight.
Alone stands the lofty emblem. Mountains and rivers enter into clouds, perilous and grim.
The Moon Palace's golden branches gleam. Frosty trees in magnificent state beam.
I shall pass through many times without fail. For the monkeys and cranes will forever prevail.
A millennium ago, Yu Xin was appointed as an official, and it is rumored that this inscription was left by him.
Within the golden case lay a precious aura, in the jade script was a secret scripture.
The sun and moon revolve around the three halls, with clouds and mist guarding the hundred spirits.
Regrettably pondering over the changes of this fleeting world, I scratch my head and bid farewell to the mountain court.
Written by Feng Weine (also known as Shaozhou) from Beihai, Shandong, on the lucky day in the first month of winter in the Gengshen year (the 39th year) (AD 1560) of the Jiajing reign.

5. *The Stone Tablet of Gan Ru's Six Poems on Revisiting Maijishan Composed Together with Hugong from Leshan*

According to the sixth part (of the Jiajing reign of the Ming Dynasty) of *Ming Shi Ji Shi*, Gan Ru, courtesy name Zhengfu, was from Fushun. He passed the imperial examination in the Jiajing reign. He was appointed as a censor and later promoted to the position of

千载庚开府,传闻此勒铭。
金函论宝气,玉字秘图经。
日月回三殿,云霞卫百灵。
空嗟浮世改,搔首别山庭。

时嘉靖庚申(三十九年)孟冬吉,北海少洲冯惟讷书。

5.《甘茹重游麦积山六首与乐山胡公同赋碑》

按《明诗纪事》:嘉靖朝已签,甘茹,字征甫,富顺人。嘉靖丁未进士,除御史,累迁山东按察副使。有《己癸草》《入秦草》《归田草》《拔茅山人草》等集。

冥搜此灵境,兴比尘游添。
群动同禅寂,千山为佛尖。
慧风吹豆甲,法雨唾松髯。
吏隐真堪寄,华簪只自嫌。
宝塔千松绕,云龛万幕悬。
丹梯斜有径,青壁峭通天。
混沌神能凿,飞翔鸟尚缘。
振衣惊蜡屐,下界等浮烟。
地因庾碣重,寺以杜诗雄。
鸟语妨僧定,毫光映日红。
浮生色相外,胜览醉歌中。
怀古情无赖,黄蒿没魏宫。
重阁浮高栋,危栏隐曲扉。
步生云片片,身共鹤飞飞。
莲宇开丹嶂,经堂俯翠微。

Deputy Inspector of the Shandong Province. He compiled collections such as *Ji Gui Cao*, *Ru Qin Cao*, *Gui Tian Cao*, *Ba Mao Shan Ren Cao*, etc.

Exploring the spiritual realm, and surpassing the worldly pleasures.
Together with the group, sharing the serenity of meditation, and regarding the thousand mountains as the pinnacle of Buddhism.
The wise breeze blows away trivialities, and the rain of Dharma moistens the beard.
Even a humble official can appreciate the true value, but only feels self-disgust for the showy hat.
A thousand pine trees encircle the pagoda, and ten thousand roofs of clouds float above the niche.
The red ladder has a slanting path, and the green cliff rises steeply to the sky.
Chaos was carved by divine power, and even birds of flight have a fateful connection to it.
Startled by a shaking robe and wax-soled shoes, one descends from this world, waiting for floating mist to surround them.
This place is important because of the inscriptions left by Yu Xin, while this temple stands proudly because of the poems of the Poetry Sage—Du Fu.
The chirping birds disturb the meditation of the monks, while the sunlight reflects the red colors of the brush strokes.
Amidst the floating world of phenomenal appearances, the drunken songs reveal the magnificent view.
Nostalgia knows no boundaries, as the yellow herbs conceal the Palace of Wei Ao.
Lofty towers rise from layers of pavilions. Where dangerous railings conceal hidden doors.
Ascending lightly on clouds like fluttering pieces. Together with cranes, my body too takes flight.
The lotus shrine reveals vermilion ridges. And from the sutra hall, verdant views below.
For a hundred years, light footsteps on perilous paths, All worldly affairs forgotten, released from the machine.
Through the vine-shaded cow cave's narrow trail. The crystal clear fall waters flow.
Flower whispers heard when the skies are still, Moonlight passes the lamp for the night to glow.
Three thousand golden grains in three realms found. Twelve floors of jade towers reach the sky.
Inscribed on cliffs far beyond account. This mountain monk treasures it high.
Climbing high with a border-colleague guide, we sight majestic Ba Mountain's pride.
With thoughts as tangled as duckweed leaf, this vista's grandeur has washed away my grief.
Serene are all things above, and even officials find here idle love.
Gazing back, three laughs we trace, unattainable memories in time and space.
In the summer of AD 1564, the 43rd year of the Jiajing reign (in the Ming Dynasty), a Sichuanese man named Gan Ru (styled as Tai Xi) recorded his experiences.

Extension and Elaboration

The background and process of the excavation of the tunnel in Cave 5 are described in the appendix *of the Stone Tablet of Gan Ru's Six Poems on Revisiting Maijishan Composed Together with Hugong from Leshan* in the cave. The appendix is as follows.

百年轻履险，万事解忘机。
牛洞藤阴细，龙湫溜色澄。
无云花自语，不夜月传灯。
金粟三千界，琼楼十二层。
摩崖未辞数，珍重此山僧。
登临依越客，指点是巴山。
萍梗牵吟思，乾坤洗俗颜。
上方诸品静，信宿一官闲。
回首追三笑，寥寥不可攀。

明嘉靖四十三年（公元1564年）夏，蜀人泰豁甘茹识。

引申与拓展

该窟《甘茹重游麦积山六首与乐山胡公同赋碑》的附文中描述了第5窟"小有洞天"过洞挖掘的背景和过程。附文如下。

小有洞天

上界右为牛堂，堂纳雾占阴雨，盖出巩记云。故有栈绕外而达，代远朽堕，不可缮补，僧始洞之。然低隘，非匍匐莫由也。乃命工稍加高广，众称便。因牛堂遂假五丁开川例之，再赋五言一律。

小有何年辟，斑斑斧凿新。
群生悲觉路，万劫启迷津。
秦蜀金牛险，阴晴玉洞春。
谁知三昧外，彼岸复无垠。

Xiaoyou Dongtian Cave

On the right of the upper realm is the Hall of Bull, where fog gathers during cloudy and rainy days, and it is covered by clouds. Therefore, a plank was built winding outside to reach it, but it has decayed and cannot be repaired. So, monks began to dig a cave there. However, the passage is very narrow and one can pass through only by crawling. Thus, workers were ordered to make it wider and higher, which was praised by everyone. For the Hall of Bull reminds me of the story of five warriors of ancient Shu who successfully opened the Golden Bull Road through the Qin and Shu mountains and a five-character quatrain was composed.

It is not known in which year the Xiaoyou Dongtian Cave was carved, only the marks left by axes being new.
The masses lament their struggles on the road, seeking enlightenment amid infinite cycles of rebirth.
The Golden Bull Road through the Qin and Shu mountains is perilous, the Cave ambience changing in spring.
Who knows what lies beyond the meditation?
The farther shore has no bounds once one has attained the ultimate state.

第169窟

第169窟位于西崖下部,与东面第69窟为双窟。两窟之间塑双龙交尾,上面影塑一尊坐佛。1953年,勘察团将两窟分开,编号第169窟。开凿于北魏(公元386年—公元534年),是麦积山石窟几组双窟形制之一。

该窟体现了麦积山双窟特征,内有两尊造像。

形制:该窟为平面方形、平拱顶。

造像:正壁塑一尊交脚弥勒菩萨坐在狮子宝座上,左侧存一身胁侍菩萨立像,共两身造像。

正壁交脚弥勒菩萨,头戴宝冠,长发垂于双肩,颈戴宽桃形项链。袒露上身,披帛覆肩并下垂,下着长裙。两臂前伸,双手残失。交脚姿势坐在狮子宝座上。后绘火焰纹头光。弥勒菩萨高雅端庄的姿态完全像一个年轻、高贵的王子。

左侧菩萨,戴宝冠,五官清秀。内着圆领服,外罩通肩衣,广袖博带。左手持帛带下垂,右手举花于胸前。

第二章　麦积山石窟汉英解说词

Cave 169

Cave 169 is located in the lower part of the western cliff, and it is a pair cave with Cave 69 to the east. Between the two caves there is a pair of dragons with heads and tails twisting together, above which a seated Buddha modelled in relief on the cliff face. They were separated by the Central Survey Team in 1953, and gave the number Cave 169. Built in the Northern Wei Dynasty (AD 386-534), it is one of several groups of pair caves at Maijishan.

In the cave visitors will enjoy the characteristics of pair caves at Maijishan, and two sculptures. Details are as follows.

Type: It is a flat square niche open to the cliff face with a flat vault ceiling.

Sculptures: The main wall contains a cross-ankled Maitreya as a bodhisattva sitting on a throne supported by a lion modelled in relief, an attendant bodhisattva standing on the left. There are two figures in all.

The Maitreya as a bodhisattva in the cross-ankled pose on the main wall bears a coronet, the rest hair cascading over the shoulders, with a wide, peach-shaped collar around the neck. The upper body is bare, the scarf covers the shoulders and falls down, a long dress on the lower body. His two arms are extended forward with hands missing. He sits in the cross-ankled pose on a throne supported by a lion. There is an aureole painted with flaming motif behind him. The grace and dignified attitude of Maitreya as a bodhisattva seems to be a young elegant prince completely.

The bodhisattva on the left wears a coronet with delicately modelled features. She is robed in an inner garment with a circular collar, an upper garment that completely covers the body and hangs in heavy folds round the shoulders, the loose and long sleeves with wide girdle. Her left hand hangs down with a ribbon passing between the fingers, and her right hand is raised to the chest holding a flower.

引申与拓展

麦积山石窟中弥勒菩萨像较多,且根据《弥勒上生经》塑造。该窟所描述的是弥勒菩萨上生兜率天宫为天人说法时的情景,这时的弥勒是菩萨装束,相貌仍旧接近印度人的形象。常有两种不同坐姿,"交脚菩萨"和"思维菩萨"。前者两脚交叉而坐;后者左腿下垂,右腿翘在左腿上,表现出一种思考问题的状态。

Extension and Elaboration

There are many images of Maitreya as bodhisattva at Maijishan Caves, which are modelled according to *the Sutra on Maitreya's Ascension*. It depicts the scene of Maitreya Ascension to Tusita Heaven preaching to the divines, then Maitreya as a bodhisattva, the appearance is still close to the image of Indians. There are often two different seated postures, cross-ankled bodhisattva and bodhisattva in pensive pose. The former figure sits in the cross-ankled pose. The latter figure sits with left leg pendent, the right leg crossed over the left, in a pensive pose.

第172窟

第172窟位于东崖中部西侧,第16窟下部。开凿于西魏(公元535年—公元556年),是麦积山常见三佛龛中少有的造像五官相同的例子。

该窟内有四身泥塑造像。

形制:该窟是平面方形、平顶窟。前壁、窟顶及右壁塌毁,现存正壁龛及左壁残龛。

造像:正壁龛和左壁龛各塑一坐佛,正壁龛外左侧立一胁侍菩萨,左壁龛外右侧立一弟子,共计四身。

正壁龛佛,磨光高肉髻,面形长方,弯眉细目,眉间有白毫相。高鼻大耳,面带微笑。内着僧祇支,外着通肩袈裟。左手施与愿印,右手施无畏印。结跏趺坐于台座上,袈裟分两片垂于座前。身后多重同心圆项光,外绘火焰纹。莲瓣形身光两侧各绘有一身弟子面佛拱手而立,以石绿、石青、赭红为主。

左壁残龛内佛,头缺失,左腿已毁。着装和坐姿与主佛相同。双手施禅定印。

正壁左侧菩萨和左壁右侧弟子,与佛同相。身后均绘多重同

Cave 172

Cave 172 is located at the middle west part of the eastern cliff, below Cave 16. It was dug in the Western Wei Dynasty (AD 535-556), is a rare example of the sculptures having the same facial features in the usual three Buddhas niches at Maijishan.

In the cave visitors can enjoy four clay sculptures. Details are as follows.

Type: It is a flat square niche with the flat ceiling. The front wall, the ceiling and the right wall have fallen away, leaving the niche into the main wall and the ruined niche on the left wall.

Sculptures: A seated Buddha is modelled in each niche into the main wall and the left wall, outside which a bodhisattva stands on the left of the main wall, and a disciple on the right outside the niche into the left wall. There are four figures in all.

The Buddha in the niche into the main wall has a polished high topknot, the rectangular face carved with arched brows sweeping above gently opened almond eyes, the white hair between the brows, the high nose flanked by pendulous ears, with a smile. He is robed in an inner vest covering the left shoulder and armpits, an upper garment that completely covers his body and hangs in heavy folds round his shoulders. With the left hand in the varada mudra and the right hand in the abhaya mudra, he sits in dhyanasana on the throne with the hem covering in two large petals. He is backed by an aureole composed of multi-tiered concentric circles adorned with flaming motif on the outer border, and on each side of the lotus petal-shaped mandorla painted a disciple in relief stands with the right hand into a fist and the left hand held straight against the fist, chiefly in a bluish grey tint, a stone green, and a reddish-brown.

心圆项光。其中正壁左侧菩萨，扇形高发髻，身躯修长。内着交领衣，外着交领束腰长衫。左手拢袖持净瓶，右手置于腹前。双足残毁，立于莲台上。左壁右侧弟子着装与主佛相同。左手捧供品于腹前，右手置于供品上。足蹬云头履，立于左龛外。

引申与拓展

该窟正壁左侧菩萨和左壁右侧弟子组合，与第121窟正壁龛外两侧两组菩萨弟子组合相似。

The Buddha in the ruined niche into the left wall is headless, with his left leg destroyed. His style of the rob and the sitting posture are identical with those of the principal Buddha. His two hands perform the dhyana mudra.

The left-side bodhisattva on the main wall and the right-side disciple on the left wall seem to be very similar to that of the principal Buddha in appearance. There are aureoles adorned with multi-tiered concentric circles behind them. Among which the left-side bodhisattva on the main wall has a high fan-shaped topknot, tall, slender and long-legged. She is robed in an inner garment of a crossing collar and an outer waist robe of a collar folded across in front. The left hand concealing in the sleeve holds a vase, and the right hand is placed on the abdomen. She stands on the lotus platform, with feet destroyed. The right-side disciple on the left wall wears the same clothes as the principal Buddha. The left hand is put to the abdomen holding up an offering, above which the right hand is placed. He stands outside the niche into the left wall in cloud head shoes.

Extension and Elaboration

The group of the left-side bodhisattva on the main wall and the right-side disciple on the left wall is similar to the two groups of bodhisattvas and disciples outside both sides of the niche into the main wall in Cave 121.

第191窟

第191窟位于西崖下部最西面,开凿于西魏(公元535年—公元556年),宋代(公元960年—公元1279年)重修,是麦积山石窟少有的依照犍陀罗风格,采用多种浮雕手法开凿的洞窟。

该窟中可见经常出现在西方建筑门楣处的"翅膀"造型布局,七身造型奇特的造像。

第191窟造像

Cave 191

Cave 191 is located on the extreme west end of the lower part in the western cliff. It was originally dug in the Western Wei Dynasty (AD 535-556) and repaired in the Song Dynasty (AD 960-1279). It is a rare niche cut in variety of relief techniques in Gandhara style at Maijishan.

Visitors can appreciate the wing-shaped layout which often appears on the gate lintel in western architectures, and seven oddly-modelled sculptures. Details are as follows.

第191窟造像

形制：该窟是麦积山石窟最奇特的一个洞窟。整组造像没有开窟或开龛，而是在崖壁上采用高浮雕、浅浮雕、圆塑、悬塑等多种雕塑手法塑造而成。

造像：现存均为宋代重修。上方圆拱龛内塑一坐佛和右侧弟子，龛外左右两侧各塑一身交脚菩萨，龛正下方塑一身化生力士，下方各塑一身蹲狮，共计七身。

龛内坐佛，倚坐于台座上，双脚踩在莲蕾上。左手抚膝，右臂上举于胸前，右手已毁。右侧弟子左手置于胸前，右手持衣角下垂。龛外两侧菩萨交脚坐在束帛座上，足踩由下方化生力士身下伸展而上的莲蕾。

龛下方化生力士，络腮胡须，双目圆瞪，挺胸鼓腹，两臂平伸，飘带缠绕，双手托龛。身下塑有一朵盛开的莲花，莲茎向左右伸展，向上与莲蕾相连，莲蕾之上各塑一菩萨。下方两身蹲狮相向而视，虽然塑造得有点粗劣，却也逼真。

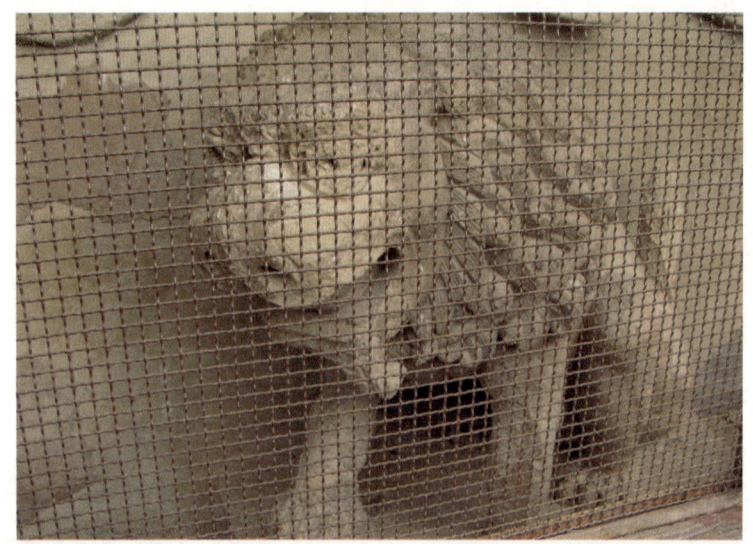

第191窟左狮子

Type: It is the most peculiar niche at Maijishan. The whole group of sculptures are not modelled in a cave or in a niche, but made or carved on the cliff face in techniques of high relief, shallow relief, three-dimensional and hanging carving.

Sculptures: All the figures are restorations of the Song Dynasty. A chaitya arched recess above the niche holds a seated Buddha and a disciple on the right, outside which sit two flanking bodhisattvas with ankles crossed, below the center of the niche is a lotus atlantid and below which are two crouching lions. There are seven figures in all.

The Buddha in the niche seated with legs pendent and feet rests on two lotus buds. His left hand rests on knee, and the right arm is raised to the chest with the hand destroyed. The disciple on the right places the left hand to the chest, and the right hand hangs down holding the corner of clothing. Outside the niche two flanking bodhisattvas sit with ankles crossed on the waist drum-shaped thrones with a ribbon tied at the waist, and feet resting on two lotus buds extending up under the body of the lotus atlantid below.

The lotus atlantid below the center of the niche is bearded with bulging eyes, squared shoulders and slightly swelling abdomen, two arms wrapped with ribbons are extended horizontally, supporting the niche on his upraised hands. Under the body there is a blooming lotus with a long lotus stem stretching up to each side and connected with the buds on which two flanking bodhisattvas rest. Below the two crouching lions facing each other, although a little roughly built, but in realistic modelling.

第191窟右狮子

引申与拓展

该窟采用外露的岩壁上直接塑造的手法,主题讲述释迦牟尼在兜率天为众菩萨讲法的场景。龛内正壁的佛已变得相当微不足道。两尊大菩萨荣耀地坐于从龛下部化生力士身下伸出的长茎莲花座上,这组菩萨像才更吸引信徒的注意力。从佛到菩萨的重心转变是后来中国佛教的特点,这一转变在该窟最显著。

该窟力士从莲花中生出,络腮胡须、双目圆瞪,极具少数民族特征。此种造型的确见证了古丝绸之路上各文化在此交融,完全不同于中国古代传统审美。

第191窟力士

Extension and Elaboration

The sculptures in the niche are directly modelled on the open cliff, and the topic illustrates the scene of Sakyamuni preaching to the bodhisattvas in the Tushita Heaven. The Buddha on the main wall has become quite insignificant. Two great bodhisattvas gloriously sit on the long stem lotus seats stretching from the body of the lotus atlantid on the lower part of the shrine, and this group of bodhisattvas attracts the attention of worshippers. The shift of focus from the Buddha to the bodhisattva was the characteristic of popular Buddhism in China. This transition is most illustrated in the shrine.

The body of the atlantid appears from the lotus, the bearded with bulging eyes, and carries more minority characteristics. This modelling indeed witnesses the blending of various cultures on the ancient Silk Road, completely different from the ancient Chinese traditional aesthetics.

本章将介绍麦积山石窟附属遗存瑞应寺和舍利塔的基本情况，所藏冯惟讷《秦州天水郡麦积崖佛龛铭川制置使司给田公据碑》《秦州雄武军陇城县第六保瑞应寺再葬佛舍利碑》和杜甫诗词《山寺》。

CHAPTER THREE

第三章

麦积山石窟附属遗存

瑞应寺

瑞应寺牌匾

瑞应寺位于麦积山石窟山脚下。唐代高僧释道世所撰《法苑珠林》第五十一卷中记载:"秦州麦积崖佛殿下,舍利山神藏之。此寺周穆王新造,名曰'灵安寺',经四十年,当有人出。"东晋曰"无忧寺",北魏曰"石岩寺",隋赐"净念寺",唐赐"应乾寺"。宋大中祥符二年(公元1009年),由迥觉大师在旧址上重建,元符年间又遭火焚,再建。宋代大观年间因山顶产灵芝三十八本,秦州经略陶龙图奏上朝廷之后,敕赐为"瑞应寺"。明清两代均称此名,一直沿用至今。

现今的寺院为明代晚期重建,清代重修。其面积约为2500平方米,坐北朝南。沿着中轴线,前面是山门,中间是天王殿,后面是大雄宝殿,左右有东西配殿。天王殿左右两侧隔偏门分别为钟鼓楼,东配殿后高台上为麦积山馆。山门前原有塔院,已被拆除。正南侧有清康熙十八年(公元1679年)建戏楼一座,亦被拆除。寺内藏碑刻、僧人墓塔及木造像等。2001年至2002年,国家文物局拨款120万元对寺院进行了整体加固和维修,同时对大雄宝殿的壁画做了修复保护。

The Ruiying Temple

The Ruiying Temple is located at the foot of the Maijishan Caves. It is said in Volume 51 of *The Encyclopaedia of the Garden of Dharma* written by the eminent monk Shi Daoshi of the Tang Dynasty, "The Buddha relic beneath the temple of the Maiji Cliff in Qinzhou was hidden by the mountain deity. This temple was newly constructed by King Mu (the fifth king of Zhou, said to have lived to 105 and reigned 976-922 BC or 1001-947 BC, rich in associated mythology) and named the Ling'an Temple. It is said that after 40 years, someone will appear." After that, it bears a different name at differt periods, the Wuyou Temple in the Eastern Jin Dynasty, the Shiyan Temple in the Northern Wei Dynasty, the Jingnian Temple during the Sui Dynasty and the Yingqian Temple during the Tang Dynasty. In the second year of the Dazhong era (AD 1009), there was Master Jiongjue who came to Maijishan, searching the old foundation of the temple and and rebuilding it. It was burned and rebuilt during Yuanfu years (AD1098-1100) of the Song Dynasty. In the first year of the Daguan era of the Song Dynasty (AD 1107), 38 lingzhi mushrooms were found near a pagoda on the mountaintop. Tao Longtu, the Qinzhou Military Commissioner, reported this miracle and it was officially named the Ruiying Temple. This name was used during both the Ming and Qing dynasties and has been used ever since.

The present Ruiying Temple was rebuilt during the late Ming Dynasty and repaired during the Qing Dynasty. Covering an area of 2,500 square meters, the building is arranged in order from south to north. It is divided into three sections: along the central axis a temple gate on the front, the Heavenly King Hall in the middle and the Mahavira Hall with two side halls in the back yard. The Bell Tower and the Drum Tower stand on both sides of the Heavenly King Hall just opposite the side doors of the temple gate, and the old shrine room in the eastern side hall is used as a small Museum at Maijishan. The original tower in front of the temple gate has been demolished. A theater building on the south of the temple gate erected in the 18 year of the reign of Emperor Kangxi(AD 1679) in the Qing Dynasty has also been removed. Many stones with inscriptions are embedded in the walls. Several Buddhist pagodas (which serve as burial sites for eminent monks) and woodcarvings are preserved in the monastery too. From 2001 to 2002, the State Administration of Cultural Heritage allocated 1.2 million yuan to reinforce and repair the monastery completely, and much repairing and preserving work of the wall paintings in the Mahavira Hall at the same time.

The gate is an archway with a single-eaved roof, three openings of 6.92 meters long, two openings of 3.3 meters deep, the central opening of 2.5 meters long and 5 meters tall, the

瑞应寺大雄宝殿

瑞应寺东配殿

第三章　麦积山石窟附属遗存

瑞应寺鼓楼

瑞应寺西配殿

山门为牌楼式单檐悬山顶，面阔三间6.92米，进深两间3.3米，正间面阔2.5米，顶高5米，两次间面阔2.21米，顶高4.08米。各间有门两扇。前后檐共有斗拱十八攒。灰板瓦覆面。正间檐前悬郭沫若书"麦积山石窟"匾额一块。

天王殿位于山门内北侧，单檐灰板瓦悬山顶，前出廊，面阔三间9.17米，进深两间6.37米，顶高6.22米，正面辟门，前后贯通，各有四扇格扇门。裙板上刻云纹、莲叶、龙纹等图案。廊前列檐柱四根，上承额枋及斗拱，计有柱科斗拱四攒，平身科斗拱三攒，均为一大斗四小斗。殿内原有木雕菩萨及韦驮像，两侧有四天王塑像，塑像1967年被毁。

大雄宝殿位于寺院中轴线最北侧，清嘉庆二十五年（公元1820年）重建。面阔五间16.8米，进深三间9.7米，高7.03米。建于高0.8米的台基上。土木结构，灰瓦单檐歇山顶，前有廊，明间与两次间开门。裙板浮雕牡丹花、宝相花及琴棋书画等图案。斗拱七攒，两侧角科斗拱两攒各为一大斗九小斗，中间柱头科斗拱四攒和平身科斗拱五攒各为一大斗二十小斗。山墙内壁存明代重绘十佛、八菩萨及诸罗汉壁画。

瑞应寺山门

two side openings of 2.21 meters long and 4.08 meters tall. Each opening has double doors. There are 18 brackets in all on the front and rear eaves. The roof is covered with gray tiles. Above its lintel hangs a wooden horizontal board inscribed with "Maijishan Caves" in the calligraphy of Guo Moruo.

The Heavenly King Hall stands inside the north section of the temple gate, with single-eaved grey tiled roof, a front corridor, with three rooms of 9.17 meters long, two rooms of 6.37 meters deep and 6.22 meters tall. There is a door on the front, which leads to the back door directly. Each bears four partition doors. Their lower boards are carved with motifs of clouds, lotus leaves and dragons. Beams and brackets are supported by a row of four stone pillars in the front of the corridor. There are four brackets on columns, three brackets between columns in total, all of which are a cap block and four small blocks. The original wood carvings of bodhisattva and Veda, images of four heavenly kings on either side in the hall were all destroyed in 1967.

The Mahavira Hall stands on the northernmost of the central axis of the monastery, and was reconstructed in the 25th year of the reign of Emperor Jiaqing in the Qing Dynasty (AD 1820), with five rooms of 16.8 meters long, three rooms of 9.7 meters deep and 7.03 meters tall. The hall is built on a base of 0.8 meters high, with civil structures, grey tiled roof with single eave, a front corridor, and a door between the main hall and the two side halls. Their lower boards are carved in relief with patterns of peonies, lotus flowers and Chinese Ku-Ch'in(Chinese seven-stringed zither) playings, Go/Weiqi playings, calligraphys and paintings. There are seven brackets, two brackets on corner embedded on both sides containing a cap block and nine small blocks, four brackets between capitals and five brackets between columns in the middle, each including a cap block and 20 small blocks. Paintings of ten Buddhas, eight bodhisattvas and Arhats repainted in the Ming Dynasty survive on the walls inside the hall.

The Inscription of the Seven-Buddha Niche on the Maiji Cliff in the Tianshui Prefecture of

瑞应寺天王殿

冯惟讷《秦州天水郡麦积崖佛龛铭并序》碑

因庾信写的《佛龛铭》的原碑已不存在，寺内石碑由陇右道冯惟讷于嘉靖甲子年间（公元1564年）重刻。此碑位于瑞应寺山门右侧。内容如下。

麦积崖者，乃陇底之名山，河西之灵岳。高峰寻云，深谷无量。方之鹫岛，迹循三禅；譬彼鹤鸣，虚飞六甲。鸟道乍穷，羊肠或断。云如鹏翼，忽已垂天；树若桂华，翻能拂日。是以飞锡遥来，度杯远至，疏山凿洞，郁为净土。拜灯王于石室，乃假驭风；礼花首于山龛，方资控鹤。大都督李允信者，籍于宿植，深悟法门。乃于壁之南崖，梯云凿道，奉为亡父造七佛龛。似刻浮檀，如攻水玉。从容满月，照曜青莲。影现须弥，香闻忉利。如斯尘野，还开说法之堂。犹彼香山，更对

瑞应寺重刻的庾信《秦州天水郡麦积山佛龛铭并序》石碑

Qinzhou · The Preface recarved by Feng Weine

The original *Tablet of the Inscription on the Seven-Buddha Niche* by Yu Xin was lost, the tablet in the temple was recarved by Feng Weine, a supervisor of the Longyou Circuit, in the year of AD 1564 during the Jiajing period of the Ming Dynasty. This monument is located on the right side of the temple gate of the Ruiying Temple. The content is as follows.

The Maijishan is a famous mountain in the Longshan mountain system, and among many beautiful peaks to the west of the Yellow River, its peak high and its valley deep. Like Mount Lingjiu, Maijishan is a sacred place of Buddhist teachings. Here you can trace the footprints of the Zen masters who have made painstaking efforts and contributions to the construction of temples in the Maijishan; they are like cranes and stars in the sky. The narrow mountain roads are dangerous and suddenly come to an end. The clouds are like the wings of big rocs, and sometimes they suddenly obstruct the sky; the trees are like the moon, and the branches seem to touch the sun when they swing. (The content of the above preface is a description of the scenery of the Maijishan.) Therefore, monks from far away came to the Maijishan to carve caves in the mountain, and built the Maijishan into a pure land of Buddhists. In the stone room, monks worshipped Vimalakirti, and then they will become immortal and walk in the wind; in the Buddhist niches on the mountain they worshipped the Bodhisattva, and then they will ascend to heaven. (The content of the above preface is that Li Yunxin used to have stone chambers and Buddhist niches on the mountain in Maijishan.) Li Yunxin, the governor of the Qinzhou Prefecture, had a profound understanding of the path to Buddhism by virtue of his good roots planted in his previous life, so he ordered on the south cliff of the Maijishan to cut the road by erecting high ladders, and respectfully build the Seven-Buddha Nich for his dead father. It's like carving river water, like processing crystal. The leisurely and soothing full moon shines on the Buddha's eyes. The Buddha statue reveals Sumeru and smells the fragrance of heaven. In this earthly world, there is also a place where masters can explain the Dharma to the monks in the world. Like the Fragrant Mountain, we still ave the Buddha who lives in peace. In the past, the Tathagata made merits for the dead, and there were scriptures to repay the kindness; when the Bodhisattva left home, there were offerings to miss his parents. I hope to follow this ritual system, so I made this inscription:

The Maijishan is the main mountain of the local area, with deep twists and turns, standing high above the sky. The Maijishan Caves are based on rock cliffs. There are ten layers on top of each other, and they are connected by plank roads, like copper beams, which make people breathless when they climb up. The Maiji Cliff is very wide and the tall pine trees are straight. The moon borrows its way, and the sun flies back. During the construction, various vehicles were loaded with materials for digging into the mountain and caves, and shuttled back and forth; skilled craftsmen were busy setting up ladders to build the Buddhist niches and the connecting plank roads. The Buddhist niches and grottoes on the cliff are brightly lit in the sun, like overlapping star rivers, gorgeous and winding. There are many scriptures on the cliff, and many Buddha images in the niches. The frescoes and caisson in

安居之佛。昔者如来追福，有报恩之经；菩萨去家，有思亲之供。敢缘斯义，乃作铭曰：

镇地郁盘，基乾峻极。
石关十上，铜梁九息。
百仞崖横，千寻松直。
阴兔假道，阳乌回翼。
载辇疏山，穿尧架岭。
紊纷星汉，回旋光景。
壁累经文，龛重佛影。
雕轮月殿，刻镜花堂。
横镌石壁，暗凿山梁。
雷乘法鼓，树积天香。
嗽泉珉谷，吹尘石床。
集灵真馆，藏仙册府。
芝洞秋房，檀林春乳。
冰谷银沙，山楼石柱。
异岭共云，同峰别雨。
冀城馀俗，河西旧风。
水声幽咽，山势崆峒。
法云常住，慧日无穷。
方域芥尽，不变天宫。

《四川制置使司给田公据碑》

此碑嵌于瑞应寺天王殿墙内，是南宋嘉定十五年（公元1222年）所立。通高1.68米，宽0.98米。方额。首题"四川制置使司给田公据碑"，碑文楷书47行，满行78字。内容记述自开禧兵火以后，由于屯田

the niches are gorgeous and exquisite, like the fairy hall with the carved moon and the beautiful hall with carved mirrors, and the incense accumulates the incense of trees. The stone walls were carved across, and the mountain beams were dug silently. The dharma drum is like thunder, and the lingering incense fly to the sky. The clear spring water flows through the valley paved with colored stones, and the light breeze comes slowly, like blowing a stone bed, green and dust-free, sounding the piano leisurely. The Maijishan is really a treasure place where celestial spirits are gathered, and a good mansion for storing scriptures. In spring orchids bloom, and in autumn the Zen houses are enveloped by red leaves, with fragrant forests, spring flowers and plenty of rain. In winter ice valley, silver sand, the silvery sight of snow and ice-covered carved mountain buildings and stone rooms are more beautiful and moving. The Maijishan in the misty rain is particularly beautiful. Here folks follow the customs of the Ji County and the land west of the Yellow River. The sound of water swallows, and the mountains are steep and strange. The Buddha dharma covering everything like a cloud is always here, and the wisdom of the Buddha shines throughout the Maijishan. The Maijishan is always a palace inhabited by Gods, free from the chaos of the worldly world."

The Stone Tablet about the Official Certificate of Returning Farmland Issued by the Sichuan Military Commissioner

The monument is inserted in the wall of the Heavenly King Hall of the Ruiying Temple. It was erected in the 15th year of the Jiading period (AD 1222) in the Southern Song Dynasty, with 1.68 meters high and 0.98 meters wide. The head of the tablet is square. The title *the Stone Tablet about the Official Certificate of Returning Farmland Issued by the Sichuan Military Commissioner* is engraved on the topmost of the tablet, the inscription is in regular script with 47 lines, a full line of 78 characters. It depicts that after the military conflict during the Kaixi period (AD 1205), for the local official in charge of farming affairs expropriated the lands of Qiuchi area to feed the army, which they belonged to the Ruiying Temple and the Shengxian Temple. It was only after the repeated appeals of the abbot and Master Mingjue of the Ruiying Temple and the monk Zhiyan of the Shengxian Temple for more than ten years that the Sichuan Military Commissioner returned two temple's land and occupied military fields and issued *the Official Certificate of Returning Farmland*, and erected the stone tablet. "February of the 15th year of the Jiading period" is inscribed at the bottom of the tablet (engraved with "Seal of the Sichuan Military Commissioner" in seal cutting).

The inscription records many historical facts in the history of Maijishan. According to the records about reclaiming the wasteland, the name of Tao Longtu, the Qinzhou Military Commissioner, who presented Lingzhi, was known through this monument. The inscription also mentions the historical facts that the local peasants Qiang De and Li Shi revolted in the area of Maijishan during Jiading years in the Southern Song Dynasty (AD 1208-1224), which is of great value to the study of local history. In addition, during the reign of Emperor Shenzong in the Song Dynasty (AD 1067-1085) Chan Master Yuantong was invited to the imperial court to give lectures on Buddhism, which is a very valuable historical material for exploring the importance of Buddhism and Maijishan in the Song Dynasty. As for the inscriptions with the longest characters on the monument at Maijishan Caves, it not only records the historical evolution of Maijishan Caves, but also involves military, litigation, regulations, administrative

官将瑞应、胜仙两寺湫池一带常驻地拘作屯田，经瑞应寺住持赐紫明觉大师重遇和胜仙寺僧智演十多年反复申诉，始由四川制置使司判准退还，发给《给田公据》，并刊石立碑的经过。尾题"知委嘉定拾伍年二月二十三日"（内有篆刻"四川安抚制置使之印"押章）。

碑文记录了许多麦积山历史上发生的史实。根据碑文关于开垦田土的记录，敬献灵芝的秦州经略陶龙图的名字是通过此碑被人知晓的。碑文还提到了当时南宋嘉定年间（公元1208年—公元1224年）麦积山一带强德、李实等农民起义的史实，对研究地方历史有重要的价值。碑文中提到，宋神宗时（公元1067年—公元1085年），麦积山高僧圆通禅师被请入朝廷讲演佛法的事，是探究佛教以及麦积山在宋代时之重要地位的非常有价值的史料。这也是麦积山石窟中文字最长的一块碑刻，碑刻中不仅记载了麦积山石窟的历史沿革，而且涉及军事、诉讼、典章制度、行政制度、寺院经济等多方面内容，具有极为重要的研究价值。摘录如下。

伏睹本寺继传名胜，因群山围绕，中间突起一峰，铸凿千龛，现垂万像，上下万仞中有三宝、文殊、普贤、观世音万民祈祷，无不感应。始自东晋起迹，敕赐无忧，给田供赡。次六国重修，敕赐名石岩寺，大隋敕赐名净念寺，大唐敕赐名应乾寺。圣朝大观元年，于绝顶阿育王塔傍地产芝草三十八本。蒙秦州经略陶龙图，具表道上，奉敕改赐名为瑞应寺。粮草诸般，非任耕犁。许本寺开坛，专一建置祝延圣寿道场，进奏功德。疏回，赐御香度牒。又奉神宗皇帝宣诏，本寺高僧秀铁壁入内，升座讲演，敕赐圆通禅师，给赐田土山田五十余顷。昨缘开禧兵火之后，于嘉定元年，有忠义首领李实、强德、张钧等，骚扰瑞应寺境之物，不

第三章　麦积山石窟附属遗存

system, temple economy and other aspects, which has extremely important research values. Excerpts read as follows.

The abbot and his associates of the Ruiying Temple on the Maijishan Mountain presented a report, stating that this famous site has been inherited. The temple is a renowned relic with mountains surrounding it, and a peak rising abruptly in the middle. Thousands of niches were carved, and countless Buddha statues are now hanging in them all the way to the bottom of the valley. Within these statues are enshrined the Three Treasures: Manjusri, Samantabhadra, and Bodhisattva. These three bodhisattvas have responded to the prayers of worshipers from all walks of life. Starting from the Eastern Jin Dynasty (about AD 317-420), it was granted the name Wuyou and land to cultivate. Later in the Seven Kingdoms period (about AD 420), it was given the name the Shiyan Temple by imperial decree. During the Sui Dynasty (about AD 581-618), it was renamed the Jingnian Temple by imperial decree, and during the Tang Dynasty (about AD 618-907), it was named the Yingqian Temple by imperial decree. In the first year of the Daguan period (AD 1107), 38 Lingzhis were produced on the land near the Asoka Pagoda at the top of the mountain. Under the recommendation of Tao Longtu, the Military Commissioner of Qingzhou, it was renamed the Ruiying Temple by imperial decree. All kinds of food and supplies are produced by ploughing the fields. Permission is granted for this temple to open its altar and preach the Buddha's teachings, devote itself to building and establishing a blessed path for the prolonging of holy life, reporting its charitable deeds. The report was answered with a decree granting imperial incense and an official permit to become a monk and join a monastery. In addition, Emperor Shenzong (AD 1067-1085) issued an edict appointing the high-ranking monk of this temple to enter the inner palace and give lectures from the platform, ordering the bestowal of a 50-hectare mountainous field to Chan Master Yuantong. Due to the past military conflict during the Kaixi period (AD 1205), in the first year of Jiading (AD 1208), loyal and righteous leaders such as Li Shi, Qiang De, Zhang Jun, etc., harassed the property within the boundaries of the Ruiying Temple. Dissatisfied with their personal interests, they plundered the temple's bell and cauldron, totaling 17,000 Jin of iron, and the culprits, armed with weapons, forcibly seized the seeds sown by the temple for two years. The temple's monks were left without food for years, and had to flee to other places seeking aid. In the second year of Jiading, the officials in charge invoked emergency measures to develop farmland and complained to various authorities. Verdict: Li Shi et al. were found guilty of forcefully taking the wheat fields, plows, bells and pots from the Maijishan Mountain, and were ordered to compensate accordingly. The decision is to order them to return the goods to the Tianshui Prefecture. Later, Qiang De, Li Shi and others were caught up with, but they only compensated with 3,000 Jins of iron. On April 11th in the 7th year of the Jiading period, after further reporting to the peacekeeping department, it was ruled to give the fields of the two temples back and allowed them to continue farming as tenants, not used for garrisoning. These matters were communicated in the form of official documents for handling. On March 14th in the 8th year of the Jiading period, the commanding officer of the general headquarters approved the issuance of a public document, which was subsequently collected and received by the temple.

满私意，使行打劫本寺钟、锅两件，计铁一万七百斤；及本寺布种二年，凶徒各持劫器强收了。当使本寺僧行，数年无食，逃外方施。于嘉定二年，宣抚主持作屯田，赴诸监司陈诉。大司钧判：照得李实等强取麦积山麦田、耕牛、钟、锅，委是分晓，合行勒令赔还，下天水军去着。嗣本军追到强德、李实等，止赔得铁三千斤。至嘉定七年四月十一日，再赴安抚司陈诉，准大使司钧判：照得二寺田砲，并系给赐条，不应作屯田，可下发还二寺，依旧作佃。牒总领。至嘉定八年三月十四日，准总领所座、准朝指挥出给公据，付本寺收执。

于嘉定十三年正月二十九日，再起随军转运司使，准合到牒天水军，差雷县尉前来交拨，即缘雷县尉与屯官雷安礼系兄弟，以此过延，未曾交下。及金人侵犯，大安王嘉定十三年正月，去年秋料收到，为国家调兵未已，遂将物斛尽数赴随军转运司，助献军粮，计二百五十石。

朝廷已给还常住田、占充营田，许重遇状上件田。于嘉定十三年，内制置大使司，括充屯田朝省陈状符下，遂给讫。去年宣司据官册拘收）作营田，缘营田系总领所赡军上件田，已先据总领所授入省符，给还去讫。今欲牒常平司照总领所已行给还本寺，奉制置台判牒使司，除已牒利州路提举常平司遵照，台判指挥，并佥厅拟定事理，照总领所已给还本寺，及移牒所召会并下天水宣照应施行。四川制置使司给田公据委。嘉定三十五年二月。

《秦州雄武军陇城县第六保瑞应寺再葬佛舍利碑》

为宋代靖康（公元1126年—公元1127年）再葬舍利所立。碑

The inscription reads, "On the 29th day of lunar January in the 13th year of the Jiading period, the army provisioning commission was established again and authorized to join the Tianshui Prefecture and the District Defender Lei was sent to handle the handover because the District Defender Lei and the local official Lei Anli were brothers, but they failed to complete the exchange as planned. When the Jin invaded, in the first month of the 13th year of the Jiading period, the crops were harvested in the previous fall and the national military mobilization was initiated. All the goods were sent to the army provisioning commission to offer military supplies, totaling 250 dans.

The inscription also said, "The court has returned the temple's land and occupied military fields, and allowed submitting a petition for the fields on behalf of Chongyu. In the 13th year of the Jiading period, the Inner Military Commissioner-in-chief Department included the request for plowing military fields in the petition, and the request was granted. Last year, the Pacification Commission took the official register to detain and conscript for army fields, due to the fact that the army fields were related to the fields mentioned by the Overseer General, which had already been granted by the Overseer General to the provincial emblem and returned. Now, it is desired to ask the Stabilization Fund Bureau to follow the Overseer General's previous return to this temple, and to set up a judge's letter to the office through the Military Commission. In addition, the letter will be sent to the summoned meeting and the Department of Tianshui. The Official Certificate of Returning Farmland of the Sichuan Military Commission. It an February of the 35th year of the Jiading period.

The Tablet of Buddha Relics Reburied in the Ruiying Temple, the Sixth Bao, the Longcheng County, the Xiongwu Prefecture in Tianshui

The tablet should have been erected during the reburial of relics in the Jingkang (AD 1126-1127) period. A corner of the tablet is missing, and now the remaining part is kept in the storehouse of cultural relics. The inscription mainly introduces the initial construction of the Ruiying Temple, the construction of Maijishan in the first year of Datong reign in the Western Wei Dynasty (AD 535), and during the Emperor Wen of the Sui Dynasty the Pagoda of Asoka was constructed, the temple was granted the name of the Jingnian Temple and important events happened in the temple after that. These words are all precious historical materials related to the Maijishan Caves. The text reads as follows.

This temple was founded during the reign of Emperor Ashoka and was known as the Temple of No Worries. By the fourth year of the Qiande reign of the Song Dynasty (AD 966), it has been in existence for 2,000 years. In the first year of the reign of Emperor Wen of the Western Wei Dynasty (AD 535), the cliff pavilions were rebuilt and the temple was restored." Furthermore, in the sixth year of the Renshou period of Emperor Wen of the Sui Dynasty (AD 606), the grottoes were renovated again, and imperial orders were issued for the burial of Buddhist relics. This pagoda was then constructed and the temple was granted the name of the Jingnian Temple. In the second year of the Dazhong period (AD 848) of the Tang Dynasty, Great Master Huijue

已残缺一角，今存文物库房。碑文主要介绍了瑞应寺的初建，西魏大统元年（公元535年）修建麦积山，隋文帝时建舍利塔赐"净念寺"及寺院随后发生的重要事件，均为石窟珍贵史料。碑文如下。

阿育王始兴建，号无忧寺。至我宋乾德四年，计二千年矣。昔西魏大统元年，再修崖阁，重兴寺宇。又至隋文皇仁寿六年，再修岩窟，敕葬舍利，建此宝塔，赐净念寺。至大中二年，有先师迥觉大师，寻□旧基圣迹，建精蓝。至乾德四年，一百二十年，及赐灵芝一百一本。其年二月，遍山花卉盛开。继至皇祐二年，一百二十八年。又元符元年，灾火堕坏寺宇。于建中靖国元年，寺主僧智俐等再建宝塔。又崇宁□年，顶产灵芝三十八本，山图进产芝，蒙恩改瑞应寺。至靖康元年管勾僧……

杜甫《山寺》

杜甫在乾元二年（公元758年—公元760年）秋天来到秦州，只待了三个多月。写了几十首诗，其中二十首杂诗尤为著名。他住在麦积山附近的东柯草堂，只写了一首题为《山寺》的诗描写瑞应寺当时的景象。诗文如下。

山寺

杜甫

野寺残僧少，山圆细路高。
麝香眠石竹，鹦鹉啄金桃。
乱水通人过，悬崖置屋牢。
上方重阁晚，百里见秋毫。

came to Maijishan to build a monastery and search for the holy sites of the past, constructing a dwelling place for monks. In the fourth year of the Qiande reign (AD 966), which was 120 years later, 101 Lingzhi (glossy ganoderma) were bestowed. In February of that year, flowers bloomed all over the mountains. Subsequently, in the second year of the Huangyou period (AD 1050), it was 128 years. In the first year of the Yuanfu period (AD 1098), a disaster fire destroyed the temple and halls. In the first year of the Jianzhongjingguo period (AD 1101), the abbot, the monk Zhichan, and others rebuilt the pagoda. In the X year of Chongning (AD 1102-1106), 38 Lingzhi were produced on the land near the Asoka Pagoda at the top of the mountain. Under the recommendation of Tao Longtu, the Military Commissioner of Qingzhou, it was renamed the Ruiying Temple by imperial decree. In the first year of Jingkang (AD 1126) the monk who was in charge of the daily affairs...(partial loss at the back)

The Mountain Temple by Du Fu

In the autumn of the second year of the Qianyuan era (AD 758-760), Du Fu arrived in Qinzhou and stayed here for only a little over three months. He wrote dozens of poems during this time, with 20 miscellaneous poems being particularly outstanding. He lived in a thatched cottage in the Dongke Valley, near the Maijishan. He only wrote a poem entitled *The Mountain Temple* in regard to the scene of the Ruiying Temple at that time. The poem reads as follows.

The Mountain Temple
Du Fu

In the wild temple, few remaining monks, with mountains round and narrow paths high.
Musk sleeping in the stone bamboo, parrots pecking at golden peaches.
Disorderly waters flow through, while houses stand secure on precipitous cliffs.
Above, lofty pavilions become heavy in the evening, where a single hair can be seen from a hundred miles in the autumn.

Readers can compare another version of the poem *The Mountain Temple* in *The Cave Temples of Maijishan* by Michael Sullivan, 1969: 7.

Mountain Temples
Du Fu

There are few monks left in these remote shrines. And in the wilderness the narrow paths are high.
The musk-deer sleeps among the stones and bamboo. The cockatoos peck at the golden peaches.
Streams trickle down among the paths; Across the overhanging cliff the cells are ranged. Their tiered chambers reaching to the very peak; And for a hundred *li* one can make out the smallest thing.

舍利塔

舍利塔位于麦积山山顶。最初建于隋朝，据《秦州雄武军陇城县第六保瑞应寺再葬佛舍利记》碑载，隋文帝仁寿元年（公元601年）"再开龛窟，敕葬舍利，建此宝塔，赐净念寺"。他们曾经建造的宝塔指的是在山顶上幸存下来的砖塔。

隋文帝曾下令在全国各地兴建舍利塔，麦积山山顶的这座塔就是建于秦州的一座。该塔于宋建中靖国元年（公元1101年）重建，并在历代进行了重修。现存为清乾隆八年（公元1743年）由麦积山瑞应寺圆慧等和尚重建。塔身在1920年海原大地震中破裂，在1983年得到了加固和修复。该塔为八角形五层密檐式实心塔，八棱覆钵形顶，顶部无塔刹。塔顶到地面高9米，八角形基座高0.4米。塔身呈棱锥形，上部略有收分，五层，每层出檐。第一层高2.38米，各面宽1.75～1.85米，正南侧有两扇浮雕的假隔门，其余七面均为横长方形假窗，二层及以上各层正南面有极小的假门，其余七面都是封闭的。

The Pagoda of Asoka

The Pagoda of Asoka stands at the top of Maijishan. It was initially built in the Sui Dynasty, according to *the Tablet of Buddha Relics Reburied in Maijishan, the Sixth Bao, the Longcheng County, the Xiongwu Prefecture in Tianshui* in the first year of the Renshou period of Emperor Wen of the Sui Dynasty (AD 601), some new caves were excavated, and imperial orders were issued for the burial of Buddhist relics. This pagoda was then constructed and the monastery was granted the name of the Jingnian Monastery. The pagoda they once built refers to the surviving brick pagoda on the top of the hill. Emperor Wen of the Sui Dynasty commanded that a temple can be erected across the country, the pagoda on the top of Maijishan is built in the commandery of Qinzhou. The pagoda was rebuilt in the first year of Jianzhong Jingguo in the Song Dynasty (AD 1101), and has been reconstructed during successive dynasties. The surviving pagoda was rebuilt by the monk Yuanhui of the Ruiying Temple at Maijishan in the eighth year of the reign of Emperor Qianlong of the Qing Dynasty (AD 1743). The tower of the pagoda was cracked by the Haiyuan earthquake in 1920 and was reinforced and repaired in 1983. It is an octagonal five-storey solid tower with the dense eave, and a ceiling with eight edges in the form of an upside-down bowl, without Tasha on the top. The pagoda rises 9 meters from floor to ceiling, and the octagonal tower base of 0.4 meters high. The body is pyramidal, with the upper part slightly narrowing, five storeys, each has an upturned eave. The first storey is 2.38 meters high, with each face of 1.75 -1.85 meters wide. There are two fake partition doors carved in relief on the south face, the other seven are horizontal rectangular fake windows, the second and above storeys have very small fake doors on the south face, and the other seven are closed.

参考文献

[1]冯国瑞.麦积山石窟志[M].天水：天水报社印刷厂承印本，1989:99-108.

[2]敦煌研究院、甘肃省文物局.甘肃石窟志[M].兰州:甘肃教育出版社，2011：277-278.

[3]马英莲.麦积山佛教石窟介绍文本英译研究[J].天水师范学院学报，2023（1）：112-119.

[4]何静珍，陈玉.麦积山石窟艺术丛书（第一辑）[M].兰州：甘肃人民美术出版社，1997：1-60.

[5]天水市文化和旅游局.天水旅游[M].天水市文化和旅游局，2019：39.

[6]天水画册编辑委员会.天水画册[M].甘肃人民出版社，1989：20.

[7] 高亚芳、秦斌峰.英语甘肃导游[M].中国旅游出版社，2008：29-33.

[8] HATIM, B. & MASON, I. Discourse and the Translator [M]. Shanghai: Shanghai Foreign Language Education Press, 2001: 223.

[9] Newmark, P. Approaches to Translation [M]. New York: Prentice Hall, 1981:39.

[10] SULLIVAN, M. Cave Temples of Maichishan [M]. London: Faber & Faber, 1969:5-6, 27, 34, 40.